Cases
in Health Care
Financial
Management

Cases in Health Care Financial Management

Edited by
James D. Suver
Charles N. Kahn III
Jan P. Clement

Published in cooperation by the
Association of University Programs in Health Administration
and Health Administration Press

This book is dedicated to Seth, whose courage
and perseverance are an example to us all.

This work is a product of the AUPHA Task Force on Financial Management Education and has been funded primarily by a grant from the W. K. Kellogg Foundation.

Library of Congress Cataloging in Publication Data
Main entry under title:
Cases in health care financial management.
    Bibliography: p.
    1. Health facilities — Finance — Case studies.
2. Health facilities — Accounting — Case studies.
3. Health facilities — United States — Finance — Case
studies.   4. Health facilities — United States — Accounting
— Case studies.   I. Suver, James D.   II. Kahn, Charles N.
III. Clement, Jan P. [DNLM: 1. Financial management —
Problems.   2. Health facilities — Economics — United
States — Problems.   3. Teaching materials.   WX 157 C338
Suppl.]
RA 971.3.C35 1984   362.1'068'1   83-25763
ISBN 0-914904-95-7

Health Administration Press
A Division of the Foundation of the
    American College of Healthcare
    Executives
1021 East Huron
Ann Arbor, Michigan 48104-9990
(313) 764-1380

Association of University Programs
    in Health Administration
1911 North Fort Myer Drive, Suite 503
Arlington, Virginia 22209
(703) 524-5500

Contents

Section I: Financial Statement Analysis

Overview

Section II: Managerial Accounting Techniques

Overview

Section III: Financing Decisions

Overview

Section IV: Investment Decisions

Preface

Managers in health care organizations confront an ambiguous and rapidly changing environment, especially regarding financial management matters. They must respond to legislation, regulation, and competing public demands, as well as most of the problems faced by managers of other business organizations. To manage health care organizations well, managers must employ tools applicable to a variety of environmental conditions.

Instructing these managers to apply such tools in actual or potential employment situations is perhaps best accomplished through the case teaching method. This method presents students with an actual or illustrative case encountered by managers. The students must then ferret out the problem, analyze the data, evaluate alternatives, and recommend a course of action.

Despite the widely professed advantages of this teaching method, health care financial management faculty have found few published case studies from which to choose assignments. At times, makeshift adaptations of business school cases have had to do. At other times, instructors have hurriedly prepared their own cases for class.

This book addresses the needs of both health care financial management faculty and students. It gathers in one place a wide variety of cases covering a range of health care financial management topics. These cases are suitable for diverse levels of academic sophistication and professional experience. Moreover, many practice settings are represented, including health maintenance organizations, home health agencies, hospitals, government agencies, and mental health agencies.

For pedagogical purposes, the book is divided into four sections: (1) financial statement analysis, (2) managerial accounting techniques, (3) financing decisions, and (4) investment decisions. Each section contains a mixture of classic and recently written cases. All focus on analytical techniques applicable to almost any environment, including both cost-based and prospective payment systems. They emphasize underlying concepts as they apply to many managerial problems.

An editorial board appointed by the Association of University Programs in Health Administration's Task Force on Financial Management Education selected the cases for this book. In addition, members of the board spent many hours assisting authors who were writing cases for the first time. The quality of the materials included is largely due to their diligence. We wish to express our appreciation for those valuable contributions. The board members are:

James D. Suver, D.B.A., C.M.A. (Chair)
University of Colorado –
Denver

Joseph S. Coyne, Dr.P.H.
University of California –
Los Angeles

R. Neal Gilbert, M.H.A., C.P.A.
Seaton Medical Center
Daly City, California

Regina Herzlinger, D.B.A.
Harvard Business School

Bettina D. Kurowski, D.P.A.
University of Colorado –
Denver

Hugh W. Long, Ph.D.
Tulane University

Bruce R. Neumann, Ph.D.
University of Colorado –
Boulder

J. B. Silvers, Ph.D.
Case Western Reserve University

Donald Simons, Ph.D., C.P.A.
Boston University

William N. Zelman, Ph.D., C.P.A.
(ex officio)
University of North Carolina –
Chapel Hill

Finally, we would like to thank Stephanie Tames and Juin Wong for their assistance. Stephanie provided the technical editing for the book as well as assisting in its organization. For the last year, Juin assisted the editors administratively.

James D. Suver
Denver, CO
Charles N. Kahn III
Arlington, VA
Jan P. Clement
Chapel Hill, NC

About the Authors

KEITH E. BOLES is an assistant professor in health services management at the University of Missouri – Columbia. Dr.Boles previously taught at the University of Colorado and has published articles on environmental economics and portfolio management. His teaching and research interests are in managerial and regulatory finance, investment analysis, and financial management of health care institutions. He holds a Ph.D. in economics from the University of Arizona.

DOUGLAS A. CONRAD is an associate professor in the departments of Community Dentistry and Health Services, and an adjunct associate professor in finance, business economics, and quantitative methods at the University of Washington. Dr. Conrad has published a number of articles on dental services and health care financial management, and has participated in several research projects. He is on the editorial board of the *Journal of Health Politics, Policy and Law* and serves as a reviewer for several other journals. Dr. Conrad earned his M.H.A. at the University of Washington and his M.B.A. and Ph.D. from the University of Chicago.

JOSEPH S. COYNE is an assistant professor in health services management at the University of California – Los Angeles, and academic assistant to the controller of the UCLA hospital and clinics. Dr. Coyne has published and consults in the area of multihospital systems. His past positions include postdoctoral research fellow at the National Center for Health Services Research, management analyst at Sonoma State Hospital, and financial analyst for a consumer finance corporation. He earned M.P.H. and Dr.P.H. degrees at the University of California – Berkeley.

KYLE L. GRAZIER is an assistant professor in Yale University's Department of Epidemiology and Public Health. Dr. Grazier is coauthor of *Decision Making and Control for Health Administration, Second Edition*. She has served as consultant to many health care organizations. Past work includes research, environmental engineering, and nursing positions in universities and health organizations. Her M.P.H. and Dr.P.H. degrees were awarded by the University of California – Berkeley.

REGINA HERZLINGER is a professor at the Harvard Business School specializing in financial and managerial accounting, and management control systems. Dr. Herzlinger has published extensively on financial management of nonprofit and health care organizations. She currently serves on the executive committee of the American Accounting Association, and as a consultant to a variety of nonprofit and for-profit organizations. Dr. Herzlinger holds a D.B.A. from Harvard Business School.

STEPHEN S. HYDE is president and chief executive officer of Health Care Management Corporation (HCM) in Colorado Springs, Colorado, which develops and manages health maintenance organizations in several states. Mr. Hyde has extensive experience in all aspects of HMO management from feasibility studies to management of operations. His past positions range from financial advisor for the Office of Health Maintenance Organizations to CEO of Peak Health Plan, Ltd. Mr. Hyde earned his M.B.A. from the Harvard Business School.

L. WILLIAM KATZ is a senior health care consultant for Arthur D. Little, Inc. In his 17 years of professional experience in the health care field, he has been actively involved in strategic and financial planning, operational assessment, and systems development. A past member of AUPHA's Financial Management Task Force, Dr. Katz previously held positions at Deloitte, Haskins and Sells, American Hospital Supply Corporation, George Washington University, and Walter Reed Army Medical Center. He holds an M.B.A. from Dartmouth College and a D.B.A. from the George Washington University.

A. KAY KEISER is an associate clinical professor in the Department of Epidemiology and Public Health at Yale University. She has provided a range of consulting services to numerous health care and professional organizations in the United States. Her experience includes employment at Harvard Community Health Plan and several hospitals. Dr. Keiser earned an M.P.H. from Yale and an Sc.D. from Harvard University.

GERALD KOMINSKI is a Ph.D. candidate at the University of Pennsylvania's School of Public and Urban Policy. He has held positions at the Leonard Davis Institute of Health Economics and the University of Chicago Hospital. Mr. Kominski is currently involved in case mix research.

BETTINA D. KUROWSKI is an associate professor and director of the Programs in Health Services Administration and an associate professor of health administration and business policy in the Graduate Business School of the University of Colorado in Denver. She holds M.P.H. and D.P.A. degrees from the University of Colorado— Denver. Dr. Kurowski serves as a consultant to many professional committees and health care organizations. She has published extensively in the areas of long-term and home health care.

HUGH W. LONG is an associate professor in the School of Business at Tulane University in New Orleans. Dr. Long taught previously at Ohio State University, San Jose State University, Stanford University, and Yale University. Dr. Long is the coauthor of a basic text in corporate finance and specializes in applying corporate finance techniques to the health and medical care industry. He has written numerous articles on corporate finance and health care management, frequently teaches at health and medical care seminars, and serves as a consultant to both governmental and private-sector organizations. Dr. Long received his Ph.D. from Stanford University.

WENDY S. LOVE is currently a strategic planning consultant in central New York. She is also assistant director of the Health Executives Development Program at Cornell, and a lecturer in the Health Administration Department at Ithaca College. She received her M.B.A. in hospital and health services from Cornell University. Formerly president of Genesee Region Family Planning, Inc., Ms. Love has also served on task forces of the Finger Lakes Health Systems Agency.

BRUCE R. NEUMANN is an associate professor of accounting and health administration at the University of Colorado. Holding a Ph.D. from the University of Illinois, Dr. Neumann has also taught at the State University of New York. He has published numerous articles on health care financial management and is the coauthor of two textbooks.

ROBERT E. SCHLENKER is the associate director of the Center for Health Services Research at the University of Colorado Health Sciences Center and an assistant professor in the Division of Health Administration at the University of Colorado. He has directed a variety of research projects concerning health care issues. Dr. Schlenker has also held positions at InterStudy and in state government. He earned M.A. and Ph.D. degrees from the University of Michigan.

J. B. SILVERS is Treuhaft Professor of Management at the Weatherhead School of Management, Case Western Reserve University. He is also professor of community health in the School of Medicine and director of the Health Systems Management Center. Dr. Silvers served previously on the faculty of the graduate schools of business at Indiana, Harvard, and Stanford universities. He has served as a consultant to federal and private health care organizations as a member of the Principles and Practices Board of the Hospital Financial Management Association. He has written a book on health care financial management and numerous articles. He earned his M.S.I.A. in industrial administration from Purdue University and his Ph.D. in finance from Stanford University.

DONALD R. SIMONS is the associate dean of graduate programs, director of the M.B.A. program, and an associate professor of accounting at Boston University. A certified public accountant, Dr. Simons holds his M.B.A. and Ph.D. degrees from the University of Wisconsin. His teaching and research interests are in financial reporting and management accounting and control in health care, public-sector, and other nonprofit organizations. He is also currently a member of the Maximum Allowable Cost Exception Review Board for the state of Massachusetts.

JAMES E. SORENSEN, a certified public accountant, is a professor of accounting at the School of Accountancy, University of Denver. Since earning his Ph.D. at Ohio State University, he has taught at Ohio State and the University of Minnesota. Dr. Sorensen is editor-in-chief of *Decision Sciences* and serves on the editorial board for *Accounting Review*. He has contributed many articles on accounting and evaluation of human service organizations to the professional literature.

KATHLEEN M. STAMM is administrative analyst for Group Health Cooperative of Puget Sound in Seattle, Washington. She has held a variety of positions in other health care organizations and on research projects. Ms. Stamm received her M.H.A. from the University of Washington — Seattle.

JAMES D. SUVER is professor of accounting and health administration at the University of Colorado — Denver School of Business. Previously he was a professor and director of the master's degree program at the Department of Health Policy and Administration, University of North Carolina — Chapel Hill. A certified management accountant, Dr. Suver speaks, consults, and publishes extensively on the financial management of health care organizations. Among his publications are two textbooks. Dr. Suver holds an M.B.A. and a D.B.A. from Harvard Business School.

THOMAS M. TIERNEY, JR. is a doctoral student in economics at the University of Washington. Previously, Mr. Tierney has held positions with the Western Center for Health Planning and the universities of Hawaii, Oregon, and California. In addition, he has consulted for many groups on a variety of health-related issues. Mr. Tierney earned his M.A. from San Francisco State University.

RALPH ULLMAN is an assistant professor of public health at Columbia University. He has held a variety of research positions and has published several articles and a book on ambulatory care. Mr. Ullman holds both an M.S. in community health and an M.B.A. from the University of Rochester.

SRINIVASAN UMAPATHY is an assistant professor in the School of Management at Boston University. He has conducted research on budgetary processes in hospitals and has been employed in corporate-divisional information and control systems in private-sector organizations. Dr. Umapathy has contributed to the professional literature in those areas as well. He earned a D.B.A. from the Harvard Graduate School of Business Administration.

JAY WOLFSON is associate professor of health finance and policy at the University of South Florida. Dr. Wolfson previously has taught at the universities of Oklahoma, South Carolina, Houston, and Texas — Houston. His areas of special interest include financial management applications in human service programs, health care cost containment in industry, and self-funding of benefit plans. Dr. Wolfson received his Dr.P.H. from the University of Texas — Houston.

DAVID YOUNG is an associate professor of management at the Harvard University School of Public Health. Earlier, he was president of Commonwealth Management Systems, a systems engineer for IBM, and a program economist for the U.S. Agency for International Development. Dr. Young has consulted widely with health and human service organizations in the United States and abroad, and has published several articles on improved management in human services and health care. Most of his recent research has been in the use of management control systems in hospitals. Dr. Young earned his D.B.A. from the Harvard Business School.

Introduction

WHY THE CASE METHOD?

The ability to select and apply appropriate management techniques is a requisite skill for managers in health care organizations. Choosing the appropriate tool is complicated, however, because the varied settings and situations in which health administrators must apply them are resplendent with ambiguities and uncertainties. Frequently, the major obstacle is simply identifying the questions.

To assist students in developing the skills to identify problems and make decisions, faculty in health care management often use teaching methods which simulate decision-making situations. One of the most effective methods is the case study. Use of the case method of instruction, however, requires careful preparation by both faculty and students. This text is designed to facilitate this process. In addition, the case studies included in this book cover an array of topical areas and decision-making situations in health care financial management.

USE OF THE CASE METHOD

An effective case study presents an actual or simulated condition of an organization or some aspect of its operations. Background is provided to enable students to make decisions concerning situations confronting the organization. Case studies may describe the environment, key factors inside or outside of the organization, and impressions of the decision-making atmosphere. It may also offer insights into formal and informal managerial and political structures. Whatever the format, the case study is designed as a vehicle through which students can learn to apply the skills and knowledge gained in technique-oriented instruction.

A case study will never give a student all the information seemingly required to apply textbook techniques for resolving organizational problems. Nor will information always be presented in an appropriate manner for the consideration of all relevant problems and decisions. The case study is designed purposely to teach students that complete information is frequently lacking in actual situations, and that they must always balance time and cost with the need for obtaining additional information. Through working with cases, students will gain an understanding, as do practicing health care managers, that many decisions are, and necessarily will continue to be, made on the basis of the best information available at the time.

In solving problems suggested in a case study, students must identify the most important issues facing decision makers. They should be able to assess the materials provided in the case study, analyze the data, determine the causes of problems, and discuss the questions they raise for the situation. With the identification of these problems and questions, students should be able to organize the facts available and formulate alternative courses of action.

Students should be able to present and defend their solutions both orally in the classroom and in written form. Such presentations should demonstrate the student's capacity to focus on the most critical issues provided by a case study and to formulate realistic resolutions. Approaches taken by students in response to decision-making situations should reflect their understanding of the strengths and weaknesses of proposed solutions as well as the requirements for implementing them.

PRESENTATION OF CASE STUDIES

It is useful to present case studies in both oral and written form. There is no universally accepted method of preparing for either type of presentation. The example case analysis format provided in this introduction offers one framework for analysis and presentation.

Oral and written presentations each have advantages. Through oral presentation, students are often given the most stimulating learning opportunity. Nevertheless, the written report may be the only available means for faculty to judge the case analyst's performance, especially if there is a large number of students in the classroom.

The objective in either format is for students to analyze management situations and derive defensible conclusions. The defense of a student's conclusions in the classroom before his or her peers is many times the best avenue for teaching the student to differentiate between essential and less important information. Frequently, the pressure of the oral presentation or a response to an instructor's queries is the most effective way students can be shown that not all written material is helpful, and that much data may be superfluous or misleading, require additional analysis, or merely represent supposition. In addition, oral presentation can be an effective simulation of a work environment.

In the classroom, the instructor is usually a known quantity for the student; students will therefore structure their written reports to fit the course parameters. In an actual work situation, however, employees may have to prepare reports on the same topic for various audiences with different biases and perspectives. Writing reports for case studies should be viewed as training for such instances. The amount and kind of background information, quantitative analysis, and recommendations provided will vary with the audience.

TECHNIQUES FOR CASE ANALYSIS

To begin, the student case analyst should read quickly the materials provided with the case study. This initial perusal will allow the case analyst to capture the flavor of the case and available materials. The next step is to identify the major questions facing the case analyst. Sometimes the case writer will provide questions, but often the case analyst is left to ferret out the most pressing problems.

The case analyst may, however, be given a role to assume. This role usually defines the case analyst's approach. The role provides a perspective from which the case analyst can organize the case material and begin the process of seeking solutions.

As the process begins, the case analyst should avoid some "big pitfalls." First, assuming a role places limitations on the analyst that must be recognized. An obvious solution to a given problem may be to fire the boss. From a practical standpoint, the assigned role may constrain such drastic suggestions. Second, cases and the types of analysis they call for may not always be obvious. If a class has as its topic for the day "working capital," the analyst would rationally anticipate that working capital problems are central to the case for that day. This may not necessarily be correct. The issue in this situation — working capital — may take only a minor position despite the title of the class. An ability to identify the major problem is as important as the ability to analyze data — "crunch numbers."

After identifying the important problems in the case — the right questions — case analysts should develop a framework around which to collect the relevant facts and begin the analysis. This framework may be based on issues ranging from the technical — for example, the comparison of the net present value of two alternative asset acquisitions — to the managerial — for example, how to reorganize a budget process.

As the case analyst "crunches the numbers" to develop alternative solutions to the issues identified, the applicability of any answer must be assessed in terms of dollars as well as the goals and objectives of the organization(s), and the key actors. Advantages and disadvantages should be identified for the subjective aspects as well as the more objective technical analysis.

Finally, the best "solution" should be chosen with an implementation plan — when required — which specifies actions to be taken to rectify the central issues in the case. These actions should be developed in sufficient detail to allow decisions to be made whether to accept the recommendations, reject them, or modify the proposal. The recommendations should be fully supported by data in the case, the analysis of the data, and, perhaps, external reference sources.

The ability of students to defend their recommendations and to modify these proposals when additional information is made available, as well as to ask appropriate questions, are important skills to develop. Frequent use of cases in the classroom, particularly orally, can enhance the development of such skills.

AN EXAMPLE CASE ANALYSIS FORMAT

Part I. Introduction

— Establish the foundation for the case analysis.
— Set the stage for sections to follow. Be concise — don't rehash the entire case.

Part II. Problem Identification

— Identify the major issues in the case and identify the problems to be solved.
— If possible, set objectives for the analysis and differentiate between short- and long-run actions implied in the identified issues.

Part III. Analysis

— Analyze the major issues and discuss the implications of the problems.
— Do not repeat the case facts, but instead evaluate the significance of available information for the section.
— Set the stage for recommendations.

Part IV. Recommendations

—State and support your recommendations for solving the major problems identified in the case study.
—Apply the background given in Part III (Analysis) to justify your recommendations.
—Do not assume that recommendations will be accepted without sufficient defense.
—Consider counterarguments.

Part V. Implementation (When Relevant)

—Develop a plan to implement Part IV (Recommendations), providing explanations for timing, responsibilities, and potential pitfalls, and how to avoid these problems.
—A consideration of costs, personnel behavior, and organizational structure should be used to help support recommendations when appropriate.
—It would be useful to generalize how the solutions chosen would apply in a broader context the next time similar situations are faced—how to avoid similar problems and obstacles in the future.

Remember, quality, not quantity should be the goal in preparing for oral or written presentations. Sufficient preparation time should be allowed to develop ideas fully, to proof final written drafts or practice oral presentations, and to meet deadlines. Disorganized presentation, errors in grammar, and mistyped words will detract from the thrust of the analysis.

In addition, there is no single correct answer to a case. Answers will vary depending on the analysis of the issues and the assumptions used in applying analytical techniques.

I

Financial Statement Analysis

Overview

Evaluating the current financial condition of an organization is a continuing concern for most health care managers. The basic financial statements — balance sheet, statement of revenues and expenses, and statement of changes in financial position — can provide valuable data for determining the financial performance of the organization. Moreover, decisions impacting future financial viability depend, to some extent, on analysis of historical data from these sources.

Quantitative techniques introduced in financial management classes that provide a structured approach for evaluating financial information include ratio, vertical, horizontal, trend, and statistical analysis. Unfortunately, data and organizational contexts are seldom as clear in work situations as in textbooks. Tools may have to be modified, assumptions made, or imperfect information used. Effective use of these tools thus requires practice in applying them in a variety of settings. The cases in this section are designed to meet this need.

The first case, "Somerville Hospital," uses actual hospital financial statements to illustrate the types of information available. It concentrates on appropriate presentation of financial data and the unique characteristics of hospital financial statements. The American Institute of Certified Public Accountant's (AICPA) *Hospital Audit Guide* is also introduced.

"Mid-State Medical Group" focuses on a large group practice. The case discusses the choice of an accounting method, business year, and organizational structure. In evaluating the organization's financial status, the student must cope with techniques for developing pro forma financial statements, comparability of data, and inflation — altogether a realistic set of decisions.

Use of cash versus accrual accounting statements for evaluating financial condition is a major topic of concern in "The New Hampshire-Vermont Hospitalization Service." In addition, the case can stimulate discussion of the financial statements of nonprofit organizations and the role of profit in a nonprofit firm. Finally, interactions between these types of institutions and public regulatory bodies are highlighted.

The fourth case in this section, "Chapel Hill Clinic, P.C.," involves analysis of the accounting information available to the decision maker. Subsequently, issues concerning the use of financial statements in the budgeting process must be resolved.

Finally, "The Demise of Good Health, Inc.," deals with the financial problems of a fledgling health maintenance organization. Providing quality health care at an acceptable price must be balanced against the financial survival of the provider organization, as well as a host of nonfinancial factors.

1

Somerville Hospital

Donald R. Simons

"When I first became treasurer of the hospital in January 1982, I found the financial reporting format used in previous years to be difficult to understand (see Tables 1.1 through 1.3). Even though I had been a certified public accountant and had previous experience in other nonprofit organizations, hospital financial statements were new to me. I also learned that senior management and the hospital's board of trustees often found our financial reporting format less than totally understandable." These comments were made by A. Keene Metzger, treasurer of Somerville Hospital, a 138-bed community hospital in an industrial suburb immediately north of Boston, Massachusetts.

"As you know," Keene continued, "in nonprofit accounting, an organization often receives assets whose uses are restricted by donors, grantors, and so on. A major concern of the old format was that the interested reader had a difficult time distinguishing between assets available for general use (unrestricted) and assets restricted for various purposes. I began examining our statements in light of recommendations contained in the AICPA's Hospital Audit Guide. With the consultation and assistance of our external auditor, Coopers and Lybrand (see Appendix 1.1), we began to discuss changing the format to that which you see in our 1981 annual report (see Appendix 1.2 and Tables 1.4 through 1.7). I wanted our statements to be simpler and more easily understood by both internal management and by our various external constituencies — lenders, trustees, benefactors, and so on."

Keene Metzger also had other objectives in mind besides changing to the new format. Now he was wondering whether the changes in format had been successful. Also, he was aware that an extremely controversial and timely issue in the corporate sector during the 1970s and early 1980s had been inflation accounting. In fact, one major health care insurer, Blue Cross, allowed for price level depreciation in reimbursing hospital care costs, such that several hundred thousand dollars in additional depreciation expense were reimbursable above the amount determined using the historical cost basis and reflected in the published annual report.

What would be the implications of including the higher amount of depreciation expense in the published annual report?

ISSUES AND PROBLEMS

1. Are the 1981 financial statements easier to interpret than those for 1980? What are the major differences between the statements in Tables 1.1 to 1.3 versus Tables 1.4 to 1.7?

2. Which financial statement items are likely to be unique to the annual report of a hospital?

3. Explain the extraordinary gain on retirement of debt in 1981.

4. How might Somerville incorporate inflation adjustments in its annual report?

5. What problems do you foresee in attempting to evaluate the financial performance in 1981, given the changes in the annual report?

Table 1.1

BALANCE SHEETS September 30, 1980

ASSETS

	1980	1979
Operating Fund:		
Cash and cash equivalents	$ 962,904	$ 572,661
Accounts receivable, net of allowances for uncollectible accounts of $1,100,000 and $1,000,000	2,411,628	1,767,648
Other accounts receivable	118,384	103,882
Interest receivable	27,036	43,901
Inventories	169,381	146,502
Prepaid expenses	116,392	124,033
Deposits and deferred expenses	25,880	153,562
Due from endowment funds	81,253	51,100
	3,912,858	2,963,289
Plant Funds:		
Cash	11,665	14,089
Investments — cash and cash equivalents	1,334,080	1,946,902
Sinking fund investments — cash and cash items (Note E)	736,528	482,574
Restricted cash and certificate of deposit (Note E)	224,031	224,031
Due from operating fund	908,200	346,456
Due from endowment funds	40,488	19,067
Construction in progress	—	14,854
Unamortized debt issue costs	823,815	879,336
Land, buildings, and equipment, at cost (Notes B, C, and E)	15,992,912	15,365,117
Less accumulated depreciation	4,607,445	3,926,787
	11,385,467	11,438,330
	15,464,274	15,362,639
Endowment Funds:		
Cash and cash equivalents	32,967	9,591
Savings bank deposits	139,477	113,943
Investments, at cost (Note D)	512,890	509,808
Loan receivable from plant funds (Note E)	345,476	345,476
	1,030,810	978,818
	$20,407,942	$19,304,746

LIABILITIES AND FUND BALANCES

	1980	1979
Operating Fund:		
Accounts payable	$ 753,062	$ 748,600
Accrued payroll	176,056	124,415
Accrued interest expense	93,359	94,578
Accrued vacation expense	294,162	244,800
Other accrued expenses	80,521	71,399
Anticipated final settlements due to major third parties	107,232	519,635
Deferred tuition and other income	212,413	293,335
Current financing — Blue Cross	177,996	169,594
Due to plant funds	908,200	346,456
Fund balance	1,109,857	350,477
	3,912,858	2,963,289
Plant Funds:		
Accounts payable	15,996	79,035
FHA mortgage loan payable (Note E)	11,178,696	11,296,521
Long-term debt (Note E)	491,898	500,278
Lease obligations (Note C)	159,646	—
Loan payable to endowment funds (Note E)	345,476	345,476
Funds invested in land, buildings, and equipment	43,043	136,683
Funds designated for plant purposes:		
Board-designated for funded depreciation	2,310,323	2,384,861
Restricted sinking fund (Note E)	736,528	482,574
Restricted	182,668	137,211
	15,464,274	15,362,639
Endowment Funds:		
Due to operating fund	81,253	51,100
Due to plant funds	40,488	19,067
	121,741	70,167
Fund balance:		
Funds functioning as endowment	207,259	207,259
Principal and income available for donor-designated purposes	66,808	66,808
Principal held as endowment, income designated by the board for sinking fund purposes	635,002	634,584
	909,069	908,651
	1,030,810	978,818
	$20,407,942	$19,304,746

Table 1.2

STATEMENT OF OPERATIONS AND CHANGES IN FUND BALANCES
for the year ended September 30, 1980

| | PLANT FUNDS | | | | ENDOWMENT FUNDS | | | | | |
	Operating Fund	Funds Invested in Land, Buildings, and Equipment	Board-Designated for Funded Depreciation	Restricted Sinking Fund	Restricted	Funds Functioning as Endowment	Principal and Income Available for Donor-Designated Purposes	Principal Held as Endowment, Income Designated by the Board for Sinking Fund Purposes	Total	Year Ended Sept. 30, 1979 Total
Expenses:										
Direct costs of patient services:										
Routine	$ 2,954,030								$ 2,954,030	$ 2,531,342
Special	3,195,310								3,195,310	2,632,804
Emergency room	377,412								377,412	333,758
Administrative and general	2,489,426								2,489,426	2,313,262
Household and property	1,683,530								1,683,530	1,391,463
Dietary	838,595								838,595	734,045
School of Nursing	527,401								527,401	459,004
Depreciation	649,461								649,461	618,078
Interest and amortization	1,218,464								1,218,464	1,213,445
Total expenses	13,933,629								13,933,629	12,227,201
Revenues:										
Patient Services:										
Routine	9,460,115								9,460,115	8,865,210
Special	10,357,350								10,357,350	8,838,225
Emergency room	802,341								802,341	738,531
Total billed revenue	20,619,806								20,619,806	18,441,966
Less unreimbursed care and contractual adjustments including anticipated final settlements	6,544,139								6,544,139	5,688,439
Net patient services revenue	14,075,667								14,075,667	12,753,527
Other operating revenues	472,099								472,099	414,932
Net operating revenues	14,547,766								14,547,766	13,168,459
Excess of net operating revenues over expenses	614,137								614,137	941,258

Continued

Table 1.2 Continued

	PLANT FUNDS					ENDOWMENT FUNDS				
	Operating Fund	Funds Invested in Land, Buildings, and Equipment	Board-Designated for Funded Depreciation	Restricted Sinking Fund	Restricted	Funds Functioning as Endowment	Principal and Income Available for Donor-Designated Purposes	Principal Held as Endowment, Income Designated by the Board for Sinking Fund Purposes	Total	Year Ended Sept. 30, 1979 Total
Nonoperating revenues:										
Investment income and other nonoperating revenues, net	(95,671)		$ 321,440						225,769	312,398
Gifts and bequests	5,250								5,250	208,701
Excess of revenues over expenses	523,716		321,440						845,156	1,462,357
Contributions, gifts, and grants					$ 45,457			$ 212	45,669	119,979
Gain (loss) on sale of investments								206	206	59
Depreciation and amortization	592,942	$ (769,231)			176,289				—	—
Additions to plant fund assets		446,778	(446,778)						—	—
Payments of plant fund debt and payables	(52,524)	228,813			(176,289)				—	—
Interfund transfers	(304,754)		50,800	$253,954		$207,259	$66,808		—	—
Net changes in fund balances	759,380	(93,640)	(74,538)	253,954	45,457			418	891,031	1,582,395
Fund balances, beginning of year	350,477	136,683	2,384,861	482,574	137,211			634,584	4,400,457	2,818,062
Fund balances, end of year	$ 1,109,857	$ 43,043	$2,310,323	$736,528	$182,668	$207,259	$66,808	$635,002	$ 5,291,488	$ 4,400,457
Total unrestricted funds									$ 3,670,482	$ 3,079,280

Table 1.3

STATEMENT OF CHANGES IN FINANCIAL POSITION OF UNRESTRICTED FUNDS
for the year ended September 30, 1980

Funds provided from operations:	
Excess of revenues over expenses	$ 845,156
Expenses not requiring current funds — depreciation and amortization, net of amounts contractually required to be funded	592,942
Total funds provided by operations	1,438,098
Funds provided by capitalized lease obligations	166,163
Funds appropriated for plant and other purposes	789,111
Total funds provided	2,393,372
Funds applied:	
Plant additions	612,941
Debt repayments	165,774
Transfer to restricted sinking fund	253,954
	1,032,669
Increase in working capital	$1,360,703
Components of increase in working capital:	
Increase (decrease) in current assets:	
Cash and certificates of deposit	390,243
Accounts receivable, net	658,482
Deposits and deferred expenses	(127,682)
Interest receivable, inventories, and prepaid expenses	(1,627)
Due from restricted funds	30,153
	949,569
Decrease (increase) in current liabilities:	
Accounts payable and accrued expenses	(50,329)
Anticipated final settlements due to major third parties	412,403
Due to restricted funds	(23,460)
Other current liabilities	72,520
	411,134
Increase in working capital	$1,360,703

Table 1.4

BALANCE SHEETS
September 30, 1981
GENERAL FUNDS

Assets	1981	1980
Current assets:		
Cash	$ 370,142	$ 962,904
Accounts receivable, net of allowances for uncollectible accounts of $1,050,000 and $1,100,000	1,828,563	2,411,628
Other accounts receivable	84,831	118,384
Inventories	193,569	169,381
Deposits and prepaid expenses	163,730	142,272
Estimated settlements due from (to) third parties (Note H)	505,316	(107,232)
Due from restricted indentured funds	200,796	—
Due from endowment funds	54,982	74,778
Total current assets	3,401,929	3,772,115
Noncurrent assets:		
Cash and certificates of deposit restricted by loan agreement	14,031	224,031
Investments, at cost which approximates market (Note D)	2,845,148	1,361,116
Unamortized debt issue costs (Notes E and F)	477,458	823,815
Property, plant, and equipment, net of accumulated depreciation of $5,325,603 and $4,607,445 (Notes B, C, and F)	11,065,575	11,385,467
Total noncurrent assets	14,402,212	13,794,429
Total assets	$17,804,141	$17,566,544

Liabilities and Fund Balances	1981	1980
Current Liabilities:		
Current portion of long-term debt and capitalized lease obligations (Note F)	$ 222,865	$ 153,632
Current portion of loan payable to endowment fund (Note F)	69,096	69,096
Accounts payable	969,943	769,058
Accrued vacation expense	366,625	294,162
Other accrued expenses	553,959	349,936
Deferred tuition and other income	164,154	212,413
Current financing— Blue Cross	113,231	177,996
Due to funds restricted for plant purposes	160,707	124,040
Total current liabilities	2,620,580	2,150,533
Noncurrent liabilities:		
Long-term debt (Note F)	9,848,575	11,530,867
Lease obligations (Note C)	128,840	145,541
Loan payable to endowment fund (Note F)	207,284	276,380
Total noncurrent liabilities	10,184,699	11,952,788
Total liabilities	12,805,279	14,103,321
Fund balances:		
Operating	2,098,951	1,152,900
Board designated for funded depreciation	2,899,911	2,310,323
Total fund balances	4,998,862	3,463,223
Total liabilities and fund balances	$17,804,141	$17,566,544

RESTRICTED FUNDS

Indentured Funds

Assets	1981	1980	Liabilities and Fund Balances	1981	1980
Sinking fund investments (Note F)	$ 1,005,720	$ 736,528	Liabilities:		
Funds held by Trustee (Notes E and F)	447,724	—	Due to unrestricted funds	$ 200,796	$ 736,528
			Fund balances:		
			Restricted sinking fund (Note F)	1,005,720	736,528
			Restricted by bond indenture (Note F)	246,928	—
			Total fund balances	1,252,648	736,528
Total assets	$ 1,453,444	$ 736,528	Total liabilities and fund balances	$ 1,453,444	$ 736,528

Plant Replacement and Expansion Fund

Assets	1981	1980	Liabilities and Fund Balances	1981	1980
Cash	160,707	11,665	Fund balance	216,788	182,668
Due from unrestricted funds	—	124,040			
Due from endowment funds	56,081	46,963			
Total assets	$ 216,788	$ 182,668	Total fund balance	$ 216,788	$ 182,668

ENDOWMENT FUNDS

Assets	1981	1980	Liabilities and Fund Balances	1981	1980
Cash and cash equivalents	172,907	172,444	Liabilities:		
Investments, at cost (Notes D and F)	587,552	512,890	Due to unrestricted funds	54,982	74,778
Loan receivable from unrestricted funds (Note F)	276,380	345,476	Due to plant replacement and expansion fund	56,081	46,963
				111,063	121,741
			Fund balances:		
			Funds functioning as endowment	207,259	207,259
			Principal and income available for donor-designated purposes	66,808	66,808
			Principal held as endowment, income designated by the Board	651,709	635,002
			Total fund balances	925,776	909,069
Total assets	$1,036,839	$1,030,810	Total liabilities and fund balances	$ 1,036,839	$ 1,030,810

The notes in Appendix 1.2 are an integral part of the financial statements.

Table 1.5

STATEMENTS OF OPERATIONS
for the year ended September 30, 1981

	1981	1980
Patient service revenue:		
Routine	$ 9,317,425	$ 9,460,115
Special	12,580,208	10,357,350
Emergency room	1,064,801	802,341
Total revenue	22,962,434	20,619,806
Deductions from patient service revenue:		
Contractual adjustments	5,463,306	4,908,730
Unreimbursed care	858,201	749,546
Provision for uncollectible accounts	712,332	885,863
Total deductions from patient service revenue	7,033,839	6,544,139
Net patient service revenue	15,928,595	14,075,667
Other operating revenues	480,802	472,099
Net operating revenues	16,409,397	14,547,766
Operating expenses:		
Routine	3,565,446	2,954,030
Special	3,850,031	3,195,310
Emergency room	443,724	377,412
Administrative and general	3,115,764	2,489,426
Household and property	1,845,573	1,683,530
Dietary	934,140	838,595
School of Nursing	580,450	527,401
Depreciation	686,063	649,461
Interest and amortization	1,247,093	1,218,464
Total expenses	16,268,284	13,933,629
Net operating revenues in excess of operating expenses	141,113	614,137
Nonoperating revenues:		
Investment income and other nonoperating revenues	588,799	225,769
Gifts and bequests	27,341	5,250
Excess of revenues over expenses before extraordinary item	757,253	845,156
Extraordinary item—gain on early extinguishment of debt (Note E)	1,294,506	—
Excess of revenues over expenses	$ 2,051,759	$ 845,156

The notes in Appendix 1.2 are an integral part of the financial statements.

Table 1.6

STATEMENT OF CHANGES IN FUND BALANCES
for the year ended September 30, 1981

GENERAL FUNDS

	Operating Fund	Board Designated for Funded Depreciation	Total
Fund balance, beginning of the year	$1,152,900	$2,310,323	$3,463,223
Excess of revenues over expenses	2,051,759		2,051,759
Proceeds of debt issue transferred to indentured funds	(595,920)		(595,920)
Payment of debt issue costs	314,538		314,538
Interest deposit from indentured funds	34,454		34,454
Transfer to restricted sinking fund	(269,192)		(269,192)
Plant acquisitions funded by funded depreciation	398,266	(398,266)	—
Transfer of investment income to funded depreciation	(599,000)	599,000	—
Other transfers to funded depreciation	(388,854)	388,854	—
Fund balance, end of the year	$2,098,951	$2,899,911	$4,998,862

RESTRICTED FUNDS

	Indentured Funds		Plant Replacement and Expansion Fund	
	Restricted Sinking Fund	Restricted by Bond Indenture		
Fund balance, beginning of the year	$ 736,528		$182,668	919,196
Contributions, gifts, and grants			34,120	34,120
Transfer from operating fund	269,192	$595,920		865,112
Transfer to operating fund for:				
Payment of debt issue costs		(314,538)		(314,538)
Payment of interest expense		(34,454)		(34,454)
Fund balance, end of the year	$1,005,720	$246,928	$216,788	$1,469,436

ENDOWMENT FUNDS

	Unrestricted Funds Functioning as Endowment	Principal and Income Available for Donor Designated Purposes	Principal Held as Endowment, Income Designated by the Board	
Fund balance, beginning of the year	$207,259	$66,808	$ 635,002	909,069
Contributions, gifts and grants			337	337
Gain on sale of investments			16,370	16,370
Fund balance, end of the year	$207,259	$66,808	$ 651,709	$ 925,776
Total unrestricted funds				$5,206,121

The notes in Appendix 1.2 are an integral part of the financial statements.

Table 1.7

STATEMENT OF CHANGES IN FINANCIAL POSITION OF UNRESTRICTED FUNDS
for the year ended September 30, 1981

Funds provided from operations:	
Excess of revenues over expenses before extraordinary item	$ 757,253
Expenses not requiring current funds:	
Depreciation and amortization	821,510
Interest expense funded by restricted fund	34,454
Funds provided by operations exclusive of extraordinary item	1,613,217
Extraordinary item—gain on early extinguishment of debt	1,294,506
Credits included in extraordinary item which did not provide working capital	(1,514,506)
Total funds provided by operations	1,393,217
Use of funded depreciation for fixed asset additions	398,266
Proceeds of issuance of MHEFA Bonds (Note E)	7,235,726
Total funds provided	9,027,209
Funds applied:	
Additions to property, plant, and equipment	398,266
Debt repayment and increase in current portion of long-term debt	222,864
Repayment of endowment fund loan	69,096
Deposits to restricted funds held by Trustee	595,920
Repurchase of debt (Note E)	6,639,806
Transfer to restricted sinking fund	269,192
Increase in assets designated for funded depreciation	1,672,298
Total funds applied	9,867,442
Decrease in working capital	$ (840,233)
Components of decrease in working capital:	
Increase (decrease) in current assets:	
Cash	(592,762)
Accounts receivable, net	(616,618)
Inventories	24,188
Deposits and prepaid expenses	21,458
Current portion of funds held by Trustee	200,796
Estimated settlements due from third parties	612,548
Due from endowment funds	(19,796)
	(370,186)
Decrease (increase in current liabilities:	
Accounts payable and accrued expenses	(404,908)
Current portion of long-term debt	(69,033)
Due to restricted funds	(36,667)
Other current liabilities	40,561
	(470,047)
Decrease in working capital	$ (840,233)

The notes in Appendix 1.2 are an integral part of the financial statements.

Appendix 1.1

AUDITOR'S OPINION

To the Trustees of
Somerville Hospital:

We have examined the balance sheet of Somerville Hospital as of September 30, 1981, and the related statements of operations, changes in fund balances and changes in financial position of the unrestricted funds for the year then ended. Our examination was made in accordance with generally accepted auditing standards and, accordingly, included such tests of the accounting records and such other auditing procedures as we considered necessary in the circumstances. We previously examined and reported upon the 1980 financial statements which are included in condensed form for comparative purposes only.

In our opinion, the aforementioned financial statements present fairly the financial position of Somerville Hospital at September 30, 1981, the results of its operations, changes in fund balances, and changes in financial position of the unrestricted funds for the year then ended, in conformity with generally accepted accounting principles applied on a basis consistent with that of the preceding year.

Our examination was made for the purpose of forming an opinion on the basic financial statements taken as a whole. The other information included in this report on pages 14 through 21 is presented for purposes of additional analysis and is not a required part of the basic financial statements. Such information has been subjected to the auditing procedures applied in the examination of the basic financial statements and, in our opinion, is fairly stated in all material respects in relation to the basic financial statements taken as a whole.

Boston, Massachusetts   Coopers & Lybrand
April 30, 1982

Appendix 1.2

NOTES TO SOMERVILLE HOSPITAL FINANCIAL STATEMENTS

A. Summary of Significant Accounting Policies

Basis of Presentation
The financial statements have been prepared on the accrual basis of accounting. To reflect observance of restrictions placed on the use of resources available to Somerville Hospital, the accounts are maintained in accordance with the principles of fund accounting. Under these principles resources are grouped for accounting and reporting purposes into funds according to their nature and use.

The financial statements for 1981 and 1980 reflect certain reclassifications and changes in format and presentation of the various funds. These changes have been made by the hospital to aggregate the financial position of unrestricted funds used in operations and to more clearly segregate unrestricted fund activities. The 1980 balances and summaries are included in the financial statements for comparative purposes only.

Third-Party Revenues and Contractual Adjustments
The hospital has various agreements with third-party payers for reimbursement on a cost basis for services provided to patients. Final settlement of these arrangements is subject to audit and adjustments by the third parties. The current and several prior years' third-party settlement reports are subject to such adjustments. The financial statements reflect estimated final audited reimbursement amounts. Differences, if any, between anticipated preliminary and actual final settlements are recognized as they are determined on a current basis.

Contributions
Contributions in kind are recorded at fair market value at the date of gift. Gifts are classified as either unrestricted or restricted in accordance with the terms of the gift. Gifts, grants, and investment income which are unrestricted are included in income when received.

Inventories
Inventories are stated at the lower of cost (first-in, first-out method) or market.

Depreciation and Capitalization
Land, buildings, and equipment are stated at cost. Depreciation is computed on the straight-line method utilizing estimated useful lives recommended by the American Hospital Association. Leases which represent equipment purchases under accounting pronouncements are reflected as such and the related assets are depreciated over the lesser of the lease term or the estimated useful lives.

The costs of repairs and maintenance are charged to operations as incurred. Debt issue costs and bond discount are amortized on the interest method.

The hospital has designated all investment income to be used for the purpose of funding depreciation. The hospital also funds current and prior years' depreciation expense through transfers to funded depreciation investments and fund balances.

B. Land, Buildings, and Equipment:

Land, buildings, and equipment at September 30 consist of:

	1981	1980
Land and land improvements	$ 584,274	$ 513,028
Buildings and building improvements	6,693,981	6,631,424
Fixed equipment	6,879,484	6,874,316
Major movable equipment	2,006,677	1,747,382
Leased equipment and leasehold improvements	226,762	226,762
	16,391,178	15,992,912
Less: Accumulated depreciation	5,325,603	4,607,445
	$11,065,575	$11,385,467

C. Lease Obligations:

The following is a schedule of future equipment lease payments under capital leases, together with the present value of the net minimum lease payments as of September 30, 1981:

Fiscal year 1982	$ 40,178
Fiscal years 1983 through 1987	187,498
Total minimum lease payments	227,676
Less: Interest	82,136
Present value of net minimum lease payments	$145,540

The hospital is also leasing space and equipment under operating leases for periods of five to seven years. Rental expense for leased space and equipment approximated $161,000 for 1981. The following is a schedule by fiscal year of future minimum rental payments required under noncancelable operating leases:

Fiscal year:	Payments:
1982	$161,000
1983	151,000
1984	83,000
1985	4,000
	$399,000

D. Investments:

Endowment funds investments at September 30 consist of:

	1981		1980	
	Cost	Market	Cost	Market
Bonds	$408,538	$317,761	$362,901	$301,109
Stocks	179,014	200,290	149,989	189,066
	$587,552	$518,051	$512,890	$490,175

Investments of the unrestricted fund consist primarily of certificates of deposit which bear interest at 14.5 percent to 17.75 percent at September 30, 1981.

E. Refinancing of Long-Term Debt:

On June 25, 1981, the hospital repurchased approximately 79 percent of the debt associated with its Federal Housing Administration (FHA) mortgage. Under the repurchase agreement, the hospital was required to pay $6,639,806 to repurchase debt with a principal balance of $8,771,876 net of unamortized discount, resulting in an extraordinary gain of $1,294,506.

The repurchase was financed through the issuance of $9,140,000 of Massachusetts Health and Educational Facilities Authority (MHEFA) Revenue Bonds, Somerville Hospital Issue, Series A, which were discounted to yield the hospital $7,235,726. From the proceeds of the bond issue, the hospital was required to deposit $595,920 with the Trustee (Shawmut Bank of Boston, N.A.) to cover debt issue costs and to provide certain debt service funds.

F. Long-Term Debt:

Long-term debt consists of the following:

	Current	Sept. 30, 1981 Long-Term	Total	Sept. 30, 1980 Total
FHA-GNMA Guaranteed Mortgage (1):				
Portion One	$ 37,607	$2,263,697	$ 2,301,304	$11,178,696
Portion Two	160,000	7,110,003	7,270,003	—
Nurses Dormitory Bonds (2)	7,000	454,000	461,000	468,000
Other (3)	1,558	20,875	22,433	23,898
	206,165	$9,848,575	$10,054,740	$11,670,594
Current portion of capitalized lease obligations	16,700			
	$222,865			

(1) *FHA-GNMA Guaranteed Mortgage*

In connection with the financing of a new facility in 1975, the hospital entered into a Federal Housing Administration (FHA) mortgage loan agreement which is insured by the U.S. Department of Housing and Urban Development and reinsured by the Government National Mortgage Association. The debt is secured by a mortgage on substantially all of the hospital's property, plant, and equipment. After the modification of the original mortgage through the issuance of MHEFA Revenue Bonds (as described in Note E), the FHA mortgage loan agreement consisted of two portions:

Portion One — Financing of Portion One was provided through the issuance of $2,500,000 GNMA-guaranteed securities with repayment over a 25-year period beginning in June of 1978 at an annual interest rate of 9 percent. The balance of Portion One at September 30, 1981, has been reduced by unamortized discount of $95,121 which is being amortized over the term of the debt.

Portion Two — Financing of Portion Two was provided through the issuance of $9,140,000 of MHEFA Revenue Bonds, Somerville Hospital Issue, Series A, which bear interest at 7.5 percent and are payable in varying semiannual installments from January 1, 1982, through July 1, 2003. The hospital's monthly principal and interest payments of $70,452 are deposited into restricted indentured funds held by the Trustee, out of which the bond principal and interest payments are made to the bondholders. The balance of Portion Two at September 30, 1981, has been reduced by unamortized discount of $1,869,997 which is being amortized over the term of the debt resulting in an effective interest rate of 10.6 percent.

Under the terms of the FHA mortgage loan agreement, the hospital is required to provide a restricted sinking fund in an amount sufficient to amortize the loan principal throughout the term of the loan. The balance in this fund was $1,005,720 at September 30, 1981. The hospital must meet the following minimum requirements at September 30 of each year:

1982	$1,291,063
1983	1,593,527
1984	1,914,139
1985	2,228,987
1986	2,562,726
1987– 1996	2,876,490 increasing to $5,009,413
1996– 2003	5,009,413 decreasing to $2,182,158

(2) *Nurses Dormitory Bonds*

The Nurses Dormitory Bonds issued on November 1, 1965, were issued in connection with the construction of a dormitory for the Nursing School. The bonds are redeemable on November 1 of each year in varying amounts to the year 2015 at an interest rate of 3 percent, and are collateralized by a first mortgage on the dormitory. Additionally, in connection with the issue, there is a first lien on, and a pledge of income from, an endowment escrow account which had a net book value of approximately $319,000 at September 30, 1981.

(3) *Other*

The hospital has entered into mortgages on certain residential properties. The mortgage agreements carry interest rates of 5.25 percent and 7 percent and have final payment dates in 1985 and 1997, respectively.

(4) In connection with the funding of original issue discount associated with the FHA mortgage loan agreement, the Board of Trustees approved a loan of endowment funds assets to the plant fund. The loan, which had a balance of $276,380 at September 30, 1981, is payable over a five-year period in equal semiannual installments beginning October 1, 1980, with interest at prime.

G. Pension Plan:

The hospital's pension plan covers substantially all regular employees over 25 years of age who have been employed by the hospital for more than one year. The total expense for 1981 amounted to approximately $132,000, which includes amortization of past service costs over a 30-year period. The hospital's policy is to fund pension costs accrued. Present values of accumulated plan benefits include an increase of $256,037 resulting from a plan amendment which increased participants' benefits adopted as of October 1, 1980.

The actuarial present value of accumulated benefits to participants of the plan and the net assets available for those benefits at October 1, 1980, are as follows:

Actuarial present value of accumulated plan benefits:

Vested	$771,530
Nonvested	176,234
	$947,764
Net assets available for benefits	$747,937

In determining the actuarial present value of accumulated plan benefits, an assumed rate of return of 5 percent compounded annually was used.

H. Third-Party Reimbursement Appeals:

The hospital has a number of appeals in process with the Rate Setting Commission for current and prior years' Industrial Accident and Medicaid reimbursement rates. The financial statements reflect an estimate of the amounts which will be successfully resolved.

2

Mid-State Medical Group

Keith E. Boles

In early spring 1983, Lew Hollis was considering how to respond to his directive from the Executive Committee of Mid-State Medical Group. Dr. Hollis was chairman of the committee which had to contend with several nonmedical issues. One had to deal with a reorganization proposal presented by Harold Calloway, the interim administrator. A related issue was the evaluation of Mr. Calloway, who had held the position of interim administrator for just over two years. The informal agreement was that he would be "interim" for a maximum of two years and that a decision would be made about his future by the end of that time period. Mr. Calloway was pressing for a decision, and his proposed structural reorganization included himself as the administrator. The committee members liked Mr. Calloway personally and knew he was a good personnel manager. However, they were unsure how to evaluate his management capabilities related to the financial aspects of the group practice. Thus, the committee had instructed Dr. Hollis to contract with an independent consulting firm with experience in the health care arena to perform an evaluation of Mid-State Medical Group. This evaluation would give the committee justification for the decision they were to make regarding Mr. Calloway and his reorganization proposal.

MEDICAL GROUP PRACTICE

History

The first medical group practice was a partnership formed between Dr. W. W. May and his two sons in Rochester, Minnesota, in 1887. Growth in the number of group practices was steady but slow until the 1930s, when there was a proliferation of specialty boards, as shown in the following table:

Year	Number
1887	1 group
1926	125 groups
1932	221 groups
1959	1,546 groups
1965	4,289 groups
1969	6,371 groups
1976	8,483 groups

With an increasing number of specialty boards and a concurrent increase in the number of physicians who continued their education to qualify for board certification, physicians sought an environment in which they could practice in their limited specialties. They also were seeking a situation where other disciplines of medicine, as well as specialized equipment and diagnostic facilities, would be readily available in the same location. Other factors which contributed to the rapid growth of medical groups included the surge in definite surgery, with its concomitant need for technical co-workers and teamwork; the early popularity of spas and sanatoria with their need for specialized staff; the development of large individual practices, with the consequent need for professional associates; and the gradual development of group patterns in clinical teaching.

The Medical Group Management Association uses the following definition of medical group practice: "the provision of health care services by a group of at least three, licensed, physician-practitioners, engaged full time in a formally organized and legally recognized entity; sharing the group's income and expenses in a systematic manner; and sharing facilities, equipment, common records, and personnel, involved in both patient care and business management."[1]

The advantages and disadvantages to physicians of belonging to a group practice can be broken down as follows:

Advantages:

1. Sharing of knowledge and responsibility

2. Best utilization of specialists' skills, as well as those of the general practitioner

3. Keeping up with the developments in medicine more easily than in a solo practice

4. High standards resulting from the interchange of ideas

5. Money and time for study and training are generally considered to be part of the remuneration of physicians in the group

6. Regular rotation of hours and sharing of after-hours emergencies

7. Entry into a ready-made practice provides immediate income to the physician who has just completed the long and costly training period

8. Relief from the business aspects of the practice of medicine, for which the individual has most likely received no training

9. Ability to present one's views concerning policy and programming within the group within a fairly short period after joining the group

10. Availability of ancillary services, personnel, and facilities

11. Cooperative spirit engendered in the "family of doctors" for the "family of patients"

Disadvantages:

1. Some loss of freedom to practice as one wishes and some loss of individuality

2. Level and method of sharing income may present problems. Most group practice salaries are based on several factors which are not relevant to solo practice

3. Conformity to established levels of practice, quality of care, and formulary and operating procedures

4. Patients are "plan patients," not a single "physician's patients"

Organization

In establishing a medical group practice, several important questions dealing with the business aspects of the practice must be addressed. The answers to these questions can have a long-term effect on the stability and ease of operation of the practice. Questions dealing with the business aspect of the group practice would include:

1. What organizational form is to be used?
2. What business year is to be used?
3. What method of accounting is to be established?

All small business enterprises must resolve these questions at one or more points in their development. However, there are several aspects unique to the delivery of health care that have implications for the resolution of these issues for a medical group practice. A medical group practice essentially consists of two separate and distinct organizations—a "professional organization" of physicians and a "management organization" of administrators. This distinction is reflected in Figure 2.1, and is an important variable in the solution of the questions listed above.

The first question has no simple answer that is correct for all situations. The advantages and disadvantages of one organizational form over another are beyond the scope of this discussion, although several points can be made. The group's professional activities require working capital only. However, the provision of facilities and equipment requires capital accumulation. Thus, the use of separate organizations to meet the group's professional needs and its equipment and facility needs offers a significant business advantage. Many group practices have two distinct firms, one consisting of the professional activities and the second consisting of the real estate and equipment ownership activities. For instance, a corporate organizational form may be used to accumulate capital and capital assets, while a professional corporation, professional association, or partnership may be used to provide medical services. In this instance, a corporation can be established with a relatively small capital outlay, with the physicians of the professional organization investing as stockholders. Capital assets may be purchased with original capital and debt financing, and may be leased to the professional organization. All or a major portion of the corporate income after taxes may be retained to meet additional capital asset needs and/or to retire any debts incurred.

If a partnership form for the professional organization is used, the second question needs to be carefully considered. Partners include in income their distributive share of the partnership income and any guaranteed payments from a partnership whose tax year ends with or within the partner's taxable year. Thus, partners would report their income for a partnership year ended January 31, 1982, on their 1982 income tax returns. The result is an effective deferral of partnership income for up to 11 months. That is, any distributions made after January 31, 1981, would not be reported until the filing of the partners' 1982 income tax returns.

The choice of the business year to be used is also important in answering the third question—whether to use cash or accrual accounting. Although a complete discussion of the advantages and disadvantages of each method is not possible here, several points can be made. Under the cash basis, the business year implications are as described in the previous paragraph. With the accrual basis, however, it becomes desirable to close the business year at a time when

Figure 2.1
MSMG ORGANIZATIONAL CHART

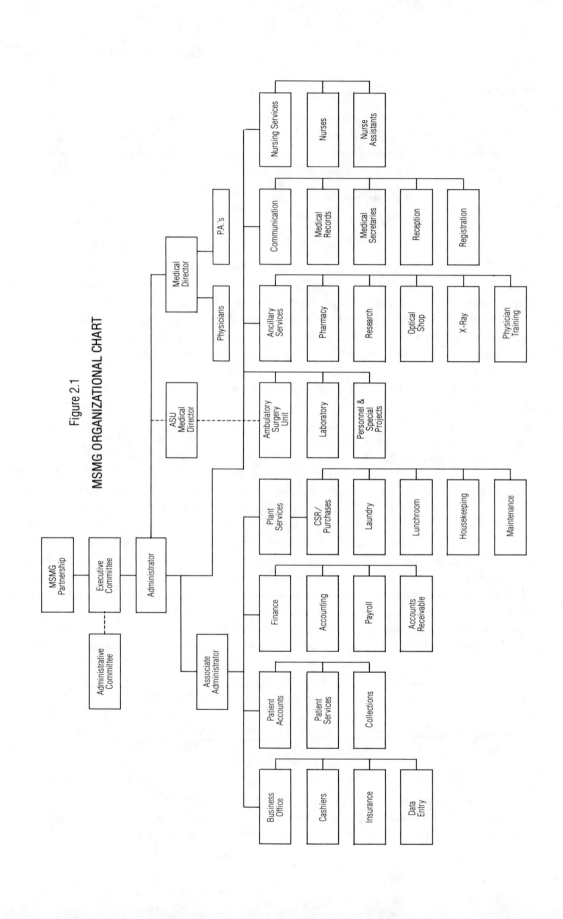

accounts receivable are at a minimum. At this time, a greater portion of the accounts receivable—upon which a tax liability exists—has been converted into funds which can be used to pay the liability. On the other hand, while the cash basis may be more advantageous from a tax standpoint, the accrual basis lends itself more readily to managerial control and analysis of current operations. There is no prolonged period between production and recognition of earnings and it is far easier to match revenues with the expenses required to generate those revenues. Further, the use of the accrual basis greatly reduces the fluctuations that occur frequently in cash-basis data as a consequence of short-term economic conditions. Unlike the cash basis, accrual accounting provides accounting records consistent with the flows of clinical activity, not short-term economic changes.

MID-STATE MEDICAL GROUP

History

Mid-State Medical Group (MSMG) was first established as a multispecialty general partnership in 1946. At that time there were 7 physician partners. Growth of the community was mirrored in the growth of the partnership to 12 members by 1955. By 1963, growth had forced the partnership to expand into an adjacent building. Profitability and willing reinvestment by the partners permitted the demolition of these two buildings in 1968 and the construction of a modern medical facility on the same site. Rapid growth in the community insulated MSMG somewhat from the shakeout being experienced by group practices in the late 1960s and early 1970s. Between 1969 and 1975, over 25 percent of the groups operating in the U.S. were dissolved, while MSMG expanded to 35 physicians. Nevertheless, MSMG suffered a setback of its own due to a declining economy, personality-caused disputes, and an unsuccessful attempt at establishing a branch clinic, all of which resulted in the loss of 13 partners by 1978. The remaining physicians maintained the aggressiveness which had kept the group viable and were able to add a successful ambulatory surgical unit in 1978 and a highly profitable branch clinic in 1979. At present, there are 30 physicians.

Several of the partners established an HMO in 1979, a period in which HMOs were not doing as well as had been anticipated in the early 1970s. MSMG has a contractual relationship with the HMO and in 1982 the HMO provided 35 percent of MSMG's patients. MSMG intended that the HMO contract would never provide more than 50 percent of the group's patient load, and the mix between HMO and fee-for-service patients would stabilize before the HMO portion of the practice reached 50 percent.

Management

The physician partners of MSMG had long been aware of the need for a nonphysician to coordinate the office, and MSMG had always had a business manager. However, during the mid- to late 1970s it also became obvious that a "business manager" did not have the requisite skills to oversee and manage the assets and finances of a group practice in a changing medical care environment. Thus, the Executive Committee decided to hire an administrator with the experience and training necessary to be a personnel-financial-accounting manager. Between 1977 and late 1980, three administrators had come and gone as Dr. Hollis and the Executive

Committee attempted to find the right person. In 1980, Mr. Calloway was hired as the fourth administrator.

Mr. Calloway was 32 years old when he joined MSMG, his third position with a group practice. After receiving his M.H.A. in 1975 he had gone to work for a group with five partners and served primarily as a business manager. Prior to joining MSMG he had worked as an assistant administrator for a 15-member group practice. He had left that position for personal reasons and been appointed interim administrator for MSMG four months later. During his tenure with MSMG he became associated with the younger members of the medical staff and his social activities tended to revolve around this group.

Dr. Hollis contacted International Healthcare Consultants, Unlimited (IHC), regarding the evaluation of the financial status of MSMG. During the initial contact, the following explanation was given by Andy Lassiter, senior consultant, in response to a question by Dr. Hollis regarding the financial analysis of a multispecialty group practice:

> Financial ratio analysis in non-healthcare fields has been an accepted methodology for many years. Hospitals have recently accepted this type of analysis and the approach is appropriate for other health-related type institutions. What we do is calculate ratios from your financial statements and then look at them from two directions. First, we determine what has been happening to these relationships over time; i.e., what is the trend? This can give us indications about where you have been and where you are going. Secondly, we generally assume that there are certain ranges for these relationships that are good, and if the values are outside of these ranges then corrective action needs to be taken in order to bring the relationship into the acceptable range. The problem is determining the acceptable range. Hospitals have been collecting and publishing ratio values under the assumption that the average of all hospitals is probably an acceptable value. Collection of this information has been simplified due to the fact that almost all hospitals are incorporated and most follow the AHA's suggested chart of accounts. This allows consistency and comparability in hospital reporting. However, the Medical Group Management Association sends out questionnaires and if enough group practices respond, can get a fairly good idea of some of these ratio values. The MGMA distributes this information in the form of a *Cost and Production Survey Report*. They also publish an *Administrative Compensation and Fringe Benefit Report* which you might wish to take a look at.

In further discussions between Dr. Hollis and Mr. Lassiter, an agreement was reached on the scope and data requirements of the study to be performed by the consulting group.

The evaluation was to be performed using the past five years of data. In addition, Mr. Lassiter convinced Dr. Hollis that it would be a fairly straightforward procedure to use the five years of data to project future cash flow, balance sheet, and income statement information. The discussion centered around the relative value of percent-of-sales and regression techniques as forecasting tools, and the value of forecasting as a strategic planning tool. A forecast, by definition, is a best guess, and the most that can be expected is to minimize the difference between the actual and forecasted value over time. Both percent-of-sales and regression techniques make implicit assumptions which must be taken into consideration in the interpretation of forecasts derived by either technique. For example, the percent-of-sales method assumes a static and constant relationship between different asset accounts and sales volume, when in fact the relationship is not and should not be constant (e.g., inventory). Regression analysis goes to the other extreme and assumes that differences and changes will continue, so that if inventory relative to sales has been decreasing in the past it will continue to decrease even more in the future. Subjectivity must be introduced to arrive at a compromise between these two mathematical techniques.

It soon became obvious to Dr. Hollis that Mr. Lassiter was hoping to generate a continuing relationship with MSMG through the development of a financial model of MSMG and the continual monitoring and updating of that model.

Organization

MSMG is made up of two separate partnerships. One owns the real estate and equipment while the other runs the medical operations, leasing the assets from the first partnership. Membership in the two partnerships is identical. Since the two partnerships have the same bookkeeping and accounting department, the decision was made long ago to establish different fiscal years for the two partnerships. This was expected to reduce the work load of the accounting department at report time.

To perform a meaningful financial analysis of MSMG, however, it is necessary to consolidate the two sets of records by putting them on the same time frame and eliminating any interpartnership transactions. Of even more consequence is the fact that MSMG records had been maintained on the cash basis until Harold Calloway was hired in 1980. Mr. Calloway changed to accrual accounting and was able to implement the change for the most recently completed fiscal year.

Although the cash basis is a simpler method of accounting, there are certain difficulties with its use. Accrual accounting information is considered to be more representative of the firm during and at the end of an accounting period. Since a major objective of published financial statements is to provide users with information to help them predict, compare, and evaluate future earning ability and cash flows, cash accounting is not generally acceptable except in the cases where the differences between the two accounting methods are immaterial.

Lew Hollis had discussed with a representative of the CPA firm the requirements of IHC for the analysis desired by MSMG. For the CPA firm to provide the required data, it was necessary first to consolidate the financial statements from the two partnerships, and then to work backwards from the cash-basis accounting statements to derive the accrual-basis accounting statements. Although the worksheets used to derive the figures were not sent to IHC, data concerning fiscal year 1982 and ratios for 1978 – 1981 were received in the mail from the CPA firm. This information is presented in Tables 2.1 and 2.2 It was against this background that an evaluation of the past and potential future financial performance of MSMG was to be made.

NOTE

1. MGMA Center for Research in Ambulatory Health Care Administration, *The Organization and Development of a Medical Group Practice* (Denver: MGMA, 1976), p. 2.

Table 2.1

MSMG FINANCIAL DATA
1982

Gross revenues ($)	6,346,562.00
Deductibles* (contractual allowances + bad debts) (%)	4.2
Total asset turnover	1.52
Current ratio	4.60
Acid-test ratio*	1.35
Average collection period (days)	63
Fixed asset turnover	2.84
Accumulated depreciation ($)	1,929,027.00
Average payment period	38.3 days
Times interest earned (%)	9.0
Return on total assets	51.9
Current assets/total assets	.42
Long-term debt to partner's invested capital	2.4
Composition of fixed assets (%):	
Land	13
Building	57
Parking lot, medical library, leasehold improvements	1.5
Furnishings and equipment	28.5
Composition of current liabilities (%):	
Accounts payable	35
Payroll taxes payable	12
Accrued wages	4
Property taxes payable	5
Long-term debt, current portion	28
Deferred revenue	8
Due to retirement plan	8
Composition of operating expenses (%):	
Nonphysician salaries	41
Medical supplies and services	26
Other supplies and services	21
Employed physician salaries	5
Building and equipment expense	6
Administrative expenses	1

*Healthcare Financial Management Association definitions.

SELECTED BIBLIOGRAPHY

Choate, G. Marc, and Tanako, Kazuaki. "Using Financial Ratio Analysis to Compare Hospitals' Performance." *Hospital Progress* 60 (12): 310– 338.

American Medical Association. *Group Practice: Guidelines to Joining or Forming a Medical Group.* Chicago: AMA, 1970.

Goodman, Lanis J., and Treshnock, Larry J. "Why Medical Groups Fail." *Medical Group Management* 25 (6): 10– 14.

Hospital Financial Management Association. *Hospital Industry Analysis Report,* Financial Analysis Service. Oak Brook, Ill.: HFMA, 1982.

Table 2.2

MSMG FINANCIAL DATA
1978 – 1981

	1981	1980	1979	1978
Return on total assets	13.5%	30.2%	40.6%	44.1%
Total asset turnover	1.28	1.27	1.26	1.32
Current ratio	2.73	3.10	5.13	4.38
Quick ratio	2.50	3.10	5.05	4.37
Acid-test ratio	2.48	1.19	3.70	2.16
Collection period	73.3 days	87.8 days	96.0 days	95.2 days
Average payment period	41.9 days	40.6 days	10.7 days	2.3 days
Ownership financing ratio	.123	.208	.322	.375
Cash flow to total debt	.36	.38	.60	.71
Long-term debt to partner's capital	6.30	3.32	2.03	1.45
Fixed asset financing ratio	1.15	1.08	1.20	.91
Times interest earned	5.34	5.36	8.72	13.6
Fixed asset turnover	1.90	1.98	2.30	2.21
Current asset turnover	4.57	4.11	3.01	3.69
Markup	1.43	1.42	1.57	1.56
Operating margin	.30	.29	.36	.56
Net profit margin	.25	.24	.32	.33

Kilpatrick, S. James, Jr. *Statistical Principles in Health Care Information.* Baltimore: University Park Press, 1973.

Koza, Russel C. *Mathematical and Operations Research Techniques in Health Administration.* Boulder: Colorado Associated University Press, 1973.

Lev, Baruch. *Financial Statement Analysis: A New Approach.* Englewood Cliffs, N. J.: Prentice-Hall, 1974.

Medical Group Management Association. *Administrative Compensation and Fringe Benefit Report: 1980.* Denver: MGMA, 1980.

Medical Group Management Association. *The Cost and Production Survey Report: 1982 Report Based on 1981 Data.* Denver: MGMA, 1982.

MGMA Center for Research in Ambulatory Health Care Administration. *The Organization and Development of a Medical Group Practice.* Denver: MGMA Center for Research in Ambulatory Health Care Administration, 1976.

Robert Wood Johnson Foundation. *Medical Practice in the United States: Special Report.* Princeton, N. J.: The Robert Wood Johnson Foundation, 1982.

Shouldice, Robert G., and Shouldice, Katherine H. *Medical Group Practice and Health Maintenance Organization.* Washington, D.C.: Information Resources Press, 1978.

3

The New Hampshire-Vermont Hospitalization Service

Regina Herzlinger

The last two paragraphs of the letter read:

> Blue Cross is at present insolvent. Its liabilities exceed its assets. It is operating, in effect, by using Peter's money to pay Paul; i.e., current expenditures are being met from funds held to meet claims incurred on which payment will be due in the future.
>
> Whatever may be said for cash basis operations for a short period in an emergency, continuation of that condition due to inadequate rates has placed Blue Cross on the verge of total collapse which is highly likely in the next three or four months if adequate rate levels are not promptly instituted.

The letter, addressed to Oliver R. Fifield, Acting President of the New Hampshire-Vermont Hospitalization Service (Blue Cross),[1] was signed by an actuary from the company's auditors, Peat, Marwick, Mitchell & Company of New York. The date was December 5, 1973. Three weeks later, New Hampshire-Vermont Blue Cross applied to the insurance commissioners of New Hampshire and Vermont for rate adjustments to go into effect on February 1, 1974.

In the rate filing, Mr. Fifield explained the purpose of the increase:

. . . the suggested rates will accomplish three things within the year 1974:

1. balance income and expense,
2. correct the present insolvent position of the Plan, and
3. provide a small reserve on December 31, 1974.

Without the proposed rate changes for the period of February 1, 1974, to January 31,

1975, Mr. Fifield warned, Blue Cross would experience a loss of more than $3 million for the year. But as public hearings on the rate filing opened in January 1974, the insurance commissioners were skeptical. They simply did not believe that Blue Cross was insolvent. In response to a previous Blue Cross rate filing (November 1972), the Vermont commissioner had written that although the Plan might become "technically insolvent from time to time," it had "sufficient cash and liquid assets to meet its current obligations."[2] Neither commissioner believed that the situation had changed in the intervening years.

BLUE CROSS

During the Depression of the 1930s, U.S. hospitals experienced a sharp drop in their major source of income, payment from clients for services rendered. Faced with unpaid bills and empty beds, hospitals in several different communities joined together to establish local non-profit corporations selling prepaid hospitalization insurance to groups of employees working for a single organization or institution. So receptive were individual subscribers as well as member hospitals to the Blue Cross concept that Blue Cross was well on its way to becoming a national institution by the end of the Depression. The principle of voluntary, community-oriented, prepayment plans for consumers using short-term general hospitals was endorsed in 1933 by the American Hospital Association (AHA), the organization that represents most of the hospitals in the United States. AHA propounded several basic principles that have been adopted by all Blue Cross Plans; namely, that the Plans should cover payment for hospital care but not physicians' services; that subscribers should have free choice of hospitals; that Blue Cross should be nonprofit; that the Plans should be "financially sound"; that all licensed hospitals in a given community should participate; and that the hospitals should retain full responsibility for patient services. AHA placed particular emphasis on the principle that each Blue Cross Plan should be organized as a "public service."

Today there are 73 Blue Cross Plans throughout the United States, covering approximately 77 million group and nongroup members. Each Plan is an autonomous, nonprofit corporation serving members in a contiguous area within one or more states. A Plan is usually established under special state legislation that exempts it from the state's laws pertaining to commercial insurance companies; e.g., from incorporation and reserve requirements and from taxes on earned income. This "enabling act" also requires that the Blue Cross governing board give representation to participating hospitals, to physicians and to the general public; that contracts be limited to properly licensed hospitals; and that hospital contracts and membership rates be approved by the state insurance department. In addition, the state insurance department usually has the right to inspect the Plan's operating records.

In return for a yearly premium, Blue Cross guarantees its members certain "benefits," total or partial payment for services received while hospitalized. Coverage is determined by the nature of the illness, surgery, or treatment for which hospitalization is required. Hospitals send each member's bills directly to the Plan. How much Blue Cross has to reimburse the hospitals for subscriber benefits is determined by the Blue Cross-hospital contract.

There are three types of Blue Cross-hospital reimbursement contract: (1) those providing that Blue Cross will reimburse the hospital for the actual cost of care provided; (2) those providing for reimbursement on the basis of regular hospital charges to noninsured patients; and (3) those that set reimbursement rates on the basis of a formula that has been negotiated by Blue Cross and the hospital, using hospital costs, charges, or some combination of the two.

In forecasting its financial experience for any given year, a Blue Cross Plan may find it difficult to predict its liabilities accurately. Revenue is known and stable; it consists of premium income and investment income. Administrative expenses are fixed. (Most Plans pay less than ten cents of every premium dollar for administration.) But the major portion of a Plan's liabilities — claims for hospital services rendered to Plan members — may vary considerably from year to year.

For any given period, a Plan must account for three types of claims:

1. claims filed by members, processed and paid;

2. claims filed but not yet processed and paid; and

3. claims that will be incurred for services *already rendered but not yet reported*.

The third type of liability is unique to the insurance industry. Claims incurred but not yet filed may equal close to 100 percent of a company's assets. If premiums received from subscribers are not adequate to cover liabilities because risk has been incorrectly projected, the problem of cash flow may become acute.

In addition to estimating the risk of incurred but unreported claims, a Blue Cross Plan must be able to project hospital costs for the premium year. When hospitals raise wages, purchase new equipment, introduce or close services or facilities, or experience unexpected changes in patterns of utilization, they inevitably charge more for their services. This will have immediate effect on a Plan's financial well-being and, eventually, on subscribers' premium rates. To counter the danger of insolvency, each Blue Cross Plan maintains a "contingency reserve," a surplus of liquid assets sufficient to cover its estimated operating expenses for a given expense period, perhaps one, two, or three months. When its contingency reserve is running lower than is considered safe, or is depleted, a Plan makes a "rate filing," a request to the insurance department under whose jurisdiction it operates for an adjustment in premium rates.

Insurance commissioners have usually considered it their primary responsibility to make sure that a Blue Cross Plan is able to meet its obligations to its members. Within the last decade, however, some commissioners have broadened their interpretation of their regulatory authority. Some are questioning the process whereby Blue Cross routinely passes along increasing hospital costs to subscribers in the form of higher premiums without first evaluating how hospitals are determining their costs and whether higher charges are justified. Some commissioners are also challenging the contingency reserve concept, asking whether Blue Cross is allowing itself too comfortable a margin for forecasting error at the expense of its subscribers. These commissioners seek to represent the public interest by demanding better management from Blue Cross, hoping that each Plan will in its turn make the same demand of the hospitals that depend on it for financial stability.

BLUE CROSS IN NEW HAMPSHIRE AND VERMONT

Since 1944, one Blue Cross Plan, the New Hampshire-Vermont Hospitalization Service (NHVHS), has served all of New Hampshire and Vermont. The New Hampshire Hospitalization Service was established in 1942, after the New Hampshire legislature passed the appropriate enabling bill. Two years later, the Vermont legislature authorized New Hampshire

Blue Cross to extend its operations into Vermont. Today, NHVHS has a total membership of more than 600,000, approximately 52 percent of the population of the two states. Two-thirds of the members live in New Hampshire, one-third in Vermont. The Plan holds contracts with all 47 regular (nongovernmental), short-term, acute-care hospitals in the two states. Approximately one-third of the hospitals' annual revenue comes from Blue Cross for services provided to members. The Blue Cross-hospital contracts give the Plan the right to audit each hospital's accounts annually and to pay for services to members on the basis of costs or charges, "whichever is lower."

In its December 26, 1973, rate filing, NHVHS noted that this was its fifth filing in two and one-half years. Before July 1971, the Plan had filed its last request for increased rates in 1963.

Blue Cross made a rate filing in July 1971, for increased rates effective October 1, 1971, because its actuaries were predicting that expenses for the next year would drain its already depleted contingency reserve. The major reason for the reduced surplus, according to NHVHS, was an expansion of benefits offered to members. If the commissioners approved its filing, the Plan expected to build up its reserve to approximately three and one-half months of operating expense as of December 31, 1971, and to two months of operating expense by December 31, 1972. In November 1971, NHVHS was forced to reduce its July rate increase request to comply with Phases I and II of the Federal Economic Stabilization Act, passed in August. The adjusted rate filing was based on an effective date of January 1, 1972.

The insurance commissioners did not respond to Blue Cross's November 1971 rate filing until May 1972. They turned down the proposed rates and ordered the Plan to reduce its contingency reserve to one month of operating expense. Blue Cross filed an adjusted request a few weeks later; its proposed rates would reduce its surplus as ordered. The filing (as later amended in public hearings) was approved by both insurance departments in July 1972 — one year after the original filing — for an effective date of September 1, 1972.

On November 1972, Blue Cross filed for a rate increase for 1973 premiums, in order to match 1973 income to projected expenses and to maintain a contingency reserve for one month of operating expense. In May 1973, both insurance departments denied the rates requested and ordered much smaller increases to go into effect on July 1, 1973. And for the first time in the Plan's history, the two insurance commissioners ordered different rates for their respective states. Blue Cross predicted that, as a result, its contingency reserve would be reduced to ten days of operating expense.

Early in June 1973, NHVHS decided to implement the rate increases granted in the commissioners' May 1973 orders and to appeal to the Supreme Court of New Hampshire and the Supreme Court of Vermont for rehearings of its November 1972 rate filing. In October, the New Hampshire Supreme Court overturned the New Hampshire insurance department's May 1973 order and granted Blue Cross the rate increase requested in November 1972. In that same month, the Vermont Supreme Court upheld the Vermont insurance department's May 1973 decision.

The December 26, 1973, Rate Filing

In its present rate filing, Blue Cross was seeking to equalize premium rates for New Hampshire and Vermont, to wipe out its deficit, and to establish a contingency reserve of 1.5 months of operating expense as of January 31, *1976*. As usual, the Plan based all its financial projections on the combined experience of members from both states.

The New Hampshire and Vermont insurance departments held public hearings in January 1974, to allow Blue Cross to present its case. Much of the testimony focused on a controversy that had over the past few years placed a considerable strain on the relationship between the state insurance commissioners and New Hampshire-Vermont Hospitalization Service: the issue of cash accounting versus accrual accounting. The insurance departments analyzed the Plan on a cash basis and found it solvent as of December 31, 1973 (Tables 3.1 and 3.2). Financial statements prepared on an accrual basis, the accounting method favored by NHVHS, showed that the Plan was insolvent (Tables 3.3, 3.4, and 3.5).

In his May 14, 1973, decision pertaining to the Plan's November 1972 filing, the Vermont insurance commissioner had written:

> Insurance Commissioners all across the country are continually faced with the "two sets of books syndrome." When companies are seeking rate increases they present financial data which understate their true financial condition; however, when management seeks praise or a raise from the board of directors, a different set of books is produced — a set of books which states much more accurately the true financial condition of the particular organization.

The major differences between accrual accounting and cash accounting are the liability items. Among these items, claims incurred but not reported account for the largest dollar amount. In the same May 14, 1973, order, the Vermont insurance commissioner had discussed the propriety of using this account as a liability:

> A review of the year-end financial statement of the Plan indicated that among the various liabilities . . . [was] a reserve for unpaid claims adjustment expense. . . . Theoretically, the reserve is intended to provide the funds necessary to cover all expenses involved in settling all outstanding claims should the Plan go out of business. As such, it is essentially a liquidation basis reserve, rather than a current identifiable liability . . . claims . . . expenses are paid as they arise . . . claims personnel . . . are working every day with both current claims and claims which arose out of illnesses months, or even years, removed. The costs of processing such old claims are included in current claims expense . . . it is inappropriate to include [this account as a liability] . . . under the circumstances.[3]

During the hearings, a Blue Cross consultant from the Harvard Business School, M. E. Barrett, was asked to discuss the accrual concept as it applies to Blue Cross. He explained that "essentially it means that the financial statements are prepared under the assumption that the income for the period will be determined by calculating the revenues earned during, say, 1973, and subtracting from them all expenses related to the 1973 coverage provided under the terms of the subscriber contracts." He further noted that in 1973 Blue Cross subscribers paid approximately $6 million less than the cost of services provided to them during that year. During 1973, he said, Blue Cross used cash received for 1973 premiums to pay claims related to 1972 experience and would have to do the same in 1974 for claims incurred for 1973 experience unless rate increases were approved. The Plan was in an especially precarious position because, in its attempt to remain solvent during 1973, it had sold virtually all its regular investment portfolio; had sold its "Shared Hospital Accounting System," a software computer program; and had recalled most of its cash advances to member hospitals (used by the hospitals to meet their cash flow needs). According to Mr. Barrett, NHVHS had very little left to work with, and the practice of using payments for next year's experience to pay current year expenses was putting "the whole concept of a 'prepaid' hospitalization plan in jeopardy."

The insurance commissioners wanted to know how Blue Cross estimated its claims expense for the two months ending December 31, 1973, and the year ending December 31, 1974. In material provided as part of the rate filing, NHVHS gave the following explanation:

> The claims expense for November and December 1973 was estimated based on claims paid through October 31, 1973. It includes correction for an estimated understatement of the October 31, 1973 unpaid claims liability of approximately $600,000. The claims expense for 1974 is based on claims incurred in the year ended June 30, 1973, trended for growth, utilization and inflation. The projected December 31, 1973 unpaid claims liability was determined by applying estimated claims incurred, claims paid and anticipated correction for November and December to the October 31, 1973 balance. The projected December 31, 1974, unpaid claims liability was determined by applying a composite 13.5 percent factor for growth, utilization and inflation to the projected unpaid claims liability of December 31, 1973. No consideration has been given to a change in the lapse time between the time a claim is incurred and time it is paid. If this lapse time is decreased, it will increase the cash outflow for the forecasted period.

The insurance commissioners were dubious about the Plan's ability to predict unpaid claims. In his May 14, 1973, decision, the Vermont commissioner noted that:

> The figures shown for claims unpaid are estimates, and for years the [Blue Cross and Blue Shield] Plans have used an actuarial technique known as "least squares per premium projection" in computing the estimate . . . [in past years] there has been an astonishing amount of variation or fluctuation between the amounts that were estimated and the actual results. . . . In computing its reserve for claims unpaid, Blue Cross took the mathematical estimate and added a "safety factor" of $100,000.

A second issue that the insurance commissioners were seeking to resolve, in addition to the question of accrual accounting, involved the contingency reserve concept. Both commissioners wondered whether it was appropriate for a nonprofit organization such as Blue Cross to maintain a surplus to protect it from possible fluctuations in its financial experience. They had expressed their doubts on several occasions. In his May 1973 order, the Vermont commissioner wrote:

> Blue Cross and Blue Shield, according to New Hampshire law, are not insurance companies. . . . In most respects they are exempted from the provisions of the code which regulates insurance companies. With respect to surplus levels, it should be noted that [the laws] do not require that Blue Cross maintain *any* surplus.

To bolster its case, NHVHS distributed a position paper on contingency reserves prepared by the national Blue Cross Association and a commentary prepared by the Plan's own consultants (see Appendix 3.2).

The Blue Cross Association identified six contingencies that might adversely affect a Plan's financial state:

1. an incorrect estimate of claims cost per contract;
2. an incorrect estimate of administration and other expenses;

3. an incorrect estimate of unpaid claims liabilities;

4. unanticipated financial demands related to improvements in health care provided by community hospitals;

5. fluctuation of stocks and bond values; and

6. natural disasters, epidemics, and other catastrophes.

Based on national experience, the Association recommended a contingency reserve of at least 17 percent of the sum of claims expense and administrative expense, both measured over the most recent twelve-month period.

In seeking to learn exactly how NHVHS had computed its current surplus, the commissioners questioned Mr. Barrett about the propriety of several of the Plan's asset and liability accounts; namely, the six accounts that do not appear in income statements prepared on a cash basis. Mr. Barrett responded to the commissioners' questions as follows:

Q. Could you comment on the propriety of the following balance sheet items? Reserve for Accrued Vacation Allowances (a liability account).

A. Let me point out that I'm not in a position to comment on the correctness of the specific dollar amount. However, the item itself is proper. It represents the amount due employees for vacation time already earned, but not taken.

Q. Unearned subscription income (a liability account).

A. This is also a legitimate liability account. In the 1973 financial statements, it should represent cash received in payment of 1974 premiums. This income has not been earned, as 1974 was not yet there and no 1974 services had been provided.

Q. Claims incurred, but unpaid (a liability account).

A. This is also a legitimate liability account. It is designed to represent claims for, say, 1973 services which will not be paid until after the end of 1973. It *must* be included to allow an accurate portrayal of the expenses related to providing service to the 1973 policyholders.

Q. Unpaid claims adjustment expense (a liability account).

A. Again, this item is included in order to present an accurate portrayal of the expenses related to providing service to the 1973 policyholders. It, and the three earlier items, are all consistent with the accrual basis of accounting.

Q. Common stock carried at historical cost (an asset).

A. With some minor exceptions, which are not applicable in this case, investments in common stock are always carried at the *lower* of historical cost or market. Blue Cross is following this concept. In addition, the ethical propriety of Blue Cross carrying these at a higher market value — in a world where the Dow Jones is known to drop by approximately 20 percent in one month's time — is highly questionable.

Q. Bonds carried at amortized cost, which is above market value (an asset).

A. Corporate bonds are most usually purchased with the intent of holding them for a period in excess of a year. In addition, they normally have a stated interest rate and a specific dollar value at a specific future date. Thus, they are normally carried at historical cost adjusted by a factor which is designed to write historical cost up (or down) to adjust for the fact that the value of bond at maturity may be more (or less) than the historical cost. Blue Cross's policy was perfectly acceptable.[4]

Blue Cross was counting on Mr. Barrett's expert testimony to justify, once and for all, its use of the accrual method of accounting and the necessity for maintaining a reasonable contingency reserve. For their part, the insurance commissioners had to determine, first, whether or not NHVHS was actually insolvent. Secondly, they had to resolve the contingency reserve issue. What is the appropriate level of surplus for a Blue Cross Plan to maintain? How much of a surplus would give NHVHS just the right amount of "cushion" — not so small that members' interests were endangered, not so large that the Plan lost its incentive to maintain rigorous management controls?

NOTES

1. Mr. Fifield is now president of the New Hampshire-Vermont Hospitalization Service. He is also president of the New Hampshire-Vermont Physicians Service, a Blue Shield plan that provides coverage for physicians' fees for services rendered in-hospital and, in some cases, for office and home visits.
2. Insurance Commissioner of Vermont, Rate Order, May 14, 1973.
3. See Appendix 3.1 for further excerpts from the Rate Order by the Insurance Commissioner of Vermont, May 14, 1973.
4. Testimony from transcript of public hearings conducted by the New Hampshire and Vermont Insurance Departments, January 28 and 29, 1974, Concord, New Hampshire, and Montpelier, Vermont.

SELECTED BIBLIOGRAPHY

New Hampshire-Vermont Hospitalization Service. "The Blue Cross and Blue Shield System in New Hampshire and Vermont." Mimeo, undated.

Somers, H. M., and Somers, A. R. *Doctors, Patients, and Health Insurance.* Washington, D.C.: Brookings Institution, May 1961.

Table 3.1

PROJECTED STATEMENT OF CASH RECEIPTS, DISBURSEMENTS, AND CASH BALANCES
for the Two Months Ending December 31, 1973

	ACTUAL RESULTS Ten Months Ended October 31, 1973	PROJECTED TOTALS 1973		PROJECTED TOTAL Year Ending December 31, 1973
		November	December	
Cash balance, beginning of period	$ 418,573	$2,612,554	$2,395,941	$ 418,573
Cash receipts from operations:				
Subscription income	$34,951,226	$3,809,069	$3,958,500	$42,718,795
Cash disbursements for operations:				
Hospital settlements	$ 1,138,550	$ —	$ 100,000	$ 1,238,550
Claims paid	35,785,398	3,708,498	3,708,497	43,202,393
Net operating expenses	2,554,330	346,157	346,143	3,246,630
Total cash disbursements	$39,478,278	$4,054,655	$4,154,640	$47,687,573
Net cash outflow from operations	$ (4,527,052)	$ (245,586)	$ (196,140)	$ (4,968,778)
Other receipts and (disbursements):				
Investment and other receivables				
from sale of investments	4,750,045	22,220	22,220	4,794,485
Return of hospital advances	1,986,520	6,753	47,833	2,041,106
Capital equipment expenditure	(15,532)	—	—	(15,532)
Other income	—	—	—	—
Cash inflow (outflow) for period	$ 2,193,981	$ (216,613)	$ (126,087)	$ 1,851,281
Cash balance, end of period	$ 2,612,554	$2,395,941	$2,269,854	$ 2,269,854

Source: New Hampshire-Vermont Hospitalization Service.

Table 3.2

PROJECTED STATEMENT OF CASH RECEIPTS, DISBURSEMENTS, AND CASH BALANCES
for the Year Ending December 31, 1974

DESCRIPTION	First Quarter January–March	Second Quarter April–June	Third Quarter July–Sept.	Fourth Quarter Oct.–Dec.	PROJECTED TOTAL Year Ending Dec. 31, 1974
Cash balance, beginning of period	$ 2,269,854	$ 2,042,461	$ 711,784	$ 1,321,019	$ 2,269,854
Cash receipts from operations:					
Subscription income	$11,939,200	$12,154,700	$12,167,300	$12,383,450	$48,644,650
Cash disbursements for operations:					
Hospital settlements	$ 500,000	$ 100,000	$ —	$ —	$ 600,000
Claims paid	10,961,538	12,788,462	10,961,538	12,788,462	47,500,000
Net operating expense	686,260	644,678	655,998	995,679	2,982,615
Total cash disbursements	$12,147,798	$13,533,140	$11,617,536	$13,784,141	$51,082,615
Net cash outflow from operations	$ (208,598)	$ (1,378,440)	$ 549,764	$ (1,400,691)	$ (2,437,965)
Other receipts and (disbursements):					
Investments and other receivables from sale of investments	69,768	69,768	69,768	69,768	279,072
Return of hospital advances	41,813	—	—	—	41,813
Capital equipment expenditure	(130,376)	(22,005)	(10,297)	—	(162,678)
Cash inflow (outflow) for period	$ (227,393)	$ (1,330,677)	$ 609,235	$ (1,330,923)	$ (2,279,758)
Cash balance, end of period	$ 2,042,461	$ 711,784	$ 1,321,019	$ (9,904)	$ (9,904)

Source: Computations based on table provided by New Hampshire-Vermont Hospitalization Service.

Table 3.3

PRELIMINARY CONDENSED STATEMENT OF INCOME AND EXPENSE
for the Period Ending December 31, 1973

	CURRENT MONTH	%	YEAR-TO-DATE	%
Operating income				
Subscriber payments	$4,167,421.20		$42,422,651.53	
Other income	23,399.26		208,527.84	
Total operating income	4,190,820.46	100.0	42,631,179.37	100.0
Claims incurred	3,679,533.74	87.8	45,441,184.93	106.5
Total operating expense	494,141.58	11.7	5,204,981.76	12.2
Less reimbursed expense	164,022.17	3.9	2,141,022.83	5.0
Net operating expense	330,119.41	7.8	3,063,958.93	7.1
Total claims and operating expense	4,009,703.15	95.6	48,505,143.86	113.7
Net operating income	181,117.31	4.3	(5,873,964.49)	(13.7)
Investment income — real estate	3,292.99		32,444.04	
Investment income — other	34,443.52	0.8	284,447.61	0.6
Gain or (loss) on sale of ledger assets	—	—	(317,705.86)	(0.7)
Net income before extraordinary items	218,853.82	5.2	(5,874,778.70)	(13.7)
Extraordinary items	(24,000.00)	(0.5)	(223,275.84)	(0.5)
Net income	$ 194,853.82	4.6	$(6,058,054.54)	(14.3)

Source: New Hampshire-Vermont Hospitalization Service.

Table 3.4

CONDENSED BALANCE SHEET
at December 31, 1973

ASSETS

Cash		
Petty cash		$ 1,300.00
Bank balances		2,595,445.10
Total cash		$ 2,596,745.10
Securities		1,587,248.48
Real estate		2,930,516.16
Less depreciation		293,622.71
Net real estate		2,636,893.45
Accounts receivable		3,629,710.18
Deposit with inter plan bank		112,548.78
Deposits — advances to participating providers		46,614.65
Equipment, furniture, fixtures		110,371.83
Less depreciation		32,109.23
Net equipment, furniture, fixtures		$ 78,262.60
Company-owned automobiles		—
Less depreciation		—
Net company-owned automobiles		—
Software programs		15,081.10
Less amortization		9,019.04
Net software programs		6,062.06
Total assets		$10,694,085.30

LIABILITIES AND RESERVES

Claims unpaid		
Reported claims in process of adjustment		$ 1,312,936.00
Hospital claims unpaid unreported		7,412,347.81
Total claims unpaid		$ 8,725,373.81
Unearned subscriber payments		997,369.38
NHVHS physician service		376,955.78
Outstanding checks		1,271,438.14
Other liabilities		1,661,088.04
Unpaid claims adjustment expense		306,616.14
Contingency reserve		(2,644,695.99)
Total liabilities, reserves, and other funds		$10,694,085.30

Source: New Hampshire-Vermont Hospitalization Service.

Table 3.5

PROJECTED BALANCE SHEET
for Selected Months in 1974

ASSETS	JANUARY	APRIL	1974 JULY	OCTOBER	DECEMBER	PROJECTED DECEMBER 1973
Cash	$ 2,103,300	$ 2,098,209	$ 898,797	$ (200,577)	$ (9,904)	$ 2,269,854
Accounts receivable from subscribers	595,650	601,200	606,750	627,300	616,350	594,000
Other receivables	2,596,392	2,596,392	2,764,616	2,702,579	2,657,719	2,596,392
Investments (securities at cost, real estate at depreciated value)	414,027	412,225	410,422	408,619	407,418	414,628
Property, plant, and equipment, at depreciated value	2,454,172	2,435,566	2,416,960	2,398,354	2,385,950	2,460,374
	$ 8,163,541	$8,143,592	$7,097,545	$5,936,275	$ 6,057,533	$ 8,335,248
LIABILITIES						
Unpaid claims	$ 8,903,987	$ 9,575,449	$ 9,064,987	$8,940,525	$ 9,801,833	$ 8,631,833
Unearned subscription income	991,638	991,638	991,638	991,638	991,638	991,638
Other liabilities	1,862,156	1,794,863	2,012,201	2,012,201	1,683,365	1,808,878
	$11,757,781	$12,361,950	$12,068,826	$11,944,364	$12,476,836	$11,432,349
(Contingency reserve)	(3,594,240)	(4,218,358)	(4,971,281)	(6,008,089)	(6,419,303)	(3,097,101)
	$ 8,183,541	$ 8,143,592	$ 7,097,545	$ 5,936,275	$ 6,057,533	$ 8,335,248

Source: Figures taken from table provided by New Hampshire-Vermont Hospitalization Service.

Appendix 3.1

THE NEW HAMPSHIRE-VERMONT HOSPITALIZATION SERVICE

Excerpts from the May 14, 1973 Order Issued by the Commissioner of Insurance, State of Vermont, in Response to Blue Cross Rate Filing of November 1972.

. . . The actuary for the Insurance Department testified that, based on his study of historical data and statistical fluctuations, and taking into account recent improvements such as more timely operating statements, annual review of rates, and prospective hospital rating, a surplus equivalent to ten days operating costs would be sufficient. Such a surplus would provide a fund of more than $1,000,000 for Blue Cross over and above normal income, to meet unforeseen contingencies.

He indicated that with such a surplus level the Plans might become technically insolvent from time to time, although this would not affect the Plans' ability to meet their current financial obligations. It was pointed out that several Blue Cross/Blue Shield Plans are currently operating, or have operated for periods of time, in a condition of technical insolvency with no adverse effect on their subscribers. He indicated that in his opinion it was most important that the Plans have sufficient cash and liquid assets to meet their current obligations. To accomplish this a level of liquid assets equivalent to one month's cash needs should be maintained. . . . I find that a surplus equivalent to ten days operating needs is adequate and reasonable . . . using the same definition of surplus as employed by Blue Cross in their filing, that is, a surplus calculated on the basis of ledger assets only. . . .

The . . . question is how much surplus [is] there to begin with. . . . Blue Cross used a so-called "ledger basis" surplus. Under this approach, they total all the assets entered on the company's books and subtract all the liabilities. The remainder is what is called surplus. This approach entirely ignores the existence of non-ledger assets. These latter assets are items which have worth, but because of their frequently changing values, or because of accounting convention, are generally not entered on a company's formal books of record.

There are only two types of non-ledger assets held by Blue Cross according to the 1972 annual statement. . . . The first is the excess of market value of stocks over their book value (original cost) . . . Adding this non-ledger asset to the book value of the stocks merely adjusts the stocks to the value they could be sold for on that date. It is obviously a reasonable adjustment.

The second . . . represents the excess of market value of the property the Plan owns over the value shown in their books. . . . Given the general rise in property values over the past few years, it is likely that the market value of this building is also greater than that shown in the Plans' financial statements. Thus, there may be even greater amounts available to the Plans.

The whole point of including such non-ledger assets is that it gives a more complete picture of the true worth of the corporation . . .

One additional asset adjustment . . . reflects the fact that the market value of the bonds owned by the Plan is substantially lower than their book value. . . . With the high interest levels prevailing today, the market value of the bonds owned by Blue Cross has decreased since the time they were originally purchased. Their true value is less than the book or ledger value, and the true financial worth of the Plan is accordingly lower.

It might be argued that certain assets should be "not admitted" in accordance with "standard insurance accounting techniques." This practice of excluding certain assets of an insurance company's balance sheet is a device used to place the assets of such companies on as conservative a basis as possible. This does not mean that the excluded assets have no worth. Rather, because of the lack of an objective or easily determinable measure of their true value, the possibility of abuse exists, and could be used to artificially inflate the apparent net worth of a company. This accounting approach is unique to insurance, and even insurance companies will generally add these assets back to surplus when preparing statements to present to their stockholders.

Not admitted assets for Blue Cross . . . at year-end 1972 according to the Annual Statement with the Insurance Department . . . consisted of . . . premiums more than 30 days overdue . . . furniture and fixtures . . . and software (computer) programs. . . . Under generally accepted accounting principles, these "not admitted" assets would be assigned a value and would be reflected in financial statements.

As was discussed above, surplus merely represents what is left over after subtracting liabilities from assets. The amount of surplus will therefore depend not only on the amount of the assets owned by the Plan but also on the degree of accuracy with which the Plans' liabilities are determined. If liabilities have been artificially overstated, or are over-conservatively determined, too much will be subtracted from assets, and the apparent surplus will be correspondingly reduced or understated. . . .

A review of the year-end financial statement of the Plan indicated that among the various liabilities were two newly created accounts, a reserve for unpaid claims adjustment expense and a reserve for accrued vacation allowances and the accrued taxes thereon. . . . theoretically, this [first] reserve is intended to provide the funds necessary to cover all expenses involved in settling all outstanding claims should the Plan go out of business. As such, it is essentially a liquidation basis reserve, rather than a current identifiable liability. . . .

The second reserve, which is for accrued vacation allowances and the taxes thereon, is likewise a "liquidation basis" reserve. Rarely, if ever, would such a reserve be called upon for making actual payments, except in the case of going out of business.

In both instances, claims and vacation expenses are paid as they arise. For example, claims personnel of the Plans are working every day with both current claims and claims which arose out of illnesses months, or even years, removed. The costs of processing such old claims are included in current claims expense. Similarly, vacations during the normal course of a working year are included in current payroll figures. In most instances, there would not be an extra payment as such to the worker. He would simply receive his paycheck as normal. The only difference would be that he would not be physically present at the office for a number of days. In the context of an ongoing public service corporation, as we have here, the likelihood of the plans being liquidated, and therefore having to call upon these full reserves to meet their obligations rather than absorbing them in current expenses, is extremely remote.

In testimony, the Plans argued that these reserves result in a more accurate allocation of expenses by year, which in turn tends to increase the amount of reimbursement from Medicare and other Federal programs, and reduce costs for subscribers. However, on an ongoing basis, the amount of such additional reimbursement would depend on the change in those reserves between accounting periods, rather than on the total dollar amount of the reserves themselves. The beneficial effect is therefore likely to be small compared to the immediate reduction of almost half a million dollars in surplus available to the subscribers of New Hampshire and Vermont. There may be other ways to reflect or create these reserves. For example, they could be treated as a special surplus account, or they could be built up over a period of years. It is not clear that all possibilities have already been explored and eliminated.

On the basis of the evidence presented at the hearings, I find that it is inappropriate to include these accounts as liabilities under the circumstances of the present rate filings. . . .

Appendix 3.2

THE NEW HAMPSHIRE-VERMONT HOSPITALIZATION SERVICE

Contingency Reserves

A. *Excerpts from "BLUE CROSS CONTINGENCY RESERVES," prepared by the Blue Cross Association, Administrative Services, January, 1974.*

The proper Blue Cross contingency reserve level varies from Plan to Plan because of differing Plan circumstances. . . . The financial standard set forth below was developed by creating a Plan model and examining the major financial contingencies faced by that Blue Cross Plan. . . .

Since the function of the reserve is to provide an offset against adverse financial contingencies, it is appropriate to attempt to identify those contingencies and estimate their likely potential financial impact . . . . several contingencies can be identified which constitute a large part of the total financial contingencies faced by a Blue Cross Plan. These are:

a. underestimate of claims cost per contract trends
b. underestimate of administrative and other expenses
c. disasters, epidemics and other catastrophes
d. underestimate of unpaid claims liabilities
e. fluctuation of stocks and bonds values
f. unanticipated financial demands related to the community function of improving health care delivery.

ESTIMATES OF POTENTIAL VALUES OF MAJOR CONTINGENCIES

Contingency	% of Claims Expense*	% of Administrative and Other Expense*
1. Claims trends	5.50	
2. Administrative expenses		5.50
3. Catastrophes	6.25	6.25
4. Unpaid claims	3.60	
5. Stocks and bonds	1.50	1.50
6. Community	5.00	5.00
	21.85	18.25

*For most recent 12-month period.

Assuming a claims expense to administrative and other expense ratio of 19 to 1, the above composites to 21.7 percent of annual claims plus administrative and other expenses.

Taking cognizance of the fact that many contingencies are not addressed above (including substantial potential termination of operations costs and substantial costs associated with potential unanticipated unfavorable court decisions), of the fact that the value of the aggregate financial contingency is not the sum of the values of each of the individual contingencies measured independently, and of the necessarily subjective nature of each of the contingency evaluations and of the aggregate contingency evaluation, a Blue Cross contingency reserve standard of 22 percent of the sum of claims expense and administrative expense, both measured over the immediately preceding twelve-month period, may be deemed appropriate.

However, recognition of the fact that reserve standards often are viewed as minimum solvency related standards suggests that the 5 percent "community contingency" be omitted, resulting in a minimum standard of 17 percent of the sum of claims expense and administrative expense, both measured over the immediately preceding twelve-month period.

B. *Excerpts from "COMMENTS ON BLUE CROSS ASSOCIATION CONTINGENCY RESERVE POSITION PAPER," by George L. Berry, Milliman & Robertson, Inc., Consulting Actuaries for NHVHS, January 11, 1974.*

In our opinion, the most important reason for holding a contingency reserve is to protect the Plan, and, therefore, its subscribers from adverse, unforeseen occurrences and thereby enable the Plan to continue as a viable organization. This need arises because future events cannot be predicted with complete precision.

There are three general areas of uncertainty which are the sources of the various contingencies.

The immediate past environment is the first area. The statistical base from which financial and rate-making projections are made comes from this environment. Some estimation of this base is required because of the time lag between the date a claim is incurred and the date it is paid. While actuarial methods of estimation are available, differences between actual and estimated results will affect projections.

The second area is the current environment. . . . It is usually expressed numerically in the cost and utilization trends used in projecting financial experience. Generally, use of these trends assumes that the forces operating in this environment will not change significantly through the end of the rating period. Rate margins and/or the contingency reserve reflect the uncertainty in precisely evaluating this environment, as well as the possibility of random fluctuations.

The future environment is the environment which will exist during the rating period. It may be the same as the current environment or it may be significantly different. The degree of uncertainty in this case would be reflected in the contingency reserve accumulation for unforeseen contingencies.

In our opinion, the contingency reserve held should reflect also (a) the ability of the particular Plan to interpret and evaluate the environments mentioned above, and (b) margins included in rate-making. Thus, it should not be considered a "maximum" reserve.

In our opinion, the most significant differences in contingency requirements will occur with respect to the time taken to detect environmental changes and the time taken to implement necessary corrective rate action.

We feel, for example, that the degree of uncertainty with respect to claim trend changes is greater for those Plans with cost-based reimbursement formulas to hospitals than for Plans with charge-based reimbursement formulas. Recent experience has made it clear that it can take two or three years to finalize liabilities under a cost-based reimbursement system. The result of this is a significant delay in identifying changes in underlying claim trends.

Plan practices also differ with respect to the degree to which actual trends are reflected in rating. We feel that one of the values of a contingency reserve is that it enables a smooth progression of trends to be used in rating. Sudden, temporary, and adverse trend changes can be absorbed through the contingency reserve. This, of course, will tend to increase the level of a suitable contingency reserve required for a Plan following this practice as compared to a Plan which attempts to reflect completely trend changes in its rating.

4

Chapel Hill Clinic, P.C.

Hugh W. Long
James D. Suver

It was a dark and dreary Monday morning when Susan Cooper, Executive Director of the Chapel Hill Clinic, started to review the materials prepared over the weekend by the clinic's business manager and the accounting staff. At its Friday evening meeting, the Executive Committee had expressed deep concern because the 1982 results were falling short of budget, especially with respect to income. The committee, which included 6 of the Clinic's 25 partners, speculated that overheads were escalating out of control and causing the income shortfall.

Prompt resolution of the partners' questions and concerns was important, since the Executive Committee expected to have a proposed calendar-1983 budget on Thursday to put forth at the regular Friday evening partnership meeting. Table 4.1 had been prepared to answer the questions about current performance, while Table 4.2 allowed a comparison of this year's performance with data from Medical Group Management Association's most recent cost survey. Ms. Cooper believed that these two pieces of data would help resolve the questions on this year's performance and could be used to make next year's budget as realistic as possible.

Ms. Cooper, a graduate of a well-known southeastern school of public health, had recently accepted the position of Clinic Executive Director after several years as a highly successful administrator of a small rural hospital. This was the first budget she had developed for the clinic and she wanted to be sure all key areas were covered and that the Executive Committee would accept the budget largely as presented.

The Chapel Hill Clinic was generally viewed as an important part of the community and was known for delivering high-quality care. Historically, its salary scales and work conditions were competitive with other providers in the area, and the clinic provided significant free and discounted care. Ms. Cooper believed she should continue these policies.

The Chapel Hill Clinic had expanded every year of its 22-year history and expected to add more physicians over the next three years. Ms. Cooper had asked the medical staff to prepare their projections of when these new physicians would be added. On the basis of this information, she had prepared a revenue forecast for 1983 – 1985 (Table 4.3). The mix of services shown in Figure 4.1 was not expected to change from 1982 to 1983. In the past, expenses had been estimated from the actual figures from the previous year adjusted for inflation.

Figure 4.1

CHAPEL HILL CLINIC PRODUCTIVITY ANALYSIS
Calendar Year 1982

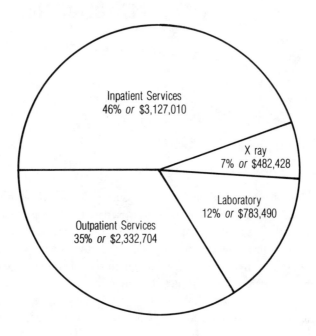

Unless a more accurate basis existed, Ms. Cooper intended to make her 1983 expense projections as follows. The projected 1982 expenses (Table 4.1) would be divided by the 1982 M.D. full-time equivalents (FTE) to obtain an average cost per M.D. The expected 1983 M.D. FTE would be multiplied by this number with an 8-percent increase added for inflation to obtain the projected 1983 expenses. The business manager had also prepared a comparison of the 1981 actual balance sheet and statement of operations with projected 1982 end-of-the-year statements (Tables 4.4 and 4.5). In addition, an analysis of the accounts receivable had been completed for the director's information (Table 4.6).

Using the data in the tables, Ms. Cooper started to prepare a 1983 budget for presentation to the Executive Committee. She knew she would have to be prepared to justify fully all of her projections and recommendations.

PROBLEM

Prepare the 1983 budget for the Chapel Hill Clinic. If you need information beyond what is provided, state your assumptions and proceed with the budget preparation.

Table 4.1

FINANCIAL REPORT (CASH BASIS)
Calendar Years 1981-1982

INCOME	1981 ACTUALS	1982 PROJECTED*	1982 BUDGET	OVER (UNDER) BUDGET
Professional fees collected	$ 6,054,862	$ 6,736,452		
Less refunds	− 109,307	− 128,337		
Net professional fees collected	$ 5,945,555	$ 6,608,115		
Other income	$+ 77,659	$+ 75,494		
Total income	$ 6,023,214 (100%)	$ 6,683,609 (100%)	$6,839,100 (100%)	$(155,491)
EXPENSES				
Personnel	$ 1,515,067 (25%)	$ 1,698,556 (25%)	$1,576,600 (23%)	$ 121,956
Medical supplies and expenses	673,085 (11%)	674,713 (10%)	723,100 (11%)	(48,387)
Building expenses	219,200 (4%)	228,614 (3%)	232,300 (3%)	(3,686)
General expenses	403,872 (7%)	477,577 (7%)	422,300 (6%)	55,277
Subtotal	$ 2,811,224 (47%)	$ 3,079,460 (45%)	$2,954,300 (43%)	$ 125,160
NON-CASH EXPENSES				
Depreciation and amortization	$+ 118,121	$+ 156,000	$ 156,000	$ —
Total operating expenses	$ 2,929,345 (49%)	$ 3,235,460 (48%)	$3,110,300 (45%)	$ 125,160
M.D. expenses	$ 3,168,795 (53%)	$ 3,255,633 (49%)	$3,429,800 (50%)	$(174,167)
Net profit (loss)	$ (74,926) (−2%)	$ 192,516 (3%)	$ 299,000 (5%)	$(106,484)
Other cash received and disbursed:				
Assets purchased	$− 165,783	$− 256,784		
Debt retirement	− 177,702	− 425,031		
Loan acquired	+ 404,411	+ 198,400		
Total other cash received and disbursed	$+ 60,926 (+1%)	$− 483,415 (−7%)		
Net productivity	$ 6,249,501	$ 6,725,632		
Collection percentage	95.1%	98.3%		
Accounts receivable change	$+ 130,374	$+ 185,041		
Accounts receivable	$ 2,430,656	$ 2,615,697		

*10 months actual plus 2 month forecast

Continued

Table 4.1 Continued

I. INCOME

Total income for 1982 increased 11 percent over 1981, an increase of $660,395. This reflects a 98.3 percent collection rate of net productivity in 1982 compared to 95.1 percent in 1981. Included in the income collected this year was $225,000, representing medical assistance payments and HMP payments that should have been collected in 1981. Therefore, the actual collection percentage in 1982 was 96 percent. Our total income for 1982 was $155,491 less than our budget for the year.

II. EXPENSES

Total cash expenses for 1982 total $3,079,460 or 45 percent of income collected. This compares to $2,811,224 or 47 percent of income collected for 1981. The increase in total expenses is $268,236 or an increase of 10 percent for 1982 over 1981. The increases for specific items are as follows:

Personnel expenses	+183,489	+12%
Medical supplies	+ 1,628	—
Building expenses	+ 9,414	+4%
General expenses	+ 73,705	+18%
	+268,236	+10%

     The major item of concern is the increase in personnel expense of $183,489. Personnel expenses also increased $121,956 over our 1982 budgeted figure. The combination of employee turnover and increase in number of employees and the addition of 1,245 overtime hours explains this increase in 1982. The Executive Director has appointed a Cost Containment Committee and they, along with the Executive Director and Medical Director, will be looking at this expense for 1983. Also, the final budget, which will be presented to the committee next Friday probably should have suggestions as to how to decrease the cost of salaries for the coming year.
     General expenses have increased for 1982, mainly due to increases of $16,689 in telephone costs, $17,087 in insurance costs, and an increase of interest expense of $18,598. The cost of telephone services has increased but also the usage of long distance telephone calls has increased. The main reason for the large increase in insurance expense is due to a late insurance premium paid in January 1982 that should have been paid in 1981, causing double payment in the calendar year of 1982. Also, insurance premium costs have increased slightly over 1981. Interest expense has increased, due mainly to the $225,000 ninety-day renewable note acquired in December 1982 and paid periodically throughout 1982 with interest at one percent over prime rate.
     Total M.D. expenses increased $86,838 or 3 percent over 1981. This was $174,167 less than the amount budgeted for M.D. expenses. Net productivity increased $476,131 or 7 percent in 1982 for a total of $6,725,632. A better collection percentage, coupled with higher productivity, could have realized our goal of covering the $3,429,800 for M.D. expenses reflected in the 1982 budget.

Table 4.2

INCOME AND EXPENSE COMPARISON—CHAPEL HILL CLINIC
TO OTHER MULTISPECIALTY CLINICS
FROM MGMA'S "COST SURVEY REPORT"
Fiscal Year 1982

| | | CHAPEL HILL CLINIC* ACTUAL (CASH BASIS) | | EAST NORTH |
		DOLLARS	%	CENTRAL**
1)	Total receipts	$6,532,773	100.0%	100.0%
	Expenses			
2)	Salaries, non-M.D.	1,317,447	20.2%	20.3%
3)	Fringe benefits, non-M.D. (see Schedule A)	246,319	3.8	4.1
	Total salaries and fringes, non-M.D.	1,563,766	24.0	24.4
4)	Computer costs	117,912	1.8	1.5
5)	Laboratory fees	7,925	0.1	1.0
6)	Radiology fees (see M.D.'s)	—	—	—
7)	Medical and surgical supplies, including laboratory and radiology	458,400	7.0	4.8**
8)	Building and occupancy expenses (see Schedule B)	310,473	4.7	7.3**
9)	Furniture and equipment expense	123,862	1.9	2.2
10)	Office supplies and services (see Schedule C)	91,074	1.4	1.3
11)	Legal and accounting	28,264	0.4	0.4
12)	Phone	100,334	1.5	1.2
13)	Insurance (see Schedule D)	200,915	3.1	3.4
14)	Consultant fees	30,133	0.5	0.4
15)	Other expenses	169,022	2.6	1.1**
	—Interest $ 40,530 = 0.6%			
	—All other (see Schedule E) 128,492 = 2.0%			
16)	Total operating expenses, non-M.D.	$3,202,080	49.0	49.0
17)	Net income before M.D. distribution	3,330,693	51.0	51.0
18)	M.D. distribution			
	—M.D. salaries (including radiologist fees)	2,680,798	41.0	(Unk.)
	—M.D. fringe benefits (see Schedule F)	558,963	8.6	6.9
	Total M.D. distribution	3,239,761	49.6	(Unk.)
19)	Total expenses (lines #16 and 18)	6,441,841	98.6	(Unk.)
20)	Net income after distribution (cash basis)	$ 90,932	1.4	(Unk.)
			100.0%	100.0%

*Data rearranged to fit MGMA format.
**Includes Illinois, Indiana, Michigan, Ohio, and Wisconsin.

Continued

Table 4.2 Continued

SCHEDULE A
Fringe Benefits, Non-M.D.'s

Retirement costs	$ 79,210
Profit sharing	6,065
Hospitalization insurance	42,316
Group life insurance	2,605
Group dental insurance	3,030
Payroll taxes	105,637
Educational meetings	4,456
Travel meetings (partial estimate)	3,000
Total fringes, non-M.D.	$ 246,319

SCHEDULE B
Building and Occupancy Expense

Fixed annual costs		
— Downtown rent (43,290 sq. ft.)		$ 63,000
— Other rent (2,200 sq. ft.)		20,343
— Parking		6,554
— Amortization of leasehold improvements		19,147
— Real estate taxes, downtown		43,657
— Utilities		47,588
— Building repairs		
Elevator	$ 4,390	
Building, general	6,426	
Heat and air	21,776	
Painting	1,109	
Miscellaneous repairs	174	
		33,875
Salary costs, maintenance man, removed from salary		10,000
Building supplies		18,547
Purchased services		47,762
Total building and occupancy expense		$310,473

SCHEDULE C
Office Supplies and Services

Office and medical record supplies	$ 21,517
Printing	37,227
Postage	32,330
Total office supplies and services	$ 91,074

SCHEDULE D
Insurance

Hazard and general liability	$ 9,811
Professional liability	187,835
Workmen's compensation	3,269
Total insurance	$ 200,915

Continued

Table 4.2 Continued

SCHEDULE E
All Other Expenses

Equipment repairs		$ 11,807
Maintenance contracts, office equipment, and general expenses		14,423
Travel, non-M.D. (partial estimate)		6,268
Collection expense		35,183
Donations		11,060
Recruitment expense— M.D.	$ 4,926	6,278
— Non-M.D.	1,352	
		6,278
Personal property taxes		14,166
Vending expenses		5,474
Miscellaneous expenses:		
— House calls	$ 427	
— Outside manpower	610	
— Purchased services	1,175	
— Bad checks	3,977	
— Cash > and <	20	
— Dues, non-M.D.	2,903	
— Books and subscriptions	1,209	
— Public relations	1,381	
— M.D. entertainment	371	
— General expense	11,760	
		23,833
Total all other expenses		$ 128,492

SCHEDULE F
M.D. Fringe Benefits

		% of Receipts
Medical — dental plan	$ 25,853	0.4%
Profit-sharing plan	132,439	2.0
Retirement plan	234,079	3.6
Group life and disability	33,932	0.5
Hospitalization	31,690	0.5
Dues and licenses	28,070	0.5
Education expenses	12,000	0.2
Travel and committee meetings	8,420	0.1
Social security taxes	51,795	0.8
M. D. exams	685	—
Total M.D. fringe benefits	$ 558,963	8.6%

Table 4.3

ACTUAL REVENUES 1980–1982,
AND PROJECTIONS 1983–1985

| | 1980 ACTUAL | | | | 1981 ACTUAL | | | |
	No. of FTE MDs	See Footnote*	$(000)	$/FTE	No. of FTE MDs	See Footnote*	$(000)	$/FTE
Gross charges	33.50	—	$5,458	$162.9	37.00	+4.1 %	$6,274	$169.6
Less: uncollectibles	—	7.7%	−421	−12.6	—	4.9%	−307	−8.3
Add: other revenue	—	—	73	2.2	—	+79.5%	131	3.5
Total receipts	33.50	—	$5,110	$152.5	37.00	—	$6,098	$164.8

| | 1982 BASE YEAR | | | | 1983 WITH AN 8% PRICE INCREASE | | | |
	No. of FTE MDs	See Footnote*	$(000)	$/FTE	No. of FTE MDs	See Footnote*	$(000)	$/FTE
Gross charges	37.14	+8.5%	$6,805	$183.3	37.90	+8.0%	$7,503	$198.0
Less: uncollectibles	—	5.1%	−345	−9.3	—	6.0%	−450	−11.9
Add: other revenue	—	−44.3%	73	2.0	—	+8.2%	79	2.1
Total receipts	37.14	—	$6,533	$176.0	37.50	—	$7,132	$188.2

| | 1984 WITH A 6% PRICE INCREASE | | | | 1985 WITH A 6% PRICE & 1% VOLUME INCREASE | | | |
	No. of FTE MDs	See Footnote*	$(000)	$/FTE	No. of FTE MDs	See Footnote*	$(000)	$/FTE
Gross charges	41.90	+6.0%	$8,794	$209.9	46.18	+7.0%	$10,372	$224.6
Less: uncollectibles	—	6.0%	−528	−12.6	—	6.0%	−622	−13.5
Add: other revenue	—	6.3%	84	2.0	—	+6.0%	89	1.9
Total receipts	41.90	—	$8,350	$199.3	46.18	—	$9,839	$213.0

*This column reports as follows:
  Gross charges line: Percentage change in gross charges from previous year attributable solely to changes in rates and volume/FTE
  Uncollectibles line: Current uncollectibles as a percentage of current gross charges.
  Other revenue line: Percentage change in other revenue from previous year.

REVENUE

Physician staffing levels will occur as projected in Table 4.3, as a minimum. The number of "full-time equivalents" (FTE's) M.D.'s estimated appears to be on the conservative side.

Revenues for the 1982 fiscal year were used as the base for estimating. Figures were obtained from the 1982 audit workpapers.

The productivity for new physicians, based on actual clinic experience, is:

  — 1st year, 50% of average full-time, established M.D.
  — 2nd year, 75% of average full-time, established M.D.
  — 3rd year, 100% of average full-time, established M.D.

Prices will increase 8 percent in 1983, at a minimum. 1982 mid-year price increases raised revenue over earlier projections. Each subsequent year fees are programmed to increase 6 percent. Considering current inflation rates of 10 percent, 6 percent is conservative.

Collections from billings are estimated to be 94 percent of gross charges for each projected year. The clinic's most recent past rates have been in the 96-98 percent range.

The projections do not take into consideration any significant changes in the reimbursement systems.

Table 4.4

BALANCE SHEETS
December 31, 1982 and 1981

ASSETS

	1982*	1981
CURRENT ASSETS		
Cash	$ 12,740	$ 83,236
Current portion of notes receivable	19,779	14,368
Land contract receivable	—	158,442
Trade receivables and unbilled charges, less allowance for doubtful receivables of $332,000 in 1982 and $200,000 in 1981	2,283,697	2,230,656
Prepaid expenses	85,286	76,285
	2,401,502	2,562,987
PROPERTY AND EQUIPMENT—AT COST		
Clinic building leasehold improvements	214,639	171,322
Furniture and equipment	1,165,655	900,423
Less accumulated depreciation and amortization	(784,300)	(651,852)
	595,994	419,893
OTHER ASSETS		
Notes receivable, less current portion	233,477	158,251
Investment in clinic building corporation—at cost	—	5,030
	233,477	163,281
	$3,230,973	$3,146,161

LIABILITIES AND CAPITAL

	1982	1981
LIABILITIES		
Current liabilities		
Notes payable to bank—unsecured	$ 92,500	$ 225,000
Current maturities of long-term debt	99,343	119,071
Trade accounts payable	148,675	95,358
Accrued liabilities	218,245	249,587
Income received in advance	81,470	—
Income taxes payable	710	—
	640,943	689,016
Deferred income taxes	841,000	745,000
	1,481,943	1,434,016
Long-term debt (less current maturities)	212,790	299,761
EQUITY		
Contributed capital		
Common stock—authorized, 5,000 shares without par value; issued, 1,550 shares in 1982 and 1,400 shares in 1981 at a stated value of $50 a share	77,500	70,000
Additional paid-in capital	99,767	143,583
	177,267	213,583
Retained earnings	1,368,573	1,198,801
	1,545,840	1,412,384
Less 50 shares of common stock in treasury—at cost	9,600	—
	1,536,240	1,412,384
	$3,230,973	$3,146,161

*Projected.

Table 4.5

STATEMENTS OF OPERATIONS
Year Ended December 31 (Accrual Basis)

	1982*	1981
REVENUES		
Net professional fees †	$6,804,972	$6,243,244
Other	73,493	130,393
	6,878,465	6,373,637
EXPENSES		
Salaries	3,865,790	3,700,182
Depreciation and amortization	138,400	118,724
Interest	40,530	35,854
Other	2,567,263	2,637,121
	6,611,983	6,491,881
Earnings (loss) before income taxes	266,482	(118,244)
INCOME TAXES		
Currently payable	710	—
Deferred	96,000	(80,000)
	96,710	(80,000)
Net earnings (loss)	$ 169,772	$ (38,244)

*Projected.
†After 1982 refunds of $116,521 and 1981 refunds of $98,793.

Table 4.6

FINANCIAL REPORT
Calendar Year 1982 – 1981

ACCOUNTS RECEIVABLE ANALYSIS

	1982	1981
Current	$ 362,379 (14%)	$ 355,874 (15%)
Over 30 days old	502,716 (19%)	390,986 (16%)
Over 60 days old	346,487 (13%)	351,687 (14%)
Over 90 days old	326,729 (12%)	201,427 (8%)
Over 120 days old	1,077,386 (42%)	1,130,682 (47%)
Total	$2,615,697 (100%)	$2,430,656 (100%)
TYPES OF BILLING:		
Family accounts	$1,647,208 (63%)	$1,594,374 (66%)
Workmen's compensation	38,436 (1%)	33,997 (1%)
Welfare accounts	514,314 (20%)	395,476 (16%)
Collection agencies	415,739 (16%)	406,809 (17%)
Total	$2,615,697 (100%)	$2,430,656 (100%)

The Demise of Good Health, Inc.

Kathleen M. Stamm
Douglas A. Conrad

INTRODUCTION

Synopsis

During its six-year history Good Health, Inc. (GHI), a health maintenance organization (HMO), was awarded more than $3 million in federal funds to cover development costs and operating expenses, and also received a federal loan to finance the purchase of a clinic. Despite this infusion of federal funds, GHI never achieved financial viability. In October 1978, its assets were purchased by a large, well-established HMO in a neighboring county.

At the highest level of analysis, the history of GHI can be thought of in terms of five underlying management issues:

1. The mechanism for developing assumptions and projections
2. The development and maintenance of the management information system
3. The mechanism for making financial decisions
4. Planning and development strategies
5. Referrals to outside providers

The details of GHI's quest for capital and the summary financial statements provide the background necessary for analysis of these management issues.

Background

GHI established itself in Burtown, a blue-collar community with a 1970 population of 150,000. The county population of 400,000 was concentrated within a ten-mile radius of Burtown. Other than its relatively high proportion of active and retired military and their dependents, the most significant economic factor was reliance on one primary industry. While there was no competing HMO in Burr County, there was a well-established HMO in a neighboring county with a much larger population base. In addition, there was a waning prepaid group practice plan in Burtown itself. That plan ceased operation in 1976. GHI had two administrators, one from its inception until October 1977, and one for the final year of its existence.

Early Financial History

GHI was incorporated in 1972. Initially, its activities were funded by an HMO planning grant awarded under Section 314(e) of the Public Health Service Act. In the months following incorporation, negotiations proceeded for the use of space and facilities at a local hospital as a base for the Good Health planning effort.

The provisional benefit package was based on the assumption that services would be provided at the same hospital. When it became clear that services and facilities would not be provided by the hospital, the GHI Board sought a contract for professional services with a well-established group practice. According to one budget projection, half of the plan's members were to be served by this group of physicians, who would be paid on a capitation basis. The contract with the physician group never materialized. As a result, GHI decided to acquire a freestanding outpatient facility to serve its members, and to purchase specialty care and inpatient services in the marketplace.

Concurrent with developmental activities, the GHI staff had to meet a deadline for a renewal application of its developmental grant. Continuing uncertainty surrounded the deadline for reapplication. How much money would be available from federal sources, and when, were frequently uncertain throughout GHI's history.

Eventually, under Section 314(e) of the Public Health Service Act, GHI was awarded funds to continue planning and development activities. The award was contingent upon several conditions. Key financial requirements were that (1) providers in the system would share the risk of providing health services on a prenegotiated basis (never fully implemented); and (2) no federal funds would be applied to direct marketing costs (one dimension of operations).

GHI received its final 314(e) planning and development funds in 1974. That same year it also received a development grant authorized by the Health Maintenance Organization Act (Public Law 93-222). Under 314(e) and P.L. 93-222, GHI received a total of $722,000 for planning and development.

SOURCES OF CAPITAL

External Sources of Funds

Local Sources of Capital

Local banks expressed an interest in loaning funds to the hospital-based HMO that was planned initially. The decision of the hospital's owners not to sell the facility, and subsequent lengthy delays in the availability of federal funding for GHI, were two major reasons that the local bank loans never materialized, except to provide operating capital for the fee-for-service segment of GHI's operation.

In 1974, GHI was still in search of working capital. The Department of Health,

Education, and Welfare (HEW) — now the Department of Health and Human Services — could loan funds only if the organization qualified as an HMO under P.L. 93-222 *and* if Congress appropriated the necessary funds. Meanwhile, developmental grant funds to GHI were expected to end or be reduced after April 1, and the fee-for-service component of GHI was not generating sufficient revenue to cover total operating expenses. A consortium of local banks attempted to develop a loan program that would provide GHI with sufficient working capital on an interim basis (until a federal loan was available), but GHI never obtained the loan. GHI also sought "equity capital" from industrialists and other sources, but such funding was not secured.

National Sources of Capital

In 1973, GHI's Chief Executive Officer traveled to other regions of the nation to explore potential sources of capital. Previously, only local sources had been approached. No funds were ever received from these out-of-area sources of private capital.

Insurance Companies

As early as January 1973, the Board considered arrangements with third-party payers to obtain funds to meet GHI's operating and capital requirements. Interest in this approach centered on Medicare and Medicaid, a participatory agreement with a third-party carrier (Blue Cross), or a prepaid program. Both direct loans and operational agreements were considered, but these discussions brought no positive results.

Internal Sources of Capital

Fee-for-Service

A local bank extended a line of credit for the fee-for-service component of GHI's operations in the fall of 1973. The fee-for-service operation required little additional capital, provided experience in operations prior to the offering of the prepaid capitation plan, and generated much-needed cash. A major component of GHI's fee-for-service activity was a contract to provide health services for a local college's students. Physician services under that contract began in August 1973. Revenues from the fee-for-service component of GHI's operations provided funds for the purchase of capital equipment and payment of operating expenses.

Capital Membership Deposit for Individual Family Membership

The Finance Committee recommended in December 1972 that GHI charge a $200 membership fee per family unit to generate cash for capital equipment purchases. The first payment ($50) was required at the time of application for membership. The balance ($150) could be paid at the rate of $50 per year over a three-year period. The membership fee bond was refundable, without interest, at the convenience of GHI, within five years of terminating membership. As of December 31, 1973, deposits in the amount of $1,200 had been subscribed; $700 in payments had been deferred and $500 received.

The resolution which initially authorized the capital membership requirement stipulated that 300 family units be enrolled before any capital could be expended. A subsequent resolution rescinded this condition. In 1974, the Board of Directors discontinued the requirement that individual family units pay a capital membership fee. The balance in the account in 1974 and succeeding years represented prior members' deposits which had not been refunded.

Subordinated Debentures

In 1973, the Board authorized the sale of up to $500,000 in subordinated debentures. At the time of issue the bonds bore a 7-percent interest rate, which the Board later increased to 8 percent. The debentures were payable on or before July 1, 1981, by which time GHI was to have been operating "in the black." Interest was due on July 1, 1974, and annually thereafter. Debentures were available in denominations of $100, $500, and $1,000. As of December 31, 1973, debentures totaling $2,400 had been issued. The proceeds from these issues were restricted for capital expenditures and the retirement of mortgage and bonded indebtedness. When the unsold debentures were withdrawn from the market in December 1976, less than $4,000 had been generated through the sale of these bonds.

Record and Evaluation Fees

In 1973, the Board adopted a record fee of $10 per member (individual or family) to be collected at or before the first patient visit. An evaluation fee of $5 per individual (up to a maximum of $30 per family) was also adopted. The purpose of these fees was to generate capital.

Board Members

Board members were expected to help raise funds to meet GHI's operating and capital expense needs. The Board, as well as GHI employees, made or secured personal loans in late 1973 and again in 1974 to meet a cash flow crisis that developed.

The Federal Government

Throughout GHI's planning, development, and years of operation, HEW was the major source of funds apart from membership dues. The other major federal program which supplied capital was the Federal Housing Authority, which loaned GHI the money to purchase a clinic.

Grants and Loans for Planning, Development, and Operations

By the end of 1974, GHI had been awarded four development grants totaling $722,000. As soon as GHI was certified by HEW as a qualified HMO, the organization received a loan of $1 million under P.L. 93-222 to supplement revenues until operations reached break-even. GHI had anticipated that an HEW loan for operations would be available much earlier.

In accordance with provisions of the loan agreement, the proceeds were deposited in an escrow account. These proceeds were to be withdrawn in monthly installments which in any year could not exceed by more than 10 percent the scheduled amounts specified in the agreement plus interest earned on the escrow. The loan was negotiated to assist GHI in meeting its operating expenses during the first 36 months of operation. At the end of that period, GHI was to have reached break-even.

Soon after the initial loan, HEW committed an additional $228,000 in loan funds under P.L. 93-222. These funds were to be made available at the end of the advance schedule for the first HEW loan. As was the case for the first note, the second was collateralized by cash in banks, accounts receivable, and the unassigned equipment of the corporation (equipment that was not used as security for any other notes). In the second year of operations, withdrawals from the escrow account totaled 37.4 percent more than the amount specified in the initial withdrawal schedule. The accelerated drawdown was needed to pay operating expenses.

In 1977, GHI was awarded a third loan of $1 million. In addition, HEW had committed funds totaling $272,000 to be made available to the corporation in 1978. In 1977, the period during which funds could be utilized (i.e., the anticipated break-even point) was extended from three to five years. In addition, the loan requirements that a restricted reserve and sinking fund be established were deferred until after the corporation had achieved break-even.

GHI was in serious financial straits by the end of 1977. Total escrow withdrawals for the year represented 24 percent of net revenues in the same year. In the first ten months of 1978, GHI applied to operations the total amount remaining in the escrow account, including interest.

FHA Loan

In addition to the $2.5 million in HEW loans, in 1975 GHI received a mortgage loan insured by the Federal Housing Authority (FHA). The loan was used to exercise GHI's option to purchase a building suitable for a clinic site, and to make necessary building improvements. Interest at 9 percent on the total loan was payable monthly beginning in January 1976. Principal payments did not begin until June 1977; the unpaid balance was payable in full in 2002. The organization which purchased GHI's assets in 1978 assumed responsibility for this loan.

Loans and Leases for Major Equipment

Early in its development, GHI financed the acquisition of major equipment through loans. Three loans were secured by radiology equipment, optometry equipment, and the personal guarantees of various members of the Board and GHI employees, respectively. There was also an unsecured note for equipment and supplies.

In 1976, GHI entered into a lease agreement for computer hardware requiring annual payments of more than $14,000 until the lease expired in 1981. The following year the corporation entered into a noncancelable lease agreement for a second building, to be used for business activities.

DECISIONS REGARDING LOCATIONS

GHI's first move was from its initial hospital quarters to a temporary location, and the search for a more permanent location continued. The Finance Committee recommended purchase of an existing building rather than construction of a new building. The site eventually selected was five blocks from a competing facility, and was in a declining neighborhood.

Board recommendations for funding included:

1. Mortgage bonds for the purchase and improvement of the building as well as fixed equipment
2. A loan from an interested agency (unspecified) or a personal loan to secure the option to purchase
3. Capital dues and purchase contracts for the purchase of nonfixed equipment
4. Loans from local banks for additional working capital, if possible

Eventually GHI's administrative offices were moved out of the clinic facility to a separate location.

The other clinic site used by GHI was a clinic in a small, remote town. It was staffed by a family practitioner and his nurse practitioner spouse. The opening of this location in 1976 was prompted by the results of a feasibility study requested by area residents, which indicated sufficient demand for a satellite GHI clinic.

Plans to expand into Burr County continued for some time. Negotiations were underway to purchase ground and a partially completed building for "a reasonable amount." A feasibility study and certificate-of-need application were also being completed. Within a year, a separate certificate of need for another satellite facility had also been submitted. This feasibility and planning analysis required a considerable commitment of staff time, which the Board questioned. (Note: GHI was never awarded any federal funds for these satellite activities.)

FINANCIAL MANAGEMENT ISSUES

Developing Assumptions and Projections

Sources and levels of revenues, enrollment, and utilization were not accurately estimated. Budgets were consistently at variance with actual levels of revenue generated, and expenses routinely exceeded estimates. Major discrepancies between projected and actual figures persisted throughout the history of the organization.

Some financial assumptions were imposed by the federal government. One early example was the requirement for matching funds for monies awarded under the Public Health Service Act. Another was the initial federal requirement that, in order to be federally qualified, an HMO had to demonstrate the ability to operate on a fiscally sound basis within 30 months. This requirement was subsequently relaxed.

Particularly in the first years, GHI pursued a wide range of financing options. Private financing was regarded as a likely source of funds with which to begin operations. The Board anticipated that substantial capital would be generated through the sale of capital membership certificates and subordinated debentures.

The Management Information System

As of September 1974, GHI maintained a double-entry accounting system. Funds were accounted for on an accrual basis. Cash receipts and cash disbursement journals had been established, and financial transactions relating to cash receipts and disbursements were being properly recorded. A general ledger with control accounts had been established. However, as of September 1974, GHI had not updated the general ledger accounts and the schedule of applicable grant expenditures since the end of March 1974. Quarterly expenditures and financial statements relating to the operations of GHI for the period ending June 30, 1974, had not been prepared.

When a marketing assessment was conducted in 1974, the federal observer found that the basic data essential to make marketing decisions had not been acquired, despite three years and $700,000 of involvement. The problem still existed three years later. Marketing and financial data were nonexistent, not current, or not organized in such a manner as to support current marketing and financial projections for GHI loan applications. At the time of a site visit in May 1977, the most recent actual cost data available were for December 1976.

Mechanism for Making Financial Decisions

The first Administrator did not delegate financial authority to any individual (e.g., Financial Director) or group (e.g., the Finance Committee of the Board). He raised financial issues, identified alternatives, and served as the primary interface with the federal HMO bureaucracy and the local financial community. The role of the Finance Committee was limited to introducing resolutions for Board action.

Persons with financial expertise were not consulted systematically. At most board meetings, the Administrator's report included financial developments. The GHI Board functioned without a Finance Committee for several months after its formation. In addition, for three periods of varying length, GHI operated without a Financial Director. The Accounting Supervisor served as Interim Finance Director during one of these intervals.

Planning and Development Strategies

Early grant proposals mentioned multiple clinic sites, but in mid-1974, the federal government began questioning plans to open additional health centers. One HEW financial analyst recommended caution and a substantial capital reserve before any new centers were considered. Despite this concern, the Chief Executive Officer proceeded with the planning and development of additional facilities and new markets.

In November 1975, the Administrator requested and received authority to apply for a certificate of need for a second facility to be located south of the current site. At the same time, GHI applied for an FHA loan to purchase and remodel the central clinic site.

In April 1976, the Board expressed concern about the need to focus all available resources on enrollment, then authorized the Administrator to negotiate a feasibility study in another county, outside GHI's market area. The Board stipulated that significant amounts of staff and monetary resources were not to be used.

At the Board meeting in December 1976 the Administrator noted the stress that "growth" was causing within the organization and reported to the Board that no federal funds would be forthcoming for the development of the neighboring county. The Administrator then proceeded to outline a two-year plan for the development of four new sites: two small offices which would provide limited services, a full-service health center, and a facility in the aforementioned county.

Referrals to Outside Providers

The summary statement of revenues and expenses indicates the proportion of total operating expenses constituted by outside referrals. Referrals to specialists in obstetrics/gynecology, orthopedics, general surgery, otorhinolaryngology, and ophthalmology predominated. Relevant factors included:

1. The lack of family practitioners on the GHI medical staff who did obstetrics/gynecology work
2. The difficulty in recruiting an obstetrician because of the high salary requirement
3. The refusal of other GHI physicians to cover and provide on-call back-up for an obstetrician
4. The relatively restricted practices of the internists in the GHI medical group
5. Referrals to hospital emergency rooms for routine care during nonclinic hours

SUMMARY FINANCIAL DATA

Financial records for the period 1973 – 1978, derived from audited financial statements, are summarized in Tables 5.1 through 5.6. These include a summary balance sheet (Table 5.1), a summary statement of revenues and expenses (Table 5.4), and horizontal (Tables 5.2 and 5.5) and vertical (Tables 5.3 and 5.6) analyses of these two financial statements. There are two reporting periods in 1978, as a result of the acquisition of GHI assets by another HMO on October 31, 1978.

ISSUES AND PROBLEMS

You are the new Administrator of the GHI operation. You are an employee of the health maintenance organization which purchased the assets of Good Health, Inc.

1. Assess and analyze the financial data using financial ratio analysis. Compare your results to industry standards and discuss a management strategy for improving each.
2. Summarize and assess the impact of major trends apparent in the horizontal and vertical analyses of the summary financial statements.
3. Using the background obtained from your analyses of questions 1 and 2, develop a management strategy which addresses each of the five underlying management issues highlighted in the case.

SELECTED BIBLIOGRAPHY

Beaver, W. H. "Market Prices, Financial Ratios, and the Prediction of Failure." *Journal of Accounting Research* (Autumn 1968): 179 – 192.

Bisbee, Gerald E., Jr., and McCarthy, Margaret M. "Planning, Budgeting, and Cost Control in HMOs." In *Managing the Finances of Health Care Organizations*, edited by Gerald E. Bisbee and Robert A. Vraciu, pp. 202 – 215. Ann Arbor, Mich.: Health Administration Press, 1980.

Caruana, Russel A., and Kudder, George. "Seeing through the Figures with Ratios." *Hospital Financial Management* 8, no. 6 (1978): 16 – 26.

Choate, G. Marc, and Tanaka, Kanaki. "Using Financial Ratio Analysis to Compare Hospitals' Performance." *Hospital Financial Management* 8, no. 6 (1978): 310 – 338.

Harrison, Deborah H., and Kimberly, John R. "HMOs Don't Have to Fail." *Harvard Business Review* (July-August 1982): 115 – 124.

Iglehart, J. K. "The Federal Government as Venture Capitalist: How Does it Fare." *Milbank Memorial Fund Quarterly/Health and Society* 58, no. 4 (1980): 656 – 666.

Lev, Baruch, and Sunder, Shyam. "Methodological Issues in the Use of Financial Ratios." *Journal of Accounting and Economics* 1, no. 3 (December 1979): 187 – 210.

Silvers, J. B., and Prahalad, Coimbatore K. "Management Control Systems." In *Financial Management of Health Institutions*, pp. 73 – 92. Flushing, N.Y.: Spectrum Publications, 1974.

Valiante, John D. "Overview of Issues Affecting Capital Investment in the Health Care Industry." Presentation to the Health Capital Conference, sponsored by the Bureau of Health Facilities, DHHS, Washington, D.C., February 19 – 20, 1980.

Vraciu, Robert A., and Starkweather, David B. "Kaiser's Financial Strategies and Some Cues for Other HMOs." In *Managing the Finances of Health Care Organizations*, edited by Gerald E. Bisbee and Robert A. Vraciu, pp. 216 – 235. Ann Arbor, Mich.: Health Administration Press, 1980.

Table 5.1

BALANCE SHEET
1973 – 1978

	DEC. 31 1973	DEC. 31 1974	DEC. 31 1975	DEC. 31 1976	DEC. 31 1977	OCT. 31 1978	DEC. 31 1978
ASSETS							
Current assets:							
Cash	$ 542	$ 57,896	$ 8,913	$ 34,273	$ 231,461	$ 382,848	$ 426,746
Accounts receivable—medical services Less allowable for fee adjustments and uncollectible accounts	2,937	18,136	25,565	103,191	277,073	329,554	345,162
Grants receivable	144,547						
Supplies inventories	2,587	3,825	8,868	13,170	14,621	24,027	
Prepaid expenses and other current assets	2,493	4,665	2,731	5,785	17,616	47,330	
Escrow account—current portion of advances		555,000	429,000	142,982	422,568		
Deposits		3,899	4,122	7,660	12,472	13,024	6,500
Restricted cash				29,057			
Receivables from purchasing HMO							370,528
Total current assets	153,106	643,421	479,199	336,118	975,811	796,783	1,148,936
Property, plant and equipment:							
Capitalized lease/option on medical center property Less allowance for depreciation	378,115						
Leasehold improvements Less amortization	13,161	17,471					
Equipment Less allowance for depreciation	56,343						
Land		78,340	78,340	78,340			
Building		301,660	316,264	464,988			
Medical equipment		35,853	38,003	139,289			
Office furniture and equipment		27,767	33,062	52,448			
Construction in progress			28,641	673			
		461,091	494,310	735,738			
Less accumulated depreciation, amortization		(17,444)	(32,823)	(56,588)			
Total property, plant, equipment	447,619	443,647	461,487	679,150	711,761	687,417	
Insolvency fund—cash				5,780	5,000	5,000	5,000
Other assets:							
Capitalized development costs	265,262						
Program development costs less amortization		310,515	276,944	243,373	209,801	181,825	
Escrow account		1,000,025	494,700				
Interest receivable		2,078	24,960				
		1,002,103	519,660				
Less current portion of advances		(555,000)	(429,000)				
		447,103	90,660				
Unamortized financing expense Net of accumulated amortization			39,069	28,268	27,152	26,222	
Total other assets	265,262	757,618	406,673	271,641	236,953	208,047	
Total assets	$865,987	$1,844,686	$1,347,359	$1,292,689	$1,929,525	$1,697,247	$1,153,936

LIABILITIES AND MEMBERS' EQUITY (DEFICIENCY)

LIABILITIES							
Current liabilities:							
Short-term notes payable	$ 11,437						
Accounts payable — trade	25,240	$ 26,897	$ 96,772	$ 238,111	$ 615,723	$ 698,322	$ 864,002
Contracts payable	27,922						
Deposit liability — federal grant	134,623	187,454	28,870	1,650	18,840[1]	2,970	3,903
Membership deposits payable		1,355	1,350		52,080	224,880	220,806
Accrued expenses	4,464	12,591	4,157	38,791			
Portion of long-term debt due within one year		33,401	9,700	11,745	16,949		
Construction contract payable				14,817			
Total current liabilities	203,686	261,698	140,849	305,114	703,592	926,172	1,088,711
Long-term liabilities:							
Long-term notes payable	12,097						
Subordinated debentures outstanding	2,400	3,700	3,700	3,900	3,700	3,200	3,200
Liability for lease/option on medical center property	368,158				42,790[2]	35,951[2]	
Notes payable — HHS		1,000,000	1,000,000	1,228,000	2,228,000	2,500,000	2,500,000
Notes payable — other		36,348	11,904	2,152			
Debt payable under purchase option		347,316	367,126	620,203	640,970	634,645	
Mortgage loan payable							
		1,387,364	1,382,730	1,854,255	2,915,460		
Less portion due within one year		(33,401)	(9,700)	(11,745)	(16,949)		
Total long-term liabilities	382,655	1,353,963	1,373,030	1,842,510	2,898,511	3,173,796	2,503,200
Total liabilities	586,341	1,615,661	1,513,879	2,147,624	3,602,103	4,099,968	3,591,911
MEMBERS' EQUITY:							
Capital membership deposits subscribed	500						
Less subscriptions receivable							
Federal development capital	276,472	346,902	346,902				
General reserve for expansion	2,674						
Fund balance (deficit)		(117,877)	(513,422)				
Members' equity (deficiency):							
Total capital	279,646						
Total members' equity		229,025					
Total fund balance (deficit)			(166,520)				
Members' equity (deficiency)				(854,935)	(1,672,578)	(2,402,721)	(2,437,975)
Total liabilities and members' equity	$865,987	$1,844,686	$1,347,359	$1,292,689	$1,929,525	$1,697,247	$1,153,936

1. And unearned revenue.
2. Obligation under capitalized leases.

Table 5.2

COMPARATIVE HORIZONTAL ANALYSIS
Summary Balance Sheet

	1973	1974	Increase (Decrease) Amount	Percent	1975	Increase (Decrease) Amount	Percent	1976	Increase (Decrease) Amount	Percent
Total current assets	153,106	643,421	490,315	300.2	479,199	(164,222)	(25.5)	336,118	(143,081)	(29.9)
Total plant, property, equipment	447,619	443,647	(3,972)	(0.1)	461,487	17,840	4.0	679,150	217,663	47.2
Total other assets	265,262	757,618	492,356	185.6	406,673	(350,945)	(46.3)	271,641	(135,032)	(33.2)
Total assets	865,987	1,844,686	978,699	113.0	1,347,359	(497,327)	(27.0)	1,292,689	(54,670)	(4.1)
Total current liabilities	203,686	261,698	58,012	28.5	140,849	(120,849)	(46.2)	305,114	164,265	116.6
Total long-term liabilities	382,655	1,353,963	971,308	253.8	1,373,030	19,067	1.4	1,842,510	469,480	34.2
Total liabilities	586,341	1,615,661	1,029,320	175.5	1,513,879	(101,782)	(6.3)	2,147,624	633,745	41.9
Members' equity (deficiency)	279,646	229,025	(50,621)		(166,520)	(395,545)		(854,935)	(688,415)	

	1977	Increase (Decrease) Amount	Percent	10 Months 1978	Increase (Decrease) Amount[1]	Percent	1978	Increase (Decrease) Amount[2]	Percent
Total current assets	975,811	639,693	190.3	796,783	(179,028)	(18.3)	1,148,936	173,125	17.7
Total plant, property, equipment	711,761	32,611	4.8	687,417	(24,344)	(3.4)	—		
Total other assets	236,953	(34,688)	(12.8)	208,047	(28,906)	(12.2)			
Total assets	1,929,525	636,836	49.3	1,697,247	(232,278)	(12.0)	1,153,936	(775,589)	(40.2)
Total current liabilities	703,592	398,478	130.6	926,172	222,580	31.6	1,088,711	385,119	54.7
Total long-term liabilities	2,898,511	1,056,001	57.3	3,173,796	275,285	9.5	2,503,200	(395,311)	(13.6)
Total liabilities	3,602,103	1,454,479	67.7	4,099,968	497,865	13.8	3,591,911	(10,192)	(0.3)
Members' equity (deficiency)	(1,672,578)	(817,643)		(2,402,721)	(730,143)		(2,437,975)	(765,397)	

1. Not Annualized.
2. Ref. 1977

Table 5.3

COMPARATIVE COMPONENT PERCENTAGE (VERTICAL) ANALYSIS:
Summary Balance Sheet

	1973	%	1974	%	1975	%	1976	%	1977	%	10 Months 1978	%	1978	%
Total current assets	153,106		643,421		479,199		336,118		975,811		796,783		1,148,936	
Cash	542	.4	57,896	9.0	8,913	1.9	34,273	10.2	231,461	23.7	382,848	48.0	426,746	37.1
Accounts receivable	2,937	1.9	18,136	2.8	25,565	5.3	103,191	30.7	277,073	28.4	329,554	41.4	345,162	30.0
Supplies inventories	2,587	1.7	3,825	0.6	8,868	1.9	13,170	3.9	14,621	1.5	24,027	3.0		
Prepaid expenses and other	2,493	1.6	4,665	0.7	2,731	0.6	5,785	1.7	17,616	1.8	47,330	5.9		
Escrow—current portion			555,000	86.3	429,000	89.5	142,982	42.5	422,568	43.3				
Total assets	865,987		1,844,686		1,347,359		1,292,689		1,929,525		1,697,247		1,153,936	
Escrow—current portion	153,106	17.7	555,000	30.1	429,000	31.8	142,982	11.1	422,568	21.9				
Total current assets	447,619	51.7	643,421	34.9	479,199	35.6	336,118	26.0	975,811	50.6	796,783	46.9	1,148,936*	99.6
Property, plant, equipment	265,262	30.6	443,647	24.1	461,487	34.3	679,150	52.5	711,761	36.9	687,417	40.5		
Other			757,618	41.1	406,673	30.2	271,641	21.0	236,953	12.3	208,047	12.3		
Total current liabilities	203,686		261,698		140,849		305,114		703,592		926,172		1,088,711	
Accounts payable—trade	25,240	12.4	26,897	10.3	96,772	68.7	238,111	78.0	615,723	87.5	698,322	75.4	864,002	79.4
Accrued expenses	4,464	2.2	12,591	4.8	4,157	3.0	38,791	12.7	52,080	7.4	224,880	24.3	220,806	20.3
Deposit liability—federal grant	134,623	66.1	187,454	71.6	28,870	20.5								
Long-term liabilities	382,655		1,353,963		1,373,030		1,842,510		2,898,511		3,173,796		2,503,200	
Notes payable—HHS			1,000,000	73.9	1,000,000	72.8	1,228,000	66.6	2,228,000	76.9	2,500,000	78.8	2,500,000	99.9
Total liabilities	586,341		1,615,661		1,513,879		2,147,624		3,602,103		4,099,968		3,591,911	
Total current liabilities	203,686	34.7	261,698	16.2	140,849	9.3	305,114	14.2	703,592	19.5	926,172	22.6	1,088,711	30.3
Total long-term liabilities	382,655	65.3	1,353,963	83.8	1,373,030	90.7	1,842,510	85.8	2,898,511	80.5	3,173,796	77.4	2,503,200	69.7
Notes payable—HHS			1,000,000	61.9	1,000,000	66.1	1,228,000	57.2	2,228,000	61.9	2,500,000	61.0	2,500,000	69.6

*Net of $5,000 Insolvency Fund

Table 5.4

STATEMENT OF REVENUES AND EXPENSES
1973 — 1978

	1973	1974[2]	1975	1976	1977	10 Months 1978	1978
REVENUES							
Operating:							
Fee for service	$ 3,517	$ 61,139	$ 64,857	$ 84,334	$ 128,775	$ 130,734	$ 147,663
Contract services	6,222	14,311	16,438	10,576			
Membership dues		44,539	290,544	1,083,710	2,814,161	3,319,313	4,046,092
Other operating revenue		3,479	15,911	49,950	64,647	163,181	187,378
Total service revenue	9,739	123,468	387,750	1,228,570	3,007,583	3,613,228	4,381,133
Nonoperating revenues:							
Federal grants earned		181,477	158,584	28,870			
Other nonoperating revenue	23[1]	238	891	3,972	14,944	32,199	140,596[3]
Gross revenue		305,183	547,225	1,261,412	3,022,527	3,645,427	4,521,729
Less revenue deductions							
Contractual adjustments		3,478	5,513	16,095			
Uncollectible accounts		4,539	5,274	9,239			
		(8,017)	(10,787)	(25,334)	(19,160)	(13,131)	(15,131)
Net revenue	9,762	297,166	536,438	1,236,078	3,003,367	3,632,296	4,506,598

	1973	1974[2]	1975	1976	1977	10 Months 1978	
EXPENSES:							
Contracted outside medical services	$ 2,035[4]	$ 44,836	$280,001	$ 873,614	$2,094,459	$2,289,800	$2,770,672
Operating expenses:							
Salaries and wages	130,786	251,815	341,082	523,491			
Employee benefits	8,606	19,130	44,291	69,349			
Depreciation and amortization	1,389	39,095	48,950	57,336			
Rent and building expenses	8,417	35,486	40,370	1,200			
Supplies	10,996	26,910	30,387	77,530			
Utilities and miscellaneous purchased services	6,237	16,252	23,308	47,112			
Professional fees		13,649	5,714	8,020			
Interest expense — net	851	8,346	42,023	141,997			
Public relations		8,483	3,348	3,256			
Insurance		7,143	20,126	41,747			
Travel	5,403	5,431	11,647	8,028			
Postage		2,087	3,928	7,077			
Consultants	2,383	1,759	5,730	2,170			
Business taxes		1,755	7,704	18,445			
Advertising		1,171	7,607	1,730			
Legal expenses	10,007						
Employee recruitment and relocation	4,941						
Other expenses	7,575	4,799	15,767	42,391			
Medical service expense					1,064,108	1,239,095	1,494,502
Supporting services					662,444	833,544	1,006,821
Total operating expenses before apportionment of program development costs	199,626	443,311	651,982	1,050,879	1,726,552	2,072,639	2,501,323
Less program development costs	(192,872)	(70,430)			—	—	—
Net operating expenses	6,754	372,881	651,982	1,050,879	1,726,552	2,072,639	2,501,323
Total expenses	6,754	417,717	931,983	1,924,493	3,821,011	4,362,439	5,271,995
Excess of revenues over expenses (expenses over revenues)	$ 3,008	($120,551)	($395,545)	($ 688,415)	($ 817,644)	($ 730,143)	($ 765,397)

1. Interest income.
2. The 1974 figures used here were taken from the 1975 Statement of Revenues and Expenses. The corresponding document from 1974 reports different figures. No explanation was given for the revisions.
3. Ordinary plus extraordinary income: $ 36,334 — interest
   4,866 — sale of assets
   99,394 — realized from sale of assets
   $140,596

4. In 1973, included in operating expenses.

Table 5.5

COMPARATIVE HORIZONTAL ANALYSIS:
Statement of Revenues and Expenses

	1973	1974	Increase (Decrease) Amount	Percent	1975	Increase (Decrease) Amount	Percent	1976	Increase (Decrease) Amount	Percent
Total service revenue:	9,739	123,468	113,729	1167.8	387,750	264,282	214.0	1,228,570	840,820	216.8
Fee for service	3,517	61,139	57,622	1638.4	64,857	3,718	6.1	84,334	19,477	30.0
Contract services	6,222	14,311	8,089	130.0	16,438	2,127	14.9	10,576	(5,862)	(35.7)
Membership dues		44,539			290,544	246,005	552.3	1,083,710	793,166	273.0
Other operating revenue		3,479			15,911	12,432	357.3	49,950	34,039	214.0
Nonoperating revenues:	23	181,715	181,692	789965.2	159,475	(22,240)	(12.2)	32,842	(126,633)	(79.4)
Federal grants earned		181,477			158,584	(22,893)	(12.6)	28,870	(129,714)	(81.8)
Revenue deductions and contractual allowances:		(8,017)			(10,787)	(2,770)	(34.6)	(25,334)	(14,547)	(134.9)
Net revenue	9,762	297,166	287,404	2944.1	536,438	239,272	80.5	1,236,078	699,640	130.4
Expenses:	6,754									
Contracted outside medical services	2,035	44,836	42,801	2103.2	280,001	235,165	524.5	873,614	593,613	212.0
Operating expenses, net of program development costs	4,719	372,881	368,162		651,982	279,101	74.8	1,050,879	398,897	61.2
Excess of revenues over expenses (expenses over revenue)	3,008	(120,551)	(123,559)		(395,545)	(274,994)		(688,415)	(292,870)	

	1977	Increase (Decrease) Amount	Percent	10 Months 1978	Increase (Decrease) Amount[1]	Percent	1978	Increase (Decrease) Amount[2]	Percent
Total service revenue:	3,007,383	1,778,813	144.8	3,613,228	605,845	20.1	4,381,133	1,373,750	45.7
Fee for service	128,775	44,441	52.7	130,734	1,959	1.5	147,663	18,888	14.7
Contract services									
Membership dues	2,814,161	1,730,451	159.7	3,319,313	505,152	18.0	4,046,092	1,231,931	43.8
Other operating revenue	64,647	14,697	29.4	163,181	98,534	152.4	187,378	122,731	189.8
Nonoperating revenues:	14,944	(17,898)	(54.5)	32,199	17,255	115.5	140,596	125,652	840.8
Federal grants earned									
Revenue deductions and contractual allowances:	(19,160)	6,174	24.4	(13,131)	6,029	31.5	(15,131)	4,029	21.0
Net revenue	3,003,367	1,767,289	143.0	3,632,296	628,929	20.9	4,506,598	1,503,231	50.1
Expenses:									
Contracted outside medical services	2,904,459	2,030,845	232.5	2,289,800	(614,659)	(21.2)	2,770,672	(133,787)	(4.6)
Operating expenses, net of program development costs	1,726,552	675,673	64.3	2,072,639	346,087	20.0	2,501,323	774,771	44.9
Excess of revenues over expenses (expenses over revenue)	(817,644)	(129,229)		(730,143)	87,501		(765,397)	52,247	

1. Not Annualized.

2. Ref. 1977.

Table 5.6

COMPARATIVE COMPONENT PERCENTAGE (VERTICAL) ANALYSIS:
Statement of Revenues and Expenses

	1973	%	1974	%	1975	%	1976	%	1977	%	10 Months 1978	%	1978	%
Operating revenues:	9,739		123,468		387,750		1,228,570		3,007,583		3,613,228		4,381,133	
Fee for service	3,517	36.1	61,139	49.5	64,857	16.7	84,334	6.9	128,775	4.3	130,734	3.6	147,663	3.4
Contract services	6,222	63.9	14,311	11.6	16,438	4.2	10,576	0.9						
Membership dues			44,539	36.1	290,544	74.9	1,083,710	88.2	2,814,161	93.6	3,319,313	91.9	4,046,092	92.4
Other operating revenues			3,479	2.8	15,911	4.1	49,950	4.1	64,647	2.1	163,181	4.5	187,378	4.3
Contractual allowances and doubtful accounts			(8,017)	6.5	(10,787)	2.8	(25,334)	2.1	(19,160)	0.6	(13,131)	0.4	(15,131)	0.3
Net revenues:	9,762		297,166		536,438		1,236,078		3,003,367		3,632,296		4,506,598	
Operating revenues (gross)	9,739	99.8	123,468	41.5	387,750	72.3	1,228,570	99.4	3,007,583	100.1	3,613,228	99.5	4,381,133	97.2
(net)[1]	9,739	99.8	115,451	38.9	376,963	70.3	1,203,236	97.3	2,988,223	99.5	3,600,097	99.1	4,366,002	96.9
Nonoperating revenues	23	0.2	181,715	61.1	159,475	29.7	32,842	2.7	14,944	0.5	32,199	0.9	140,596	3.1
Expenses:	6,754		417,717		931,983		1,924,493		3,821,011		4,362,439		5,271,995	
Contracted outside medical services	2,035	30.1	44,836	10.7	280,001	30.0	873,614	45.4	2,094,459	54.8	2,289,800	52.5	2,770,672	52.6
Operating expenses	199,626		443,311											
Program development costs	192,872		70,430											
Operating expenses, net	6,754		372,881	89.3	651,982	70.0	1,050,879	54.6	1,726,552	45.2	2,072,639	47.5	2,501,323	47.4

1. Net of contractual allowances and allowances for doubtful accounts.

II

Managerial Accounting Techniques

Overview

Effective and efficient management of health care resources requires an understanding of basic management accounting techniques. Decisions on cost control, rate setting, and performance measurement can be influenced by the proper application of management accounting techniques such as cost-volume-profit models, standard costing, and flexible budgeting. Although the tools themselves are fairly simple in their design, their application in a health care organization is considerably more complex. The cases in this section are designed to develop familiarity with fundamental management accounting techniques and to stress their application to diverse organizational settings and problems.

The first case in this section, "Rosemont Hill Health Center," deals with the importance of defining cost objectives, cost centers, and the cost allocation system in establishing rates. Rosemont Hill is a community health center primarily serving inner-city clients. Cutbacks in financing and the requirements of third-party reimbursers have made the administrator concerned about cost determination. The case allows students to practice using managerial accounting tools and to formulate policies based on the results.

Similarly, "Good-by Columbus Community Mental Health Center" applies managerial accounting techniques to a midwestern community mental health center. The center is in the unenviable position of not having broken even in the preceding year. Nevertheless, its managers are contemplating expansion.

In a shift of emphasis, "Lakeside Hospital" focuses on full versus incremental costing techniques in deciding whether to continue to offer a service. Although the service discussed in the case is hemodialysis, the case illustrates a pressing decision commonly confronted by managers of health care organizations. The appropriateness of this type of analysis for health care in different situations can be examined.

The budgeting process is explored in "Carney Hospital," as is the relationship between the control system and implementation of the organization's strategy. Both internal factors and the external environment impinge upon these processes.

"University Hospital," the fifth case, requires the use of cost-volume-profit techniques, cost allocation methods, and incremental analysis to evaluate whether a hospital should establish an independent group practice. In addition, it serves as a review for most of the major management accounting techniques.

The development of diagnostic related groups (DRGs) and the political process of implementing the system are the focus of "Hospital Rate Setting by Per-Case Methods: DRGs and the New Jersey Department of Health." Emphasizing the impact of public policy on the health care industry, the case provides a thorough chronology of the events leading to the New

Jersey experiment. Moreover, it presents the statistical procedures used to partition cases into DRGs and illustrates rate setting for three different DRGs. A range of classroom uses for this case is apparent.

"Healthcare, Inc." is the final case in this section. Among the issues it addresses are the application of cost accounting techniques to health care organizations, product definition, product costing, internal versus external accounting information systems, and the design of a management information system. A health maintenance organization is the setting for this case.

6

Rosemont Hill Health Center

David Young

In March 1976, Mr. Frank Mitchell, Administrator of the Rosemont Hill Health Center, expressed concern about Rosemont Hill's cost accounting system. The extensive funding Rosemont Hill had received during its early years was decreasing and Mr. Mitchell wanted to prepare the center to be self-sufficient, yet the center lacked critical cost information.

At a meeting with Mr. Robert Simi, Rosemont Hill's new accountant, Mr. Mitchell outlined the principal issues:

> First of all, our deficit is increasing. We obviously have to reverse this trend if we're going to become solvent. But, for that, we have to know where our costs are.
>
> That leads to the second problem: we don't know the cost of each of the services we offer. I mean, our patients receive a variety of services yet we charge everyone the same per-visit fee.

Mr. Mitchell provided a further motivation for analyzing Rosemont Hill's cost in that federal and local funding was available for family planning and mental health programs, but to qualify, Rosemont Hill would need a precise calculation of cost per visit in these departments. Likewise, to receive third-party reimbursement for patient visits, Rosemont Hill's fee schedule had to be reasonably related to costs.

BACKGROUND

Rosemont Hill Health Center was established in 1968 by a consortium of community groups. Situated in Roxbury, an inner-city residential neighborhood of Boston, Massachusetts, the health center was intended to provide comprehensive health care to residents of Roxbury and neighboring communities. Eight years after its inception, the health center maintained strong ties with the community groups responsible for the center's development and subsequent acceptance in Roxbury.

Funding for Rosemont Hill was initially provided by the federal government as part of the Department of Health, Education, and Welfare's attempt to equalize health care in the United States. When these operating funds were depleted in 1974, the city of Boston supplemented Rosemont Hill's income with a small three-year grant. Because Mr. Mitchell realized that government support could not continue indefinitely, he intended to make the health center self-sufficient as soon as possible. Rosemont Hill's financial statements are contained in Table 6.1.

Table 6.1

FINANCIAL STATEMENTS FOR 1975
Balance Sheet
as of December 31, 1975

ASSETS			LIABILITIES AND FUND BALANCES		
Cash	$30,934		Accounts payable	$32,754	
Accounts receivable	8,800		Accrued wages	3,466	
Inventory	40,540		Total current		$36,220
Total current		$80,274			
			Bank loan		27,550
Furniture and equipment	21,700		Total liabilities		$63,770
Less: accumulated					
depreciation	8,788		Fund balances:		
Total fixed		12,912	Designated by board for		
Total assets		$93,186	Special outreach project	25,000	
			Purchases of new equipment	3,000	
			Undesignated	1,416	
			Total fund balances		$29,416
			Total liabilities and fund balances		$93,186

INCOME STATEMENT
1975

Revenue from patient fees		$345,450
Other revenue		5,000
Total revenue		350,450
Expenses:		
Program services	235,000	
Utilities	10,000	
Laboratory	25,000	
General and administrative	92,000	
Total expenses		$362,000
Surplus (deficit)		(11,550)

Rosemont Hill Health Center is composed of eight departments: Pediatrics, Adult Medicine, Family Planning, Nursing, Mental Health, Social Services, Dental, and Community Health. In addition, the center has a laboratory and medical records department. Community Health, which was designed by Rosemont Hill's consumers, is a multidisciplinary department providing a link between the health and social services at Rosemont Hill and the schools and city services of the community. The department is staffed by a part-time speech pathologist, a part-time learning specialist, and a full-time nutritionist. The center has 22 paid employees and a volunteer staff of 6 to 10 students acquiring clinical and managerial experience.

THE EXISTING INFORMATION SYSTEM

Rosemont Hill's previous accountant had established a cost system to determine the charge fee for patients. According to this method, shown in Table 6.2, the fee was derived from the average yearly cost of one patient visit. The accountant would first determine the direct cost of each department. He would then add overhead costs, such as administration or rent and utilities, to the total cost of all the departments to determine the health center's total costs. Finally, he would divide that total by the year's number of patient visits. Increased by an anticipated inflation figure for the following year (approximately 8 to 10 percent), this number became the charge per patient visit for the subsequent year.

In reviewing this method with Mr. Simi, Mr. Mitchell explained the problems he perceived. He said that although he realized this was not a precise method of determining charges for patients, the center's charge had to be held at a reasonable level to keep the health services accessible to as many community residents as possible. Additionally, he anticipated complications in determining the cost per patient visit for each of Rosemont Hill's departments:

> You have to consider that our overhead costs, like administration and rent, have to be included in the cost per patient visit. That's easy to do when we have a single cost, but I'm not certain how to go about it when determining costs on a departmental basis. Furthermore, it's important to point out that some of our departments provide services to others. Nursing, for example. There are three nurses in that department, all earning the same salary. But one works exclusively for Adult Medicine, another divides her time evenly between Family Planning and Pediatrics. Only the third spends his entire time in the Nursing Department seeing patients who don't need a physician, although he occasionally refers patients to physicians. In the Social Service Department, the situation is more complicated. We have two M.S.W.'s, each earning $12,000 a year, and one bachelor degree social worker earning $8,000. The two M.S.W.'s yearly see about 1,500 patients who need general social work counseling, but they also spend about 50 percent of their time in other departments. The B.A. social worker cuts pretty evenly across all departments except dental, of course, where we don't need social work assistance.

Mr. Simi added further dimensions to the problems:

> I've spent most of my time so far trying to get a handle on allocating these overhead costs to the departments. It's not an easy job, you know. Administration, for example, seems to help everyone about equally, yet I suppose we might say more administrative time is spent in the departments where we pay more salaries. Rent, on the other hand, is pretty easy: that can be done on a square-foot basis. We could classify utilities according to usage if we had meters to measure electricity, phone usage, and so forth, but because we don't we have to do that on a

square-foot basis as well. This applies to cleaning, too, I guess. It seems to me that record keeping can be allocated on the basis of the number of records, and each department generates one record per patient visit.

Laboratory work is the most confusing. Some departments don't use the laboratory at all, while others use the laboratory regularly. I guess the fairest would be to charge for laboratory work on an hourly basis. Since there are two people in the laboratory, each working about 2,000 hours a year, the charge per hour would be about $4.00. But this is a bit unfair, since the laboratory also uses supplies, space, and administrative time. So we should include those other costs in the laboratory hourly rate. Thus, the process is confusing and I haven't really decided how to sort it out. However, I have prepared totals for floor space and laboratory usage (Table 6.3).

THE FUTURE

As Mr. Mitchell looked toward the remainder of 1976, he decided to calculate a precise cost figure for each department. The health center was growing and he estimated that total patient volume would increase by about 10 percent during 1976, spread evenly over each department. He anticipated that costs would also increase by about 10 percent. He asked Mr. Simi to prepare a step-down analysis for 1975 so that they would know Rosemont Hill's costs for each department. He planned to use this information to assist him in determining charge fees for the remainder of the year.

Table 6.2

COSTS AND PATIENT VISITS[1] FOR 1975
by Department

Department	Number Patient Visits	EXPENSES		
		Salaries[2]	Others[3]	Total
Pediatrics	5,000	$ 20,000	$ 8,000	$ 28,000
Family planning	10,000	5,000	15,000	20,000
Adult medicine	2,100	30,000	16,000	46,000
Nursing	4,000	27,000	6,000	33,000
Mental health	1,400	15,000	8,000	23,000
Social services	1,500	32,000	8,000	40,000
Community health	2,500	5,000	10,000	15,000
Dental	6,400	20,000	10,000	30,000
Sub-total	32,900	154,000	81,000	235,000
Administration		38,000	2,000	40,000
Rent			36,000	36,000
Utilities			10,000	10,000
Laboratory		16,000	9,000	25,000
Cleaning			6,000	6,000
Record keeping		7,000	3,000	10,000
Total		$215,000	$147,000	$362,000
Number of patient visits				32,900
Average cost per visit				$11.00

1. Patient visits rounded to nearest 100; expenses rounded to nearest 1,000.
2. Includes fringe benefits.
3. Materials, supplies, contracted services, depreciation, and other nonpersonnel expenses.

Table 6.3

FLOOR SPACE AND LABORATORY USAGE[1]
by Department

Department	Floor Space[2]	Laboratory Usage[3]
Pediatrics	1,000	1,000
Family planning	1,300	200
Adult medicine	1,800	2,400
Nursing	300	100
Mental health	1,000	—
Social services	500	—
Community health	1,100	100
Dental	1,000	200
Administration	500	—
Record keeping	300	—
Laboratory	1,200	—
Total	10,000	4,000

1. Rounded to nearest 100.
2. In square feet.
3. In hours/year.

7

Good-by Columbus
Community Mental Health Center

James E. Sorensen

The Good-by Columbus Community Mental Health Center (CMHC), located in a large midwestern state, operates a full-service mental health program including a highly successful partial hospitalization unit (PHU). Last year, however, the CMHC did not break even and the loss of $72,000 had to be covered by a federal operations grant. The CMHC charges each separate service for direct costs and for indirect services such as meals, laundry, depreciation, and administrative services, including billing costs and bad debts. All uncollectible accounts are charged to the service giving rise to the receivable. Space and bed costs are fixed for the year.

For the year ending June 30, the PHU at Good-by Columbus CMHC charged each client a standard fee of $65, but collected only about $42 on the average, even when fees were partially offset by a state grant. The PHU had a capacity of 30 beds and operated 182.5 days during the year ending June 30. Revenues (at standard) amounted to $284,700.

Expenses for the current fiscal year (other than salaries) prepared by the accounting office are shown in Table 7.1.

Personnel in the PHU include supervising clinicians, clinicians, and mental health workers. Table 7.2 shows the staffing patterns used, with the unit having a minimum capacity to produce 4,000 annual client days of care.

These staffing levels represent full-time equivalents (FTEs) and the PHU employs only the minimum number of FTEs required to produce the actual volume experienced. Annual salaries for each class of employee are:

Supervising Clinicians	$36,000
Clinicians	$26,000
Mental Health Workers	$10,000

Table 7.1

EXPENSES FOR THE CURRENT FISCAL YEAR
(Other than Salaries)

| | BASIS OF ALLOCATION | |
	Client Days	Bed Capacity
Dietary	$21,000	
Janitorial		$10,000
Laundry	14,000	
Lab charges	11,200	
Pharmacy	16,000	
Repairs and maintenance	5,000	5,000
General administration*		20,000
Rent/depreciation		25,000
Bad debts	10,000	
Other	10,400	
	$87,600	$60,000

*Allocated by hospital

Table 7.2

PHU STAFFING PATTERNS

Annual Client Days	Mental Health Workers	Treating Clinicians	Supervising Clinicians
4,000 - 4,500	2	2	1
4,501 - 5,000	3	2	1
5,001 - 5,500	3	3	1
5,501 - 6,000	4	3	2

The PHU operated at 100 percent capacity during the last quarter ending June 30. During those 90 days, the demand averaged two clients more than capacity and even went as high as four clients on some days.

The PHU currently rents space from University Hospital and could add an additional two beds at a fixed cost of $30 per bed day for a minimum of 182.5 days. This rate does *not* include any costs related to client days or any PHU staffing costs.

ISSUES AND PROBLEMS

1. Calculate the minimum number of client days required for the PHU to break even for June 30 if the extra beds are *not* rented. Use last year's costs but add a 10 percent inflation factor adjustment.

2. If the extra demand experienced during the fourth quarter can be expected to continue, should the Director press for an expansion of capacity? Document your conclusion with a financial analysis.

3. Analyze the cost structure of salary, other direct costs, and allocated costs. Are the proportions in balance?

8

Lakeside Hospital

David Young

"A hospital just can't afford to operate a department at 50 percent capacity," said Dr. Peter Lawrence, Director of Specialty Services at Lakeside Hospital. "If we average 20 dialysis patients, it costs us $257 per treatment and we are only reimbursed for $138. If a department like this can't cover its costs, including a fair share of overhead, it isn't self-sufficient and I don't think we should carry it."

Dr. Lawrence was meeting with Dr. James Newell, Chief Nephrologist of Lakeside Hospital's Renal Division, about the recent change in the Medicare reimbursement policy regarding hemodialysis treatments. At the outset of the current fiscal year (1978) Medicare had begun reimbursing independent dialysis clinics for standard dialysis treatments. (Lakeside's fiscal year [FY] ran from October 1 to September 30. FY 1978 began on October 1, 1977.) Consequently, they had modified their hospital reimbursement policy to cover only treatments for start-up or overflow patients, inpatients, emergencies, and treatments with complications. Effective October 1, 1977, all standard dialysis treatments were to be performed at independent dialysis centers at a significant cost savings to Medicare.

The change in policy had caused the dialysis unit's patient volume to decrease to 50 percent of capacity and produce a corresponding increase in per-treatment costs. By February 1978, Dr. Lawrence and Lakeside's Medical Director were considering phasing down or closing the dialysis unit. At the end of February, Dr. Lawrence met with Dr. Newell to discuss the future of the dialysis unit.

Dr. Newell, who had been Chief Nephrologist since helping to establish the unit in 1972, was opposed to cutting down renal disease services and even more opposed to closing

This case was prepared by Patricia O'Brien under the direction of David W. Young, Harvard School of Public Health. It is intended as a basis for class discussion rather than to illustrate either effective or ineffective handling of an administrative situation.

Table 8.1

COST ALLOCATION
For Year Ended Sept. 30, 1977

#	Cost Center	Direct Expenses	Apportioned Expenses	Total for Appnmt.	Depreciation (Sq. Footage)	Admin. & General (Payroll $)	Employee H & Welfare (Payroll $)	Operation of Plant (Sq. Footage)	Laundry & Linen (Lbs. Processed)	House-keeping (Sq. Footage)	Dietary (No. of Meals)	Maint. of Personnel (Payroll $)	Nursing Service (Hrs. of Service)	Physician Sal. (Hrs. of Service)	Medical Supplies (Dir. Supp. $)	Pharmacy (Phrm. Rev. $)	Medical Records (No. of Records)	Social Services (Hrs. of Service)	Intern-Res. Serv. (Hrs. of Service)	Total Expense
	General Services																			
1	Depreciation	3,185,102		3,185,102																
2	Admin. & General	7,416,669	85,998	7,502,667	85,998															
3–4	Employee Health & Welfare	4,774,196	956	4,775,152	956	72,626														
5	Operation of Plant	2,379,838	295,941	2,675,779	177,092	23,334	46,223													
6	Laundry & Linen	530,249	106,312	636,561	35,036	344,372	15,233	32,109												
7	Housekeeping	1,364,177	642,554	2,006,731	38,221	349,174	219,179	35,053	5,729											
8	Dietary	98,735	989,973	1,088,708	153,203	17,106	222,236	140,211	17,187	107,962										
9–10	Maintenance of Personnel	204,327	838,166	1,042,493	306,725		10,887	280,957	6,366	216,125	10,887									
	Prof. Care—Gen.																			
11	Nursing Service	604,183	84,327	688,510	27,392	251,790	160,254	25,152	1,591	19,305	33,750	39,302								
12	Physician Salaries	1,237,980	485,096	1,723,076	181,869	306,859	195,304	166,701	14,641	128,230	136,089	47,850								
13	Medical Supplies	352,954	1,041,454	1,394,408	36,310	105,037	66,852	33,180	891	25,566		16,367			1,645					
14	Pharmacy (gen.)	932,181	285,848	1,218,029	53,510	114,791	73,060	48,967		37,727		17,410								
15	Medical Records	276,355	345,465	621,820	23,888	125,144	79,650	21,941		16,857		19,495								
16	Social Services	221,804	286,975	508,779		143,676	91,444					23,039								
17–18	Intern-Resident Services	438,547	630,658	1,069,205	89,820			82,146	1,082	63,292					70					
19																				
	Prof. Care—Special																			
20	Operating Rooms	1,589,868	1,877,383		178,366	424,651	270,274	163,490	177,601	100,337		66,615		143,015	78,645	114,008			160,381	3,467,251
21	Electrocardiology	174,776	101,372		18,155	27,760	17,668	16,590	159	12,843		4,378		1,723	418	609			1,069	276,148
22	Anesthesiology	616,494	807,737		37,983	327,866	208,674	28,898	1,082	26,489	15,242	54,210		12,062	2,468	108,405				1,424,231
23	Radiology	1,454,540	1,622,683		188,876	656,483	368,642	173,123	14,577	134,451		90,384		5,169	7,251	45,067			695	3,077,223
24	Laboratory	2,086,649	1,878,882		245,890	131,297	417,826	225,301	7,639	173,181		102,373			3,904	46,285				3,965,531
25	Blood Bank	444,595	414,876		65,932	61,822	83,565	60,473	1,719	46,556		20,433			516	4,385				859,471
26	Physical Therapy	387,735	183,484		22,296		39,347	20,336	6,175	15,653		9,591		5,169	42			3,053		571,219
27	Pharmacy (spec.)	254,426	673,570													673,570				927,996
28	Renal Dialysis	525,142	277,267		4,778	69,550	44,266	4,281	1,782	3,411	9,471	10,842		65,477	279	1,827		50,878	10,425	802,409
29	Oxygen Therapy	532,757	30,086		5,733	7,728	4,918	5,352	318	4,013		1,251			42	731				562,843
30																				
31																				
	Prof. Care—Ambulatory																			
32	Emergency	223,082	921,647		16,881	118,542	75,447	15,252	12,094	11,839		18,452		177,477	28,864	20,706	52,233	7,123	366,737	1,144,729
33	Other (OPD)	796,023	1,854,084		168,492	316,613	201,511	155,195	2,419	118,397		49,414		286,031	10,319	13,520	171,000	132,791	228,382	2,650,107
34																				
35																				
	Routine Servs.—Inpatients																			
36	Adults & Children	4,810,077	8,902,811		438,589	1,546,300	984,159	401,367	327,861	321,077	883,269	241,233	688,510	937,353	1,191,424	138,977	310,910	285,425	206,357	13,712,888
37	Intensive Care	388,417	1,456,321		102,879	492,925	313,727	94,187	35,011	72,242		76,415			68,186	48,721	27,360	29,509	95,159	1,844,738
38	Non-patient		3,015,094		480,632	887,415	564,806	445,517	637	351,178		133,439		89,600	335	1,218	60,317			3,015,094
39																				
40	**Total**	38,301,878			3,185,102	7,502,667	4,775,152	2,675,779	636,561	2,006,731	1,088,708	1,042,493	688,510	1,723,076	1,394,408	1,218,029	621,820	508,779	1,069,205	38,301,878

he was convinced that Lakeside's unit was necessary for providing back-up and emergency services for the outpatient centers. Furthermore, although the unit could not operate at the low costs of the independent centers, Dr. Newell disagreed with Dr. Lawrence's cost figure of $257 per treatment. He resolved to prepare his own cost analysis for their next meeting.

BACKGROUND

At Dr. Newell's initiative, Lakeside had opened the dialysis unit in 1972 in response to the growing number of patients with chronic kidney disease. The hospital's renal division had long provided acute renal failure care and kidney transplants, but by the 1970s, the most common treatment for end-stage renal disease was hemodialysis. During dialysis, a portion of a patient's blood circulates through an artificial kidney machine and is cleansed of waste products. Used three times a week for four to five hours, the kidney machine allows people with chronic kidney disease to lead almost normal lives.

Lakeside's dialysis unit had 14 artificial kidney machines but they were limited by their certificate of need to using 10 per hour and reserving 4 for breakdowns and emergencies. Open six days a week with two shifts of patients daily, the unit could provide 120 treatments a week or accommodate 40 regular patients. From 1973, the year that Medicare began reimbursing for dialysis, all of Lakeside's dialysis patients were covered by Medicare. By 1975, the unit was operating close to or above 100 percent capacity, extending its hours and staff to accept emergency cases and avoid turning away patients.

When Medicare began reimbursing for dialysis, they reimbursed hospitals exclusively, paying 80 percent of charges up to the "reasonable charge" ceiling as determined by a Medicare carrier. (Medicare's payment policy is detailed in Appendix 8.1.) In FY 1977 and FY 1978, Medicare paid up to $138 per dialysis treatment. The hospital was then free to bill the patient or next insurer for the remaining 20 percent of the charge, but because dialysis was so expensive, hospitals frequently waived this portion. Although Medicare was hesitant about setting a precedent for reimbursing nonhospital facilities, in FY 1978 it began reimbursing independent centers for dialysis treatments because of the significant cost savings. Beginning in October 1977, patients spent their first three months of dialysis in a hospital facility; if there were no complications when the "start-up" period had passed, patients were then required to transfer to independent centers.

The independent dialysis centers were developed in the mid-1970s throughout the United States. Centrally owned and operated, they were organized in satellite groups of eight or ten spread throughout metropolitan and suburban areas. The centers' facilities were modern and attractively designed and, because they were separate from hospitals' institutional environments, they offered psychological advantages to patients dependent on dialysis. Centrally managed with low overhead, the independent centers could achieve economies unobtainable by similar hospital units. Supplies and equipment were purchased in bulk and administrators watched staff scheduling and cost efficiency closely. As a result, the cost per treatment in outpatient centers was significantly lower than comparable treatments in a hospital facility. For example, treatments in a center operating at 100 percent capacity with 40 patients could cost the center as little as $80. Center charges varied from $113 to $150, depending on the center's volume and location.

LAKESIDE DATA

In FY 1978, Lakeside charged $172.50 per dialysis treatment, the maximum allowed in its geographic region (Appendix 8.1). Lakeside's retrospective costs for the renal dialysis unit in FY 1977 are detailed in Table 8.1, line 28. Dr. Newell also obtained the unit's FY 1977 cost center report that was prepared annually by Lakeside's Fiscal Affairs Department (Table 8.2).

Table 8.2

COST CENTER REPORT—DIALYSIS UNIT
(Actual Expenses, October 1976 – September 1977)

Expense	Oct.-Nov.	Dec.-Jan.	Feb.-Mar.	Apr.-May	June-July	Aug.-Sept.	Totals
Medical supply							
Dialyzers	1,792	1,750	1,728	1,720	1,750	1,759	
C-dak coils	5,772	5,631	5,560	5,537	5,629	5,654	
Needles and syringes	6,370	6,290	6,136	6,108	6,213	6,250	
General supplies	12,446	12,070	11,981	11,938	12,142	12,190	
Concentrate	2,058	2,008	1,982	1,974	2,014	2,018	
Saline	4,390	4,283	4,229	4,211	4,283	4,301	
Blood tubing	5,743	5,602	5,532	5,468	5,564	5,633	
Miscellaneous	3,381	3,258	3,257	3,243	3,298	3,312	
Total	41,952	40,892	40,405	40,199	40,893	41,117	245,458
Purchased lab services	2,116	2,026	2,000	1,994	2,042	2,060	12,238
Salaries and wages							
Nursing	17,500	17,500	17,500	17,500	17,500	17,500	
Technicians	15,340	15,340	15,340	15,340	15,340	15,340	
Administration	3,560	3,560	3,560	3,560	3,560	3,560	
Total	36,400	36,400	36,400	36,400	36,400	36,400	218,400
Employee expense	2,350	2,350	2,350	2,350	2,350	2,350	14,100
Water usage	1,764	1,740	1,728	1,720	1,748	1,748	10,448
Minor equipment	1,904	1,904	1,904	1,904	1,904	1,904	11,424
Major equipment depreciation	2,188	2,188	2,188	2,188	2,188	2,188	13,128
Number of treatments	980	956	944	940	956	960	5,736

Dr. Newell intended to use the FY 1977 costs to calculate the per-treatment cost at various volume levels for FY 1978. More importantly, he wanted to find the point at which the unit's revenue would meet its costs. He planned, however, to use only those costs that could be traced directly to dialysis treatments, omitting all overhead expenses. According to Dr. Newell, if the unit's revenue met those costs, the unit was self-sufficient. Dr. Newell considered Dr. Lawrence's treatment cost of $257 misleading because it included substantial overhead. He argued that the FY 1978 overhead would differ from that of FY 1977 because of the dialysis unit's changes in volume and revenue. However, Dr. Newell knew that the FY 1978 overhead could not be calculated until the end of the fiscal year. Dr. Newell felt that an accurate cost analysis would first calculate the "real" cost of a treatment and, from there, define a "fair share of overhead."

In reviewing the cost center report, Dr. Newell realized that the nature of the costs varied. He defined three types of costs for his analysis: those that varied in proportion to volume, those that varied with significant changes in volume, and those that remained the same regardless of the unit's volume.

He first separated the costs of medical supplies, purchased laboratory services, and water usage because they changed according to the number of treatments provided. He then examined the salary and wages and employee expense costs; although these costs had not changed during FY 1977, the unit's number of treatments had also remained fairly steady. Dr. Newell thought that the significant change in volume, caused by the new Medicare policy, might cause a corresponding change in salary and employee expenses. In FY 1977, the unit had employed eight hemodialysis technicians, seven nurses, and two administrative staff (its eight consultant nephrologists were on the hospital's physicians' payroll). However, anticipating that the unit's volume would fall, Dr. Newell had not replaced the nurse or the two technicians who had left in January 1978. Consequently, by February, the unit's monthly salaries and employee expenses had decreased by some $3,000. Dr. Newell determined that the remaining costs on the cost center report would remain essentially the same regardless of the number of treatments.

As a final preparation for his meeting with Dr. Lawrence, Dr. Newell called a hospital equipment supply manufacturer to discuss the resale value of Lakeside's 14 artificial kidney machines. The company informed him that machines used for four years or more could not be sold, even for scrap. Lakeside had purchased the 14 machines in 1972 for $105,000.

Appendix 8.1

MEDICARE PAYMENT POLICY FOR RENAL DIALYSIS

The federal Medicare program pays 80 percent of the dialysis charge up to the "reasonable charge" ceiling as it is determined by the Medicare carrier. Each regional Medicare division contracts with a local carrier (usually a health insurance agency) to determine the "reasonable charge" level.

The carrier determines the reasonable charge from three regional charges:

1. actual charges

2. customary charges (midpoint of all charges)

3. prevailing charges (75th percentile of charges)

The lowest of these becomes the region's "reasonable charge."

For Lakeside's region, the reasonable charge ceiling was $172.50. Accordingly, the Medicare reimbursement limit was 80 percent of 172.50, or $138.

9

Carney Hospital

Srinivasan Umapathy

Early in January 1981, John Logue, Executive Vice President and Chief Operating Officer of Carney Hospital, was reviewing the budgetary control system used by the hospital. He was particularly concerned by the fact that the budget for fiscal 1981 (October 1980 to September 1981) was finalized only in December 1980, even though everyone had actively participated in the process. Logue felt that further refinements were desirable, even though substantial improvements had been made in the budgeting process during the two years he had been at Carney.

THE CARNEY HOSPITAL: BACKGROUND INFORMATION

The Carney Hospital, which was founded in South Boston in 1863, had been located in Dorchester since 1953. It was one of 41 hospitals established and administered by the Company of the Daughters of Charity in the United States.

The foundation of the Daughters of Charity was laid in Paris in 1633 in the context of the extensive crime, poverty, sickness, and hunger that ravaged seventeenth-century France. Vincent de Paul established the religious organization to perform service to the poor and needy. Elizabeth Ann Seton, later known as Mother Seton, laid the groundwork for the American branch of this international order in 1809.[1] The influence of the religious women was strongly felt throughout Carney Hospital. The sisters lived on the eighth floor of the building, and the walls throughout the hospital were decorated with mementos of their beliefs and history.

With 376 beds and 1,950 employees, Carney Hospital was a teaching community hospital that included the general hospital, an adjoining medical office building, and six neighborhood health centers providing a full spectrum of health services. The hospital had 321 medical-surgical beds, 5 respiratory care beds, 6 coronary care beds, and 21 progressive coronary care beds. The 1979 occupancy rate was close to 90 percent, with an average length of stay of 12.1 days. There were 123,393 patient days in the 1979 fiscal year. Visits to the Outpatient Department clinics, affiliated health centers, and the emergency room numbered 116,174 in 1979.

Thomas Devane, Director of Public Affairs, commented on the plans for future growth at Carney Hospital:

> We have been pursuing a certificate of need for a $36 million project. Originally we wanted to finish the garage, add three floors to the front to expand fiscal-dietary, add three stories to the northeast wing to hold a 46-bed psychiatric unit, add a new intensive care unit and respiratory care unit, add space in materials management, renovate nursing units, and redo the outpatient-emergency area to change the flow of patients for triage.

> The hospital retained Ernst and Whinney to do an independent audit so that we could go through the Health and Educational Facilities Authority of Massachusetts (HEFA), the state bonding agency, for financing. Ernst and Whinney suggested a less costly renovation program, as did the Health Systems Agency. The hospital worked with these agencies and reduced the project to $18.5 million. We deleted the garage, some nursing unit changes, and some of the space for materials management. We have to commission an energy study before we can build a new boiler plant. The hospital intends to go ahead with the psychiatry unit and new intensive care unit.

POPULATION SERVED BY THE CARNEY HOSPITAL

In 1978, 41.4 percent of inpatient discharges originated from Dorchester, 20 percent came from other Boston neighborhoods such as Hyde Park and Roslindale, and 25.5 percent came from south suburban communities such as Milton, Quincy, and Braintree. Sixty percent of all outpatient visits came from Dorchester.

The population in Carney's service area contained groups with distinctive socioeconomic characteristics. Dorchester and the other Boston neighborhoods using Carney had a higher percentage of females of childbearing age which led to a particular demand for pediatrics and gynecology. Dorchester had a large minority population (28.5 percent), predominantly black and Hispanic. Minorities made up 23 percent of the city-wide population. The Boston neighborhoods also sent a significant number of elderly patients to Carney. These patients had an unusually long length of stay because of their propensity for multiple diagnoses, their lower socioeconomic status, and the occasional shortage of nursing home beds. The nearby suburban communities such as Milton and Quincy had populations with a higher income level, a lower percentage of people over 65, and a higher percentage of white population than the Boston neighborhoods.

MEDICAL STAFF

Approximately 360 physicians used Carney's facilities. Ten percent of the doctors were fully salaried; 90 percent earned their incomes from fees for services provided to patients. The hospital was a teaching facility for medical students. It had a house staff of 47 resident physicians and 3 fellows as of 1978. The medical students were drawn from Tufts University, Boston University, University of Massachusetts, and from out of town. According to Mr. Mitchell Carroll, Director of the Emergency Room and Coordinator of the Surgical Teaching Program:

> We're a half-breed in a sense. We're not a major teaching affiliate, but we do a great amount of teaching. Our physicians want to maintain their identity with teaching, but they don't want to be taken over lock, stock, and barrel by medical schools.

Carney was very involved in teaching nurses and provided clinical education for many allied health profession students in fields such as dietetics and respiratory therapy. Thus, it drew students from many of the schools in Boston. The hospital also sponsored Laboure Junior College which had programs in nursing and in other allied health professions. Table 9.1 provides statistics for patient treatment according to medical specialty.

ORGANIZATIONAL STRUCTURE

During the late 1970s, Carney made several organizational changes to increase effectiveness and efficiency. Prior to 1977, all divisions were headed by assistant administrators who reported directly to the Administrator (see Figure 9.1). The sister who held the position of Administrator was directly involved in all operations of the hospital. In addition, she had major religious responsibility as the Religious Superior of all the sisters in the convent on the eighth floor.

John Logue explained that the increasing complexity of the hospital required that the sister-in-charge delegate some of her direct involvement in hospital decision making. This was a trend in many hospitals. He also noted that, over time, fewer women entered the convent. Thus, the Company of the Daughters of Charity was growing smaller in size, contributing to the impetus for decentralization.

Dr. John Coldiron, Vice President of Ambulatory and Community Services, remembered the extent of centralization in many of the divisions before the organizational change:

> The Fiscal Division was late in bringing in a Budget Director and a Controller. Paul Vielkind used to do it all. When he does something he does it well. He's a very capable man. However, it got to be too much for one person.

In 1977, the hospital was organized in a corporate format (Figure 9.2). Sister Margaret Tuley, President, was no longer involved in the daily operations of the hospital, nor was she the Religious Superior on the eighth floor. Sister Anna Marie, Assistant to the President in hospital matters concerning volunteers and special projects, was the local Superior.

Sister Margaret was the Chairman of the Board of Trustees and a member of all Board committees. The Board at Carney consisted of Daughters of Charity from other hospitals and schools; a former chief of the medical staff at Carney; a layperson who headed St. Vincent's Hospital in Bridgeport, Connecticut; and two practicing attorneys. According to Carney Hospital administration, it was the Board that approved major program changes, the one-year and five-year plans and the budget, and made decisions about top-level personnel hiring and salaries. The Associate Board was comprised almost entirely of lay people. These people augmented various hospital committees with specific expertise.

Sister Margaret delegated responsibility for operations to John Logue and for fiscal affairs to Paul Vielkind, Senior Vice President of Fiscal Services. The Director of Planning and Public Affairs reported to her. The rest of her duties involved the community. According to Thomas Devane, Director of Public Affairs:

> Sister Margaret is involved with the Massachusetts Hospital Association as Secretary of the Board of Trustees; the Council of Boston Teaching Hospitals (she is chairperson); a Corporation member of University Hospital Inc.; member of the Board of the Eastern Cooperative Services of the Daughters of Charity; Chairman of the Board of LaBoure Junior College; and Board member of St. Mary's in Troy, New York.

Figure 9.1

THE 1973 ORGANIZATIONAL CHART

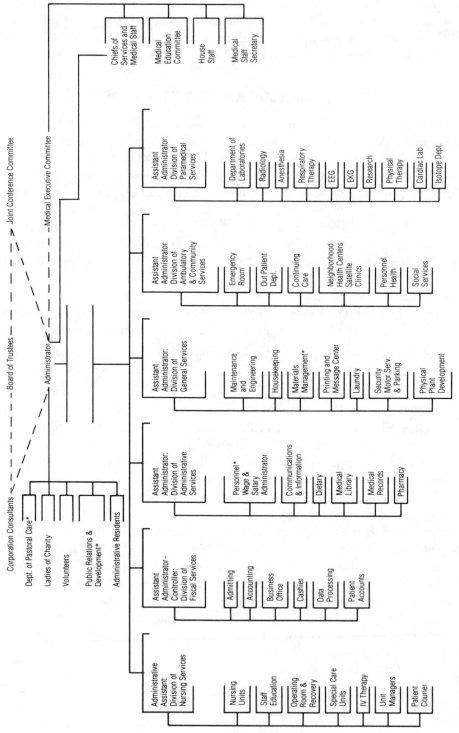

*Also has staff function.

Figure 9.2
THE 1980 ORGANIZATIONAL STRUCTURE

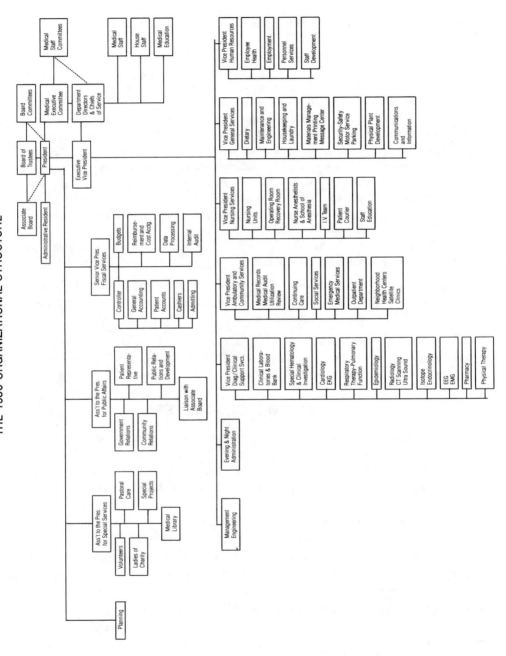

John Logue managed daily operations at Carney. His position was created during the change in organizational structure. He held a Master's of Hospital Administration and had a number of years of experience in hospital administration. Reflecting over his two years at Carney, he commented:

> My belief is that there are multiple theoretically sound organizational structures which could work in any one organization. What makes the difference is how well our relationships are defined and developed. The organizational chart itself is only one means of expressing a multifaceted relationship between people. Interpersonal relationships are not easily described upon a chart. If a person looks at an organizational chart and says that should not work, it is important to look further and understand what is behind the structure and why it would not work, or why it would work. I believe that our organization is successful because it is theoretically sound and because we continue to work at building relationships which are open and trusting. We have tried to develop an administrative staff which is open, which is trusting, and which bases its relationships on cooperation and collaboration rather than on competitiveness. Excessive administrative competitiveness would not be appropriate to a Catholic hospital. We have specifically chosen people who are able to work in this kind of corporate model. If we set a model for our staff which is one of friction among ourselves, that process will be passed through the organization and eventually felt by the patients. The patient is entitled to a peaceful environment in which healing is promoted. In the long run the patient would be hurt by the lack of our ability to be cooperative with each other.

Logue felt that an organization's structure and procedures had to be adaptive to its culture. Since joining the Carney Hospital administration, he observed that the people in the organization tended to avoid direct confrontation. He commented:

> A good manager must understand the organizational culture. One of my roles at Carney is to facilitate a more trusting environment where people can openly disagree with each other. Genuine resolution of conflict will ultimately enhance cooperation.

HOSPITAL COMMITTEES

John Logue sat on a number of hospital committees and chaired the Administrative Council and the Budget Steering Committee. According to Patricia Nelson, Director of Planning, the Budget Committee structure at Carney was such that budgetary recommendations were made in the departments and then submitted by the division directors to the Budget Steering Committee.

Among the hospital's committees, those which had the most direct input into the annual budget were the Long-Range Planning Committee, the Development of Hospital Services Committee, the Operating Room Committee, and the Budget Steering Committee. According to several administrators, the Long-Range Planning Committee considered the conceptual aspects of new programs which the hospital might undertake, such as a hospice program. The Development of Hospital Services Committee (DHSC) was concerned with similar issues from a more practical standpoint. It was this committee which would examine the actual feasibility of proposed ideas. The Operating Room (OR) Committee dealt with the capital needs of the OR. The DHSC and OR Committee recommended to the Budget Steering Committee large capital equipment expenditures based on replacement or programmatic needs. The Budget Steering Committee was made up of many of the members of the Administrative

Council, DHSC, and Long-Range Planning Committee. Its function was to make specific recommendations regarding the hospital's operating and capital budgets to the Administrative Council and the Board. The Administrative Council was made up of division vice presidents. It dealt with most matters concerning operations. Pat Nelson viewed the Management Executive Committee as an "airing place" which considered larger hospital issues and channeled important matters to the Board.

THE HEALTH CARE ENVIRONMENT IN 1980

The regional medical environment in which Carney operated was extensive. It consisted of large and well-known teaching hospitals which were affiliated with Harvard, Tufts, and Boston universities. In addition, there were many smaller community hospitals serving the Boston metropolitan area. Table 9.2 illustrates this network of hospitals. According to the Carney Hospital administration, the competition for personnel was great, putting an upward pressure on salaries.

The National Health Planning and Resources Development Act was enacted by Congress in 1975. The law mandated the creation of a network of nonprofit health planning groups, called Health Systems Agencies (HSAs), supported by federal funds. Each HSA was designed to evaluate the health care needs of the population, list available resources, identify areas of unmet needs, establish priorities, and recommend goals and objectives. The certificate-of-need (CON) process was the HSA's primary method of containing costs. The CON regulations required that any capital investment by a health facility costing over $150,000, or any substantial change in service, had to be approved by the State Health Planning and Development Agency of the Department of Public Health. The HSA staff and Board of Directors recommended denial or approval of the CON application.[2]

Another regulating influence on Carney was the Department of Public Health of the Commonwealth. According to William James, Budget Director, this agency sometimes mandated a policy which increased costs. He commented:

> For example, the Public Health Department requires that you have one nurse for every two patients in intensive care. We have five intensive care beds and found two nurses to be adequate. However, we had to hire a third because of the state's regulation.

The Joint Commission on the Accreditation of Hospitals (JCAH) was also a powerful influence on hospitals. It did not have the authority to enforce regulations, but could publicly cite an institution for violation of its standards which would lead to a loss of prestige. Thus, hospitals incurred the cost of compliance.

Paul Vielkind offered an example of internal cost-containment problems in hospitals. As he saw it:

> Hospitals are unique in that there can be an "uncontrolled" partner in the form of the medical staff physician. This certainly influences costs. Many of the physicians here are not paid by Carney and use several hospitals. The practicing physician frequently wants his hospital to provide the best possible facilities. Then there are developments in technology. The doctor may be on your doorstep before the old equipment is obsolete. You make a plan to write off a piece of equipment in six years, but the doctor feels he needs a replacement in three years.

Prior to 1975, hospital charges were not regulated. Charge-paying patients and the commercial insurance companies that paid full charges provided enough revenue to support high expenditures and expansion. In effect, the charge-payers subsidized hospitals for revenue which could not be collected from cost-based payers. The increased expenditures subsequently became part of the historical cost base, increasing future years' levels of Medicaid, Medicare, and Blue Cross reimbursement.

Since 1975, all hospital charges were regulated through state regulation known as Chapter 409, which established the Massachusetts Rate Setting Commission (MRSC). The impetus for the legislation came from the Governor's desire to curb rising Medicaid expenditures. Medicaid reimbursement was based on an assessment of "reasonable costs" which were determined by adding an inflation factor to the previous year's costs. The Medicaid program reimbursed a hospital for the costs incurred in treating a patient, as opposed to a hospital's charges for services. Medicare and Blue Cross had similar cost-based reimbursement procedures. The ultimate objective of Chapter 409 was to reduce cross-subsidization by full-charge payers and slowly reach a point where total hospital charges equaled total costs. However, this legislation placed a ceiling on revenue and aggravated the problem of allocating already scarce resources (Tables 9.3 and 9.4 contain financial information on the Carney Hospital.)

Each year, Carney submitted its budget to the MRSC on or before August 1. On the basis of an examination of the proposed budget, MRSC determined allowable costs and maximum charges that the hospital could collect during the budget year. This meant that the Carney administration did not know how much money was available for spending until about one month before the new fiscal year. According to William James, Budget Director, matching costs and revenues was a difficult task:

> The Rate Setting Commission is talking about categorizing hospitals according to size, patient days, and types of procedures. This might mean that Carney would lose money. Carney would want to be with the big teaching hospitals whose per diem costs and revenues are higher. However, Carney has little tertiary care compared with the big teaching hospitals.
>
> The charge/pay mix is 15 percent of patients at Carney. For each additional dollar of revenue the operating room generates, we see an income of 33 cents because of the charge-based payers, while the laboratory sees only 17 cents because its revenue comes mainly from cost-based payers. Here, it makes sense to raise the prices in the OR before raising them in the lab. Some hospitals have computers which tell them about the income sensitivity of departments.

CARNEY HOSPITAL'S BUDGETARY PROCESS, 1980

There were three components to the budget: supplies and general expense, personnel, and capital equipment. Department heads prepared requests for supplies, expenses, and personnel in collaboration with their respective division vice presidents and William James. They were eventually submitted to the Budget Steering Committee. There were three methods for dealing with requests for capital equipment. Requests for items costing less than $5,000 were submitted to the Budget Steering Committee. Requests for equipment amounting to more than $5,000 had to be presented to the Development of Hospital Services Committee, where they were ranked by the committee members and submitted to the Budget Steering Committee. The Operating Room Committee dealt with requests which pertained only to the operating room.

Requests from surgeons, nurses, and technicians were ranked and sent to the Budget Steering Committee.

The budgetary process at Carney Hospital was coordinated by the Fiscal Services Department and by William James. Working closely with James was Andrew Kowal, Controller. James's duties involved coordinating and developing the budget calendar, consultating with department heads about budgetary problems, submitting the budget to the Massachusetts Rate Setting Commission, and integrating data into pro forma budgets for review by the Board of Trustees. Kowal served a broader accounting and finance function involving the compilation of monthly financial reports. James and Kowal collaborated regarding the analysis of variances in departmental budgets. Both reported to Paul Vielkind, who spent a large part of his time negotiating with third parties and state regulators and seeking external financing for the future expansion of the hospital. (See Figure 9.3 for an organizational chart of fiscal services.)

Figure 9.3

CARNEY HOSPITAL: FISCAL SERVICES

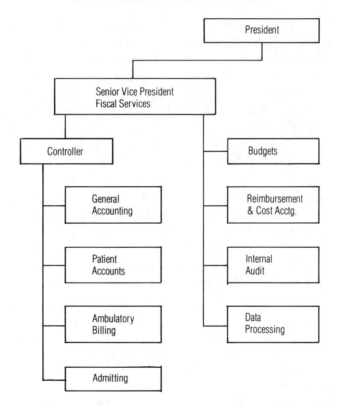

The Budget Steering Committee was made up of the following members in 1980:

John Logue (Chairman) — Executive Vice President and Chief Operating Officer
Andrew Kowal — Controller
Florence McLeod, R.N. — Vice President of Nursing Services
James Morrisey — Vice President of General Services

Mark Kochanowski — Vice President of Human Services
John Coldiron, M.D. — Vice President of Ambulatory and Community Services
Mitchell Carroll, M.D. — Director of the Emergency Room and Coordinator of the
Surgical Teaching Program
Frank O'Donnell — Vice President of Clinical and Diagnostic Services

Staffed by:
Patricia Nelson — Director of Planning
William James — Director of Budgets
Robert Harris — Management Engineer

The 1980 budget calendar is presented in Table 9.5 and the schedule of activities for the
Budget Steering Committee is displayed in Table 9.6. This report was prepared by Andrew
Kowal, Controller, and was targeted for the third Monday of each month. The hospital used
a Financial Management Reporting System (FMRS). The report was prepared by each cost
center and analyzed the revenues, accounts payable, and payroll of the previous month. The
actual expenses were compared with the budget in the report.

The Budget Steering Committee convened, as planned, on May 29, 1980, and continued
to meet once a week until June 20, 1980. Early in July 1980, the MRSC implemented its
plan to group hospitals according to number of beds, kinds of procedures performed, and
number of patient days. Carney, to its dismay, was not classified in Group 1 among the large
teaching hospitals. Instead, it was placed in Group 2, where it was classified as a "cost outlier"
because its costs were more than one standard deviation above the mean costs of the group.
The consequences of this event were uncertain, although the possibility of not being reimbursed
for all its expenses worried the Carney administration. The Budget Steering Committee ad-
journed from June 20, 1980, to August 8, 1980.

During the Budget Steering Committee meetings held in the second half of 1980, Carney
Hospital vice presidents had presented their requests for new personnel, supplies, and general
expenses. The Development of Hospital Services Committee along with the Operating Room
Committee presented requests for large capital expenditures. Given the 12 percent limit on
the next year's increase in revenues and the need to show a gain of at least $500,000 from
operations to help the sale of bonds for expansion, the Carney management had to make some
tough decisions. William James discussed some of the difficult decisions:

> Sister Margaret, John Logue, and Paul Vielkind made a decision that we could add only three
> new positions for the next year — a Senior Vice President for Medical Affairs and two new
> purchasing agents for our new purchasing program which will involve using cathode-ray tubes
> (CRTs). The division heads were understandably upset that they couldn't have new personnel.
> We never got around to ranking our requests because we were not able to add any new people.
>
> Though the overall requests for capital items were quite large, a decision was made to
> restrict the capital budget to $1 million. This amount was allocated to various departments in
> proportion to the dollar value of their requests.
>
> Thus, the only area left for negotiation during the final Budget Steering Committee
> meetings was supplies and general expenses. By achieving a reduction of $150,000 in bad debts
> and free care, a $100,000 cutback in overtime, and a $170,000 savings from expected attrition
> in the personnel budget, the supplies and general expenses could be permitted to increase by
> 7.1 percent. Though this was much lower than the departmental needs, the Budget Steering
> Committee decided to adhere to its financial plan.

LONG-RANGE PLANNING AND THE BUDGETARY PROCESS

Patricia Nelson, Director of Planning, described the functions of the Planning Department as follows:

The Planning Department:

1. coordinates a hospital-wide planning system through the development and coordination of all committees
2. develops feasibility studies for new programs, e.g., an inpatient psychiatric unit, a hospice program, and an alcoholism program
3. prepares and documents all CON requirements
4. prepares the One- and Five-Year Plans
5. is involved in various special projects and studies
6. is responsible for space planning, and development and maintenance of various operations statistics
7. maintains liaisons with planning agencies to keep abreast of all regulations and to advise administration of same

Fiscal Services and the Planning Department are trying to develop a coordinated program. Through the five-year planning process we are trying to improve the linkage between planning and budgeting.

Some excerpts from the One- and Five-Year Plans are presented in Table 9.7.

SOME PERSPECTIVES ON BUDGETING AT CARNEY

Florence McLeod, Vice-President of Nursing Services, described the process of budgeting in her division:

While estimating nursing staff requirements, we start with existing staff and build on it or recommend change from mix. We do not have a patient classification system on which the number, mix, and allocation of personnel are based. An acuity-based classification system would be beneficial. Carney uses the judgment of first- and middle-line management as it relates to the mix of patients in the unit, as well as the desired delivery system. We have a framework of 4.5 hours of nursing care per day per patient, on an average. This varies somewhat, but we do not have a scientific data base. Variables such as the patient census of the unit are considered. We don't have many peaks and valleys. We know that the census on the surgical floors drops over the weekend. We also consider the turnover of patients while estimating nursing requirements.

Regarding budgeting, the head nurse reviews needs, projects, and makes a recommendation to her supervisor and to us. I have been the one to present those needs to the Budget Committee. These are considered along with requests from all other hospitals. We don't really have a good method of choosing. We've tried ranking and weighting. This is hard with nursing because there really isn't solid data to back up requests, and usually the request is not related to an increase in volume, but rather it is to improve quality. Some decisions are obvious, but some are more subjective.

The Ernst and Whinney study wasn't that helpful regarding nursing. It is difficult when inputs aren't quantifiable. The unit of measurement was patient days, which is not an accurate measure of patients' needs and necessary nursing care.

In the past two years, the quality of our decisions has improved. They have been based on better material and the composition of the Budget Committee has changed. There is less competitiveness and more discussion.

A different point of view was expressed by another administrator:

Our budgetary process is weak. Input is strong but the feedback during the year is useless. Each learning cycle has not been used to build better budgets. Additionally, there is not enough support from data processing. Very little educational effort is made in terms of making us knowledgeable about the 409 process. What does volume do to allowable revenues? More people should understand these matters. Knowledge is power. You can't question certain fiscal decisions if information isn't shared with you. Consequently, department heads cannot be intelligent budgeters.

Another administrator commented:

Our budget system is ineffective and too time-consuming. I favor program budgeting and there is finally some support for it.

The Senior Vice-President of Fiscal Services stated:

In our long-range planning efforts, we do not have as much financial analysis, such as modeling, as necessary, and some important areas, such as marketing, are not given adequate priority as far as action is concerned.

Another administrator declared:

The Financial Management Reporting System (FMRS) is meaningless to us because of the way the data is communicated. The report breaks income down to where the patient was when he had the procedure[3] — e.g., inpatient or outpatient. The income is not classified according to procedure. . . . I don't use the FMRS as a management tool, since I can't predict costs and revenues from it.

NOTES

1. From Daughters of Charity brochures.
2. Blue Cross and Blue Shield of Massachusetts, "Health Planning Agencies," January 1979.
3. The term *procedure* refers to the medical procedure performed on the patient.

Table 9.1

DISTRIBUTION OF INPATIENT DISCHARGES BY SPECIALTY, SERVICE, PATIENT DAYS

Specialty	PRIVATE #	PRIVATE %	SERVICE #	SERVICE %	TOTAL #	TOTAL %	TOTAL PATIENT DAYS #	TOTAL PATIENT DAYS %	AVERAGE LENGTH OF STAY #
Pediatrics	382	4.5	20	1.3	402	4.0	2,074	1.7	5.2
Medicine	3,225	37.7	804	53.0	4,029	40.0	56,832	45.7	14.2
Cardiology	282	3.3	49	3.2	4,317	3.4	4,317	3.4	13.0
Neurology	196	2.3	1	.1	197	2.0	2,372	1.9	12.0
Surgery	1,530	17.9	380	25.1	1,910	19.0	22,484	18.1	11.8
Thoracic surgery	98	1.1	15	1.0	113	1.2	1,560	1.2	13.8
Ophthalmology	179	2.1	0	0	179	1.8	839	.7	4.7
ENT	244	2.9	3	.2	247	2.4	546	.4	2.2
Dental	69	.8	8	.5	77	.8	281	.2	3.6
Neurosurgery	811	9.5	20	1.3	831	8.3	12,327	10.0	14.8
Orthopedics	801	9.4	81	5.3	882	8.8	14,242	11.4	16.1
Urology	448	5.2	34	2.3	482	4.8	4,556	3.7	9.5
Gynecology	283	3.3	102	6.7	385	3.8	1,968	1.6	5.1
Totals	8,548 84.9%	100.0	1,517 15.1%	100.0	10,065 100%	100.0	124,398	100.0	12.4

Table 9.2

COMPARATIVE STATISTICS ON BOSTON AREA HOSPITALS
(1978)

Hospital	No. of Beds	Patient Days	Discharges or Admissions	No. of Discharges of Persons over 65	Average Length of Stay	Average Length of Stay of Persons over 65	Occupancy Rate
Beth Israel	452	138,288	15,956	4,826	8.6	12.4	87.5
Massachusetts General	1,082	348,789	29,810	8,469	11.8	13.8	88.3
Cambridge	182	53,868	6,960	1,353	7.9	13.6	80.2
Faulkner	259	85,788	7,040	3,137	12.3	15.7	90.7
Mt. Auburn	300	88,603	9,576	3,338	9.3	12.4	80.9
South Shore	280	83,635	12,050	2,742	6.9	11.8	83.9
Milton	161	44,550	4,747	1,929	9.2	13.1	75.8
Carney	376	122,638	9,977	3,445	12.0	17.4	89.4
St. Elizabeth's	385	116,368	11,561	3,636	10.0	14.7	82.8

Source: Massachusetts Hospital Association.

Table 9.3

BALANCE SHEETS
September 30, 1979 and 1978

UNRESTRICTED FUNDS

Assets	1979	1978	Liabilities and Fund Balances	1979	1978
Current:			Current:		
Cash	$ 6,400	$ 6,300	Notes payable, bank (note 5)	$ 320,000	$ —
Receivables	10,026,416	8,467,519	Current installments of mortgage and loans payable (note 4)	440,473	455,030
Less estimated uncollectibles and allowances	(2,774,265)	(1,981,562)	Accounts payable and accrued expenses (note 6)	3,180,838	2,424,241
Net receivables	7,252,151	6,485,957	Accrued payroll	397,986	329,820
Due from restricted funds	7,822	—	Estimated final settlement due to third-party payers	825,119	202,625
Inventories	265,109	248,091	Advances from third-party payers	346,784	357,601
Prepaid expenses	377,130	253,730	Due to restricted funds	—	1,739
Total current assets	7,908,612	6,994,078	Total current liabilities	5,511,200	3,771,056
Other:			Long-term portion of mortgage and loans payable (note 4)	13,174,715	13,407,724
Cash	97,892	48,292	Fund balances:		
Investments (note 2)	2,786,714	2,678,417	Operations	2,517,627	2,971,596
Property, plant, and equipment (notes 3 and 4)	36,190,519	34,809,991	Board-designated	3,527,619	3,399,347
Less accumulated depreciation	(14,189,104)	(12,873,568)	Plant	8,063,472	8,107,487
Net property, plant, and equipment	22,001,415	21,936,423	Total fund balances	14,108,718	14,478,430
Total unrestricted funds	$32,794,633	$31,657,210	Total unrestricted funds	$32,794,633	$31,657,210

RESTRICTED FUNDS

	1979	1978		1979	1978
Specific purpose funds:			Specific purpose funds:		
Cash in savings accounts	39,997	36,365	Due to unrestricted funds	4,466	—
Grants receivable	4,768	1,313	Fund balances	40,299	39,417
Due from unrestricted funds	—	1,739			
Total specific purpose funds	$ 44,765	$ 39,417	Total specific purpose funds	$ 44,765	$ 39,417
Building fund:			Building fund:		
Pledges receivable, net of estimated uncollectibles	3,340	49,588	Fund balance	3,340	49,588
Total building fund	$ 3,340	$ 49,588	Total building fund	$ 3,340	$ 49,588
Endowment funds:			Endowment funds:		
Cash in savings certificates (note 2)	135,187	135,187	Due to unrestricted funds	3,356	—
Accrued interest receivable	3,356	—	Fund balances	135,188	135,188
Interest in perpetual charitable trust, at nominal value	1	1			
Total endowment funds	$ 138,544	$ 135,188	Total endowment funds	$ 138,544	$ 135,188
Debt amortization fund:			Debt amortization fund:		
Cash in savings certificates (notes 2 and 4)	219,629	103,444	Fund balance	219,629	103,444
Total debt amortization fund	$ 219,629	$ 103,444	Total debt amortization fund	$ 219,629	$ 103,444

Table 9.4

REVENUE AND EXPENSE STATEMENTS

Operating Revenue	1979	1978	1977	1976
Room, board, general services	23,528,360	19,794,100	18,816,262	16,932,728
Special professional services	20,637,970	16,500,200	15,828,167	14,292,534
Outpatient and emergency				
room services	5,162,512	3,977,100	3,761,369	3,303,921
Subtotal	49,328,842	40,271,400	38,405,798	34,529,183
Less allowances	14,796,067	9,477,700	10,176,354	8,207,614
Net patient revenue	34,532,775	30,793,700	28,229,444	26,321,569
Other operating revenue	1,666,765	1,331,600	909,447	857,217
Total operating income	36,199,540	32,125,300	29,138,891	27,178,786
Operating Expenses				
Salaries and wages	21,453,943	19,647,800	17,770,813	16,106,959
Food, medical and surgical				
supplies, and other expenses	12,362,686	10,599,600	9,729,595	9,035,837
Subtotal	33,816,629	30,247,400	27,500,408	25,142,796
Depreciation and mortgage				
interest expense	2,778,192	2,495,800	2,161,476	2,057,115
Total operating expenses	36,594,821	32,743,200	29,661,884	27,199,911
Operating gain or (loss)	(395,281)	(617,900)	(522,993)	(21,125)
Nonoperating Income				
Gifts, endowment fund income,				
investment income, and				
donated services	377,086	332,800	371,956	314,563
Accrued vacation pay applicable				
to prior years of service	284,519			
Total net gain or (loss)	(302,714)	(285,100)	(151,037)	293,438

Table 9.5

SIGNIFICANT DATES ON BUDGET DEVELOPMENT CALENDAR
FOR DEPARTMENT HEADS AND DIVISION DIRECTORS, FISCAL 1980

DATE 1980	PARTICIPANTS	SIGNIFICANCE
5/09	Department Heads/Division Directors	Due date for submitting salary and wages worksheets to Budget Director.
5/16	Department Heads/Division Directors	Due date for submitting supply expense worksheets to Budget Director.
6/01	Department Heads/Division Directors	Due date for submitting *all* capital equipment requests to respective committees (Development of Hospital Services, Operating Room and Budget Review Committees).
6/06	Department Heads	Due date for submitting recommended charges for the budget year.
10/01	All personnel	Begin operations under new budget.

Table 9.6

SCHEDULE OF ACTIVITIES FOR CARNEY HOSPITAL
BUDGET STEERING COMMITTEE

Agenda for May 29 Budget Steering Committee Meeting
1. Review of supplies and expenses as submitted by hospital department managers.

2. Review of new personnel:
   a. President's departments
   b. Executive Vice President's departments
   c. Senior Vice President — fiscal services departments
   d. Vice President — nursing's departments

Agenda for June 6 Budget Steering Committee Meeting
1. Review of new personnel (continuation of May twenty-nine meeting):
   a. Carry — over from previous meeting
   b. Vice President — general services' department
   c. Vice President — ambulatory services' departments
   d. Vice President — clinical and diagnostic services' departments

Agenda for June 13 Budget Steering Committee Meeting
1. Review of new personnel
   a. Carry — over from previous meeting
2. Ranking of new positions by each division
3. Review of capital equipment under $5,000
4. Ranking of capital equipment under $5,000 by each division

Agenda for June 20 Budget Steering Committee Meeting
1. Review of capital equipment by the respective chairmen
   a. Development of Hospital Services Committee recommendations
   b. Operating Room Committee recommendations
2. Discussion of recommendations by Budget Steering Committee
3. Ranking of recommendations from each committee by Budget Steering Committee

Agenda for June 27 Budget Steering Committee Meeting
1. Review and finalization of operating and capital budget recommendations

Table 9.7

EXCERPTS FROM ONE- AND FIVE-YEAR PLANS

	Description	National Health Priority
Goal #1	Integrate and strengthen hospital-wide programs stressing the healing ministry.	8, 10
Goal #2	Plan and market a linked program of primary care services for populations in Dorchester, Hyde Park, and the South Metro: This system will include private physicians, group practices, neighborhood health centers, and the hospital's ambulatory clinics and emergency services.	2, 4, 5
Goal #3	Monitor quality of patient care to provide maximum patient benefits	6
Goal #4	Continue to develop improved management and development systems.	4, 9
Goal #5	Complete HMO — IPA Feasibility Study.	3
Goal #6	Develop multi-institutional arrangements in order to regionalize the utilization of resources.	2, 5
Goal #7	Plan comprehensive mental health services for service area.	
Goal #8	Complete facility energy saving renovations, parking accommodations, and cost control systems.	
Goal #9	Evaluate medical education programs and introduce necessary changes.	8, 10

Continued

Table 9.7 Continued

	Description	National Health Priority
Goal #10	Provide a spectrum of services to meet specified needs of service area—acute care, specialized, and ancillary services.	1, 6
Goal #11	Define and develop appropriate role of Carney Hospital as a teaching/community/regional hospital.	2, 5, 10

GOAL #1: Integrate and strengthen hospital-wide programs stressing the healing ministry.
Program 1A: Coordinate hospital-wide programs planned to reflect the church's healing ministry.
Program 1B: Continue to provide Chaplain services and provide appropriate accommodations for private counseling.
1. Provide grieving room in the Emergency Room.
Program 1C: Implement recommendations developed from 1979 Catholic Criteria Seminars.
Program 1D: Continue to analyze services from a mission viewpoint, emphasizing quality patient care.
Program 1E: Maintain human services network which reflects Daughters of Charity ministry.
1. Develop battered wives program and seek funding.
2. Upgrade psychiatric counseling services in coordination with plans for new inpatient/outpatient psychiatric services.
GOAL #2: Plan and market a linked program of primary care services for populations in Dorchester, Hyde Park, and the South Metro: This system will include private physicians, group practices, neighborhood health centers, and hospital's ambulatory clinics and emergency services.
Program 2A: Continue to plan and further penetrate underserved populations. Task force will:
1. Set levels of penetration for Dorchester, Hyde Park, South Metro, Randolph, Quincy, and other communities.
2. Designate needed programs.
3. Delegate marketing of services to Public Relations and Planning.
Program 2B: Provide appropriate system which offers treatment follow-up and referrals at the patient's place of entry into the system.
1. Set patient referral goals which relate to specialty needs.
Program 2C: Continue outpatient service augmentation of comprehensive ambulatory program:
1. Increase basic dental services. Increase service hours per week including time for coordination. Obtain office for dental coordinator, dental hygienist, and dental assistant.
2. Increase nurse practitioner sessions in Outpatient Department Medical II.
3. Set plan for expansion of social work services in Outpatient Department and Emergency Room (counseling).
    a. Expand services in Pediatrics.
    b. Provide additional concrete, tangible services to Emergency Room and Outpatient Department.
Program 2D: Review emergency room personnel functions to satisfy past complaints.
Program 2E: Continue to increase primary and secondary pediatric care services to surrounding communities of Hyde Park, Codman Square, Hough's Neck, and others.
Program 2F: Support the growth of existing primary care at Little House Health Center and Bowdoin Street Health Center.
Program 2G: Reorganize Outpatient Department in order to develop a family-oriented primary care program.
1. Audit family health process in order to improve quality access in Dorchester, Hyde Park, and other service areas.
2. Solve urgent problem of Outpatient Department space needs in order to effect program.
3. Explore methodologies for family health evaluation.
4. Support family approach with medical record coding system.
5. Maintain back-up system for specialty referrals.
Program 2H: Designate level of primary outreach to South Metro needed for satisfactory levels of occupancy.
1. Augment present primary physician placement in order to sustain inpatient capacity.
2. Maintain favorable patient origin balance.
3. Maintain feasible financial mix.
Program 2I: Provide an upgraded ambulatory psychiatric program to meet community needs.
1. Coordinate program with community mental health services.
2. Cooperate with the Dorchester Mental Health Center.
3. Provide increased level of mental health counseling.
Program 2J: Develop new comprehensive primary care thrust into Hyde Park.
1. Plan physician placement for needed primary care programs.
Program 2K: Coordinate and upgrade Referrals for Alcoholics.
1. Refine alcoholism educational program in hospital staff.
2. Plan alcoholism prevention programs throughout the system.

10

University Hospital

Regina Herzlinger

BACKGROUND

University Hospital is a relatively small (373-bed complement) teaching hospital located in the heart of Boston's South End. Directly adjacent to it is the Boston City Hospital, a municipal hospital serving the city at large but especially the depressed areas of the inner city. University Hospital, on the other hand, is primarily a referral hospital for difficult cases, drawing its admissions from a much wider area including the more affluent suburbs. Most of its inpatients—about 80 percent, according to recent estimates—are admitted by specialists with offices at the hospital, to whom the patients were referred by physicians elsewhere.

Although University Hospital offers a full range of surgical and medical care, because it is a teaching and research institution it has specialized in treating certain diseases, many of which require lengthier and more costly inpatient care than the average illness.

In addition to the inpatient services, University Hospital operates a series of ambulatory outpatient clinics that serve mostly the local community. A detailed breakdown of the patient mix by source of payment is shown in Table 10.1 and the utilization patterns in Table 10.2.

Table 10.1

PATIENT BREAKDOWN BY THIRD PARTY
(Fiscal Year Ending September 28, 1974)

Third Party	Department of Medicine Inpatients	Medical Clinic Outpatients
Blue Cross/Blue Shield	35%	8%
Medicaid/Welfare	32%	40%
Medicare	13%	22%
Self-pay and commercial insurance	20%	30%

Table 10.2

UNIVERSITY HOSPITAL STATISTICS
(10th Period Year to Date Ending 7/5/75)

		Medicine	MICU	CCU	Surgery	SICU	Neur./ Neurosg.	PSY.	Rehab.	TOTAL	ECU
Admissions	1975	1,957	181	267	3,351	53	424	166	73	6,652	459
	1974	1,965	169	305	3,415	73	403	140	81	6,551	524
Discharges	1975	2,170	79	61	3,667	43	438	180	75	6,713	462
	1974	2,217	54	58	3,523	44	416	149	89	6,550	527
Days care	1975	25,351	1,620	1,696	34,005	2,319	5,938	6,011	4,424	81,364	9,696
	1974	25,932	1,448	1,870	32,453	2,351	5,494	6,161	3,999	79,708	9,729
% Change	1975 to 1974	−2.3	11.9	−10.3	4.7	−1.4	8.1	−2.5	10.6	2.1	−.3
Daily average	1975	90.5	5.8	6.1	121.4	8.3	21.2	21.5	15.8	290.6	34.6
	1974	92.6	5.2	6.7	115.9	8.4	19.6	22.0	14.3	284.7	34.7
Length of stay	1975	9.6	5.2	5.1	8.1	4.2	11.0	31.0	52.1	12.1	21.0
	1974	—	—	—	—	—	—	—	—	12.2	18.5
Occupancy%	1975	89.7	75.6	75.7	88.5	83.8	80.9	89.4	98.8	88.1	86.5
	1974	98.5	86.2	83.5	85.2	84.2	85.3	91.7	89.3	89.8	86.9
Deaths	1975									321	22
	1974									277	25
Operations	1975							Hrs. 6,216.0		3,735	28

(ADMISSIONS) AND DAYS OF CARE BY SERVICE

		Acute		ECU					Acute		ECU	
Medicine	1975	(2,375)	28,350	(175)	3,750	Surgery						
	1974	(2,404)	29,185	(183)	3,390							
Neur./Neursg.	1975	(431)	6,206	(45)	806	General surg.	1975	(1,459)	17,584	(118)	2,213	
	1974	(410)	5,792	(49)	790		1974	(1,340)	17,003	(105)	1,945	
Psychiatry	1975	(166)	6,010			Gynecology	1975	(55)	308	(2)		
	1974	(140)	6,162				1974	(80)	463	(6)	164	
Rehab.	1975	(73)	4,406	(31)	1,385	Ophthalmology	1975	(353)	2,063	(18)	101	
	1974	(80)	3,844	(44)	1,210		1974	(366)	2,312	(35)	384	
						Orthopedics	1975	(665)	6,666	(29)	596	
							1974	(617)	5,665	(57)	908	
						Otolaryngology	1975	(357)	1,292	(19)	437	
							1974	(380)	1,542	(18)	460	
						Stomatology	1975	(134)	419			
							1974	(127)	316			
						Thoracic	1975	(189)	3,727	(7)	181	
							1974	(246)	4,271	(15)	303	
						Urology	1975	(395)	4,333	(15)	214	
							1974	(361)	3,153	(12)	139	

		OPD	ADRC	6 HR.				INPT.	ECU	OUTPT.	PA.
First Visits	1975	8,910	7,628	128	Laboratory	1975	530,733	13,198	89,057	30,618
	1974	9,598	—	—	Exams	1974	472,080	14,041	69,598	33,985
Revisits	1975	15,575	2,028	164	X-ray Exams	1975	24,979	447	8,603	1,161
	1974	16,246	—	—		1974	23,656	484	7,067	1,399
Total Visits	1975	24,485	9,656	292						
	1974	25,843	9,094	—						

University Hospital's outpatient clinics have a capacity for 35,000 patient visits a year, roughly one-tenth the capacity of Boston City Hospital's nearby outpatient clinic. In the last fiscal year, University Hospital handled 31,831 outpatient visits, as well as 12,932 visits to the emergency room.

Although there are some 800 "staff physicians" (physicians who can admit patients to the hospital) connected with University Hospital, only about 120 of these have offices in the hospital and work there full time. These 120 divide their time among research, seeing patients in the hospital, overseeing the training of residents and interns, administering their departments, and teaching at Boston University School of Medicine, with which University Hospital is affiliated. (Boston City Hospital is also affiliated with Boston University School of Medicine.) Many of these physicians also maintain a private practice, often using hospital facilities.

Although University Hospital does compensate its full-time physicians for administrative duties, they are not paid by the hospital for patient care. As a consequence, their incomes come primarily from three sources: teaching salaries, salaries from research grants, and fees from their private practices. (This includes fees for seeing their private inpatients as well as their private ambulatory practices.) The breakdown of this income varies widely from individual to individual, but a physician earning $45,000 per year might receive 25 percent from teaching, 25 percent to 50 percent from research grants, and most of the remainder from private practice. The amount received from the hospital is virtually negligible in most cases.

HOSPITAL FINANCING

The hospital itself receives revenues from several sources. A large part comes from so-called third parties, the public and private insurers such as Blue Cross, Medicare, and Medicaid. The third parties reimburse the hospital for the costs of care to patients covered by them. This reimbursement is usually subject to certain restrictions; for example, Medicare has set a ceiling at $109.26 on the daily rate of reimbursement for routine inpatient care. Current charges for routine inpatient care are $131 (average semiprivate room rate) and current average costs are $126 per patient day. Medicare, however, reimburses for ancillaries (services such as radiology, pharmacy, or medical laboratories) and ambulatory (outpatient) care at current costs.

Medicaid, controlled by the state Rate Setting Commission, reimburses the hospital for outpatient care on a ratio of all outpatient costs to all outpatient charges (RCC), determined from statements of costs from two years prior to the year of concern. For University Hospital, the RCC currently used for reimbursement is 89.68 percent. Medicaid reimburses for inpatient care including ancillaries on the basis of an "all-inclusive per diem." This is determined from the actual costs from two years prior to the year of concern divided by the total number of patient days for that year. This figure is then inflated, using relevant indices, to set the all-inclusive per diem for the current year. The all-inclusive per diem currently being used for University Hospital is $230.06 per patient day, while current charges are $286 per patient day and costs currently average $246 per patient day.

Blue Cross, the other major third party, reimburses the hospital on the basis of current allowable costs. Allowable costs are based on previous years' costs adjusted for inflation by using data from other businesses and industry in the same geographic region. Until this time, University Hospital has been reimbursed by Blue Cross for virtually 100 percent of costs.

However, for the first time there is an indication that Blue Cross may disallow certain costs at University Hospital and may not reimburse it for the full 100 percent of costs.

Patients who are not covered by any insurance or who have certain types of commercial insurance (or who are subject to a "deductible" part of Medicare) are billed by University Hospital on the basis of their ability to pay, which averages 53.7 percent of the hospital's costs. The incidence of bad debt, virtually zero under all third-party payments, has been quite high for uninsured patients, averaging 17.9 percent.

Another major source of hospital funds is the government, which provides research grants, used to pay the salaries of physicians and staff and purchase equipment and facilities, and "capitation money," a subsidy of teaching salaries paid to medical institutions on a per-student basis. (Currently, this is $2,000 per student per year.)

The vast majority of funds available to the hospital is controlled by outside agencies, usually governmental.

FINANCIAL PRESSURES

Recently, two things have put University Hospital in general, and the physicians in particular, under financial pressure. First, government grant money is becoming more difficult to obtain, and there is the possibility that Congress, under pressure to restrict government spending, will put an end to "capitation money."

Second, Medical Department admissions have shown a very slight decline over the last five months, which James Dorsey, administrator for fiscal affairs for University Hospital, feels may be a trend rather than a short-term fluctuation. John Betjemann, hospital administrator, explained it this way:

> University Hospital, like many other teaching hospitals, has been essentially working to bring about its own demise. It used to be that the only place a patient could go for specialized care was to the teaching hospital. Now, the suburban hospitals are staffed with the specialists we have trained, and there is no longer the need to go into the city for specialist care. What we need to do to survive is to find a new way of doing business.

University Hospital's problem is clear from its most recent financial statements (Tables 10.3 and 10.4). As can be seen, the hospital had an operating deficit of $597,419 for the past fiscal year, and the Evans Fund (a restricted fund for the support of research but under the control of Dr. Norman Levinsky, chief of medicine and a trustee) had an operating deficit of $710,021.

Since John Betjemann and Dr. Levinsky took over their respective positions a few years ago, the problem of shrinking funds compounded by the need to keep physicians' compensation competitive with private practice has become of increasing concern. The alternative of reducing hospital costs and allowing both inpatient care and research to shrink has been considered and rejected. Some of the third parties allocate costs to a minimum percentage of bed complement; thus, for example, if the minimum were an average bed occupancy of 317 and the actual average were 300, the costs would be spread over 317 rather than 300 in determining the per diem costs to be reimbursed for inpatient care. In addition, many of the overhead costs, such as administration, accounting, and records, are relatively fixed and will not vary much with

Table 10.3

BALANCE SHEET
September 28, 1974 and September 30, 1973

ASSETS	1974	1973
UNRESTRICTED FUNDS		
Current Assets:		
Cash	$ 13,523	$ 374,469
Accounts receivable — less allowance for uncollectible accounts: 1974, $1,282,763; 1973, $1,264,238	9,061,012	7,790,701
Pledges receivable — less allowance for uncollectible pledges: 1974, $43,372; 1973, $34,000	65,273	81,402
Inventories of supplies — at cost	298,308	319,081
Prepaid expenses	99,602	87,962
Total current assets	9,537,718	8,653,615
Funds Held by Others under Lease-Purchase Agreement	936,678	1,227,809
Property, Plant and Equipment — At cost:		
Construction in progress	89,801	216,530
Land, buildings, and equipment — net	15,515,211	15,352,422
Property, plant, and equipment — net	15,605,012	15,568,952
Total	$26,079,408	$25,450,376
RESTRICTED FUNDS		
Specific Purpose Funds:		
Cash	$ 1,130,900	$ 229,160
Grants receivable	2,505,143	2,578,317
Accounts receivable — less allowance for uncollectible accounts: 1974, $10,727; 1973, $500	89,524	165,595
Pledges receivable — less allowance for uncollectible pledges: 1974, $1,810; 1973, $500	4,753	65,416
Apportioned pooled investment securities	6,982,848	7,209,193
Due from unrestricted funds	2,085,868	2,024,736
Funds held by others under lease-purchase agreement	261,972	
Property, plant, and equipment — net, at cost	8,774,323	9,283,387
Total Specific Purpose Funds	$21,834,331	$21,555,804
Plant Replacement and Expansion Funds:		
Cash	$ 289,446	$ 54,543
Pledges receivable — less allowance of $6,050 for uncollectible pledges in 1974		271,514
Total Plant Replacement and Expansion Funds	$ 289,446	$ 326,057
Endowment Funds:		
Cash	$ 59,235	$ 189,510
Accounts receivable	5,281	14,844
Prepaid real estate taxes		52,981
Apportioned pooled investment securities	3,648,547	3,450,805
Real estate, equipment, and furnishings — at cost less accumulated depreciation: 1974, $529,422; 1973, $484,475	4,131,157	4,250,778
Due from unrestricted funds	4,154,498	4,444,565
Total Endowment Funds	$11,998,718	$12,403,480

LIABILITIES AND FUND BALANCES	1974	1973
UNRESTRICTED FUNDS		
Current Liabilities:		
Notes payable	$ 800,000	$ 3,513,951
Accounts payable and accrued liabilities	3,561,129	331,062
Current installments of long-term debt	333,807	280,817
Advances from third-party payers	161,900	
Total current liabilities	4,856,836	4,125,830
Due to Restricted Funds:		
Specific purpose funds	1,307,868	1,246,736
Endowment funds	4,154,498	4,444,565
Total Due to Restricted Funds	5,462,366	5,691,301
Long Term Debt:		
Mortgage note payable	1,466,069	1,499,876
Due to Restricted Funds — specific purpose funds:		
Note payable	633,000	633,000
Advance	115,000	115,000
Lease-purchase obligation, net of deferred lease-purchase agreement costs: 1974, $179,283; 1973, $188,324	8,045,717	8,336,676
Total Long-Term Debt	10,289,786	10,614,552
Fund Balances	5,470,420	5,018,693
Total	$26,079,408	$25,450,376
RESTRICTED FUNDS		
Specific Purpose Funds:		
Accounts payable and accrued liabilities	$ 124,710	$ 181,450
Fund balances:		
General account	3,023,358	2,387,078
Evans account	18,686,263	18,987,276
Total Specific Purpose Funds	$21,834,331	$21,555,804
Plant Replacement and Expansion Funds:		
Fund balances	$ 289,446	$ 326,057
Total Plant Replacement and Expansion Funds	$ 289,446	$ 326,057
Endowment Funds:		
Accounts payable	$ 25,500	$ 203,929
Mortgage note payable	2,815,179	2,865,471
Fund balances:		
General account	6,240,687	6,283,061
Evans account	2,917,352	3,051,022
Total Endowment Funds	$11,998,718	$12,403,483

Table 10.4

STATEMENT OF REVENUES AND EXPENSES, BY ACCOUNTS
For the Years Ended September 28, 1974, and September 30, 1973

	1974			1973		
	General Account— Unrestricted	Evans Account— Restricted	Combined (for Information)	General Account— Unrestricted	Evans Account— Restricted	Combined (for Information)
PATIENT SERVICE REVENUE:						
Inpatient	$24,666,702		$24,666,702	$21,302,969		$21,302,969
Outpatient and private ambulatory	3,755,429		3,755,429	3,079,496		3,079,496
Total patient service revenue	28,422,131		28,422,131	24,382,465		24,382,465
Less free care, provision for uncollectible accounts, contractual adjustments, etc.	2,110,952		2,110,952	2,057,066		2,057,066
Net patient service revenue	26,311,179		26,311,179	22,325,399		22,325,399
Other operating revenue — transfer from Specific Purpose Funds, etc.	2,189,046	$1,705,731	3,894,777	2,216,109	$2,351,121	4,567,230
Total patient and other operating revenue	28,500,225	1,705,731	30,205,956	24,541,508	2,351,121	26,892,629
OPERATING EXPENSES:						
Professional care of patients:						
Routine	10,419,960		10,419,960	8,012,150		8,012,150
Special	6,801,258		6,801,258	6,780,055		6,780,055
Administration and general	4,711,590		4,711,590	4,665,813		4,665,813
Household and property	3,528,256		3,528,256	3,116,510		3,116,510
Research and training	885,474	1,422,634	2,308,108	1,030,142	1,814,053	2,844,195
Dietary	1,203,551		1,203,551	1,033,608		1,033,608
Depreciation of buildings and equipment:						
General account	849,627		849,627	563,975		563,975
Evans account	414,550		414,550	407,246		407,246
Interest	1,276,496		1,276,496	648,173		648,173
Total operating expenses	30,090,762	1,422,634	31,513,396	26,257,672	1,814,053	28,071,725
Allocation of operating expenses to Evans account (Note 1)	(993,118)	993,118		(1,052,151)	1,052,151	
Operating expenses — net	29,097,644	2,415,752	31,513,396	25,205,521	2,866,204	28,071,725
Loss from patient and research operations	597,419	710,021	1,307,440	644,013	515,083	1,179,096
NON-OPERATING REVENUES (LOSS):						
Income from investments of Restricted Funds:						
General account — unrestricted	308,193		308,193	221,664		221,664
Evans account — restricted		599,131	599,131		507,400	507,400
Donations and grants	34,946		34,946	9,055		9,055
Gains (losses) on sales of investments — Evans account — restricted		(227,855)	(227,855)		177,099	177,099
Income (loss) from operation of Doctors' Office Building (including depreciation of $122,629 in 1974 and $124,033 in 1973) (Note 8)	44,561		44,561	(178,471)		(178,471)
Nonoperating revenues — net	387,700	271,276	758,976	52,248	684,499	736,747
Excess (deficiency) of revenues over expenses	$ (209,719)	$ (338,745)	$ (548,464)	$ (611,765)	$ 169,416	$ (442,349)

the bed complement. The only reasonable alternative is to find some way to increase both admissions and income for the physicians from nongovernment sources.

Mr. Betjemann and Dr. Levinsky feel that both objectives can be best accomplished by increasing the private practices of the 120 full-time hospital-based physicians. Most physicians at the hospital would rather teach and do research than see private patients; they maintain private practices primarily to supplement their incomes and to provide enough cases for their research activities. However, as teaching and research funds become tighter, economics may force them to accept a larger patient load.

THE GROUP PRACTICE

Mr. Betjemann and Dr. Levinsky think that the increase can be brought about most simply by establishing a group practice, at least for the full-time physicians in the Department of Medicine (the department most affected by funding cutbacks). At present, physicians handle their private practices individually on a part-time basis, which has led to inefficiencies in patient scheduling and tied up physicians' time in managerial tasks. The group practice, to be called the Evans Group, is designed to increase the volume of private patients seen by the Medical Department without increasing greatly the physicians' time required, by assigning routine and administrative duties to a professional administrator and staff. The group would occupy a vacant floor of the recently constructed Doctors' Office Building that houses a number of private practices, and would be an organization separate from the hospital.

At present, referrals come to individual physicians. But with the establishment of a group practice, it is hoped that the referrals would come to the group instead, which, like the Lahey and Mayo Clinics, could in time obtain its own professional reputation.

In addition, hospital administrators plan to close the medical clinics of the Outpatient Department (OPD), now housed in the dilapidated Talbot building, and have their operations subsumed under the new Evans Group. This part of the plan caused two problems in setting up the new group practice. First, in order to establish any new health care facility, by law a certificate of need had to be obtained from, among others, a designated local community group. Community residents, who feared that the Evans Group would not be as responsive to poor patients as the Talbot Clinic had been, initially refused to grant a CON, and only agreed after repeated assurance from the hospital that this would not be the case.

Second, because most third parties reimburse 100 percent of cost for outpatient care and only a portion of costs for inpatient care, hospitals try to assign a large part of their overhead costs to outpatient operations, in which category it will be reimbursed in full. Since inpatient costs at University Hospital are already at or over Medicare's cost ceilings for reimbursement, and are reimbursed by Medicaid at a per diem rate that is fixed for at least the next two years, little of the overhead now borne by the OPD will be reimbursed if it is shifted to inpatient care.

The amount of overhead carried by the medical clinics can be seen in the "step-down" of expenses (Table 10.5), the procedure used by the hospital to allocate expenses from non-revenue-producing departments to revenue-producing departments. It begins by listing the direct expenses for all cost centers. Then, expenses for non-revenue-producing departments are "stepped down" (or allocated) to other departments successively proportional to floor space, payroll dollars, or percentage of time spent in that department. For example, Administration and General Expenses are distributed to Employee Health and Welfare, Operation of Plant, Laundry and Linen, etc. Then, Employee Health and Welfare, including the portion of Administration and General Expenses allocated to it, is distributed to Operation of Plant, etc. This is continued until all expenses from non-revenue-generating departments have been distributed to revenue-generating departments.

The step-down does not show the costs of the medical clinics separately from the rest of the OPD. When asked how these might be separated to isolate the effect of reorganizing the medical clinics, Charles Macdonald, assistant to the administrator for fiscal affairs, replied, "The only defensible way that we could separate these costs would be proportional to charge revenue, but even that would be only an approximation."

Charge revenue is the revenue that would be received if all charges were billed and if all billings were collected. Table 10.6 shows the charge revenue for the medical clinics against the rest of the OPD, and the allowances for uncollectible billings.

Although the direct expenses of most departments consist of salaries and wages (primarily) and supplies and outside services, not all of these expenses vary with department volume. The estimate of variable expenses for the departments that would be affected by a move of the medical clinics' patients into a group practice are shown in Table 10.7. It is estimated that nursing salaries to support the present medical clinics' patient volume would come to $55,400 per year (four nurses at $13,850). Fringe benefits average 14 percent of salaries and wages for University Hospital and are charged to Employee Health and Welfare on the step-down.

However, to offset the potential loss of revenue when the medical clinics no longer absorb the hospital overhead, the hospital's administration is planning to require the Evans Group to use hospital ancillaries for 100 percent of its procedures. At present, the Department of Medicine physicians use the clinical laboratories for about 80 percent, radiology for about 15 percent, of their private ambulatory procedures.

In addition, fringe benefits for the $55,000 in nurses' salaries for the medical clinics will no longer be paid by the hospital. Fringe benefits, which are charged to Employee Health and Welfare on the step-down, average 14 percent of salaries.

Physicians and others feel that the total number of ambulatory patients seen at the hospital will increase by 10,000 within the first year that the group is in existence. This is predicated on plans to bring several new physicians into the department over the next year, in addition to the present 35 members. The volume for the medical outpatient clinics during the last fiscal year was 8,600 patient visits; the volume for the department's private ambulatory practices, 15,000 patient visits.

It is estimated that the rate of inpatient admissions by Department of Medicine physicians will respond proportionally to changes in the size of their ambulatory patient load. In the last fiscal year, the hospital provided 36,855 days of inpatient "medicine" care, which was 89.7 percent of capacity.

ALTERNATIVE MODELS

The four alternatives under consideration for the group practice would all require that the present outpatient medical clinics be closed and their function taken over by the Evans Group.

Table 10.5 COST APPORTIONMENT

COST APPORTIONMENT—GENERAL SERVICES

Line No.	Cost Center (Omit cents)	Total Direct Expenses for Apportionment (from Sched. A Col. 6, Lines 1-35)	PROVISION FOR DEPRECIATION — Bldg. and Fixtures, Etc. ECU	Hosp.	Sub-total	Admin. Gen'l Not Applicable to Research	Administration and General	Employee Health and Welfare	Operation of Plant	Mainte-nance of Plant	Laundry and Linen Service
		1	1(a)		1(b)	2	3	4	5	6	7
	General Service Cost Centers										
1a	Provision for	$ 2,450,079	$238,916	$2,211,163							
1b	Depreciation										
2	Administration & General	2,728,207	8,526	67,332	$2,804,065	($400,692)	$2,403,373				
3	Employee Health & Welfare	2,151,863	6,331	479	2,158,673	35,304	196,718	$2,390,695			
4	Operation of Plant	1,984,491	4,639	119,949	2,109,079	34,493	192,199	128,576	$2,464,347		
5	Maintenance of Plant									$	
6	Laundry and Linen Service	407,884	1,744	7,590	417,218	6,824	38,020	7,755	25,076		$494,895
7	Housekeeping	1,049,367	4,257	16,302	1,069,926	17,499	97,501	125,976	23,398		
8	Infection and Quality Control	70,581	1,263	61,583	133,427	2,183	12,159	8,719	6,311		
9	Other	1,116,089	14,646	30,520	1,161,255	18,992	105,824	93,879	80,449		
10	Cafeteria	75,950	7,237	17,220	100,407	1,643	9,150	14,016	57,428		
11	Maintenance of Personnel			14,961	14,901	246	1,363		40,590		7,489
12	Nursing Service Admin.	464,756	3,638	12,175	480,569	7,860	43,794	75,434	33,331		
13	Medical Supplies & Expense	271,503		7,500	279,083	4,565	25,432	12,146	10,053		2,814
14	Pharmacy	563,216		166,939	730,155	11,942	66,538	21,251	56,769		47
15	Medical Records	212,581		108,592	321,170	5,253	29,268	27,249	53,565		
16	Social Service	134,179	2,525	3,322	140,026	2,291	12,760	20,684	13,361		
17	Nuclear Med.	161,749		6,123	167,872	2,746	15,298	10,810	16,790		1,313
18	Intern-Resident Service	1,568,113	7,576	99,191	1,674,880	27,392	152,630	208,632	118,742		78
19	Hemodialysis	251,030	3,823	537	255,390	4,178	23,273	22,850	8,431		1,423
20	I.V. Therapy	125,294		2,902	128,196	2,098	11,682	2,693	8,640		
	Cardiac Cath.	250,843			250,843	4,103	22,859	16,066			
	EEG	56,467		1,516	57,983	949	5,284	6,958	2,208		
	Special Service Cost Centers	16,094,242									
21	Operating Rooms	1,222,975		59,523	1,282,498	20,975	116,873	113,555	57,082		26,640
22	EEG	134,443	1,499	25,622	161,564	2,642	14,723	18,748	32,488		1,188
23	Anesthesia	474,266		10,098	484,954	7,931	44,193	92,949	5,926		
24	X-Ray	1,118,877		72,105	1,190,982	19,477	108,533	125,529	56,424		6,611
25	Laboratory	1,605,115	12,787	448,147	2,066,123	33,789	188,284	118,304	190,671		266
26	Blood Bank	341,996		15,870	357,866	5,853	32,612	10,152	4,272		
	X-Ray Therapy	144,496		5,196	203,692	5,331	18,562	41,477	24,948		5,785
27	Oxygen Therapy	409,813	180	12,313	422,306	6,906	38,484	49,788	12,382		
28	Physical Therapy	298,258	3,831	9,359	311,448	5,094	28,382	42,730	28,810		3,002
29	Cost of Medical Supplies Sold										
30	Cost of Drugs Sold										
	Ambulance	402			402	7	36				
	Inpatient Cost Centers CCU	259,881		13,474	273,355	4,470	24,910	38,086	24,611		12,481
32	Inpatients	3,700,059	48,276	222,721	3,981,056	65,106	362,790	552,045	598,245		324,545
33	MICU	248,471		12,647	261,118	4,270	23,795	34,658	24,603		12,481
	SICU	392,912		14,912	407,834	6,670	37,165	57,141	21,808		12,481
34	Extended Care	298,782	100,160		398,942	6,524	36,355	42,560	187,258		58,784
35	Emergency & OPD	783,927		258,461	1,042,388	17,047	94,992	75,152	223,054		16,134
36	Research	1,679,078	5,051	219,867	1,903,996		170,717	174,127	410,625		1,329
	Nonpatient		927	1,435	2,362	39	215		6,006		
37	TOTAL	$29,208,073	$238,916	$2,211,163	$29,208,073	$400,692	$2,403,373	$2,390,695	$2,464,347		$494,893

PERIOD: FYE 9/30/74   WORKSHEET B

House-keeping	Infection & Quality Control	Dietary Other	Cafe-teria	Mainte-nance of Per-sonnel	Nursing Service	Medical Supplies and Expense	Phar-macy	Medical Records	Social Services	Nursing School	Intern-Resident Service	TOTAL (Cols. 2 thru 19, Lines 21-37) (To Sched. C)	Line No.
8	9	10	11	12	13	14	15	16	17	18	19	20	
													1a
													1b
													2
													3
													4
													5
													6
$1,334,300													7
1,528	$164,327												8
45,450		$1,505,849											9
17,187		301,169	$501,000										10
20,624				$85,273									11
6,493			10,996		$658,477								12
6,875			3,959			$344,927							13
12,082			4,838			1,178	$924,800						14
10,694			10,557					$457,759					15
4,965			5,718						$199,805				16
16,805						448	144					$ 232,226	17
56,144			49,704	57,685		673	1,133				$2,347,698		18
14,132			4,399		14,296	4,432	4,658					357,462	19
			880			151	148					154,488	20
						396	34					284,301	
72,949			20,234	7,524	75,842	94,778	23,663				375,633	2,288,246	21
13,610			5,718			2,476	1,942					275,099	22
6,875			10,117	7,524		23,996	54,419					738,878	23
58,054			30,350	7,524		7,241	4,763					1,615,480	24
71,804			48,824	5,016		8,121	1,809					2,733,000	25
			2,199			1,870	603					415,427	26
17,775			7,478									323,048	
6,875			12,756			9,687	802					559,986	27
12,222			9,677			375	116					441,856	28
						66,810						66,810	29
							723,518					723,518	30
												445	
12,970	3,485	25,416	7,038		26,768	9,068	4,502	5,915			37,563	510,638	
391,100	136,118	997,477	165,827		418,135	70,544	60,991	225,657	75,290		1,241,929	9,666,855	32
12,969	2,663	19,418	9,237		20,454	6,928	3,441	4,503			30,519	471,050	33
11,415	4,260	31,060	10,117		32,722	11,088	5,504	7,239			46,954	703,533	
59,969	17,801	131,311	19,794		37,550	10,835	4,654	29,840	21,350		145,557	1,209,071	34
119,163			14,955		32,710	11,512	18,467	181,426	103,165		469,538	2,419,700	35
212,737			35,628			2,331	9,489	3,179				2,924,158	36
764													
$1,334,300	$164,327	$1,505,849	$501,000	$85,273	$658,477	$344,927	$924,800	$457,759	$199,805		$2,347,693	$29,208,073	37

Table 10.6

OUTPATIENT DEPARTMENT (OPD) CHARGE REVENUES AND BILLING ALLOWANCES
(Includes Ancillary Charge Revenue)
(Fiscal Year Ending September 28, 1974)

Clinic	Charge Revenue	Allowance	Net Billing
Total OPD	$2,605,200	$469,100	$2,136,100
Med. clinics	450,000	61,300	388,700
Other OPD	2,155,200	407,800	1,747,400
Emergency	715,200	5,600	709,600

OUTPATIENT DEPARTMENT (OPD) CLINIC VISIT CHARGE REVENUES AND BILLING ALLOWANCES
(Does Not Include Ancillary Charge Revenue)
(Fiscal Year Ending September 28, 1974)

Clinic	Charge Revenue	Allowance	Net Billing
Total OPD	$1,354,400	$335,500	$1,018,900
Med. clinics	249,600	34,900	215,700
Other OPD clinics	1,104,800	300,600	803,200
Emergency	282,400	1,300	281,100

OUTPATIENT DEPARTMENT (OPD) ANCILLARY CHARGE REVENUES AND BILLING ALLOWANCES
(Fiscal Year Ending September 28, 1974)

Ancillary*	Charge Revenue	Allowance	Net Billing
Radiology			
Med. clinics	$ 44,000	$ 4,900	$ 39,100
Other OPD	320,300	10,200	310,100
Clinical Labs			
Med. clinics	84,900	9,100	75,800
Other OPD	310,800	12,600	298,200

*Other ancillaries, such as pharmacy are not affected by the move of the medical facilities.

Table 10.7

DEPARTMENTS AFFECTED BY REORGANIZATION OF MEDICAL CLINICS

Department	Total Expense	% Variable
Ambulatory accounting*	$ 167,700	69%
Medical records	163,600	50%
Nursing service (outpatient)	182,400	68%
Ancillaries:		
Radiology	1,705,000	53%
Clinical labs	2,225,000	56%

*Part of Administration and General Expenses, which are apportioned on the basis of payroll dollars. Even though this is not apportioned directly to the outpatient department in the step-down, nearly the entire expense is due to Emergency and Outpatient Department accounting.

The group would provide a single standard of care for all ambulatory patients, both private practice and hospital outpatient, and patients would make appointments to see individual physicians.

The four models offer a variety of possible arrangements for the Evans Group, ranging from a practice to be operated and administered by the hospital with the physicians placed on a salary, to a completely independent group practice with no other ties to the hospital than to contract to handle the hospital's medical outpatients.

The arrangement most likely to be adopted would establish the Evans Group as an independent nonprofit organization, with the following provisions:

1. University Hospital renovates and furnishes a 10,000 square feet floor in the Doctors' Office Building, at an estimated cost of $420,000.

2. University Hospital rents 10,000 square feet of this space to the Evans Group at the current rental price of $10 per square foot per year.

   The yearly cost to the hospital for that space is estimated by the building manager to be:

   a. Building cost: ½ of 8-floor building costing $2,538,000 with a 45-year life
   b. Shell development cost: $150,000 with a 20-year life
   c. Suite development cost: $270,000 with a 10-year life
   d. Financing cost: 85 percent of building cost financed by an 8.25 percent loan. Remaining costs financed by internal funds earning 15.0 percent return
   e. Utilities cost: $1/sq. ft.
      Cleaning cost: $1.25/sq. ft.

3. The Evans Group purchases from University Hospital its medical records, accounting, and ancillary services, and is required to use hospital ancillaries for all of its procedures.

4. The Evans Group pays for its own nursing staff and all other expenses, and absorbs the bad debt for all its billings. It does not absorb the hospital's fixed costs.

One uncertainty is the charge per patient visit for the group. The hospital is now charging $37 per visit to the Outpatient Department and would like not to increase it, but other hospitals in the area are reportedly charging as much as $45 per visit.

Since University Hospital is hoping to increase revenues over the long run by the move to a group practice, trade-offs may have to be made by balancing a possible short-term loss of revenue from the move against a long-term increase in admissions to inpatient care.

Although there is no deadline for setting up the group practice, the board of trustees has approved it, and almost all of the physicians in the Medical Department have committed themselves to join. Mr. Betjemann and others feel that the group, if it is to be established, should be put in operation within a year while enthusiasm is still high.

ISSUES AND PROBLEMS

1. What economic factors weigh on the decision?
2. What other factors should be considered?
3. What course of action would you recommend?
4. Analyze the financial condition of University Hospital from Tables 10.2 and 10.3.

11

Hospital Rate Setting by Per-Case Methods: DRGs and the New Jersey Department of Health

Ralph Ullman
Gerald Kominski

On June 17, 1974, Joanne E. Finley, M.D., M.P.H., was appointed Commissioner of Health by the newly elected Governor of the State of New Jersey, Brendan T. Byrne. Dr. Finley's particular interest in hospital financing initiated what was to become a period of unparalleled activism by the state in trying to control the $2-billion-a-year hospital industry. This activism resulted in the development of an innovative method of rate setting based upon classification of hospital cases and patterns of treatment. For the regulatory staff responsible for implementing this program, both a heightened sensitivity to political factors and an increased technical capability were to become essential.

BACKGROUND

The new role of the New Jersey State Department of Health can be traced to the significant public interventions in the quality, availability, and accessibility of health services during the 1960s. The federal Hill-Burton program, which had been enacted in 1946, continued to provide the funds for a massive replenishment and expansion of hospital facilities. Assurance that the aged would have adequate access to care was the intention of the Medicare legislation of 1965. The concurrent enactment of Medicaid as a federal-state partnership endeavored to finance similar access for the low-income segment of the population. But, partly as a result of the capital expansion and the increased demand, the total cost of health care rose dramatically, and, as the most expensive component, hospital inpatient services received particular scrutiny.

Support for an earlier version of the case was provided by the Sloan Foundation through the Public Policy Curricular Materials Development Program, administered jointly by the Duke Institute of Policy Sciences and Public Affairs and The Rand Graduate Institute.

In the early 1970s, response by the United States Congress to the explosion of hospital costs resulted in two major programs. First, local Health Systems Agencies (HSAs) were established and directed to review any proposed significant expansion of hospital facilities, although final approval (through the granting of a certificate of need) was still reserved for the states. Second, Professional Standards Review Organizations (PSROs), also locally based, were developed to evaluate the medical appropriateness of publicly financed hospitalizations. In addition to these highly visible, nationwide programs, however, the restraint of hospital costs also began to be investigated through a less publicized, decentralized series of "demonstrations" conducted by federal Medicare and Medicaid officials. These demonstration projects allowed standard payment procedures to be waived for state governments that were willing to design innovative reimbursement mechanisms to control costs.

The standard methods of hospital reimbursement were considered to constitute a major part of the overall problem, since they were based on the costs actually incurred in providing services. While the "reasonableness" of specific costs might be challenged retroactively, the system provided little incentive for the hospital sector in general to restrain its inflationary tendencies. The demonstration projects thus sought to establish arrangements in which hospitals would agree to *prospective* budgets within which they would function for a given period of time, and on which reimbursement rates would be based, regardless of the costs eventually incurred.

The state of New Jersey moved somewhat in advance of the general trend toward increased governmental involvement with hospital reimbursement. As early as 1963, the Commissioner of Insurance had established a ceiling above which the per diem payments made to hospitals by the state's dominant private health insurer — Blue Cross — would be disallowed. As a ratio of total inpatient costs to total inpatient days, the per diem rate is just a variation on the cost-reimbursement approach, and it was therefore considered highly prone to inflation in the absence of regulatory restraints. Nonetheless, the rate ceilings initiated in 1963 were quite lenient and appeared to have little effect.

The continuing rise in New Jersey hospital per diems and the resulting increase in Blue Cross premiums brought about considerable public concern. In 1969 the Commissioner of Insurance responded by establishing a voluntary budget-review mechanism and creating an advisory committee of hospital industry experts. Given the endorsement of the New Jersey Hospital Association, which provided staff support through its Hospital Research and Educational Trust, the voluntary review program met with cooperation from the industry but did little to change the overall inflationary trend.

Legislative dissatisfaction with the organization of health sector activities culminated in the Health Care Facilities Planning Act of 1971. The act began with the following statement:

> It is hereby declared to be the public policy of the state that hospital and related health care services of the highest quality, of demonstrated need, efficiently provided and properly utilized at a reasonable cost are a vital concern to the public health.

The 1971 act vested in the Department of Health the centralized responsibility for virtually all regulatory functions, some of which were transferred from other agencies. With respect to hospital reimbursement, any payments made by the state, notably through the Medicaid program, were to be at "rates established by the Commissioner of Health, based on elements of costs approved by him," while Blue Cross rates were to be "approved as to reasonableness by the Commissioner of Insurance with approval of the Commissioner of Health." However, final review of any rules and regulations proposed by the Commissioner of Health to implement the provisions of the act was vested in a new entity, the Health Care Administration Board. The Commissioners of Health and Insurance were to sit on this board along with 11 members representing the health industry and the public at large.

Few provisions of the 1971 act were implemented through the early part of 1974. No new funding had accompanied the mandate, and little cooperation had been forthcoming from the hospital leadership, who much preferred to continue the existing budget-review system. The state's reluctance to move forward received widespread attention with the publication of a consumer research center's report entiled *Bureaucratic Malpractice*. This report characterized the 1971 law as a significant attempt to gain public supervision of a chaotic and increasingly expensive industry but criticized it as "no more than an unkept promise" resulting from "governmental lassitude and pressures from the regulated industry."[1]

In addition to presenting a classic example of a regulated industry, itself performing the regulatory function, *Bureaucratic Malpractice* discussed some of the features of the existing reimbursement system that would be expected to lead to excessive costs. The per diem payment was criticized particularly as creating an incentive for hospitals to extend the lengths of inpatient stays beyond the point of justifiable medical need. The report suggested that reimbursement by case, instead of by day, be tried as a means of encouraging greater efficiency.

The underlying ills of hospital reimbursement, of course, were not at all unique to New Jersey. In fact, the basic functioning of the state's health sector appeared fairly representative of the nation as a whole. Perhaps the major difference that Brendan Byrne faced as he assumed the governorship in 1974 was that New Jersey had recognized the inherent problems and had begun to act upon them, but thus far had failed to meet its expectations for reforming the hospital industry.

PROCESS AND POLICY

Governor Byrne's appointment of Joanne Finley as Commissioner of Health at first elicited relatively little discussion, except with respect to Dr. Finley's non—New Jersey background. Yet Finley's initial encounters with the press clearly indicated her aggressive stance regarding the hospital industry: "The first priority of her administration will be to bring the health planning, budget review, and rate-setting powers of her department into a cohesive package that can control costs and improve the health delivery system."[2]

In the wake of *Bureaucratic Malpractice* and similar subsequent criticisms, the hospital industry had little chance of defending its own budget-review system against the state's renewed enthusiasm to control health care costs. Media attention to a letter of resignation from one of the few public members on an existing review committee further publicized charges that the budget review system had been concerned primarily with assuring that "each hospital is in line with the expenditures of other institutions of similar size and clientele," with no consideration given to "encouraging any kind of innovative program" or to "improved conditions for either the patients or the staff." Further, the dominance of hospital personnel on the review committees had lead to "incestuous mutual evaluations" and a "serious conflict of interest."[3]

The first major task undertaken by Finley and her staff was finalizing a contract with a public accounting firm for developing a uniform hospital accounting system as a prerequisite to prospective budget review. The system was called SHARE (Standard Hospital Accounting and Rate Evaluation) and was to be ready for implementation by 1976. SHARE required hospitals to submit annual cost reports and budget projections based on 34 identified cost centers. After establishing "peer" categories within which hospitals of similar structural and organizational characteristics could be compared, Department of Health staff challenged any cost center figures that substantially exceeded the peer medians. If a challenged hospital did not provide satisfactory justification for the discrepancy, then the excess cost could be disallowed and the reimbursement rates lowered accordingly.

Through 1980, SHARE remained the primary mechanism for rate review in New Jersey and attained nation-wide attention as a model of prospective reimbursement.[4] The program was viewed as at least modestly successful in restraining increases in the rates that the state had been authorized to regulate, i.e., Blue Cross and Medicaid. Further, for overall hospital costs, one study showed New Jersey to have experienced consistently lower levels of inflation than those experienced by nonregulated states during the years of 1974 to 1978.[5]

While contracting for the development of SHARE in 1974, consideration was given to establishing criteria by which the types of cases treated in a given hospital could be incorporated into the rate-setting process. Without such criteria, a hospital that treated a mix of cases requiring a particularly complex level of service would have appeared excessively costly. Further, if a fixed reimbursement could be established for the medically appropriate services required to treat a specific case, then the hospital's incentive to prolong the length of stay would be eliminated.

As City Health Officer of New Haven, Connecticut, Joanne Finley had become acquainted with a method of hospital case-mix assessment developed by a group of researchers at the Yale School of Public Health, originally for the purpose of utilization review. Finley was eager to see whether this system could be applied to reimbursement, and she began negotiations with its originators soon after coming to New Jersey. Shortly thereafter, rules that required hospitals to submit the medical abstracts necessary for a case-mix developmental effort were formulated and approved. Soon after that, the effort was merged into a proposal to the federal Social Security Administration, then responsible for Medicare, for support as a demonstration project in prospective payment. The project was awarded $1.4 million for the period 1976 to 1978; an additional grant for implementating the resulting system could follow.

The Yale case-mix method was designed to apportion hospital admissions into a set of mutually exclusive categories, or "diagnosis related groups" (DRGs), each of which would be both readily interpretable from a medical viewpoint and homogeneous with respect to the resources consumed in treatment. The Department of Health proposal called for DRGs to be identified on the basis of the New Jersey inpatient abstracts being collected, followed by a determination of appropriate costs associated with each DRG and establishment of prospective payment formulas. Thus, for example, a hospital eventually might receive $500 for an appendectomy, and $700 for a hysterectomy, regardless of the costs actually incurred in treating an individual patient. Given these new definitions of output and price, hospital administrators and physicians would begin to think more critically about how their decisions influence the cost of care, while state regulators now would share a language with which to evaluate performance of the hospital industry.

The Department of Health had numerous political problems to overcome before DRG payment could be implemented. In particular, the Social Security Administration wanted private payers, not just Medicare and Medicaid, to be included in the demonstration. While the state already had the authority to regulate Blue Cross rates and did so through SHARE, no such authority existed for control over charges made to commercial insurers or to patients who were responsible for their own bills. In fact, the department's staff believed that whatever monies SHARE had saved for Blue Cross and Medicaid had been partly at the expense of increases in the itemized charges made to commercial subscribers and self-payers, roughly 20 percent of all hospitalizations. (Blue Cross and Medicaid covered 27 percent and 13 percent, respectively, and Medicare the remaining 40 percent.) Joanne Finley reportedly told a legislative committee that "non—Blue Cross or non-Medicaid covered persons are charged anywhere from 20 to 400 percent more for their care."[6]

Not surprisingly, commercial insurance companies voiced support for legislation drawn in 1976 to extend the state's rate-setting authority to all payers. But Blue Cross, fearing damage to its own advantageous position, opposed the move. The New Jersey Hospital Association, already critical of the constraints imposed by SHARE, joined in opposition to any further expansion, and the suggested legislation was withdrawn.

Joanne Finley attacked the position of the New Jersey Hospital Association on two fronts. First, she released the results of a survey that portrayed most hospitals as retaining profits under the SHARE system. "It certainly gives a clearer picture of who needs help and who is blowing smoke," she was quoted as saying.[7] Second, she tied the issue of equitable treatment of payers to another perceived problem, the plight of the inner-city hospitals. These institutions *were* incurring large deficits, she suggested, because many of their patients were "medically indigent," that is, unable to purchase private insurance but not poor enough to qualify for Medicaid. While hospitals might try to recapture the revenues lost from serving these "non-payers" by inflating the unregulated charges made to commercial insurers, the inner-city institutions treated too few commercial subscribers to achieve a balance. Only if the state were authorized to distribute the costs of indigent care equitably across all payers could these needed services be preserved.

Support by the urban hospitals for a new, comprehensive rate-setting bill effectively dissipated the industry's unified opposition and was a key factor in the bill's being passed by the legislature and signed by the newly reelected Governor Byrne in July 1978. The New Jersey Hospital Association was mollified further by the establishment of a five-member commission, on which the Department of Health would retain only one seat, for final approval of all reimbursement rates. An additional compromise involved Blue Cross, for which a companion bill allowed the retention of surplus funds as contingency against detrimental effects. Passage of the overall package undoubtedly represented a major coup for Commissioner Finley: "Everybody got a little piece of what they wanted, and I didn't lose a thing."[8]

Although the 1978 legislation made a general reference to the need for consideration of a hospital's case mix in setting an equitable rate of reimbursement, no mention was made of the DRG method specifically. Only in the ensuing months did the Department of Health's commitment to this approach become evident publicly. Again, the issue of subsidization of care for the medically indigent was particularly salient. The department had assumed that the status of the project as a Medicare demonstration implied a waiver of the usual federal payment procedures in favor of the new state regulations. There was some concern, however, that this waiver might not cover the full share of the indigent subsidies unless the project achieved commensurate savings in other areas. That is, total Medicare expenditures might be "capped," and significant financial risk would then fall upon other payers and the hospitals themselves. By late 1978, a department official attempting to lessen the impact of such an eventuality was quoted as expressing a view sharply different from what had been expressed during the legislative hearings:

> The purpose of the indigency provision . . . is only to pick up that portion of indigency not being paid by anybody else or being disproportionately paid by commercial insured and self-paying patients. . . . We would hope that the freeholders [county commissioners] will recognize that the hospitals are treating patients from their jurisdictions who can't afford to pay for all their care and somebody has to pay . . . otherwise what will happen is that all the people who have insurance will have to pay the hospital bills for people who can't afford any, and that doesn't seem very fair.[9]

Despite the uncertainty surrounding the Medicare cap, a five-year, $3.86-million contract to implement DRG-based reimbursement in New Jersey was negotiated between the state and the U.S. Department of Health, Education, and Welfare. In February 1979, soon after announcing this contract, the state Senate committee responsible for monitoring performance under the rate-setting legislation held a hearing to find out more about DRGs and the federal-state relationship. State health officials emphasized to the committee that adoption of the DRG-based method was a necessary condition for a waiver of the Medicare payment principles that otherwise would prohibit the inclusion of the costs of care rendered to the medically indigent. Despite warnings from the New Jersey Hospital Association that the anticipated increase in funds from Medicare would not materialize and that the new system would be exceedingly complex, the committee took no action to deter implementation.

The concern over Medicare funding proved to be justified. In March 1980, the *New York Times* reported a federal official as agreeing that Medicare funds could support indigent care in New Jersey. However, the official added that Medicare would " 'essentially pay no more than it would without the experiment' . . . that the Federal Government had never agreed to pay more money . . . that, if Medicare paid out too much, the hospitals would have to pay back the excess at the end of the four-year experiment." The same report presented two responses by state officials to the resulting alarm expressed among hospital administrators. The Assistant Commissioner of Health responsible for management of the project stressed his projection that the improved efficiency of hospitals under DRG incentives would lower costs to the point where no paybacks would be necessary. However, one official, "who asked not to be identified, said he had been telling hospitals: 'Nobody is going to be able to do the kind of calculations needed to enforce the paybacks. So don't worry, there won't be any.' "[10]

While the Medicare cap was the major source of public controversy between federal and state officials involved in the DRG demonstration, a second point of debate—the method of payment—also would have a great impact upon implementation. The case-mix assessment provided by DRGs could be used as just another part of a complex formula for establishing prospectively a hospital's budget and later for computing any reconciliation needed to adjust for actual experience. Going somewhat further, per-case rates could constitute the basis for this prospective budget, although the rates themselves also might be determined partly by the hospital's location, physical plant, nonservice components such as teaching, and whatever other considerations the state would view as fair. But even then the regulatory process of budgeting, reimbursement, and reconciliation did not necessarily have to alter the basic transaction between *payer* and hospital. Although the state surely would control a hospital's charges to assure the equitable treatment of each payer, the method of payment could remain the same as before. Federal officials, however, apparently wanted a more visible demonstration in which each payer would be billed a flat charge based upon the patient's DRG. Department of Health staff eventually capitulated to this demand, although they generally believed it would create unnecessary complexity, particularly in the reconciliation process. Others wondered what would happen when a DRG rate was sent to a discharged patient whose treatment clearly had involved *less* than the usual amount of resources.

Despite the considerable controversy, by late 1979 the DRG-based system was close to being ready for implementation. "This is kind of like a dream come true for me," Joanne Finley was quoted as saying. "It's something I've been working on for a number of years."[11] Still, the hospital industry was reluctant, at best. Of the 26 hospitals identified as initial participants in the system, only 10 — mostly urban institutions — had been "volunteers"; the rest had to be "drafted." Then 25 of the 26 participants joined the Hospital Association in lawsuits against the Department of Health, seeking to delay implementation pending more favorable resolution of the Medicare issue. Nevertheless, by the time of the deadline that was finally imposed, 18 hospitals of the initial group had accepted "conditionally" the rates distributed to them by the state. On May 1, 1980, reimbursement by DRG began. By the end of the federal grant period in 1983, all 118 of New Jersey's acute-care hospitals were to be phased into the new system.

The implementation of the New Jersey program brought renewed attention to the technical formulation of the regulatory language — the DRGs and their assigned rates. In a highly critical pamphlet entitled *The DRG Maze,* the New Jersey Hospital Association termed the program "untested," "unevaluated," and "unproven."[12] And, in truth, tremendous uncertainty did exist as to what would transpire. An attempt by the Department of Health to mount a smaller-scale experiment under the original federal grant had failed several years previously; the behavior of physicians and hospitals under the incentives of DRG payment remained open to speculation and hypothesis. In essence, the department gambled that what was known was "good enough." If DRGs were not perfect, they surely were better than the system that they replaced.

DRGs—THE NEW LANGUAGE OF RATE SETTING

The Formulation of DRGs

The importance of case mix in explaining variations in hospital costs was first demonstrated by Martin Feldstein in his study of British hospitals in the mid-1960s.[13] Although data limitations forced him to use a case-mix measure based simply upon the percentages of patients housed in various specialty wards, Feldstein argued that the patients' actual diagnoses would constitute a more suitable basis. He also argued that the resources used during treatment should be measured on a per-case rather than on a per diem basis, so that hospitals might be encouraged to recognize the trade-off between service intensity and length of stay for each episode of hospitalization. Feldstein concluded that two criteria were essential for case-mix measurement: (1) patient categories should be meaningful medically, not merely convenient administratively; and (2) patterns of resource consumption should be as homogeneous as possible within each patient category.

Both of Feldstein's suggested criteria were incorporated by the Yale researchers into the DRG classification scheme. A two-stage approach was employed. First, the *International Classification of Diseases* (8th edition) was partitioned into "Major Diagnostic Categories" (MDCs), each of which comprised medical problems either located in the same organ system, or caused by similar pathophsyiological mechanisms (such as infectious disease or cancer), or requiring similar surgical procedures. Eighty-three MDCs resulted. The second stage of analysis partitioned these MDCs into final categories—the DRGs—by using a combination of statistical evaluation as to the homogeneity of resources consumed and continued clinical judgment as to medical meaningfulness.[14]

To facilitate the derivation of the DRGs, the Yale researchers used an interactive computer program called AUTOGRP,[15] which incorporates a partitioning algorithm based on the Automatic Interaction Detector (AID).[16] The algorithm requires the identification of a dependent variable—in this instance, a measure of resource consumption—upon which to evaluate homogeneity and a set of independent variables for defining the partitions. As the dependent variable, the Yale team used length of stay. As independent variables, the researchers selected primary diagnosis, secondary diagnosis, primary surgical procedure, secondary surgical procedure, and patient's age. These variables are readily available from most hospital discharge abstracts and pertain to the three general factors that were considered necessary for prediction of resource consumption: (1) the patient, (2) the disease condition, and (3) the treatment process. Restriction to the identified set of independent variables was intended to simplify the definition of the DRGs and to limit them to a manageable number, something fewer than 500.

Figure 11.1 presents the sequence of steps used by AUTOGRP to partition each MDC into DRGs for a given set of hospital cases. After measuring the total variation in length of stay within the MDC (step 1), each of the independent variables is searched to find the grouping of categories that yields the greatest reduction in variation (steps 2a through 2d). As it is presented, this process would require an enormous computational effort for those independent variables that contain more than a few categories of cases. By first ordering these categories according to their mean values on the *dependent* variable, however, and then by performing a series of binary splits—each selected to minimize the resulting within-group variation—the optimal solution is found with relative efficiency.[17]

After the optimal statistical partition on each independent variable is identified, a clinician working interactively with AUTOGRP might simply select the variable and partition that provide the greatest overall reduction in variance, and then the entire process would be repeated on the new groups thus formed (step 3). However, the interactive capability of AUTOGRP allows the clinician to evaluate the initial suggested partitions on the basis of medical meaningfulness (step 2e). If the clinician believes that the partitions that achieve the greatest reductions in variance are not instructive from a medical viewpoint, he can then choose to alter

Figure 11.1

PARTITIONING PROCEDURE OF THE AUTOGRP ALGORITHM

1. Compute the total sum-of-squares (TSSQ) within the MDC as the total of squared deviations of all observations from the grand mean, or:

$$TSSQ = \sum_{j=1}^{J} \sum_{i=1}^{M_j} (Y_{ij} - \bar{Y})^2,$$

where

> Y_{ij} = LOS of the ith patient in the jth category of the independent variable,
>
> M_j = number of patients in the jth category of the independent variable,
>
> J = number of distinct categories of the independent variable, and

$$\bar{Y} = \frac{\displaystyle\sum_{j=1}^{J} \sum_{i=1}^{M_j} Y_{ij}}{\displaystyle\sum_{j=1}^{J} M_j} = \text{MDC grand mean.}$$

2. Then, for each independent variable:
   a) Consider mappings of the J categories, each containing the set of patients R_j, into K groups S_k such that:

   $S_k \Omega \, S_{k_1} = \varnothing, k \neq k'$; and

   $$\bigcup_{k=1}^{K} S_k = \bigcup_{j=1}^{J} R_j, 1 \leq K \leq J.$$

   b) Compute the within-group sum-of-squares (WGSSQ) for the kth group as the total of squared deviations of the group's observations from the group mean, or:

   $$WGSSQ(k) = \sum_{i=1}^{N_k} (Y_{ik} - \bar{Y}_k)^2,$$

   where

   Y_{ik} = LOS of the ith patient in the kth group;
   N_k = number of patients in the kth group; and

   $$\bar{Y}_k = \sum_{i=1}^{N_k} Y_{ik} = k\text{th group mean.}$$

   c) Compute the total within-group sum-of-squares (TWGSSQ) for the k groups as the sum of the total squared deviations of each group's observations from the respective group mean, or:

   $$TWGSSQ(K) = \sum_{k=1}^{K} WGSSQ(k)$$
   $$= \sum_{k=1}^{K} \sum_{i=1}^{N_k} (Y_{ik} - \bar{Y}_k)^2.$$

   d) Select the K groups such that *TWGSSQ* is minimized and such that no finer partition—a larger K—achieves a reduction in variance that is greater than a predetermined amount. This step is equivalent to maximizing $1 - (TWGSSQ/TSSQ)$, which is the proportionate reduction in variance.

   e) If the K groups in step 2d are not medically meaningful, alter them accordingly and compute the corresponding *TWGSSQ*.

3. Select the independent variable and the medically meaningful partition that achieve the greatest reduction in variance. Repeat step 2 within each of the new groups, using the independent variables that remain.

Source: R.B. Fetter, *AUTOGRP Patient Classification Scheme and Diagnosis Related Groups (DRGs)* (Washington, D.C.: U.S. DHEW, Health Care Financing Administration, 1979). Adapted.

or disregard them. Subsequent partitions are evaluated similarly, and the process continues as long as the following criteria are met:

1. The new groups provide a significant reduction in variance
2. Each new group includes a sufficient number of patients
3. The group length of stay means remain significantly different
4. The number of groups within the MDC is still manageable

When the process is completed, the groups that remain are the DRGs.

In order to derive DRGs for use in New Jersey, AUTOGRP was applied to a data set that consisted of approximately 500,000 inpatient records from the state's 118 participating hospitals, plus about 150,000 records from one Connecticut hospital and 52,000 records from 50 hospitals within a separate PSRO region. The data had been screened for clinical and statistical "outliers," which were removed in order to enhance the likely stability of the resulting DRG categorization. Clinical outliers included patients who died in the hospital, since their treatment patterns could be considered atypical for the diseases or conditions being partitioned. Statistical outliers included records with obvious coding errors or missing data and, most importantly, patients with extremely high lengths of stay.

The AUTOGRP procedure applied to the given data set resulted in a partitioning of the 83 MDCs into 383 DRGs. Figures 11.2 and 11.3 illustrate how the DRGs were constructed for the 1,545 patients who were categorized broadly by primary diagnosis into MDC 68 — diseases of bone and cartilage. As shown, the "best" independent variable for the initial partition was primary surgical procedure, and the split was made simply on the basis of whether or not any surgery at all had been performed. The distinction here by medical treatment was obvious, and a modest differentiation in length-of-stay distribution was also achieved. Subsequently, patients with no surgery were partitioned further into three groups according to the primary surgical procedure performed. No additional partitioning of these five final groups met all of the criteria listed above.

DRGs and Rate Setting

In order to set equitable rates of reimbursement for cases treated in each DRG, the Department of Health conducted various analyses of historical costs. For the most part, costs were allocated according to principles already well established in hospital accounting. Thus, some categories of hospital costs, such as administrative and capital expenses, were considered as fixed regardless of inpatient type and were excluded entirely from the DRG calculations, as were the costs of outpatient services. Physician expenses were also kept separate. Of the remaining categories, which comprised about half of all hospital costs, some such as housekeeping and dietary services were allocated to DRGs on the basis of existing measures of use. Services used in direct patient care, such as radiology and laboratory, were allocated on the basis of proportionate charges.

For purposes of illustration, results of the historical (1978) cost allocations to three representative DRGs treated by the initial 26 participating hospitals are shown in Tables 11.1, 11.2, and 11.3. It was argued that the generally higher DRG costs demonstrated by teaching hospitals were due to legitimate differences in the types of services rendered, not to "inefficiency" per se, and therefore should be reflected in differential rates. It also was argued that

Figure 11.2

PARTITIONING A MAJOR DIAGNOSTIC CATEGORY

(a) Length-of-Stay Distribution for MDC 68:
Diseases of Bone and Cartilage

Mean	Std. Dev.	No. of Patients
7.71	4.50	1545

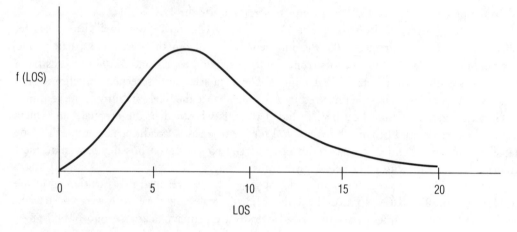

(b) Partitioning by Presence or
Absence of Surgery

	Mean	Std. Dev.	No. of Patients
no surgery:	7.21*	3.89	858
surgery:	8.33	5.16	687

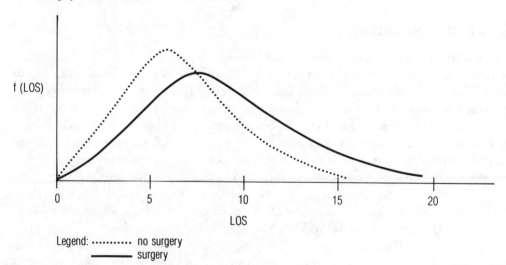

Legend: ·········· no surgery
—————— surgery

Figure 11.2 (continued)

(c) Partitioning by Primary Diagnosis of
Patients with No Surgery

	Mean	Std. Dev.	No. of Patients
A1:	5.23	3.02	338
A2:	8.50	4.37	520

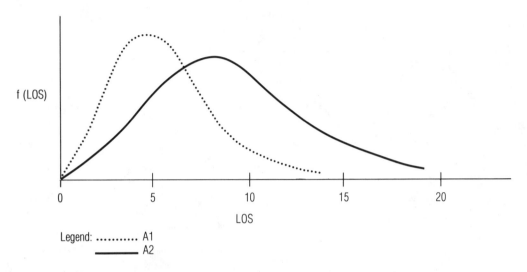

Legend: ·········· A1
 ────── A2

(d) Partitioning by Specific Surgery of
Patients with Surgery

	Mean	Std. Dev.	No. of Patients
B1:	5.91	3.24	278
B2:	7.54	4.50	290
B3:	15.90	8.92	119

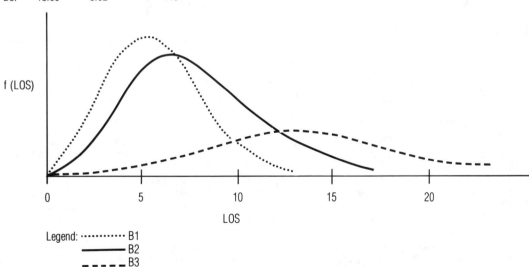

Legend: ··········· B1
 ────── B2
 ── ── ── B3

Source: New Jersey State Department of Health, *A Prospective Reimbursement System Based on Case-Mix for New Jersey Hospitals 1976 – 1981*, Annual Report, Vol. 1 (1977), pp. 13 – 15.

*Recomputed to correct an error in the original table.

Figure 11.3

DRGS 297 TO 301

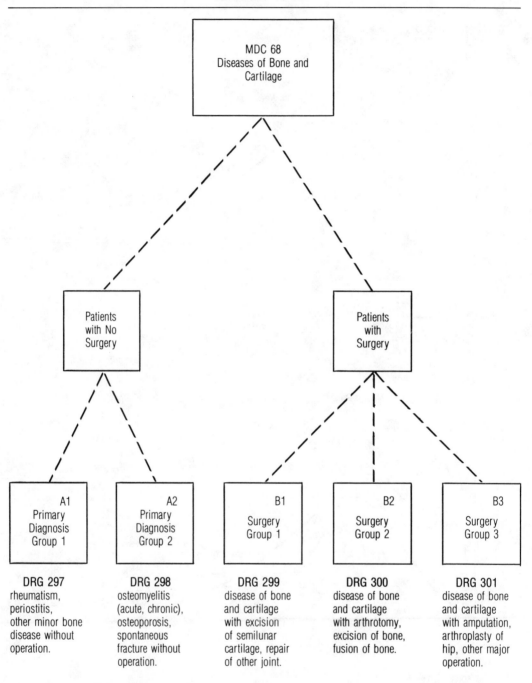

MDC 68
Diseases of Bone and
Cartilage

Patients
with No
Surgery

Patients
with
Surgery

A1
Primary
Diagnosis
Group 1

A2
Primary
Diagnosis
Group 2

B1
Surgery
Group 1

B2
Surgery
Group 2

B3
Surgery
Group 3

DRG 297
rheumatism,
periostitis,
other minor bone
disease without
operation.

DRG 298
osteomyelitis
(acute, chronic),
osteoporosis,
spontaneous
fracture without
operation.

DRG 299
disease of bone
and cartilage
with excision
of semilunar
cartilage, repair
of other joint.

DRG 300
disease of bone
and cartilage
with arthrotomy,
excision of bone,
fusion of bone.

DRG 301
disease of bone
and cartilage
with amputation,
arthroplasty of
hip, other major
operation.

Source: New Jersey Department of Health, *A Prospective Reimbursement System Based on Case-Mix for New Jersey Hospitals 1976–1981*, Annual Report, Vol. 1 (1977), p. 16.

some of the cost differences among hospitals resulted from differences in the market costs of labor inputs, for which the hospitals should not be held responsible. Among the same 26 participants, Table 11.4 indicates the cost differences that might be accounted for in this way, based upon a division of the state into 11 labor-market areas.

Relatively early in the development of the New Jersey program, it was decided that a hospital's own historical cost (initially lagged by two years) would become a factor in the actual DRG per-case reimbursement, rather than the rate being determined entirely by a statewide, standard amount. The resulting payment then would be adjusted to reflect both realized and

Table 11.1

BASE-YEAR (1978) COSTS FOR DRG 121
(Acute Myocardial Infarction)

Hospital[1]	Total Cases[2]	Average LOS	Total Cost	Average Cost (C_{ijk})	Stand. Dev. of Cost
A	312	14.5	$536,328	$1,719	$ 740
B	146	13.8	416,976	2,856	2,041
C	214	13.7	451,968	2,112	1,653
D	178	15.7	412,248	2,316	1,381
E	276	12.4	569,388	2,063	1,098
F	264	14.6	669,240	2,535	1,490
G	159	14.6	347,097	2,183	1,494
Teaching Hospitals	1,549	14.2	$3,403,245	$2,197	$1,353
H	103	14.0	$209,811	$2,037	$1,157
I	150	14.5	285,900	1,906	897
J	112	13.9	215,600	1,925	1,129
K	271	16.2	452,670	1,670	918
L	224	15.3	433,888	1,937	1,129
M	91	13.7	155,519	1,709	1,042
N	135	15.4	275,670	2,042	1,358
O	75	17.4	187,575	2,501	1,275
P	192	13.9	334,080	1,740	972
Q	218	13.6	357,738	1,641	1,103
R	242	12.3	341,704	1,412	808
S	278	14.5	584,356	2,102	1,458
T	165	14.7	272,415	1,651	839
U	128	14.2	197,248	1,541	837
V	54	16.4	99,576	1,844	933
W	121	16.6	272,008	2,248	1,332
X	147	14.0	242,991	1,653	850
Y	143	13.6	247,390	1,730	1,096
Z	68	13.4	115,532	1,699	905
Nonteaching Hospitals	2,917	14.5	$5,281,571	$1,811	$1,104
All Hospitals	4,466	14.4	$8,684,816	$1,945	$1,203

Source: New Jersey State Department of Health.

1. Initial 26 participating hospitals.

2. Outliers excluded: LOS greater than 45 days.

Table 11.2

BASE-YEAR (1978) COSTS FOR DRG 278
(Normal Delivery)

Hospital[1]	Total Cases[2]	Average LOS	Total Cost	Average Cost (C_{ijk})	Stand. Dev. of Cost
B	771	3.4	$461,829	$599	$153
D	980	3.3	529,200	540	94
E	1,185	4.3	734,700	620	125
F	721	4.3	396,550	550	99
G	574	3.7	371,952	648	272
Teaching Hospitals	4,231	3.8	$2,494,231	$590	$147
H	348	3.6	$167,040	$480	$102
I	272	3.5	145,248	534	113
J	618	4.0	239,784	388	90
K	1,298	3.7	481,558	371	61
L	436	3.9	224,976	516	96
M	322	3.3	117,208	364	111
N	310	3.2	187,240	604	136
O	843	3.4	462,807	549	311
P	452	3.4	247,244	547	106
R	646	3.6	319,770	495	110
Nonteaching Hospitals	5,545	3.6	$2,592,875	$468	$161
All Hospitals	9,776	3.7	$5,087,106	$520	$162

Source: New Jersey State Department of Health.

1. Of the initial 26 participating hospitals, 11 have been excluded because mother and infant charges were not reported separately.

2. Outliers excluded: LOS greater than seven days or less than two days.

anticipated inflation, with an eventual reconciliation mechanism available to correct for any misprojections. Another adjustment would increase each payment by a ratio sufficient to reimburse all fixed costs, which would be subject to a separate review. The unadjusted rate setting formula was a weighted sum of the historical cost and a standard cost, as follows:

$$R_{ijk} = (1 - w_{jk}) \cdot C_{ijk} + w_{jk} \cdot S_{ijk},$$

where

R_{ijk} = unadjusted reimbursement rate for a patient in the kth DRG treated in the ith hospital in the jth hospital category (e.g., teaching vs. nonteaching);

C_{ijk} = average (mean) cost of treating a patient in the kth DRG by the ith hospital in the jth hospital category, during a given base year;

S_{ijk} = standard cost of treating a patient in the kth DRG by the ith hospital in the jth hospital category, during the same base year, as determined by statewide patterns of costs; and

w_{jk} = a proportion, which varied by the hospital category and by the DRG.

According to the above weighting procedure, an "inefficient" hospital would not be penalized the entire amount of its cost over the standard; likewise, an "efficient" hospital would not reap the entire potential gain. To some extent, this was considered necessary to allow the industry a reasonable period of time for adjustment to the new system. The weighted formulation, however, also gave the Department of Health an opportunity to refine the structure of incentives and to adapt somewhat to the recognized problems imposed by deficiencies in the DRGs themselves. Some of these problems are described in the sections that follow.[18]

Recognizing the Problems

Length of Stay as the Dependent Variable

Because the DRG method had been developed initially for utilization review, in which the major concern is the appropriateness of extending a patient's period of hospitalization, the use of length of stay as the dependent variable in the classification algorithm had been easy to

Table 11.3

BASE-YEAR (1978) COSTS FOR DRG 368
(Severe Burn)

Hospital[1]	Total Cases[2]	Average LOS	Total Cost	Average Cost (C_{ijk})	Stand. Dev. of Cost
A	36	17.7	$111,096	$3,086	$3,882
B	27	9.4	24,624	912	953
E	16	21.6	38,704	2,419	2,578
F	127	21.1	887,222	6,886	7,880
G	14	14.4	16,758	1,197	815
Others	14	13.2	19,166	1,369	986
Teaching Hospitals	234	18.4	$1,097,570	$4,690	$6,275
I	11	16.4	$ 16,500	$1,500	$1,647
K	11	15.9	11,781	1,071	912
L	17	18.1	36,329	2,137	2,885
M	11	10.2	8,525	775	498
N	11	5.3	5,236	476	269
Q	19	6.8	11,590	610	367
R	10	10.3	9,850	985	998
S	10	18.8	20,580	2,058	2,566
U	11	6.9	5,577	507	526
W	12	14.1	13,968	1,164	1,537
Y	16	5.8	6,944	434	222
Others	44	8.9	37,664	856	844
Nonteaching Hospitals	183	10.8	$ 184,544	$1,008	$1,373
All Hospitals	417	15.5	$1,282,114	$3,075	$5,085

Source: New Jersey State Department of Health.

1. Initial 26 hospitals; those with less than ten cases in the DRG are grouped as "others."

2. Outliers excluded: LOS greater than 73 days.

Table 11.4

LABOR-WAGE INDEX

Hospital	Index	Hospital	Index
A	99.0%	N	100.5%
B	111.2	O	111.6
C	103.9	P	92.7
D	97.8	Q	93.7
E	103.2	R	93.3
F	104.9	S	110.4
G	104.7	T	90.2
H	98.0	U	92.4
I	97.0	V	97.2
J	97.5	W	97.5
K	95.0	X	93.4
L	101.4	Y	95.5
M	103.4	Z	90.2

The labor-wage index measures the relationship between the total costs of a hospital that pays its nonphysician employees wages representative of its own labor-market area and the total costs that would be incurred if statewide average wages were paid, all other factors being held constant. For example, Hospital B above is located in a high-wage area, to which an extra 11.2 percent in total costs (1978) can be attributed. The labor-wage index α_{ij} for the ith hospital in the jth hospital category is computed as follows:

$$\alpha_{ij} = \frac{\sum_{m=1}^{8} (L_{ijm} \times w_{ijm}) + G_{ij}}{\sum_{m=1}^{8} (L_{ijm} \times w_m) + G_{ij}},$$

where L_{ijm} is the number of hours worked by employees in job class m, w_{ijm} is the average hourly wage for job class m in the hospital's labor-market area, w_m is the statewide average wage for job class m, and G_{ij} is the total cost of all other nonfixed, nonphysician inputs to inpatient care. The eight job classes are:

m		m	
1	Registered Nurses	5	Technicians
2	Licensed Practical Nurses	6	Therapists
3	Attendants	7	General Services
4	Clerical	8	Administrative

Source: New Jersey State Department of Health. Modified for illustration.

justify. The program of rate setting and reimbursement in New Jersey, however, was intended to provide a hospital with an equitable return based on the *resources consumed* in appropriate treatment of the patient. Clearly, length of stay cannot be a precise measure of resource consumption, because the intensity of service is likely to vary across patient conditions and may vary also across hospitals and individual attending physicians. In such instances, the total cost per case represents an obvious alternative measure.

The developers of DRGs recognized that length of stay "may not be as accurate an indicator of the level of output as actual costs" but justified its use because "it is still an important indicator of utilization as well as being easily available, well standardized, and reliable." Further, clinical judgments might be brought into the system more easily, at least initially, if length of stay rather than cost was the unit of measurement. Nevertheless, "if cost information is readily available and well standardized, that would be a preferable alternative to length of stay as the output utilization measure."[19]

Standardized, statewide cost information was unavailable at the time the DRGs were initially developed for New Jersey. But, in order to establish rates of reimbursement, a uniform accounting system (based upon SHARE) and collection of cost and billing information were part of the program's requirements. It was envisioned that these cost data would serve as the basis for a future reformulation of the DRGs. However, there seems to have been no serious consideration given to postponing implementation until such time as the DRGs could be based upon cost.

Homogeneity and Prediction

The ultimate goal of the Yale DRG team was to identify "classes of patients for whom consistent, stable, and reliable patterns of resource consumption could be predicted during any episode of care."[20] Thus, a criterion employed by AUTOGRP in the creation of DRGs was the reduction in variance of a measure of resource consumption. But, if length of stay was not a precise indicator of resource consumption, then prediction would be hampered accordingly. Further, even if length of stay was accepted as a valid measure, the resulting DRGs differed considerably as to their homogeneity. For example, of the standard deviations in the five DRG length-of-stay distributions illustrated in parts (c) and (d) of Figure 11.2, three are less than that of the "parent" MDC, one is greater, and one is equal. Finally, the DRGs were derived from a given set of data obtained from several sources, and their ability to predict patterns of resource consumption strictly within the state of New Jersey remained an open question. All these issues had to be addressed by the state when it adopted the DRGs as the basis for prospective payment.

To some extent, a lack of homogeneity in resources and costs was fully expected, given the counterproductive incentives of the existing reimbursement system. And in fact, the Department of Health made such diversity a major target of its new program:

> If, regrettably, John Jones has another heart attack five years from now, the situation in payment for his hospital stay should be very much different. The costs of the stay will not vary nearly so much as they do now depending on who is paying for them nor on the particular hospital John chooses.[21]

But the objectionable diversity clearly pertained to the cost of treating the *same* medical condition. While the DRGs were portrayed as being "medically meaningful," the medical conditions included within each DRG were not the same, as even a cursory examination could reveal (see Figure 11.3, for example). Reducing the array of possible diagnoses to a "manageable" number was the intent of the whole process. Thus, a lack of homogeneity in resources consumed could not be due entirely to differences in treatment patterns.

In public presentations, the state gave little recognition to homogeneity or to any of the other technical issues that affect the use of a given set of DRGs in the rate-setting process. For example, the Department of Health stated in a summary paper distributed prior to a public hearing in late 1979 that "all the cases within a DRG are identical in the kinds of medical treatment they should require."[22] The actual regulations, however, did include a mechanism designed to allow for problems in homogeneity and prediction. Department of Health staff had examined empirical length-of-stay distributions for each DRG and had developed a set of high and low "trim" points. Just as outliers were removed from the data used to derive the DRGs, patients whose lengths of stay fell outside the trim designations were excluded from the process of reimbursement by DRG. Hospitals would receive "fair" payment from these patients on the basis of itemized charges for services rendered. To illustrate, DRGs 297 to 301 (Figures 11.2 and 11.3) were initially assigned upper trim points of 28, 47, 18, 40, and 67 days, respectively; only DRG 301 was also assigned a lower trim point—2 days. Over all DRGs, the cases excluded by the initial trim points accounted for approximately one-tenth of the recognized inpatient costs.

Homogeneity across Payers

The formulation of the New Jersey DRGs did not specify a patient's source of payment as an independent variable for analyzing resource consumption. This strategy avoided the recognition of a relationship that might have been due entirely to the effects of the method of payment, cost-based vs. charge-based, which would be irrelevant upon implementation of a new, uniform reimbursement policy. Yet, variation in resource consumption may also have been attributable to patients' social and demographic characteristics, which might relate systematically to the source of payment and would not be altered by a change in the payment mechanism.

Blue Cross officials pointed to the "special" characteristics of their subscriber population in arguing for retention of a differential similar to what previously had existed between the Blue Cross per diem and the average charges made to commercial insurers. They contended that, in the "public interest," Blue Cross's willingness to provide coverage for individuals and small employee groups resulted in a higher-risk population than that selectively covered by the commercial companies.[23] Eventually, the rate-setting commission did agree to a small adjustment—4.05 percent.

Given rejection now of the principle that all payers would be treated "alike," the rates charged to the governmental payers might also be questioned. Since these payers covered *only* the low-income and the elderly, would the medical-social problems of their subscribers generally require a greater intensity of service within certain DRGs? Under the old system, in fact, Medicare had paid an 8.5 percent addition to a hospital's usual per diem charge for nursing services. Yet only a minority of the DRGs were defined by an age characteristic, and very few employed a "split" in the sixties that would broadly distinguish Medicare subscribers from other patients.

The equitable allocation of nursing costs represented a general challenge for the rate-setting process. These costs had been measured only by patient days within large specialty services (medical-surgical, obstetric, etc.), which is probably not a sensitive enough indicator of resource consumption. To provide a better method, the Department of Health engaged in several special studies. One of these measured the time spent by nurses in direct care for 3,497 patients treated at three hospitals. Since this population did not provide samples large enough for analysis of each of the 383 DRGs, the MDCs were used instead. A multiple-regression model was developed to explain nursing activity for an MDC as follows:

$$Y = a + b_1U + b_2V + b_3W + b_4X + e,$$
where

Y = total nursing minutes over the entire length of stay (LOS),

U = LOS squared,
V = LOS,
W = patient's age,
X = presence ($=1$) or absence ($=0$) of surgery,
a = constant term, and
e = error term.

The equation estimated for MDC 28 (arrythmia and slowed conduction) is shown below (standard errors are in parentheses; only statistically significant coefficients were reported):

$$Y = 5288 + 27U - 89W + 3161X, n = 22, R^2 = .77.$$
$$\quad\quad (4)\quad (34)\quad (1454)$$

This equation is typical in that the Department of Health indicated all three independent variables (LOS whether squared or not) as generally influential in the directions shown (although few individual equations actually contained this many significant coefficients).[24] The relationships involving length of stay and surgery were fully expected, but the *negative* coefficient of age was a surprise. Certainly the extra payment from Medicare appeared inappropriate under this circumstance.

The nursing-cost studies provided justification for disallowing any additional charge to Medicare, but the regression equations were not otherwise used in setting rates, for the following reasons: (1) the small sample sizes in some MDCs, (2) the "pilot study" nature of the allocation technique, and (3) anticipated improvements through further proposed analyses.[25] Thus, for the 1980 rates, nursing costs were allocated to DRGs on a per diem basis, with no differentiation by payer or by any other characteristic.

Homogeneity and Payment

Even if conclusive evidence had existed showing that the costs of treatment within DRGs were not likely to vary systematically by payer, the DRGs' general lack of complete homogeneity would become a more salient issue to some payers than to others. Primarily this was due to the decision to use the DRG rates for billing and payment, not just for budgeting and reconciliation, and to include all payers in the process.

For the large-volume payers—Blue Cross, Medicare, and Medicaid—who previously had dealt with complex cost formulas, the DRG computations could be viewed as a different way of organizing the same set of information. Given the large volume of claims expected in each DRG, the reimbursement methodology would yield predictable aggregate payments, much as the per diem mechanism had done. These payers thus did not have to be concerned with the *actual* cost of care for specific patients whom they had insured, since the "losses" on claims with costs below the DRG rates would be balanced by the "savings" on claims with costs above the DRG rates. However, self-pay patients and insurers with small numbers of New Jersey subscribers, who had formerly been billed itemized charges, now faced the prospect of having to pay a rate based upon average costs without the statistical "protection" against deviations from the mean that accompanies large samples. Protests were foreseeable from those whose costs of treatment fell substantially below the DRG billings but whose lengths of stay exceeded the lower trim points specified for exclusion from the system. Of course, these trim points could be raised, but at the disadvantage of excluding large numbers of cases from reimbursement by DRG. Further, protection of the *hospitals'* financial positions might require similar trims at the other end of the DRG distributions.

Although the initiative for including self-payers and commercial insurers in a payment-by-case system appears to have come from the federal level, there is evidence that state officials did not appreciate fully the extent of the potential problem. In critiquing SHARE within the initial DRG proposal to the Social Security Administration, the Department of Health wrote: "The 'per diem' reimbursement for all classes of patients, as presently constructed, is unfair and misleading. Since the per diem system is essentially a system of aggregating and averaging, it is unfair to the consumer who is paying effectively for all services, not just those he uses." Yet the DRG reimbursement formulas also clearly constituted a "system of aggregating and averaging," and the services for which the patient would pay need not be "just those he uses." In fact, whether the grouping procedure per se would lessen the discrepancy between the "cost" and the "price" of a given hospital case was unclear. Under the old system, in which a payer was charged the product of the hospital's per diem and the patient's actual length of stay, variations in the intensity of service could not be recognized. Under the new DRG system, recognition of the intensity of service probably would increase, but variation in length of stay within DRGs would be ignored.

Stability and Manipulation

The capability of DRGs to predict resource consumption rested not only on their homogeneity with respect to the dependent variable but also on the stability of clinical and administrative decisions made over time. In particular, if a new system of reimbursement were based upon DRGs, then the altered incentives might change the behavior of physicians and administrators to the point where resource allocations exhibited little resemblance to those in the data base originally used to construct the groupings. Again, of course, creating incentives for change was precisely what the Department of Health hoped to accomplish. And if over time some DRGs became less useful than others as predictors of resource consumption, then the reimbursement formulas might be adjusted accordingly. Nevertheless, it seemed likely that sequential reformulations would be necessary if the initial properties of the DRGs were to be maintained.

The potential instability of DRGs would probably have been regarded as a very minor annoyance if it could have been attributed entirely to changed behavior in accordance with the objectives of the reimbursement program. But counterincentives may be envisioned also. Primarily these concern the extent to which the demographic, diagnostic, and therapeutic characteristics that were used to classify patients can be manipulated for reimbursement purposes. As the only demographic variable used to assign patients to DRGs, age clearly is exogenous to a hospital's classification process. However, the therapeutic characteristics — primary and secondary surgical procedures — in theory can be manipulated, placing more patients into high-reimbursement DRGs by increasing the frequency of costly, perhaps dangerous surgery. Even then, however, professional standards and malpractice judgments should restrain such practices.

The major area of concern regarding the classification of patients involved the primary and secondary diagnoses. These variables would be determined primarily by the judgment of the attending physician, given the symptoms presented by the patient. In "gray" areas of diagnosis, the physician might be persuaded to act systematically in the financial interests of the hospital. Even if not, multiple diagnoses often would be made quite properly, leaving discretion as to which the hospital would report. Further, some DRGs were distinguished purely by the presence or absence of *any* secondary diagnosis, whether or not clinically related to the primary condition. In *The DRG Maze,* the New Jersey Hospital Association suggested that "the financial status of hospitals could be impaired" by the unfamiliarity of medical records departments with the need to "determine which of all a patient's diagnoses is critical in terms of resource consumption." Other observers, however, hypothesized that medical records personnel would learn the system very quickly, given their opportunity to select from several possible DRGs the one that would result in maximum net reimbursement to the hospital.

State health officials believed that "end runs" and "gamesmanship" by participating hospitals would not create major difficulties, for two reasons. First, blatant manipulation, perhaps as evidenced by wide shifts in a hospital's case mix from year to year, would be uncovered by the normal process of review. Second, since part of the hospital's reimbursement would be determined by its own historical cost, the "coding up" of a low-cost case into a higher-reimbursement DRG would be reflected by a lower rate in a succeeding year. And, if all hospitals behaved similarly, the statewide standard would also be reduced. Thus, after several years, an equilibrium would be reached, which would present no further incentives for manipulation in DRG coding.

IMPLEMENTATION AND CONJECTURE

What would be the future of hospital rate setting by DRG in the state of New Jersey? As in any question of implementation, assessment of the technical character of the policy components must be coupled with assessment of the likely behavior and political strength of the various affected actors. Envisioning a set of possible scenarios may be helpful. For example, the *best* eventuality may be the following:

Shortly before each hospital is brought into the DRG system, physicians and administrators begin meeting to discuss patterns of treatment and the resulting financial effects upon their institution. Excessive laboratory tests and other procedures that cannot be demonstrated as favorable to patient outcomes are eliminated. Rather quickly, differences in treatment patterns within the hospital are reduced. Over time, differences across hospitals are lessened also, and the reimbursement rates for individual DRGs become more and more dependent upon statewide standard amounts. A few notoriously ill-managed hospitals cannot meet their expenses and are forced to close, thereby increasing the occupancy rates at less costly neighboring institutions, which in turn creates additional economies. Some hospitals begin to specialize in treating certain DRGs and acquire a reputation for high-quality, cost-effective care. Reimbursement by DRG is extended to cases that may be treated more efficiently in an outpatient setting, and corresponding reductions in the incidence of hospitalization are observed. Inflation in total health care costs for the state of New Jersey is constrained dramatically, while research ascertains no negative effects upon clinical outcomes of care. Patient surveys indicate a heightened understanding of medical diagnoses and treatments and a greater satisfaction with the overall process of care. Finally, adoption by the federal Medicare and Medicaid programs of policies similar to the New Jersey demonstration leave the state's hospitals, now experienced with per-case payments, in a highly advantaged position.

Conversely, the *worst* scenario might resemble this:

Complaints from patients and insurers who believe their DRG charges are excessive compared to the services actually received are given wide publicity by the media. Organized groups of physicians begin an intensive lobbying effort to discredit DRG reimbursement as an intrusion on individualized treatment and the practitioner-patient relationship, while their statistical consultants affirm the inability of DRGs to account fully for legitimate differences in medical conditions. The Department of Health also adopts a critical attitude, but primarily toward hospitals that it accuses of questionable diagnostic recording, improper patient referrals, and inappropriate discharges and readmissions of the same patients. Elsewhere, reports of skimping on care, particularly that rendered to Medicaid and medically indigent patients, become widespread. Hospital administrators criticize the state's reports as hopelessly out of date for management purposes and become frustrated over continual changes in DRG defi- nitions, "outlier" specifications, and reimbursement formulas. Penalties and appeals delay the setting of new rates, and some hospitals threaten to deny admission to patients in certain diagnostic categories unless reimbursement is increased. Faced with the loss of services con- sidered essential to their communities, New Jersey state legislators hold hearings preliminary to terminating DRG rate setting. The governor and other state officials, feeling little com- mitment to a program initiated by their predecessors, offer only token resistance. The system collapses.

Among the many *intermediate* scenarios is the following:

After a long series of complaints, the billing of patients and insurers on a DRG basis is discontinued, and a system of state-controlled, per-service charges is instituted instead. DRG utilization and cost data continue to be collected statewide and are used in the prospective setting of hospital budgets. But specific rates are established for only a small number of common, relatively uncomplicated diagnoses. For the rest, a DRG index is computed to represent a hospital's case-mix complexity and is used in conjunction with numerous other factors to determine peer groups for comparison of rates. Subsequent to an initial flurry of activity, hospitals are able to cut back a bit on the additional numbers of accountants, statis- ticians, and lawyers who were hired to achieve maximum reimbursement under the DRG system. The regulatory task force at the state level is also able to stabilize. The student of public policy comes to regard the DRG approach as an admirable attempt to define a "product" where an industry had been unable to do so previously but, as used for allocating actual dollars, a regulatory device caught up in a never-ending struggle with the complexity of its subject.

NOTES

1. R.S. Powell, *Bureaucratic Malpractice* (Princeton, N.J.: Center for the Analysis of Public Issues, 1974).
2. *Newark Star-Ledger*, June 18, 1974.
3. *Newark Star-Ledger*, September 22, 1974.
4. U.S. General Accounting Office, *Rising Hospital Costs can be Restrained by Regulating Payments and Improving Management*, Report No. HRD-80-72, September 19, 1980; N. Worthington et al., *National Hospital Rate-Setting Study, Vol. VI: Case Study of Prospective Reimbursement in New Jersey* (Washington, D.C.: U.S. DHEW, Health Care Financing Administration, 1980).

5. B. Biles, C.J. Schramm, and J.G. Atkinson, "Hospital Cost Inflation Under State Rate-Setting Programs," *New England Journal of Medicine* 303 (1980):664.
6. *Newark Star-Ledger*, March 15, 1977.
7. *Atlantic City Press*, March 21, 1977.
8. *Bergen Record*, July 21, 1978.
9. *Newark Star-Ledger*, December 3, 1978.
10. *New York Times*, March 2, 1980.
11. *Bergen Record*, August 30, 1979.
12. New Jersey Hospital Association, *The DRG Maze: Unravelling the Mysteries of Hospital Reimbursement in New Jersey* (Princeton, N.J.: New Jersey Hospital Association, 1979).
13. M.S. Feldstein, *Economic Analysis for Health Services Efficiency* (Amsterdam: North-Holland Publishing, 1967). Preliminary findings concerning the impact of case-mix on cost appeared in M.S. Feldstein, "Hospital Cost Variations and Case Mix Differences," *Medical Care* 3 (1965):95.
14. R.B. Fetter, *AUTOGRP Patient Classification Scheme and Diagnosis Related Groups (DRGs)* (Washington, D.C.: U.S. DHEW, Health Care Financing Administration, 1979).
15. R. Mills et al., "AUTOGRP: An Interactive Computer System for the Analysis of Health Care Data," *Medical Care* 14 (1976):603.
16. J.N. Morgan and J.A. Sonquist, "Problems in the Analysis of Survey Data, and a Proposal," *Journal of the American Statistical Association* 58 (1963):415.
17. W.A. Ericson, "A Note on Partitioning for Maximum Between-Group Sums of Squares," in *The Detection of Interaction Effects*, ed. J. Sonquist and J. Morgan (Ann Arbor, Mich.: University of Michigan, Institute for Social Research, 1964).
18. Published critiques of DRGs and their use in reimbursement, available by the time of implementation in New Jersey, include the following: D.J. Belding, "DRG Reimbursements Being Rushed," *Modern Healthcare* 9, no. 7 (1979):74; P.L. Grimaldi, "Physicians and the DRG Model," *Journal of the Medical Society of New Jersey* 77 (1980):279; S.D. Horn and D.N. Schumacher, "An Analysis of Case Mix Complexity Using Information Theory and Diagnostic Related Groupings," *Medical Care* 17 (1979):382; D.N. Schumacher et al., "Hospital Cost per Case: Analysis Using a Statewide Data System," *Medical Care* 17 (1979):1037; H. Smejda, "N.J. to Test Payment by Case Mix," *Hospital Financial Management* 31, no. 7 (1977):10; and W.W. Young, R.B. Swinkola, and M.A. Hutton, "Assessment of the AUTOGRP Patient Classification System," *Medical Care* 18 (1980):228.
19. R.B. Fetter et al., "Case Mix Definition by Diagnosis-Related Groups," *Medical Care* 18 (February 1980, supplement).
20. Fetter, *AUTOGRP and DRGs*, p. 1.
21. New Jersey State Department of Health, "Summary of Senate Bill 446," August 29, 1979.
22. Ibid.
23. *New York Daily News*, January 20, 1980.
24. New Jersey State Department of Health, "The Allocation of Hospital Inpatient Nursing Costs Using Case-Mix Sensitive Relative Intensity Measures: A Description of the Method and Its Application to 1979 Rate-Setting," 2d revision, February 1, 1979.
25. New Jersey State Department of Health, "A Prospective Reimbursement System Based on Patient Case-Mix for New Jersey Hospitals 1976-1983," Tenth Quarter Report, Volume 1 (September 10, 1979), p. 81.

12

HealthCare, Inc.

Kyle L. Grazier

Ed: We've been in this position many times before, Pat, and I just don't see how it can be resolved rationally. HealthCare has provided you with what we consider a fair capitation for our enrollees. But you claim it's not adequate.

Pat: But it's not, Ed. Our records at MediCenter show increasing utilization by the HMO enrollees and we must adjust to cover these costs.

Ed: But if you could get control over your physicians . . .

Pat: Control! MediCenter's physicians are not only productive, they are efficient!

Donna Roche, Director of Marketing for HealthCare, watched and listened. It was not the first debate of this kind she had witnessed during the "negotiation" phase for setting capitation rates for the group practice–HMO contract. And it was not the first time she had felt the frustration of inadequate management data. By the end of the second day, she vowed that next year the process—and outcome—would be different. She interrupted their debate:

Ed, Pat, let me make an observation. HealthCare needs MediCenter to provide services, and your history is a good one for good-quality care to these people. The families in the area like the physicians; the facilities are good; we are responsive. HealthCare provides MediCenter with an important source of patients—a growing source, I might add. What neither of us have is the means to measure accurately the products of our businesses. If we had a supporting data structure which allowed us to identify the resource use that the products entail, we could price the services more accurately and, in turn, set more equitable rates. Once this major task was complete, we could further refine our information system to assist us with budgeting, planning, and productivity evaluation. Just in accomplishing this first phase, with rate-setting improvement as our goal, these negotiations could rely less on guesses and more on facts.

Ed Danish, Chief Executive Officer (CEO) of HealthCare, Inc., and Patricia Flanders, Executive Director of MediCenter, listened to Ms. Roche as she explained how she envisioned an information system which would support a cost accounting system for each organization. She explained the parallels she had observed with ACME manufacturing, her former employer. If the appropriate data were collected reliably and retrieved easily, she explained, product costing could be achieved.

Ed and Pat seemed to buy, in theory, the ideas and explanation of a cost-accounting model for a health care facility, but they were skeptical whether the concepts could be applied to an ambulatory care setting. Ms. Roche suggested they share in the costs of a consultant to examine the feasibility of the ideas and the potential for designing a computer-based system to support the mechanics.

John McGuire, an accountant and information systems specialist, was introduced to the administrative staffs at both organizations. Through informal discussions with many of the staff, he learned the history of HealthCare and MediCenter, and details about the present information system.

HISTORY OF HEALTHCARE

HealthCare, Inc., is a federally qualified health maintenance organization (HMO) which has been in existence since July 1980. As a group model HMO, it contracts for ambulatory care services with a multispecialty group practice, MediCenter. Ten of the twenty-seven physicians from MediCenter were the incorporators and original shareholders of the for-profit HMO. Dr. Carson, one of the founders, frequently relates with a smile how he and his colleagues decided after ten years of practicing with a large multispecialty group practice that they wanted to "try the prepayment idea." The group was confident that with some good management behind them they could control the use of unnecessary services, give good medical care, and make a profit.

After investigating several HMO/fee-for-service plans in Colorado, Minnesota, and Wisconsin, they hired Ed Danish, a former administrator from one of these plans, to arrange legal and medical details with the objective of beginning enrollment in mid-1980. Mr. Danish procured the services of an attorney who prepared the articles of incorporation and filed with the state, forming HealthCare, Inc., on January 1, 1980. Mr. Danish became CEO and, at the outset, chose to operate with a small administrative organization in which a few individuals were responsible for well-defined functions. The financial director, marketing director, and medical director were the key actors and met with him frequently on formal and informal bases (see Figure 12.1 for organizational chart).

The Board has been pleased with the success of the HMO (see Tables 12.1 and 12.2 for financial statements). Since its establishment, member enrollment has grown from 5,000 after six months to 26,000 members after two and one-half years. Disenrollment has averaged less than 3 percent per year. Four additional specialists have been offered equity positions in the HMO since its inception. The plan's competition, a one-year-old Independent Practice Association (IPA) and a ten-year-old staff model HMO, have remained a minimal threat to its growth.

The services the HMO initially offered to its group and individual subscribers were and still are fairly standard; it has most likely been MediCenter's reputation for high-quality accessible care in the city which has made the HMO an attractive option for employers. Ambulatory care facilities include specialist offices, a laboratory, pharmacy, radiology services, and an urgent care unit—all open six days a week, 7:00 A.M. to 7:00 P.M. Telephone consultation with a nurse practitioner is available 24 hours a day.

Inpatient services are provided with a $50 deductible/day in any of three hospitals in

Figure 12.1

HEALTHCARE, INC., ORGANIZATIONAL CHART
July 1982

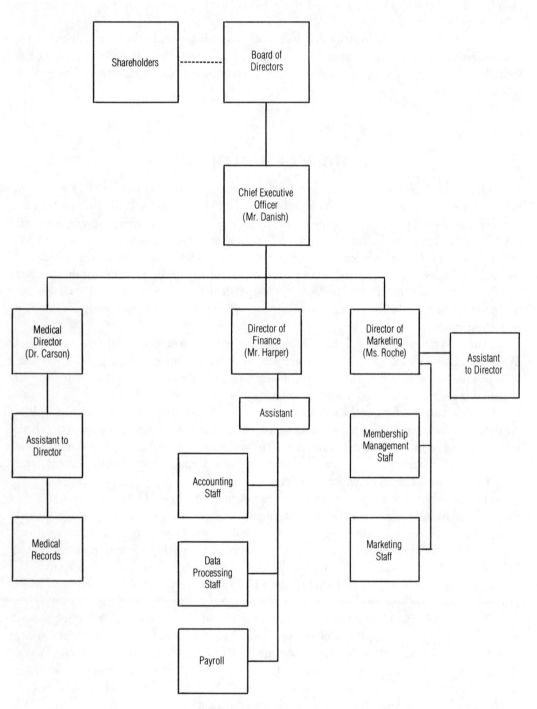

the vicinity: St. Bernard's Hospital, a 300-bed community hospital; Marion Community Hospital with 400 beds; and City General, a 600-bed teaching hospital. The HMO has contracted with St. Bernard's to discount charges for HealthCare enrollee inpatient services by 9 percent, and an attempt is made to pay St. Bernard's within 30 days of use. The other two hospitals bill charges and are paid anywhere from 45 to 90 days after care is rendered. There is a $15 copayment required of the enrollee for each emergency room visit. All hospitals bill charges for emergency room use. Costs to the enrollees as group members are competitive with the Blue Cross/Blue Shield plan, the HMOs, and the commercial carriers in the area (see Table 12.3 for rates). Group members can convert to individual-based coverage upon a health screening examination; however, only 3 percent of the members are not part of an employer group.

Utilization of services by HealthCare enrollees is below national norms, averaging 3.02 ambulatory visits/member/year and 400 patient days/1000 members/year. The HMO attributes the low rates partly to its policy regarding the use of the primary care physician — all members of a family must select a physician and have all care provided or approved by that physician for the care to be covered. This helps to assure continuity of care to the patient and sufficient physician knowledge of the patient's history to minimize redundant or ineffective services.

HISTORY OF MEDICENTER

MediCenter has been a multispecialty group practice serving the city for 15 years. It has grown from 5 primary care physicians to 27 full- and part-time physicians representing most specialties and subspecialties. Assisting in the care provided are 25 nurses, 4 physician's assistants, and 30 health technicians. MediCenter uses the same staff for fee-for-service (FFS) and HealthCare, Inc., capitated patients.

Administratively, MediCenter is organized similarly to the HMO (see Figure 12.2). Patricia Flanders, the Executive Director, answers to the Board of Directors, and oversees the activities of her director of finance, health services and operations directors, marketing/member services director, and medical director. The Medical Director, Dr. Spring, and the Director of Finance, Ms. Marici, have been in their positions for about four years; however, turnover in the membership and health services directors' positions has been active, with both positions now filled by relative newcomers to the organization (membership director — 8 months; health services director — 13 months). Turnover in leadership of these departments mirrors the turnover of their staff, with average terms of employment being less than 18 months.

HealthCare, Inc., is viewed as one of MediCenter's ten profit centers, similar to the departmental profit centers such as Obstetrics-Gynecology, Surgery, and Pharmacy. An attempt is made to make each profit center self-supporting. The capitation fees paid by HealthCare comprise a pool of money out of which services provided to the HMO patient are covered. In the two and one-half years of HealthCare's existence, the proportion of Medicenter's patient visits accounted for by HMO enrollees has increased from 5 percent in January 1981 to almost 30 percent at present (Tables 12.4 and 12.5).

Figure 12.2

MEDICENTER ORGANIZATIONAL CHART
July 1982

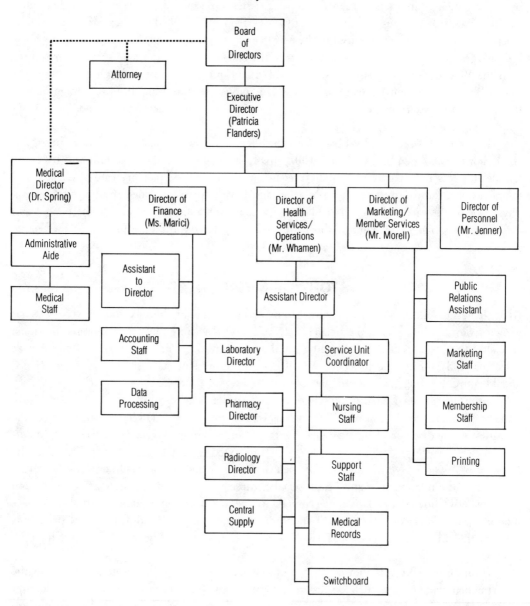

THE INFORMATION SYSTEM: SERVICE DELIVERY

Registration

HMO enrollees who use the group practice for services are treated in the same manner as the FFS patients. Upon entering the facility, they are greeted by a receptionist whose responsibility it is to establish the membership in HealthCare, Inc. If the enrollee has a member identification card, the task becomes one of verification, comparing a card number with the number on a printout generated monthly by the service bureau contracted by MediCenter to aggregate member information. If, however, the enrollee has joined the plan within the last month, does not have a card, or has an unrecognizable ID number, the process becomes much more time-consuming and difficult for all concerned. Without an ID number, medical records cannot be obtained, no patient history is available, and at least partial payment must be obtained upon receipt of services. Few enrollees are tolerant of the delay. They are required to complete another application form (in addition to the one completed at their job site), and a patient medical history, and to provide the cashier with a $25.00 deposit, which, they are told, will be returned once membership has been verified. For many enrollees, deductions for the HMO benefits have already appeared on their paychecks, and many have been told by their supervisors or unions that out-of-pocket expenses will be minimal. The identification procedures required of approximately one-fourth of the incoming patients prior to receipt of care are often disillusioning to enrollees and staff.

Provision of Services

In some cases, arrival at the service unit (having conquered the registration process) does not guarantee service. Often, termination information does not filter back to registration for two to three months. If an enrollee has been terminated as an HMO member two to three months prior to a visit, registration will have no record of it unless the provider makes a note on the encounter form on an earlier visit. If the receptionist at the service unit notes such a termination in the medical record, she must call the data processing or medical records department to verify its accuracy. If it is accurate, then the patient must return to the registration desk and agree to pay for the services received that day, or establish his coverage by another carrier.

The fee-for-service organization of MediCenter permits the HMO to collect information on charges per service; both service and charge are recorded on charge slips generated at each service site. The patient's name and enrollment (ID) number, the ordering or attending physician's name, the code for service, and service charges appear on triple-carboned charge slips. The top sheet remains in the medical chart, the second sheet is sent nightly to data processing, and the third goes to the service unit and eventually to the billing department, where all such sheets are batched and sent to St. Bernard's Hospital. At St. Bernard's, the billing data are keypunched and a report is generated for each account. These reports then become the basis for the manual billing process, which is handled at MediCenter and at HealthCare, Inc.

The encounter form also contains a wealth of member data (see Appendix 12.1). Upon each visit or use of service, an encounter form is completed by the nurse, physician, or technician who has had contact with the enrollee. Reason for visit, procedures ordered, and prescriptions recommended are written in longhand; codes for common diagnoses and procedures are listed and can be checked (x) to simplify recording. Often, the physician's assistant completes the charge slips from the information recorded by the physician on the encounter forms. The form is considered one of the most useful documents in the chart; it is referred to by consulting physicians, the pharmacist, or in telephone care requests. At this time, there are no carbons of the encounter form, although several practitioners have expressed their desire to see more than one copy on file.

Medical Records

The medical record, or chart, contains a wealth of information on eligibility for care, medical history, services provided, payment mechanism, and charges. Theoretically, all information relative to the patient should appear in the chart in an accurate, timely manner. However, understaffing in the medical records department often makes personnel responsibilities overwhelming. While charts are filed in an alphabetic, color-coded scheme, much time is spent tracking down charts which have been held in a unit for additional information, held in the laboratory or in the X-ray unit for results to be added, or held in the nurse-practitioner's office in response to a phone call until the physician can review it and the patient's call can be returned. Charts are often gone from medical records for over a week. For those charts that are available, organization of forms within the chart is haphazard; information on address, telephone number, or enrollment status is often incomplete or inaccurate.

The person in charge of medical records would like to maintain a minimum data set similar to that kept by hospitals (see Appendix 12.2), but the work load is so great that planning for these changes is not possible.

THE INFORMATION SYSTEM: MARKETING

HealthCare's Marketing Director, Ms. Roche, has been working most of the accounts herself with the assistance of an administrative intern and clerical staff. After initial contact by telephone, she visits the benefits director of a company and explains the plan. This has made her familiar with the majority of coverage packages being offered in the area so that benefit comparisons can be made and hopefully used to support the acceptance of the plan.

The majority of the time and effort spent by Ms. Roche in her role as Marketing Director involves selecting the employer groups believed to be a good risk for the plan. Because of the paucity of utilization data available for new groups and the inability to track and identify similar groups already enrolled, her decisions as to the risk level of the potential enrollees are often not as informed as she would like. In addition, the delays in data processing often make it difficult to notify the group practice of the numbers and characteristics of new enrollees, information which might be useful in their personnel and program planning.

THE INFORMATION SYSTEM: FINANCE

The Director of Finance, Mr. Harper, shares Ms. Roche's concerns about high-risk groups. The rates that he calculates and sends to the insurance commissioner must reflect the potential costs to the plan of providing services and administering the accounts. If he could accurately document past utilization experience, diagnostic mix, and demographic characteristics of past or potential enrollees, he could substantiate requests for particular partitioning of rates. He is also aware that the Health Care Financing Administration is determined to have case mix reflected in the amounts paid by them for outpatient services provided to Medicare beneficiaries, as is now done for inpatient care through the use of the Medicare case-mix index. Although Medicare enrollees are currently only a small percentage of the HMO enrollment, the experience of other HMOs has shown that the cost of providing services to the aged can be controlled to the point where this might be a profitable market. More complete medical and financial data on enrollees might also aid in the negotiations with the state for Medicaid patients. Up until now, no agreement has been reached on acceptable prospective reimbursement levels for the AFDC population. Although Mr. Danish would like to serve more of the Medicare/Medicaid population, the Finance Director has discouraged too rapid advances into that market without adequate data.

The directors of finance and marketing at both organizations recounted to John McGuire their concerns about a series of events over the past three months which affected the operations and markets of MediCenter and HealthCare, Inc. In September 1982, HealthCare, Inc., received bills from the three hospitals in town and from physicians outside MediCenter for services provided to their members during the previous quarter. Both the volume and amount of bills were approximately 25 percent higher than budgeted. In addition, MediCenter billed HealthCare, Inc., for about 15 percent more services provided to HMO enrollees than for the previous month, the majority being services to patients whose enrollment could not be verified at the time of delivery. And finally, a new IPA had been formed by a local life insurance company. This plan was to be a "primary care network" type of plan, in which all enrollees must choose a primary care physician who either provides or approves all care. Since the physicians practice in their own offices, in most cases there is no need for enrollees to change their usual source of care to enroll in the plan. It is expected that the new IPA will capture some of the same market of interest to HealthCare.

Having completed his discussions with the staffs of both organizations, John McGuire reviewed the documents he had collected during his meetings: income statements and balance sheets (Tables 12.1 and 12.2), departmental revenue and expense reports (Tables 12.6 through 12.11), utilization records (Tables 12.4, 12.5, 12.13, and 12.14), physician productivity reports (Table 12.12), and copies of the critical forms for data collection. He was not sure that, given these reports, he could determine the costs of providing medical services to the enrollees. There were also no procedures to capture practitioners' time with patients or in other related activities. Indirect expenses were allocated using a somewhat arbitrary weighting method devised by one of MediCenter's first accountants. There was no organized accounting of materials and supplies.

John called a meeting of the administrators and explained that he had reviewed the history and present condition of each organization by interviewing staff and physicians, reading manuals, and collecting reports and forms used in generating those reports. But before he could proceed, he explained, he needed to know their needs as managers and the priorities of those needs. Were each of them getting the information they needed to understand the utilization of resources and thus to control their organizations? Ms. Roche recalled the negotiation session which prompted the decision to hire John.

It was *their* decision, he continued, as to what form the information system should take. The strategies for collection and aggregation of data might support any number of objectives:

product costing, utilization assessments, manpower planning, ancillary service usage, quality of care determinations, or some combination of these. With a properly designed management information system, many of these objectives could evolve over time following the implementation of the first objective—product costing. Once resource use was identified and priced accurately, the system could be perfected to meet these other very important goals.

Pat Flanders and Ed Danish listened intently to John McGuire's lecture on product costing, which was followed by a fairly technical discussion of hardware and software options and accompanying costs for the computer information system. As each absorbed the consultant's words, each related them to the problems of which they were acutely aware: Ed couldn't help remembering the report on excess hospital utilization by his members; Pat knew if she could accurately cost a visit or encounter for care, she could substantiate her rate requests and strengthen her negotiating position with HealthCare and possibly with other HMOs in the area. John McGuire finished his report and asked that they think about his questions and meet with him the following week to express their desires as to whether and how he should proceed.

Ed and Pat contemplated the information and agreed to meet together in an attempt to come to a consensus on how to use the consultant. After a long dinner meeting, they came to partial agreement: the first priority for a system should be product costing. Each agreed that their respective problems could be attenuated, if not alleviated completely, by the ability to accurately assess and price their limited resources. But they could not agree beyond this priority. Neither was willing at this stage to pay for the costs of collecting data not useful to their organizations. In addition, who would own this computer equipment and control its use?

John McGuire heard their views and was not surprised by the disputes. His experience had included similar conflicts between supposedly synergistic organizations. He knew as he left the meeting with contract in hand—for the design of a cost accounting system supported by computer technology—that these were not the only conflicts that would be faced.

ISSUES AND PROBLEMS

1. Present a cost analysis using visit as the product unit.
   a. Are there other data which might add to the accuracy of the analysis?
   b. What problems surround using "visit" rather than "episode" (the series of visits all relating to the same medical complaint or problem) as the unit of analysis?

2. How does the present information system support your product costing analysis?
   a. How would you design a management information system to meet the product costing need? Outline the major decision criteria related to:
      1. acquiring a computer system to support cost accounting, and
      2. implementing its use in these two organizations.
   b. What recommendations for management changes might you make to support your proposed MIS and product-costing objective?

3. How might your analysis improve cost prediction for MediCenter? for HealthCare, Inc.?

4. Given the organizational difficulties, should John McGuire have accepted this contract? What problems/opportunities should he foresee?

Table 12.1

HEALTHCARE, INC., BALANCE SHEET, UNAUDITED
As of June 30, 1982

ASSETS

Current Assets:	
Cash	$ 144,643
Securities (short-term)	500,000
Receivables:	
Premiums	1,377,814
Reinsurance claims	121,604
Interest	4,568
Prepaid expenses	4,973
Total current assets	$2,153,602
Long-Term Assets:	
Office equipment, furniture, and fixtures, at cost	$ 130,892
Less accumulated depreciation	(57,018)
Net office equipment, furniture, and fixtures	73,874
Other assets	
Long-term securities	350,000
Organizational costs, net of amortization of $9,125	9,125
Total long-term assets	432,999
Total assets	$2,586,601

LIABILITIES AND SHAREHOLDERS EQUITY

Current Liabilities:	
Hospital claims payable (St. Bernard)	$ 323,985
Hospital claims payable (others)	602,701
Out-of-area hospital allowance	32,861
Payable to MediCenter	218,706
Total current liabilities	1,178,253
Deferred income	1,146,548
Total liabilities	$2,324,801
Stockholders Equity:	
Common stock:	
Authorized: 4000 shares, $10 par	
Issued and outstanding, 1400 shares	$ 14,000
Capital contributed in excess of par	136,000
Retained earnings	111,800
Total stockholders equity	261,800
Total liabilities and shareholders equity	$2,586,601

Table 12.2

HEALTHCARE, INC., INCOME STATEMENT
Fiscal Year Ending June 30, 1982

Revenue		
Premium income		$16,187,364
Reinsurance recoveries		217,307
Coordination of benefits		9,874
Application fee income		11,212
		$16,425,757
Operating expenses		
Capitation	$7,587,552	
Administrative expenses	2,139,876	
Hospital expense	5,577,201	
Reinsurance premium	144,514	
Hospitalization incentive	309,736	
Depreciation	24,869	
Organizational costs — amortization	3,650	
Insurance expenses	10,617	$(15,798,015)
Operating income		$ 627,742
Interest income		89,518
Income before tax		717,260
Income tax		(283,966)
Net income		$ 433,294

Table 12.3

HEALTHCARE, INC., RATE TABLE (INDIVIDUAL CONVERSION)
Effective July 1, 1982

COVERAGE A	THREE-TIER
Regular	**Monthly Rate**
Single	51.95
Subscriber and 1 dependent	101.90
Family	134.11
Medicare	
Single	32.82
Subscriber and 1 dependent	82.77
(1 Medicare eligible)	
Subscriber and 1 dependent	63.64
(2 Medicare eligibles)	
Family (1 Medicare eligible)	114.98
Family (2 Medicare eligibles)	95.85
Group	**Composite Rate**
01	117.33
02	115.31
03	112.65

Table 12.4

MEDICENTER UTILIZATION REPORT
Clinical Patient Visits and Ancillary Visits and Exams
by FFS/HMO Payment Source

	July 1981	July 1982	Total FY 80-81	Total FY 81-82
Clinical Patient Visits				
Fee for service	6,943	6,091	82,859	79,800
HMO	427	2,362	14,506	34,200
Total	7,370	8,453	97,365	114,000
Total Ancillary Visits				
(A) Patients				
Fee for service	5,436	5,333	66,268	63,996
HMO	750	3,488	21,682	38,397
Total	6,186	8,821	87,950	102,393
(B) Exams				
Fee for service	5,084	6,062	66,054	78,744
HMO	467	2,084	14,198	58,599
Total	5,551	8,146	80,252	137,343

Table 12.5

MEDICENTER: VOLUME PATIENT VISITS
Fiscal Year 1981—82, One Quarter

DEPARTMENT	May	June	July
Clinical Visits			
(1) Internal Medicine			
FFS	1,595	1,475	1,708
HMO	849	814	983
Combined	2,444	2,289	2,691
(2) Pediatrics			
FFS	1,518	1,457	1,450
HMO	670	723	700
Combined	2,188	2,180	2,150
(3) Obstetrics-Gynecology			
FFS	1,097	1,206	1,193
HMO	351	454	437
Combined	1,448	1,660	1,630
(4) General Surgery			
FFS	118	103	130
HMO	62	53	45
Combined	180	156	175
(5) Urology			
FFS	291	277	284
HMO	55	63	64
Combined	346	340	348

Continued

Table 12.5 Continued

DEPARTMENT	May	June	July
(6) Ophthalmology			
FFS	485	508	447
HMO	23	41	32
Combined	508	549	479
(7) Otolaryngology			
FFS	181	219	151
HMO	66	68	36
Combined	247	287	187
(8) Orthopedic Surgery			
FFS	156	142	138
HMO	89	63	62
Combined	245	205	200
(9) Occupational Medicine			
FFS	536	617	590
HMO	3	9	3
Combined	539	626	593
Total Clinical Visits			
FFS	5,977	6,004	6,091
HMO	2,168	2,288	2,362
Combined	8,145	8,292	8,453
Ancillary Visits			
(1) Ambulatory Surgical Unit			
FFS	24	37	24
HMO	25	23	14
Combined	49	60	38
(2) Research			
FFS	16	28	21
(3) Optical			
FFS	149	148	136
(4) Physical Therapy			
(A) Patients			
FFS	382	418	498
HMO	133	178	163
Combined	515	596	661
(B) Exams			
FFS	856	978	1,219
HMO	272	414	366
Combined	1,128	1,392	1,585
(5) Laboratory			
(A) Patients			
FFS	1,700	1,748	1,838
HMO	567	723	645
Combined	2,267	2,471	2,483
(B) Exams			
FFS	3,703	3,569	3,863
HMO	1,564	1,890	1,451
Combined	5,267	5,459	5,314
(6) Pharmacy			
FFS	1,815	1,860	1,867
HMO	2,195	2,392	2,376
Combined	4,010	4,252	4,243

Continued

Table 12.5 Continued

DEPARTMENT	May	June	July
(7) Radiology			
(A) Patients			
FFS	965	864	879
HMO	268	256	225
Combined	1,233	1,120	1,104
(B) Exams			
FFS	1,075	962	980
HMO	301	296	267
Combined	1,376	1,258	1,247
(8) Allergy			
FFS	37	61	70
HMO	54	69	65
Combined	91	130	135
Total Ancillary Visits			
(A) Patients			
FFS	5,088	5,164	5,333
HMO	3,242	3,641	3,488
Combined	8,330	8,805	8,821
(B) Exams			
FFS	5,634	5,509	6,062
HMO	2,137	2,600	2,084
Combined	7,771	8,109	8,146
Registrations			
FFS	544	629	605
HMO	306	589	394
Visitors	143	188	185
Combined	993	1,406	1,184

Table 12.6

MEDICENTER: INDIRECT EXPENSES
July 1982

Account Description	CURRENT MONTH			YEAR TO DATE		
	Actual	Budget	Variance	Actual	Budget	Variance
Physician administrative salaries	1,237	1,450	213	3,047	4,350	1,303
Physician administrative expense	1,187	640	(547)	2,874	1,920	(954)
Physician benefits	3,762	4,750	988	8,106	14,250	6,144
General and administrative salaries	53,309	49,379	(3,930)	159,244	152,127	(7,117)
Employee benefits	12,183	9,409	(2,774)	32,273	29,226	(3,047)
Supplies expense	10,194	3,150	(7,044)	21,163	9,495	(11,668)
Occupancy and use expenses	73,284	76,802	3,518	178,145	221,678	43,533
Fixtures and equipment expenses	7,864	7,016	(848)	18,245	21,052	2,807
General and administrative purchased services	9,124	7,850	(1,274)	14,506	19,350	4,844
General and administrative expenses	3,700	4,076	376	9,908	13,718	3,810
Finance charges	129	-0-	(129)	205	-0-	(205)
Interest expense — HMO	4,794	4,886	92	13,786	14,316	530
Discount expense — HMO	13,620	10,159	(3,461)	37,968	29,853	(8,115)
Occupancy income	(57,714)	(57,714)	-0-	(115,428)	(173,142)	(57,714)
Other (income)/expenses	(3,049)	2,800	5,849	(3,295)	8,400	11,695
Total indirect expenses	133,624	124,653	(8,971)	380,747	366,593	(14,154)

Table 12.7
MEDICENTER: INDIRECT EXPENSE ALLOCATION
July 1981 (actual)

Department	M.D.'s	%	Patient Visits	%	Gross Revenue	%	Employee	%	ALLOCATIONS M.D.'s	Patient Visits	Gross Revenue	Employee	Total
General surgery	1	0.04	175	0.01	15,844	0.03	1	0.01	1,063	635	1,017	286	3,001
Occupational medicine	1	0.04	593	0.05	18,392	0.03	3	0.04	1,063	2,151	1,181	858	5,253
Internal medicine	7.7	0.29	2,691	0.21	132,791	0.24	18	0.23	8,184	9,760	8,525	5,150	31,618
Obstetrics-gynecology	4.7	0.18	1,630	0.13	91,884	0.16	11	0.14	4,996	5,912	5,899	3,147	19,953
Ophthalmology	1	0.04	479	0.04	43,962	0.08	1.5	0.02	1,063	1,737	2,822	429	6,052
Orthopedics	1	0.04	200	0.02	16,876	0.03	1.5	0.02	1,063	725	1,083	429	3,301
Pediatrics	5	0.19	2,150	0.17	67,521	0.12	8	0.10	5,315	7,798	4,335	2,289	19,736
Urology	1	0.04	348	0.03	24,084	0.04	1.5	0.02	1,063	1,262	1,546	429	4,300
Otolaryngology	1	0.04	187	0.01	14,424	0.03	2.5	0.03	1,063	678	926	715	3,382
Radiology	2	0.08	1,104	0.09	49,994	0.09	6.3	0.08	2,126	4,004	3,209	1,802	11,142
Laboratory	0	0.00	2,483	0.19	44,704	0.08	8.8	0.11	0	9,006	2,870	2,518	14,393
Research	0	0.00	21	0.00	396	0.00	1	0.01	0	76	25	286	388
Ambulatory surgical unit	1	0.04	38	0.00	16,589	0.03	4.5	0.06	1,063	138	1,665	1,287	3,553
Pharmacy	0	0.00	0	0.00	8,218	0.01	5.5	0.07	0	0	528	1,574	2,101
Optical shop	0	0.00	0	0.00	2,457	0.00	1.5	0.02	0	0	158	429	587
Physiotherapy	0	0.00	661	0.05	12,874	0.02	3.2	0.04	0	2,397	826	916	4,139
Allergy	0	0.00	135	0.01	991	0.00	.6	0.01	0	490	64	172	725
Total	26.4	1.	12,895	1.	562,001	1.	79.4	1.	28,061	46,768	36,078	22,716	133,624

Indirect expenses = 133,624
M.D.'s % = 0.21 = 28,061
Patient visits % = 0.35 = 46,768
Gross revenue % = 0.27 = 36,078
# Employee % = 0.17 = 22,716
1.00 = 133,624

Table 12.8

MEDICENTER: DEPARTMENT REVENUE AND EXPENSE REPORT—OBSTETRICS-GYNECOLOGY
July 1982

Account Description	CURRENT MONTH			YEAR TO DATE		
	Actual	Budget	Variance	Actual	Budget	Variance
Gross charges	91,884	62,664	29,220	262,168	218,324	43,844
Less: credit adjustments	(2,741)	(2,565)	(176)	(5,994)	(8,938)	2,944
Less: bad debts	(3,162)	(2,506)	(656)	(8,689)	(8,733)	44
Net charges	85,981	57,593	28,388	247,485	200,653	46,832
Net revenue	85,981	57,593	28,388	247,485	200,653	46,832
Direct Expenses						
Physician salaries	2,500	2,000	(500)	2,500	2,000	(500)
Physician benefits	829	1,222	393	2,156	3,192	1,036
Physician extender salaries	1,750	1,750		5,571	5,250	(321)
Employee expense	9,336	9,860	524	26,833	28,113	1,280
Supplies expense	2,174	1,715	(459)	5,711	5,145	(566)
Occupancy and use expense	4,518	4,518	-0-	13,554	13,554	-0-
Fixtures and equipment expense	614	758	144	1,749	2,274	525
Purchased services — medical and laboratory	20	50	30	185	150	35
Professional liability insurance	2,985	3,735	750	8,956	10,460	1,504
General and administrative expenses	834	464	(370)	1,266	1,392	126
Total direct expenses	25,560	26,072	512	68,481	71,530	3,049
Profit before indirect expenses	60,421	31,521	28,900	177,004	129,123	49,881
Total indirect expenses	19,953	15,258	(4,695)	53,094	46,411	(6,683)
Profit before physician allocation	40,468	16,263	24,205	125,910	82,712	43,198
Profit/net revenue	47.07%	29.24%		50.88%	41.22%	
Total expenses	45,513	41,330	(4,183)	121,575	117,941	(3,634)
Expense/net revenue	52.93%	71.76%		49.12%	58.78%	

Table 12.9

MEDICENTER: DEPARTMENT REVENUE AND EXPENSE REPORT—GENERAL SURGERY
June 1982

Account Description	CURRENT MONTH			YEAR TO DATE		
	Actual	Budget	Variance	Actual	Budget	Variance
Gross charges	15,844	15,905	(61)	50,293	52,231	(1,938)
Less: credit adjustments	(1,118)	(610)	(508)	(2,394)	(2,002)	(392)
Less: bad debts	(543)	(795)	252	(1,668)	(2,611)	943
Net charges	14,183	14,500	(317)	46,231	47,618	(1,387)
Net revenue	14,183	14,500	(317)	46,231	47,618	(1,387)
Direct Expenses						
Physician benefits	189	270	81	566	810	244
Employee expense	1,178	1,295	117	3,954	3,885	(69)
Supplies expense	632	320	(312)	1,141	960	(181)
Occupancy and use expense	946	946	-0-	2,838	2,838	-0-
Fixtures and equipment expense	50	22	(28)	150	66	(84)
Professional liability insurance	518	519	1	1,555	1,557	2
General and administrative expenses	163	248	85	355	744	389
Total direct expenses	3,676	3,620	(56)	10,557	10,860	301
Profit before indirect expenses	10,507	10,880	(373)	35,672	36,758	(1,086)
Total indirect expenses	3,001	2,889	(112)	8,766	8,788	22
Profit before physician allocation	7,506	7,991	(485)	26,906	27,970	(1,064)
Profit/net revenue	52.92%	55.11%		58.20%	58.74%	
Total expenses	6,677	6,509	(168)	19,325	19,648	323
Expense/net revenue	47.08%	44.89%		41.80%	41.26%	

Table 12.10

MEDICENTER: DEPARTMENT REVENUE AND EXPENSE REPORT—PHARMACY
July 1982

Account Description	CURRENT MONTH			YEAR TO DATE		
	Actual	Budget	Variance	Actual	Budget	Variance
Gross charges	8,218	46,749	(38,531)	25,805	136,796	(110,991)
Less: credit adjustments		(59)	59	(25)	(172)	147
Less: bad debts	(411)	(467)	56	(1,288)	(1,367)	79
Net charges	7,807	46,223	(38,416)	24,492	135,257	(110,765)
Other income	37,046		37,046	114,125		114,125
Net revenue	44,853	46,223	(1,370)	138,617	135,257	3,360
Direct Expenses						
Ancillary department salaries	7,951	8,625	674	23,348	25,875	2,527
Employee expense	1,357	1,321	(36)	3,620	3,963	343
Supplies expense	416	220	(196)	975	660	(315)
Ancillary department supplies	27,703	25,712	(1,991)	83,978	75,218	(8,760)
Occupancy and use expense	1,345	1,345	-0-	4,035	4,035	-0-
Fixtures and equipment expense	633	965	332	1,899	2,895	996
Purchased services — medical and laboratory	478			478		(478)
General and administrative expenses	535	694	159	1,116	2,082	966
Total direct expenses	39,940	38,882	(1,058)	119,449	114,728	(4,721)
Profit before indirect expenses	4,913	7,341	(2,428)	19,168	20,529	(1,361)
Total indirect expenses	2,101	1,814	(287)	6,147	5,250	(897)
Profit before physician allocation	2,812	5,527	(2,715)	13,021	15,279	(2,258)
Profit/net revenue	6.27%	11.96%		9.39%	11.30%	
Total expenses	42,041	40,696	(1,349)	125,596	119,978	(5,618)
Expense/net revenue	93.73%	88.04%		90.61%	88.70%	

Table 12.11

MEDICENTER: DEPARTMENT REVENUE AND EXPENSE REPORT—HEALTHCARE, INC.
July 1982

Acct. #	Account Description	CURRENT MONTH			YEAR TO DATE		
		Actual	Budget	Variance	Actual	Budget	Variance
3470	Copayments	8,679	8,789	(110)	25,413	25,748	(335)
3475	Capitation	151,114	139,015	12,099	434,116	407,244	26,872
3477[1]	Hospital savings/due from HMO	(7,868)	-0-	(7,868)	(14,438)	-0-	(14,438)
3478	Retroactive adjustments[2]	7,372	-0-	7,372	7,372	-0-	7,372
	Net revenue	159,297	147,804	11,493	452,463	432,992	19,471
	Expenses						
	Outside purchased services/gross	67,638			148,573		
	Outside purchased services/discounts	(1,333)			(3,858)		
7100	Net outside purchased services	66,305	35,894	(30,411)	144,715	104,032	(40,683)
7100	Inside purchased services	136,196	126,986	(9,210)	440,556	373,170	(67,386)
7812	Reinsurance recoveries	(4,695)	-0-	4,695	(4,695)	-0-	4,695
7814	Disallowed charges	-0-	-0-	-0-	-0-	-0-	-0-
	Total expenses	197,806	162,880	(34,926)	580,576	477,202	(103,374)
7822	Interest income[3]	(4,794)	(4,886)	(92)	(13,786)	(14,316)	(530)
7823	Discount income[4]	(13,620)	(10,159)	3,461	(37,968)	(29,853)	8,115
	Miscellaneous adjustments[3]	2,967	-0-	(2,967)	YTD IN ACCT #7822		
	Total adjustments	(15,447)	(15,045)	402	(51,754)	(44,169)	7,585
	Net expenses	182,359	147,835	(34,524)	528,822	433,033	(95,789)
	Prior year expense adjustment[5]	15,883	-0-	15,883			
	Profit before physician allocation	(7,179)	(31)	(7,148)	(76,359)	(41)	(76,318)
	Enrollees	10,393	9,701	692			

1. Due June 1982: $27,785.
2. Recalculation of March 1981 capitation. To be paid in August 1982.
3. Interest discount is now calculated as 3% of actual copayment and capitation received as this is the actual "cash in advance" received. A correcting entry for May 1982 and June 1982 is on line 17 and is reflected in the year-to-date column on line 15 (Acct. #7822).
4. This represents 8% of inside expenses for bad debt and write-offs plus 2% of inside expenses representing the difference between "Fee for Service" and HMO charges. Thus the total of 10% of inside expenses.
5. Represents outside expenses incurred in FY 1981 that were carried forward to FY 1982 in error. Year-to-date figure adjusted (line 9).

Table 12.12

MEDICENTER: PHYSICIAN PRODUCTIVITY

(Sample includes only Pediatrics, Obstetrics-Gynecology, Surgery, Occupational Medicine, and Pharmacy)

June 1982

Physician #	Dept.	Medic Gross Charges	Medic Adj.	Medic Net Charges	HMO Gross Charges	Total Dept. Gross Charges	Medic Credit Adj.	5% Bad Debts	Net Charges
42	Occu.	20,376	—	20,376	710	21,087	(134)	(1,018)	19,933
53	Peds.	14,747	(1,564)	13,810	308 (NB) 6,242 (DT)	20,360	(684)	(769)	18,907
54	Peds.	9,399	626	10,026	308 (NB) 4,013 (DT)	14,347	(240)	(501)	13,606
55	Peds.	4,479	626	5,105	308 (NB) 1,338 (DT)	6,751	(193)	(255)	6,303
56	Peds.	11,243	626	11,869	308 (NB) 6,180 (DT)	18,358	(561)	(593)	17,204
57	Peds.	9,876	626	10,503	308 (NB) 3,012 (DT)	13,823	(1,214)	(525)	12,084
21	OB/GYN.	10,760	1,498	12,258	12,549	21,469	(575)	(612)	20,281
22	OB/GYN.	10,804	2,384	13,188	8,978	21,186	(577)	(659)	19,949
23	OB/GYN.	17,838	(2,781)	15,057	5,971	23,276	(817)	(752)	21,706
24	OB/GYN.	7,347	367	7,714	4,454	12,285	(3,844)	(385)	11,861
25	OB/GYN.	On Leave							
10	Surg.	11,299	-0-	11,299	6,186	17,485	(409)	(564)	16,510
92	Pharm.	9,585	-0-	9,585	-0-	9,585	(25)	(479)	9,080

Table 12.13

HEALTHCARE, INC.: HOSPITAL UTILIZATION MONTHLY PAYMENT VOUCHER

Produced through June 30, 1982

Hospital	Patient Name	Admit Date	Discharge Date	Total Charges	Discount	Net Charges	Diagnosis
St. Bernard	A	6/01/82	6/04/82	1,125.00	101.25	1,023.75	Pregnancy
St. Bernard	B	6/01/82	6/06/82	2,019.30	181.71	1,837.56	Peri-Abd. Abscess
Marion	C	6/03/82	6/08/82	2,454.04		2,454.04	Skull Fx
St. Bernard	D	6/04/82	6/07/82	1,084.57	97.61	986.96	Tonsillitis
City	E	6/05/82	6/07/82	1,267.19		1,267.19	Cysto-TUR
St. Bernard	F	6/09/82	6/15/82	2,079.57	187.16	1,892.41	Ovary-Cyst
City	G	6/10/82	6/12/82	1,192.65		1,192.65	PID
St. Bernard	H	6/14/82	6/16/82	1,186.69	106.80	1,079.89	Bunion
St. Bernard	I	6/16/82	6/21/82	2,630.54	236.75	2,393.79	Corneal Transplant
Marion	J	6/16/82	6/17/82	454.88		454.88	Spon Abortion
City	K	6/16/82	6/16/82	575.00		575.00	Myoc Inf
St. Bernard	L	6/23/82	6/25/82	925.82	83.32	842.50	Ulnar Fx
St. Bernard	M	6/24/82	6/29/82	586.28	52.77	533.51	Fx Hip
St. Bernard	N	6/25/82	6/27/82	1,214.79	109.33	1,105.46	Tympanot.
City	O	6/26/82	6/28/82	975.00		975.00	Poss Liver Abscess
City	P	6/27/82	6/29/82	1,053.04		1,053.04	Poss PID
St. Bernard	Q	6/27/82	6/30/82	1,421.50	127.94	1,293.56	Pregnancy

Table 12.14

HEALTHCARE, INC.::OUT-OF-AREA HOSPITAL UTILIZATION SUMMARY

June 1982

Patient	Admit Date	Discharge Date	Days	Net Charges	ER Charges	Other Charges	Amout Paid	Admitting MD	Admitting Diagnosis
1. F. Franks	6/10/82	6/30/82	20	8,692.60				Jones	Expl. Lap.
2. M. George	6/01/82	6/06/82	5	1,206.35				Searly	Pneumonia
3. S. Smith	6/03/82	6/05/82	2	1,010.30	72.50			Mairne	Cerv. Disc.
4. P. Frinde	6/06/82	6/12/82	6	1,535.30				James	Retinal Detachment
5. J. Hathaway	6/14/82	6/15/82	1	5,600.32				Smith	Hernior.
6. G. Macy	6/28/82	6/29/82	1	4,200.40				Carroll	Rule Out Pneumonia

Appendix 12.1

ENCOUNTER FORM

Date of encounter
Member/nonmember/temporary
Name of patient
Patient ID number
Appointment/walk in
    Date
    With whom
Provider number
Diagnosis code (1)
Procedure code (1)
Primary reason for visit
    Routine
    Nonroutine
    Follow-up
    Procedure (provider-initiated)
Disposition

Copies to: Medical records
           Registration
           Data processing

Appendix 12.2

UNIFORM HOSPITAL DISCHARGE DATA SET

Personal identification
Date of birth
Sex
Race and ethnicity
Residence
Hospital identification
Admission and discharge date
Physician identification:
   attending and operating
Diagnoses
Procedures and dates
Disposition of patient
Expected principal source of
   payment

Source: Public Health Service, Report of the National Committee on Vital and Health Statistics: Uniform Hospital Discharge Data Set, DHEW Publication No. (PHS) 80-1157, April 1980.

III

Financing Decisions

Overview

Meeting the financing needs of the health care organization is a prime responsibility of managers. Determining and implementing the optimal capital structure—if one exists—requires an understanding of the various sources of funds available to the health care organization. Naturally, there are costs associated with each source. The impact of debt, the cost associated with equity capital, economic conditions, the risk aversion of management, and the type of health care organization all play important roles in establishing the financial management strategy of the firm. The cases in this section provide an opportunity for the student to make financing decisions for varying economic conditions and health care settings.

"Voluntary Villa" presents the problem of finding money for replacement or renovation of a skilled nursing home facility. The organization, which confronts the problem as a result of noncompliance with the state's health and life safety code, is also concerned about the impact on patient care costs. Various political and planning considerations are present as well.

"Home Health Aide Services." switches the focus to working capital requirements and how accounts receivable collection policies influence financial requirements. The managers have felt encouraged by the apparent recent success of the agency. Yet they must now decide quickly whether to seek a bank loan or a cash advance from United Way.

Analysis of relevant financial issues for a diversification decision is the point of the third case, "Hospital Diversification into Long-Term Care." Internally generated funds will be affected by the decision to expand into long-term care through Medicare and Medicaid regulations.

The impact of organizational design and patient care modalities on working capital requirements is the focus of "Midtown Mental Health Center." Several alternatives to alleviate the accounts receivable problem must be evaluated under varying conditions of certainty. In addition, any recommendations must be acceptable to the public. This further complicates any quantitative ranking of the alternatives.

Starting a new health maintenance organization is the topic of "Bay Health Plan." At this point, a wide range of financial analyses must be performed—including start-up financing needs and cash flow analysis—and the business plan evaluated. Despite the prevalence of HMOs, most health care managers know very little about their financial management. Thus, this case provides a valuable teaching resource.

"Brant Clinic" continues the exploration of start-up financing requirements as applied to a satellite clinic for a group practice, which is examined in part A of the case. Part B requires that a choice be made among three investment alternatives representing a spectrum of medical care technologies. Finally, part C involves the decision of whether to contract with a town's major employer to provide medical care services at a discount.

The seventh case, "Manchester Community Hospital," provides many opportunities for both quantitative and qualitative analysis. It highlights the importance of short- and intermediate-term fiscal and operational planning in an uncertain environment. The case also illustrates the use of a variety of financing sources.

"The CCD Cost-Sharing Case" investigates common public-sector financial management difficulties. In response to financial shortfalls, a cost-sharing policy has been implemented for a service that had previously been free to all with qualifying medical conditions. The impact on receivables management, on other financial procedures of the agency, and on access to care have not been evaluated.

"Failure to Orchestrate an HMO: The Case of One HMO's Reorganization under Chapter 11 of the Federal Bankruptcy Law," the final case in this section, presents myriad financial issues besides the most obvious one—bankruptcy. Determining why the HMO failed and potential solutions to its problems requires application of many financial management techniques.

13

Voluntary Villa

Wendy S. Love

INTRODUCTION

Francis Fencesitter, the newly appointed administrator of Voluntary Villa, a 72-bed skilled nursing facility, was not looking forward to his first meeting that evening with the Board of Trustees' Building Committee. He had just received a letter from the state saying that they would no longer waive the health and life safety code requirements that the home had been violating for the past ten years. The Villa had to submit a certificate of need (CON) for the needed renovations within three months or be closed.

He had also just received a copy of next year's proposed budget showing a projected $83,000 deficit. Mr. Fencesitter hurriedly called the head of the Building Committee, trustee Doug Blueprinz, and asked him to make a presentation at the meeting that night. He was somewhat comforted by the fact that his head nurse, Florence Nightcap, and his bookkeeper, Debbie Credit, were also members of the committee.

ALTERNATIVES

That evening, Mr. Blueprinz explained to the committee the only alternatives he envisioned:

1. Close the facility.
2. Renovate the existing facility.
3. Build a new patient care wing next to the 1961 (32-bed) wing which would be converted to offices and demolish the 1919 wing (containing 26-bed and 14-bed units). The projected new wing would have two or three floors with 40 beds on a floor, for a total of 80 or 120 beds.
4. Buy the old hospital on South Hill and convert it to an 80-bed skilled nursing facility.

Doug Blueprinz felt that remodeling the present facility was not a good option. To satisfy space requirements, three rooms would have to be put together to create two patient rooms.

Even then, it would not be possible to correct some of the other health and safety violations. Florence Nightcap, the head nurse, wondered where the elderly patients would be relocated during such a major renovation. Debbie Credit, the head bookkeeper, added that the Villa could not afford the loss of patient revenue during renovation. The Board quickly voted to eliminate that option.

Erma Cutter, whose husband was on the county board of supervisors, suggested that they close the Villa. The supervisors were against any project that would raise taxes. She had heard that Proprietary Peak, on the outskirts of town, had a 20-percent vacancy rate in its 100-bed health-related facility (HRF). Their skilled nursing section of 160 beds, however, was always full.

It was Erma's understanding that the number of residential care beds in the surrounding small towns was growing rapidly. Home health visits were making it possible for many of these people to be cared for at home rather than go to health-related facilities. When they got very sick, they entered a skilled nursing facility. Erma also understood that Proprietary Peak was considering converting 80 of its HRF beds to SNF level. No capital costs would be involved in such a conversion. She reminded the Board that 80 percent of the people in skilled nursing homes in the country were Medicaid recipients. County taxes paid 25 percent of their care. Since the area was very rural, the burden of the local and state taxes fell on individuals, many of whom were on fixed incomes.

Lottie Bucks, who had been on the Board for 40 years, was horrified at the suggestion of closing the Villa. The Villa had a proud history, first as a rehabilitation center for polio victims and now as the only voluntary nursing home within a 100-mile radius. She wanted to make sure that the doors were kept open. Therefore, she would personally give the Villa $600,000 toward a new patient care wing. She personally favored building a wing containing 80 beds. She noted that the most popular nursing home in town, Valley View, was also the smallest, with only 60 beds. It was also the most popular home with staff. With 80 beds they could retain an intimate, friendly atmosphere. She knew of 80-bed nursing homes in the big city which had no financial difficulties.

Dr. Goodheart, a local general practitioner and part-time medical director of the Villa, said that he felt the Villa should build a 120-bed wing. He was concerned about the number of elderly Medicaid patients backed up in the local hospitals waiting for nursing home placement. He said that "Meals on Wheels" and the senior citizen nutrition programs were fine for people living in town but could not be used by his many rural patients. Likewise, the state's emphasis on increasing home health care would not help many of his elderly patients living alone in the country.

Joe Ivy, a sociology professor at the local college, noted that a 17-percent increase in the 75+ population was expected between 1980 and 1985. He also felt that because of current federal Medicare trends which increased copayments and deductibles, people were going to arrive at nursing homes with less money and would convert to Medicaid sooner. He noted that the proportion of Medicaid patients in Proprietary Peak's SNF was already 93 percent. If the Villa were to increase its bed number to 120, it would probably go to 90 percent Medicaid patients. He thought that it was important that the Villa continue to exist since it was the only voluntary nursing home in the area, but he wondered whether it would be financially viable to have a nursing home with 90 percent Medicaid patients. He understood that Proprietary Peak was having terrible financial problems.

Marian Middlerock was also a member of the local Health Systems Agency. She pointed out that suitable existing alternatives would be explored before the HSA would approve a CON for new construction. She suggested that they consider moving the Villa to the old hospital at the edge of town. It would certainly be cheaper to remodel the old hospital than to build a new patient wing.

Ms. Nightcap disagreed, however, arguing that the old hospital was entirely unsuited for nursing home care. The halls were long and dark, and the building had no common room areas. The old hospital was located on the edge of town; her patients wouldn't have anything to look at but birds and trees. Many of her nurses walked to work and in good weather they wheeled patients to the main shopping area, one block away. The old hospital was at the end of the bus line. Buses ran infrequently.

Freddie Reserve, a local banker, said that he was concerned about financing new construction. It was his understanding that there was no conventional mortgage money available for projects of this sort. His bank couldn't handle a project of this nature, especially with the uncertainties surrounding Medicaid reimbursement. He thought Lottie's offer was very generous. He doubted, however, whether a fund drive would raise enough additional capital.

Mr. Fencesitter suggested that they needed professional help. As a new administrator, he couldn't assemble the data and write a CON within the next three months. He suggested that they hire a professional consultant. As the hour was growing late, the committee authorized Mr. Fencesitter to engage a consultant.

THE CONSULTANTS

Sam Turnkey arrived at the next Building Committee meeting prepared with tables, charts, and an overhead projector, but no answers. Mr. Turnkey started the meeting by discussing need and demand for long-term-care nursing beds in the area. He explained that the state was revising its bed-need methodology to reflect its belief that more day care and home health care should be given and that the state was meeting its mandate to control costs by curtailing bed supply (Table 13.1). According to the new methodology, the county had too many beds already. However, since no proposals had reached the state yet, he didn't know what would happen if the Villa asked for a 48-bed increase.

He then presented a table showing the present budget, a proposed 80-bed budget, and a proposed 120-bed budget (Table 13.2). He noted that the current facility was very inefficient. The nursing units were small — 32, 26, and 14 beds, respectively. Forty-bed units could be more efficiently run. Current practice also suggested using more licensed practical nurses and fewer registered nurses and supervisors. He also felt that some administrative staff could be cut. An 80-bed facility did not need an assistant administrator. The billing, medical records, inventory, and payroll could be handled by a leased computer. In a 120-bed facility, economies of scale would also be a factor.

New construction was currently running about $45,000 per bed. The old hospital could probably be renovated for $25,000 per bed. Conventional mortgages were no longer available for nursing homes. Two methods of financing were currently available. The FHA 232 mortgage insurance program basically provided an AAA rating so that the nursing home could enter the tax-exempt bond market at 12.5 percent. The government charged a 0.8 percent application and inspection fee and required a monthly insurance premium of 0.5 percent per

Table 13.1

CANFIELD COUNTY BED NEED

1985 Population Age 65+ 8527	1985 Beds Available 472	1985 Proposed Ceiling 443

Table 13.2

PRESENT AND PROPOSED BUDGETS

Revenue	Present (72 beds)	Proposed (80 beds)	Proposed (120 beds)
Charges	$1,752,653		
Adjustments	209,270		
Net revenue	$1,543,383		
Expenses			
Nursing	$ 754,251	$ 668,547	$ 889,607
Social work and therapies	73,376	73,376	101,376
Dietary	209,736	220,176	306,576
Plant and maintenance	87,451	77,451	100,000
Housekeeping and laundry	115,200	117,660	181,560
Administration and benefits	334,064	267,176	356,661
Interest and depreciation	51,948	51,948	51,948
(Current) Total expenses	$1,626,026	$1,476,334	$1,987,728
# Patient days	26,159	28,616	42,924
% Occupancy	99.5+	98	98
Cost per diem	$62.16	$51.59*	$46.30*

*Excludes annual expenses associated with capital costs of project such as interest, depreciation, amortization of financing fees, and mortgage premium insurances.

annum of the outstanding principal. The process could often take a year or more to complete. Federal building regulations could also increase costs. A Debt Service Reserve Fund consisting of one year's principal and interest was required. The mortgage and bond placement firms usually charged a total of 3.5 percent.

If one did not want to go the FHA route, it was very easy to place a 16-percent (30-year) unrated tax-exempt bond within two months. Although a Debt Service Reserve Fund was required, there were no government fees or insurance premiums. Placement fees were only 2.5 percent. Tables 13.3 and 13.4 show how to calculate bond size and figure annual interest, depreciation, amortization, and insurance premiums.

Mr. Turnkey explained that well-managed, efficient facilities were still being reimbursed for costs incurred by Medicaid patients. In order to control costs, the state had started placing facilities in clusters by size. Discrete ceilings were set for certain items. Some items such as utilities were passed through. Group averages were calculated and facilities were reimbursed accordingly. Since proprietary homes were often more efficiently run, many voluntary facilities were not receiving full reimbursement for their costs. The proposed budgets were designed not to exceed ceilings. However, private patients had to be charged at least the Medicaid rate. Table 13.5 shows the private charges and Medicaid rates for the other facilities in the county, as well as the private-Medicaid patient mix.

Mr. Turnkey stated that there were many variables involved in deciding what to do— some quantitative, some qualitative. He felt that he could not make a recommmendation to the Board. He provided the facts; the Board would have to make the final decision.

THE DECISION

Freddie Reserve thought that it was important to separate out capital operating expenses. These expenses were a function of construction costs, interest rates, mortgage requirements, and fees. He wanted to see how these variables would affect the per diem cost per patient. He wanted to examine the 80- and 120-bed options with 12.5 percent and 16 percent interest rates. He was concerned about the FHA regulations. He wanted to know what the effect on the per diem cost would be if building costs went up 6 percent as a result of time delay and 10 percent as a result of federal building regulations. He thought they could probably lower the construction cost per bed if they didn't have to follow federal codes. He wanted to know how low they would have to lower construction costs for the FHA 232 12.5-percent, $45,000-per-bed project to equal a 16-percent unrated mortgage project.

Debbie Credit was skeptical that the state would reimburse all costs for Medicaid patients. She worried about being competitive with the other facilities for private patients and wondered how much they could charge private patients. What would happen if they had 80 percent Medicaid patients? 95 percent?

Erma Cutter was very concerned about the cost to the taxpayers. She wanted to know what the cost would be if the state allowed Proprietary Peak to convert 80 of their 100 HRF beds to SNF level, and did not allow them to rebuild the Villa. She also wanted to know the cost if the state allowed the Villa to build 80 beds and the Peak to convert 40 HRF beds to SNF level.

These concerns could not be answered readily. The committee members asked Mr. Fencesitter to research their questions and develop criteria for making their final decision. The decision would not be an easy one even if he did his homework, so Mr. Fencesitter was, again, not looking forward to another meeting of his committee.

Table 13.3

BOND ISSUE COMPUTATION (SIMPLE)

		Example*	
Cost to be bonded	$G-H$	5,400,000 - 600,000	4,800,000
Capitalized interest	$+A(x)\dfrac{T}{12}$	$.125(x)\dfrac{18}{12}$	$.1875x$
Debt service reserve fund	$+\dfrac{x}{F} + Ax$	$\dfrac{x}{30} + .125x$	$.1583x$
FHA 232 fees[1]	$+.008x$		$.008x$
Mortgage fees[1]	$+.01x$		$.01x$
Placement fees[1 & 2]	$+.025x$		$.025x$
Bond issue amount		$x =$	4,800,000 + .3888x
		$x = \$7,853,403 = \$7,860,000$	

x = Bond issue amount
G = Construction cost
H = Equity = $600,000 for new wing
A = Borrowing rate = 12.5% or 16%
F = Term of bond = 30 years
T = Construction period = 18 months
B = Earned interest rate = 11%
D = Depreciable life = 33
M = Amortization factor = .0645

*FHA 232, 12.5% bond, 120-bed facility, $45,000 per bed.
1. FHA 232 only.
2. 16% unrated bonds.

Table 13.4

ANNUAL CAPITAL EXPENSES

		Example	
Depreciation	$(G +A(x)\dfrac{T}{12}) \div D$	$(5,400,000 + 1,473,750) \div 33$	$208,295
Interest expense	$+A(x)$	.125 (7,860,000)	982,500
Interest earned on DSRF	$-B[\dfrac{x}{F}+A(x)]$	$-.11\ (.1583)\ (7,860,000)$	(136,866)
Annual amortization[1]	$+M(.043x)$	(.0645) (.043) (7,860,000)	21,800
or			
Annual amortization[2]	$+M(.025x)$		
Mortgage insurance[1]	$+.005\ x$	.005 (7,860,000)	38,300
Annual capital expenses			$1,115,028

1. FHA 232 only.
2. 16% unrated bonds.

Table 13.5

CURRENT CHARGES AND PATIENT MIX

Facility	# Beds	Private rate (# pts)	Medicaid rate (# pts)
Proprietary Peak			
SNF	160	$74(11)	$62(149)
HRF	100	$60(20)	$47(60)
Valley View			
SNF	60	$60(30)	$50(30)
Voluntary Villa			
SNF	72	$67(14)	$57(58)
Rural Rest			
SNF	40	not open yet	
HRF	40	rates unknown	
		(at the far end of the county)	

14

Home Health Aide Services

J. B. Silvers

Although the crocuses were beginning to bloom and the sailboats again plied Rhode Island's Narragansett Bay, the mood at the Home Health Aide Services of Rhode Island (H/H) was more befitting of winter than spring. The April 1979 board meeting of the nonprofit provider of various health and housekeeping services (see Appendix 14.1 for a description) was in discord. Many of the directors were perplexed and alarmed by the need to seek a $50,000 bank loan in spite of the recent operating surplus of the agency.

GROWTH AND FINANCING

The mood of euphoria prevailing in recent months was due to the exceptional recovery of H/H since 1976, the low point of its six-year life (see Table 14.1 for a five-year summary). Revenues in 1979 were expected to reach almost $500,000, about four times the 1976 level, while hours of service provided were expected to grow by a factor of five. However, all of this was clouded by the report of Ed Perre, the Executive Director, that the informal loan provided to H/H by the Federal Bank as an overdraft to their checking account had reached $30,000 at the end of March. While small overdrafts were granted as a courtesy to such nonprofit community service agencies, an advance of this size was unacceptable to the bank (previous temporary overdrafts had never exceeded $5,000). Something would have to be done. In short, H/H could no longer pay its bills in spite of the fact that it was breaking even or even generating some surplus. Mr. Perre estimated that current external financing of at least $50,000 was needed, although he did not provide any explicit financial forecasts. Without some amount of cash injection, he did not think that H/H could even meet its payroll expenses for April.

ALTERNATIVE SOLUTIONS

After the magnitude of the financial crisis had been presented, the Board quickly split into several camps. One director suggested that the answer lay with the United Way. Revenue from this source had fallen off in percentage terms from 48 percent of total revenue in 1976 to only 13 percent in 1978 (see Table 14.1). He could see no reason why they would be unwilling to either advance H/H cash on an accelerated schedule within their 1979 planned allocation, or actually increase the H/H allocation from the 1979 budgeted amount of $63,636. In the past, United Way had, in fact, granted small requests up to $10,000 to meet the payroll.

Mr. Perre, however, didn't think that this alternative was desirable. He was certain that a $50,000 advance was out of the question since both the United Way and other agencies with partial United Way funding had financing problems of their own. Even the minimum $30,000 advance would severely limit the autonomy of H/H with respect to hiring and expansion. With less than 15 percent of the agency's financing, United Way would gain an effective veto power.

The Board and Mr. Perre had ambitious growth plans, projecting more than a doubling of service hours to approximately 135,000 hours in 1979, followed by another large increase to 300,000 hours in 1980. Subsequent years were thought to hold the potential for at least an additional 100,000 hours each year. Many board members felt a strong moral obligation to provide at least this much service in the face of a perceived far greater market need. Any limitation — even a temporary one — would constitute a serious setback to their aspirations and growth plans.

On the other hand, a retired executive on the Board felt that there was no other alternative but to freeze expansion, at least temporarily. He was immediately overwhelmed, however, by opposition to that idea. In particular, one strong consumer advocate, who was a community representative on the Board, argued forcefully that even a public campaign to marshal community support to put pressure on the United Way and the bank would be superior to a freeze. Zero growth or retrenchment would impose a great hardship on the elderly and sick who were expecting H/H assistance in their homes. This would be unacceptable in her opinion.

On a less impassioned level, Mr. Perre noted that a freeze on services, which was also advocated by United Way officials, would mean that the agency's contractors (such as the various state and city welfare departments, the Veterans Administration, and several visiting nurse associations in Rhode Island) would find other providers to meet their needs and might even cancel their current contracts with H/H. Furthermore, a March 1977 survey conducted by the Health Systems Agency had found a tremendous current need in the area. In response to this, a number of well-financed, for-profit competitors had sprung up and, in fact, were competing with H/H for these public contracts. In addition, they were making serious inroads into the private services provided by H/H to individual clients.

A bank officer who was on the Board thought that if the bank could get an assurance from United Way for continued future funding for the agency, a $50,000 line of credit might be arranged on the terms listed in Appendix 14.2. Unfortunately, with the current prime rate at 13 percent, this financing would be very expensive. His concern, however, went beyond the current need. He saw no problem if the $50,000 would be the limit of the agency's need for the immediate future and could be paid back over a reasonable period as H/H generated more of its financing through retained earnings and other funding sources. However, he wondered how quickly this would occur. Already, as of March 31, 1979, the loan had risen to over $30,000 (see Table 14.2).

FORECAST OF NEED

A nursing home administrator on the Board indicated that repayment should be no problem. In less than four years (15 quarters), if the rate of the first quarter ($3,420, from Table 14.3) were maintained, enough surplus would be accumulated to repay the full $50,000. This first-quarter surplus was based on 22,717 hours of service (see Table 14.4). The Board then turned to a discussion of whether the nature of costs and revenues would allow such an accumulation.

Although professional and clerical salaries were largely fixed with respect to volume, health aide wages, benefits, and payroll and unemployment taxes were variable (see Table 14.3 for recent months). For the first quarter, direct expenses — which were thought to be variable with hours served — averaged $3.52 per hour. Professional and clerical salaries, which depended upon the number of office staff, averaged about $590 per staff member per month. Mr. Perre thought that these levels would probably prevail for the remainder of the year.

Since variable costs were large, they would rise with volume, thus making a large surplus very difficult to generate. Furthermore, inflation and slow payment by both public assistance agencies and the visiting nurses associations caused him worry.

Yet, others on the Board saw no problem once the current crisis was past since there were no deficits on the horizon. With the loan, the H/H program would be saved.

As they left the meeting, Mr. Perre was still concerned about future financing. He knew he would have to recommend some sort of financing plan at the emergency meeting the following Monday.

Appendix 14.1

HOME HEALTH AIDE SERVICES: HOME HEALTH AIDE'S DUTIES

THE HEALTH AIDE CAN DO THE FOLLOWING WORK

Housekeeping

1. Routine Light Housekeeping — such as making and changing beds, dusting, washing dishes, wet mopping kitchen and bathroom floors, vacuuming, defrosting refrigerator and cleaning stove.
2. Prepare and Serve Meals
3. Marketing and Simple Errands — (Consult with supervisor if car is to be used.)
4. Light Laundry — Hand wash light personal laundry, use automatic washer and dryer and iron.

Personal Care

In the area of PERSONAL CARE they may:

1. Give or assist with sponge or bed bath including back rubs, care of mouth and hair.
2. Give shampoo to ambulatory patient on doctor's order.
3. Feed patient or assist with meals.
4. Dress or assist dressing patient.
5. Remind patient to take medication at specified times.
6. Remind patient to do prescribed exercises.
7. Give and remove bed pan.
8. Help patient in and out of bed (lifting not permitted.)
9. Care for children.

THE HEALTH AIDE SHOULD NOT

1. Scrub and wax floors on hands and knees.
2. Wash walls and woodwork.
3. Move heavy furniture.
4. Do heavy laundry by hand.
5. Wash windows outside.
6. Stand on anything except firm stepladders.
7. Fix electrical equipment.

Appendix 14.2

HOME HEALTH AIDE SERVICES:
FEDERAL BANK LOAN PROPOSAL FOR
HOME HEALTH AIDE SERVICES OF RHODE ISLAND

Maximum Borrowing Available: $50,000.00 (Line of Credit Agreement)

Rate: Bank's Prime Rate plus 4.5%, with a floor of 13% and ceiling of 17%.

Collateral: First security interest under the Rhode Island Uniform Commercial Code of all Accounts Receivable not owned or hereafter acquired.

Terms and Conditions:

1. In conjunction with the maximum line, the outstanding loan balance must be fully collateralized by 80 percent of those accounts receivable aged less than 90 days old. The company will provide the Bank with a detailed aging of accounts receivable within 10 days of the end of each month.*

2. Annual audited financial statements prepared by a certified public accountant will be required within 90 days of the fiscal year-end. Also, the Bank requests unaudited quarterly statements within 60 days of the end of each fiscal quarter.

3. We will require a letter from the United Way stating that the above borrowing will in no way endanger the organization's ability to be a recipient this year and any future years.

4. No change in management in the organization without permission of the Bank.

5. No borrowing/leasing without permission of the Bank.

6. Any legal expenses incurred in the preparation and closing of the above loan will be paid by the company at the time of the closing.

---

*Aging Schedule as of March 31, 1979

Accounts Receivable Due From:	Dollar Amount	AMOUNT AND PERCENTAGE OUTSTANDING FOR			
		0-30 days	31-60 days	61-90 days	over 90 days
Public assistance	$46,224	$22,188 (48%)	$5,547 (12%)	$4,622 (10%)	$13,867 (30%)
Visiting Nurse Assn.	32,360	9,061 (28%)	7,119 (22%)	6,472 (20%)	9,708 (30%)
Private	3,944	1,814 (46%)	513 (13%)	355 (9%)	1,262 (34%)
Other	8,153	2,038 (25%)	2,772 (34.5%)	897 (11%)	2,446 (30%)
Total and percent	$90,681	$35,101	$15,951	$12,346	$27,283
	(100%)	(39%)	(17%)	(14%)	(30%)
Assumed average days outstanding	57 days	15 days	45 days	75 days	110 days
Weighted average days of revenue outstanding in accounts receivable			67		

Table 14.1

INCOME STATEMENTS AND OPERATING STATISTICS
1974 – 1979

	1974	1975	1976	1977	1978	Budget 1979
Income Statement						
Total revenue	$92,979	$149,749	$121,344	$203,404	$325,659	$478,703
Total expenses	92,178	146,620	123,987	203,311	325,958	478,703
Surplus (or deficit)[1]	801	3,129	(2,643)	83	(299)	—
Operating Statistics						
United Way allocation	$31,900	$ 25,287	$ 58,180	$ 52,656	$ 53,636	$ 63,636
(Percentage of total revenue)	(34%)	(19%)	(48%)	(30%)	(13%)	(13%)
Total hours served	20,602	29,897	20,720	38,804	62,436	96,000
Hours — private payment	1,400	10,600	8,800	11,000	17,250	
Percentage hours — private payment	7%	36%	43%	28%	28%	
Cost per hour served	$4.04	$4.90	$5.98	$5.02	$5.22	$4.99

1. The United Way reduces its allocation to H/H by any amount of surplus over $100. Thus, after the implementation of this policy in 1976, a surplus greater than $100 was literally impossible.

Table 14.2

BALANCE SHEETS
January – March 1979

Assets	Jan. 31, 1979	Feb. 28, 1979	Mar. 31, 1979
Cash	$ 0	$ 0	$ 0
Accounts receivable	55,444	76,249	90,681
Prepaid insurance	5,016	3,408	2,791
Total assets	60,460	79,657	93,472
Liabilities and retained earnings			
Bank loan (overdraft)	$13,063	$26,611	$30,415
Accounts payable	20,616	19,380	23,013
Payroll withholding tax due	1,405	1,651	2,544
Advances from United Way	—	5,304	10,607
Retained earnings			
Balance at beginning of month	23,602	25,376	26,711
Plus net income (loss) for month	1,744	1,335	182
Balance at end of month	25,376	26,711	26,893
Total liabilities and retained earnings	60,460	79,657	93,472
Accounts receivable due from:			
Public assistance	$20,971	$37,298	$46,224
Visiting Nurse Assn.	25,707	27,403	32,360
Private	2,987	3,474	3,944
Other	5,779	8,074	8,153
Total	55,444	76,249	90,681
Percentage of total expenses outstanding in accounts payable	55.5%	51.5%	53%

Table 14.3

INCOME STATEMENTS
1979

	MONTH ENDING			Actual First Quarter Total	Original Total 1979 Budget (before revisions)
	January 31	February 28	March 31		
Revenue					
Public assistance	16,143	17,124	19,821	53,588	214,577
Visiting Nurse Assn.	9,644	10,137	11,011	30,792	144,655
Private	2,154	2,353	2,642	7,149	34,117
Other	5,133	3,996	4,798	13,927	21,718
Operating revenue	33,574	33,610	38,272	105,456	415,067
(Per hour served)	($4.90/hr)	($4.59/hr)	($4.48/hr)	($4.64/hr)	($4.32/hr)
United Way subsidy	$5,303	$5,304	$5,303	$15,910	$63,636
Total revenue	$38,877	$38,914	$43,575	$121,366	$478,703
Expenses					
Health aide staff wages	21,642	21,880	25,961	69,483	208,665
Employee benefits	1,225	676	1,910	3,811	13,801
Payroll & unemployment taxes	2,539	1,952	2,186	6,677	27,086
Direct expenses	25,406	24,508	30,057	79,971	249,552
(Per hour served)	($3.71/hr)	($3.35/hr)	($3.52/hr)	($3.52/hr)	($2.60/hr)
Professional and clerical salaries	$8,685	$8,971	$9,357	$27,013	$108,894
Other operating expenses	3,012	4,101	3,979	10,962	120,257
Total expenses	$37,103	$37,580	$43,393	$117,946	$478,703
(Per hour served)	($5.41/hr)	($5.14/hr)	($5.07/hr)	($5.19/hr)	($4.99/hr)
Surplus (or deficit)	$ 1,774	$ 1,335	$ 182	$ 3,420	$ 0
Operating Statistics					
Professional and clerical staff	15	15	16		
Health aide staff	75	84	90		
Hours served	6,854	7,318	8,545	22,717	96,000
Total cases	427	449	463		
Professional and clerical salaries per staff member	$579	$598	$585	$587	

Table 14.4

1979 STAFF AND VOLUME

Actual First Quarter	Professional and Clerical Staff	Health Aide Staff	Hours Served	Total Cases
January	15	75	6,854	427
February	15	84	7,318	449
March	16	90	8,545	463
Subtotal — Quarter I			22,717	
Forecasted Balance of 1974*				
April	22	115	11,000	500
May	22	125	11,500	575
June	22	130	12,000	600
Subtotal — quarter II			34,500	
July	22	140	12,500	600
August	22	140	12,500	600
September	23	140	12,500	600
Subtotal — quarter III			37,500	
October	23	145	13,000	600
November	23	145	13,500	600
December	23	145	14,000	600
Subtotal — quarter IV			40,500	
Total			135,217	

*Revised from original budget in Table 14.1 on the basis of the first quarter's experience.

15

Hospital Diversification into Long-Term Care

Robert E. Schlenker

THE SITUATION

This case deals with the possible diversification of a small, rural, acute-care hospital into institutional long-term care. The 40-bed hospital is considering whether or not to provide nursing-home-type care to patients. There is no long-term care facility in the hospital's service area, and preliminary surveys by the hospital suggest that a need for such care exists.

Two options for providing long-term care are available to the hospital. The first is to create a "distinct part" unit. This would be a physically identifiable unit (such as a separate building, floor, wing, or corridor) that could be certified as a Medicare and Medicaid provider if it meets specific health, safety, and related requirements. Such a unit is reimbursed separately from the rest of the institution through the cost-allocation process (explained later in the case).

The second option available to the hospital is the recently implemented "swing-bed" program. This program allows small rural hospitals (of 50 beds or less) to use their beds interchangeably as either hospital or long-term-care beds, and involves a simplified reimbursement process under Medicare and Medicaid. (The regulations are presented in the *Federal Register*, July 20, 1982, pp. 31518–28.) The swing-bed concept is intended to provide small rural hospitals with greater flexibility to meet the fluctuating demands for inpatient hospital and nursing home care.

The hospital has determined that ten beds could be converted to long-term care, either as a distinct part or as swing beds. The assignment for this case is to utilize the available information to determine the short-run financial impacts of both long-term-care options. This requires determining the impact of each option on annual hospital revenues and costs. For simplification, the case deals only with the impacts on routine (and not ancillary) services, costs, and revenues. Also, inflation can be ignored in the analysis.

ACUTE CARE

Acute-care utilization in the hospital has been fairly stable at 7,300 patient days per year, representing a 50 percent occupancy rate. Medicare utilization is typically 4,000 of those patient days (or approximately 55 percent of total utilization).

The nursing cost for routine care in this hospital amounts to $90 per patient day. All other routine costs are $60 per patient day, so that total routine cost is $150 per patient day. These represent allowable costs under Medicare after allocation to the routine care cost center. Since Medicare has recently eliminated the nursing differential, Medicare reimbursement for routine inpatient care is the average cost per patient day multiplied by the number of Medicare days.[1]

Medicaid acute-care utilization is 2,000 patient days. In the hospital's state, Medicaid hospital reimbursement for acute routine care is based on a fixed prospective rate set at $130 per patient day (below average cost).

Private-pay acute-care utilization is 1,300 patient days. This group includes patients covered by Blue Cross and commercial insurers, and self-pay patients, and all payment is assumed to be based on charges. After taking into account bad debts, the hospital realizes an average net revenue for routine care services to this group of patients of $180 per patient day.

LONG-TERM CARE

Levels of Care

Long-term care is typically categorized into two levels: skilled care and intermediate care. The Medicare program covers only skilled care, since its intent is that such care should be provided only as post-acute care. Skilled care is also referred to as SNF care, alluding to its provision in a "skilled nursing facility."

Skilled care is also a required service under Medicaid. However, since the Medicaid definition of skilled care is determined by each state, Medicaid SNF care differs among states, and SNF care typically differs between the Medicaid and Medicare programs within a state. For purposes of this analysis, it is assumed that the Medicare and Medicaid SNF benefits are the same, and that the ten beds to be used for long-term care will be certified as SNF beds under both Medicare and Medicaid.

Intermediate care is a lower level of care than skilled and is not covered by Medicare. However, most states cover intermediate care as an optional Medicaid benefit. Intermediate care is also referred to as ICF care, denoting its provision in "intermediate-care facilities." Although hospitals can and do provide both levels of long-term care, this case assumes that the hospital will provide only skilled-level care.

Long-Term Care Utilization

The hospital's projections of expected long-term care utilization are the same for both the distinct part and the swing-bed options. The expected annual utilization (all skilled days) is 500 Medicare days, 800 Medicaid days, and 200 private patient days, for a total of 1,500 long-term-care days.

The hospital administrator feels that the projected need for long-term care can be provided without any increase in the nursing staff. The hospital's low but fluctuating occupancy rate results in staffing levels which are higher than necessary during much of the year, and this "excess" staff can be utilized to provide long-term care. Thus, the hospital projects no increase in nursing cost to provide long-term care. Additional (nonnursing) routine operating costs for long-term care are projected at $5 per patient day. This includes the cost of food, laundry and linen services, basic medical supplies, and related items.

In addition, under the distinct-part option, the facility will need certain renovations, primarily the development of a patient activities room. The renovations will cost $100,000, including interest expenses. These expenses will be capitalized and depreciated over a ten-year period on a straight-line basis.

Under the swing-bed option, these renovations will not be necessary, since the swing-bed provisions provide more flexibility than the distinct-part regulations in meeting standards for the provision of long-term care. Hence, no additional capital expense will be required.

REVENUE IMPACTS

Non-Medicare Revenues

Medicaid long-term-care reimbursement varies among states. The state in which this hospital is located uses a prospectively determined SNF rate, set at $35 per patient day. The hospital also estimates that the average charge for private patients will be $60 per long-term-care patient day. As noted above, this case assumes that long-term-care patients will not utilize any ancillary services.[2] Hence, the addition of long-term care will affect only routine hospital revenues and costs.

Medicare reimbursement for long-term care differs between the distinct-part and swing-bed options. Further, Medicare reimbursement for acute care is altered under both options. The Medicare reimbursement procedures for each option are thus described in the next two sections. Table 15.1 summarizes the data presented up to this point.

Medicare Distinct-Part Reimbursement

Under the distinct-part option, all appropriate costs are allocated to the long-term-care unit, an average cost per day is determined, and that amount is paid for each Medicare patient day. Thus, routine costs must be allocated between the acute- and long-term-care units of the hospital, and this will affect Medicare acute-care reimbursement as well.

For this case, nursing cost is allocated between acute and long-term care in proportion to the amount of nursing time spent in each unit. Since less nursing care is required by long-term than by acute-care patients, it is assumed that each day of long-term care requires half the nursing cost of a day of acute care.

The cost attributable to the renovation is allocated entirely to the long-term-care unit. The allocation of the remaining routine cost utilizes different bases for different cost components. Total hospital depreciation expense is $200,000, and is allocated on the basis of square feet. (Assume that the distribution of square feet is the same as the distribution of beds.) The remaining routine costs are allocated in proportion to patient days.

Medicare Swing-Bed Reimbursement

Medicare reimbursement under the swing-bed approach is quite different from the distinct-part procedure. To begin with, Medicare payment for long-term-care services is at the average

Table 15.1

COST AND UTILIZATION DATA FOR ACUTE ROUTINE CARE AND POTENTIAL LONG-TERM ROUTINE CARE

Hospital Characteristics		
Number of beds	40	
Available bed days	14,600	
Acute patient days	7,300	
Medicare acute patient days	4,000	
Occupancy rate	50%	
Routine Acute-Care Utilization and Payment	**Patient Days**	**Per Patient Day Payment**
Medicare	4,000	$150
Medicaid	2,000	130
Private pay	1,300	180
Total	7,300	
Routine Acute-Care Costs	**Per Patient Day**	
Nursing cost	$ 90	
Other routine costs	60	
Total routine cost	150	
Expected Long-Term Care Utilization and Payment	**Days (all SNF)**	**Per Patient Day Payment**
Medicare	500	To be determined
Medicaid	800	$35
Private patients	200	60
Total	1,500	
Added Routine Costs for Long-Term Care		
Renovations (cost per year)		
Distinct part	$10,000	
Swing beds	0	
Nursing cost	0	
Other routine operating costs	$5 per patient day	

state *Medicaid* rate for routine SNF services during the previous calendar year. For this case, that amount is assumed to have been the same in the previous year, $35 per patient day.

Medicare reimbursement for acute-care services to hospitals providing swing-bed care is determined using the "carve-out" method. Under this method, no allocation of cost between the acute-care and long-term-care components of the hospital is carried out. Instead, an estimate of long-term-care costs is "carved out" of total routine costs (including acute- and long-term-care costs), and the remaining amount is assumed to be the portion attributable to acute care. The carve-out amount is calculated as the Medicaid cost per day times the number of long-term-care days, regardless of payer. (If both SNF and ICF care were involved, then the separate average SNF and ICF Medicaid rates would be utilized.) The total routine cost from which the long-term-care cost estimate is carved out is then the total cost including acute-care and long-term-care services; no cost allocation is carried out. The carve-out amount for this case is, therefore, the $35 per day times the total number of long-term-care days. The remaining routine costs are attributed to acute care.

NOTES

1. The nursing differential was a provision under Medicare that assumed that above-average nursing intensity was required for Medicare patients (because of their typically higher age and more intense case mix). This led to a higher Medicare reimbursement per routine-inpatient day than the average for all patients. Medicare reimbursement for routine care has also been subject to a routine operating cost limit. This limit was recently expanded to cover all Medicare inpatient services — routine and ancillary. For simplicity, this case assumes that the hospital is well under such limits.
2. A more realistic assumption would be that long-term-care patients use some ancillary services. A complete analysis would therefore include the impacts of the added ancillary services utilization on revenues and costs. The process and analytic techniques would be similar to those required for this case, although the specific reimbursement mechanisms differ from those applied to routine care.

16

Midtown Mental Health Center

J. B. Silvers

Rob Totten, the controller of the Midtown Mental Health Center, had pulled together the relevant information on data-processing alternatives. Although none were inexpensive, the problem was pressing and something had to be done. The degree of the need became apparent in early spring of 1978 when the critical paperwork process almost ground to a stop. Now, in April, he had to pull together a recommendation on the best method of upgrading the fiscal system with a particular eye to accelerating the collection of accounts receivable.

THE CENTER AND ITS FUNDING

Midtown Mental Health Center is a large inpatient/outpatient psychiatric treatment facility located within a substantial (650-bed) general hospital operated by the county government. Affiliated with one of the country's largest medical schools, the mental health center derived its operating income from a number of sources, including federal grants, state and local taxes, Title XX funds,[1] and donations from community organizations, as well as fees from consulting services rendered to other health-related institutions and patient charges to Medicare, Medicaid, insurance carriers, or the patients themselves. The contribution of the various funding sources to the total Midtown budget is shown in Table 16.1. The direct patient service costs (see Table 16.2) were not fully supported by the patient charges as a deliberate policy decision consistent with the philosophy of the center in serving an inner-city population.

In light of the presence of partially or totally indigent patients, the state funding had been devised as a way to allow free or discounted care to patients otherwise unable to pay. The state funding also was designed to pay for services of many sorts, such as community education, that did not generate any revenue.

In recent years, the dollar amount and the proportion of the state funds available had expanded greatly. Unfortunately, because of this dependence, state budgeting limitations were now severely restricting the growth of Midtown's services. This forced a greater attention to obtaining funds from other sources. The local taxing authorities, however, had a statutory

Table 16.1

PERCENTAGE CONTRIBUTION OF VARIOUS SOURCES OF FUNDS

Source	1976	1977	Projected 1978
Federal grants	38%	22%	6%
State tax receipts	26	47	51
Local tax receipts	16	10	15
Title XX payments	0	2	10
Donations	0.5	0.5	0.5
Consultation fees	0.5	0.5	0.5
Patient charges	19%	18%	17%
Total budget (in millions)	$2.85	$3.18	$3.41

Table 16.2

BUDGETED COSTS
1976 – 1978

	1976	1977	Projected 1978
Patient care staff costs	$1,679,313	$1,755,293	$2,147,086
Direct services costs	824,726	860,633	755,823
Subtotal	2,504,039	2,615,926	2,902,909
Support staff costs	233,368	411,192	276,534
Support services costs	71,554	86,594	53,066
Data processing costs	43,174	65,282	78,991
Total	$2,852,135	$3,178,994	$3,311,500
Percentage of growth over prior year		11%	4%

limit on property and income tax which had been reached in 1976. Several federal grant applications had been submitted, but none had been funded. Of the federal grants in effect, the amount available for use was shrinking each year.

STATUS OF THE COLLECTION SYSTEM

These developments left only patient charges as a source of additional funds to finance the center's growing needs for operating capital. Fortunately, because of historical imperfections in the billing system, there was a lot of opportunity to increase collections from this source. The main difficulty in improving collections of patient charges lay in the necessity to investigate delinquent accounts and initiate all follow-up without the aid of computerized systems.

A further complication was the mental state of Midtown's customers. Minor attempts at somewhat more aggressive collection efforts had backfired in the past, aggravating the patients' unstable condition. On one occasion, a patient asked a second time for payment went berserk in the office area and had to be restrained. On another, a patient relapsed into fits of crying and depression. As a result, the rule of thumb was that all accounts more than 30 days delinquent were just written off as uncollectible. Furthermore, the billing office took into account advice from the therapist concerning the patient's mental ability to pay, and acted accordingly.

In spite of these constraints, Mr. Totten felt that a significant improvement in actual collections was possible through improvement in the billing process within the center and its parent hospital. In fact, over half of the write-offs were now from commercial insurers due to improper or incomplete documentation. The degree of improvement, in terms of extra cash generated, depended on the method chosen but approached a cumulative total of around $500,000 (over the five-year period of analysis) for each of the three alternatives. This represented about 15 percent of the current year's budget.

In addition, over the past few years, requirements for more complicated billing, alterations in accounting procedures, and needs for special reports had increased tremendously. Confounding their problems was the fact that most of the funding sources required reporting using individualized accounting practices. Furthermore, nonbilling accounting work of the mental health center was done manually while billing was done by the host hospital's large computer system. For this service, the center paid a fee, which was increasing each year— especially in relation to the amount collected through its use.

By the end of January, the controller's office was sufficiently behind schedule that Mr. Totten sent a memorandum to the administrator of the center:

> We're on borrowed time right now in meeting our reporting and budgeting deadlines. There seem to be only two ways to keep on top of this work and still try to achieve some improvement in collections: either add staff to my department (four people right now), or perform major surgery on the data-processing system we're using.

THE ALTERNATIVES

As a result, Mr. Totten was asked to perform a study of Midtown's needs for information processing, both manual and automated, to determine the feasibility of Midtown's implementing an automated data-processing system designed to handle most of the financial and reporting requirements of the center. He concluded that there were three alternatives: (1) adding more staff, or upgrading computer services by (2) adding to the hospital's system or (3) purchasing a specialized computer.

Addition of more staff seemed a less desirable solution since it represented an ongoing and annually increasing cost with very limited capacity for expansion without more cost. Electronic data-processing improvements looked more promising, as evidenced by this memorandum from the controller to the administrator:

> From my review of available methodology, I am most impressed not by the difficulty of our problems, but by the rich selection of totally acceptable methods to solve them. The alternatives appear to fall into three major categories:
>
> 1. Addition of substantial staff resources to enable our current manual system to respond to the demand. Over the next 60 months (five years) seven accounting personnel would be added. (Table 16.3 summarizes these costs.)
> 2. Enhancement of the hospital's mainframe computer system by development of a software application and the addition of any necessary hardware to the computer. Because

of conflicts in scheduling of systems development personnel, it will be necessary to utilize data-processing consultants for this task. (Table 16.4 provides data on this alternative.)

3. Acquisition of a specialized medical management computer system consisting of a minicomputer to be installed in Midtown's offices along with a purchased software package. We also have the option to purchase this outright or to lease at a rate of 2 percent of the purchase price per month over the 60 months of its useful life, although purchase would require a three-month delay while the proposal cleared the hospital and county capital budgetary authorities. Leases, on the other hand, are operating expenses and fit within existing fiscal authorization. (See Table 16.5.)

With this financial information, Mr. Totten felt that he had the basis to make a preliminary evaluation. However, there were several additional factors which could not be ignored. First was the element of risk involved. Although most of this was subjective it nevertheless was a real factor. The proposals (Tables 16.3, 16.4, and 16.5) all included some of his subjective estimates.

RISKS INVOLVED

At one level, Mr. Totten felt that the minicomputer was more risky since it involved the installation of new hardware and systems, while the existing hospital mainframe and the addition of new personnel were known commodities. Furthermore, the main hospital computer costs would be shared (and paid) by users other than just Midtown. On the other hand, the new software systems to be developed on the main computer, although they would be compatible with a future minicomputer which might be added, were new and thus were subject to typical delays and start-up problems.

Unfortunately, even personnel costs were unusually variable in Midtown due to the constantly changing mix of professionals in the mental health field. This was partially due to an imbalance between supply and demand. The state now had 27 mental health centers with up to 40 forecast by 1980, producing a big demand for therapists. However, the colleges in the state were graduating only 100 therapists on the bachelor's and graduate level combined. The resulting turnover in personnel reached 60 percent in 1977. In the accounting area, however, Mr. Totten thought that the instability would be much less, although accounting and data-processing personnel were also in high demand. He guessed that labor costs throughout his analysis might vary by 10 percent to 20 percent from his estimates, with the variation growing larger in later years.

The biggest risk, however, lay in the forecast for collecting the extra billings (which produced the "cash benefits" under each alternative). Historically, over the 24 months of 1976−1977, collections had varied widely from month to month. About two-thirds of the *actual* monthly collections fell in a range of 37 percent above or below the *average* monthly collections (i.e., standard deviation = 37 percent). If the "benefits" from the better billing systems followed the same pattern, then the results could be significantly different from that forecast in the tables.

Table 16.3
ALTERNATIVE I: PROPOSAL FOR ADDITION OF STAFF TO CONTROLLER'S DEPARTMENT
Forecast Cash Flows—Months 1 to 60 (5-Year Project)

	YEAR 1												YEAR 2			YEAR 3			YEARS 4-5		5 Year Cumulative Total
	1	2	3	4	5	6	7	8	9	10	11	12	13 ...	24	25	26 ...	36	37	38 ...	60	
Cash Outflows																					
2 Accountants, 2 Clerks (mo. 1)	$4,667	4,667	4,667	4,667	4,667	4,667	4,667	4,667	4,667	4,667	4,667	4,667	4,667 ...	4,667	4,667	4,667 ...	4,667	4,667	4,667 ...	4,667	280,020
1 Accountant, 1 Clerk (mo. 25)															2,292	2,292 ...	2,292	2,292	2,292 ...	2,292	82,512
1 Clerk (mo. 37)																		450	958 ...	958	22,992
Office furniture purchased	$4,000	0	0	0	0	0	0	0	0	0	0	0	0 ...	0	2,000	0 ...	0	1,000	0 ...	0	7,000
Subtotal— outflows	8,667	4,667	4,667	4,667	4,667	4,667	4,667	4,667	4,667	4,667	4,667	4,667	4,667 ...	4,667	8,959	6,959 ...	6,959	8,917	7,917 ...	7,917	392,524
Cash Benefits (Inflows)																					
Increased collections	2,000	2,000	2,000	4,000	4,000	6,000	8,000	10,000	10,000	10,000	10,000	10,000	10,000 ...	10,000	10,000	10,000 ...	10,000	10,000	10,000 ...	10,000	558,000

NOTES:

Summary:
The proposal is basically a straightforward addition of accounting professionals and clerks to extend the current manual system to include a more exhaustive follow-up and a more rapid initial processing.

Cash-Flow Benefits
The primary benefit to be derived will be increased collections from patient charges due to an increased ability to review bad debt listings to determine accounts to be turned over to an agency.

Subjective Evaluation: From the standpoint of being a social service agency, one goal of our management is to provide a working environment in which employees are free to perform their job in the best manner possible, without pressures arising from potential layoffs or other disasters. The future of Midtown Mental Health Center funding is quite political. Personnel already account for over 70 percent of the total budget. In the future, extreme pressure will be placed on all health-care agencies to trim this down by increasing emphasis on automation. A large increase in staffing, as suggested by this proposal, would be much harder to sustain in such conditions than would increased staff in direct patient-contact areas.

Table 16.4

ALTERNATIVE 2: PROPOSAL FOR ENHANCEMENT OF MAINFRAME COMPUTER SYSTEM OF PARENT HOSPITAL
Forecast Cash Flows — Months 1 to 60 (5-Year Project)

	YEAR 1												YEARS 2-5			5 Year Cumulative Total
	1	2	3	4	5	6	7	8	9	10	11	12	13	....	60	
Cash Outflows																
Development costs	4,000	4,000	18,500	6,000	21,000	4,000	2,000	2,000	2,000	14,000	8,000	8,000	0		0	103,500
Operating costs	0	0	2,000	2,000	3,000	3,000	6,000	6,000	8,000	10,000	10,000	10,000	3,000		3,000	256,000
Subtotal — outflows	4,000	4,000	20,500	8,000	24,000	7,000	8,000	8,000	10,000	24,000	18,000	18,000	3,000		3,000	359,500
Cash Benefits (Inflows)																
Increased collections	0	0	0	6,000	8,000	8,000	12,000	12,000	12,000	12,000	12,000	13,000	13,000		13,000	723,000

NOTES:

Summary:
Develop and implement a computer system which will allow the acquisition and processing of financial and patient-identification data and the printing of necessary management reports. The system must be implemented on the hospital's IBM 370/135 computer system, augmented as necessary by additional peripherals or core capacity. The system as implemented must allow easy development of special or "one-time" reports.

Cash-Flow Benefits:
The primary benefit to be derived will be increased collections from patient charges due to an increased ability to review bad debt listings to determine accounts to be turned over to an agency.

Subjective Evaluation: The primary risk here is technological obsolescence. This is considered to be quite low, since the entire hospital is utilizing systems which are required to be run on IBM equipment. In addition, all new systems for Midtown will be developed using ANS Cobol which can be transferred to a large number of different machines with little conversion cost. In addition, we have received in writing an agreement from the data processing department that future hardware problems necessitating conversion of our system will be resolved by their personnel at no cost to Midtown. Financial risk has also been reduced, because of a written agreement from data processing that limits our costs of running on their machine to the amount stated in the proposal for the length of the project (60 months). In any event, bankruptcy risk is *eliminated* because of "in-advance" funding of the development costs and our ability to stop using the computer at our option at any time.

Table 16.5

ALTERNATIVE 3: PROPOSAL FOR IN-HOUSE MINICOMPUTER SYSTEM
Forecast Cash Flows Months 1 to 60 (assumed at end of month)

| | | YEAR 1 | | | | | | YEARS 2-5 | | 5 Year |
	0	1	2	3	4	5	6...12	13...59	60	Cumulative Total
CASH OUTFLOWS										
Operating Costs										
Data entry personnel/computer operator		1,000	1,000	1,000	1,000	1,000	1,000... 1,000	1,000... 1,000	1,000	60,000
Additional data transfer cost to/from main hospital computer		700	700	700	700	700	700... 700	700... 700	700	42,000
Subtotal — operating cost	0	1,700	1,700	1,700	1,700	1,700	1,700... 1,700	1,700... 1,700	1,700	102,000
Capital Costs										
Computer system lease cost (due at beginning of month)	3,000	3,000	3,000	3,000	3,000	3,000	3,000... 3,000	3,000... 3,000	0	180,000
(a) Subtotal — total costs if leased	3,000	4,700	4,700	4,700	4,700	4,700	4,700... 4,700	4,700... 4,700	1,700	282,000
Initial purchase expenditure (lease/mo. = 2% of purchase)	150,000	—	—	—	—	—	— ... —	— ... —	—	150,000 *
Depreciation (straight line; zero salvage value = 150,000/60 months)	0	2,500	2,500	2,500	2,500	2,500	2,500... 2,500	2,500... 2,500	2,500	
(b) Subtotal — total costs if purchased	150,000	4,200	4,200	4,200	4,200	4,200	4,200... 4,200	4,200... 4,200	4,200	252,000
CASH BENEFITS (INFLOWS)										
Increased collections	0	4,000	6,000	8,000	8,000	8,000	12,000...12,000	12,000...12,000	12,000	694,000

NOTES:

Summary: Develop and implement a computer system with the same specifications as above, except that the hardware will be a dedicated minicomputer to be installed in Midtown's offices. The operating system will be a standard "package."

Cash Flow Benefits:
The primary benefit to be derived will be increased collections from patient charges due to an increased ability to review bad debt listings to determine accounts to be turned over to an agency.

Subjective Evaluation: This is a project carrying high risk. Midtown, in agreeing to a long-term lease, is assuming a financial liability which is fixed, regardless of the level of benefits derived. The cost to break the lease is very high. Inquiries at other Mental Health Centers indicate only very slight interest in purchasing computer time from us.

*Note: $150,000 initial expenditure represents *cash outflow* while $2,500/month depreciation is the accounting recognition of this outlay as a *cost* of business in each month.

POLITICAL AND FUNDING PROBLEMS

Another factor that bothered Mr. Totten was the political one of the autonomy of the center versus centralized data processing (and general management) under the hospital umbrella. While this trade-off was hard to evaluate, Midtown would have greater control with the minicomputer system — as long as it could find sufficient funding.

In fact, it was the funding issue which typically created the greatest problem for both existing and new program efforts. However, from the point of view of the center, if implementation were phased to coincide with the regular budgeting cycle, then no extra cash-flow problems would be encountered (assuming that the project were approved). This resulted from the center's cost-based payment system which was utilized for federal reimbursement and state and local budget allocations. Both development and operating costs (which were basically all labor) and capital costs (lease payments or interest and depreciation costs) were included. Currently, federal payments were 10 percent of the budget, state appropriations about 50 percent, and local allocations about 15 percent; thus, about 75 percent of all Midtown's receipts were based on accounting costs.

Presumably, the $60,000 capital cost of the minicomputer (if it were not leased) would be paid by a regular lump sum appropriation from the county. The hospital source of these capital funds could be interpreted either as borrowing by the county hospital at the current 5 percent rate for tax-exempt securities or as receipts of income and property tax levies at the state and local level. Both of these sources provided cash which could be used to fund the appropriation. But, in any event, Mr. Totten felt that in essence the taxpayers would be paying for the project's capital cost either immediately (in the case of purchase) or over five years (in the case of lease or gradual upgrading of the hospital's main system). In terms of budgetary politics, however, it was much easier to spread the cash outlay over several years than to request an initial lump sum.

THE DECISION

As Mr. Totten summarized the data and began his analysis and report for the board, he faced several issues. The first had to do with determining the expected advantage of one alternative over the others in terms of dollar benefits and costs over the 60-month (five-year) useful life of the equipment. He thought that the benefits were so superior that the question was not one of whether to do something, but rather which way was best. However, since the benefits varied among the three alternatives, he planned to compare the net present value (of cash benefits less cash outlays) using an opportunity rate of 5 percent (see Table 16.6). However, he was unsure as to the variation in the cash flows and the appropriateness of the interest rate used. This would require further analysis. He also needed to come to some conclusion regarding whether the minicomputer should be leased or purchased, if it were to be acquired at all.

He knew that the board would require substantial explanation of both the technical and subjective factors. However, in resolving the problem, the hospital's vice-president of finance indicated that this sort of problem occurred frequently and had in the past been evaluated in a very sloppy fashion. He was under pressure from all sides, but particularly from federal and state auditors, to become more sophisticated in order to satisfy "prudent buyer" standards

Table 16.6

MONTHLY PRESENT VALUE FACTORS AT 5% ANNUAL RATE
(Present Value of $1 Received at the End of the Month)

	Month Received	Present Value at 5% Annual Rate (0.417%/month)[1]	Cumulative within Year[2]	Cumulative from Outset[3]
Initial	0	$1.0000	--------	--------
1st Year	1	0.9959		
	2	0.9917		
	3	0.9876		
	4	0.9835		
	5	0.9794		
	6	0.9754		
	7	0.9713		
	8	0.9673		
	9	0.9633		
	10	0.9593		
	11	0.9553		
	12	0.9513	11.6812	11.6812
2nd Year	13	0.9474		
	:	:		
	24	0.9050	11.1127	22.7939
3rd Year	25	0.9013		
	:	:		
	36	0.8610	10.5718	33.3657
4th Year	37	0.8574		
	:	:		
	48	0.8191	10.0573	43.4230
5th Year	49	0.8157		
	:	:		
	60	0.7792	9.5677	52.9907

1. The practice is usually to state monthly rate as $\frac{1}{12}$ of the annual rate. However, technically the monthly rate if compounded would result in a higher annual rate than 12 times the monthly rate.
2. "Cumulative within Year" represents the present value at time zero (now) of $1 received each month for the twelve months of *only* the year in question.
3. "Cumulative from Outset" represents the present value at time period zero (now) of $1 received each month for *all* months up to the end of the year in question.

increasingly being applied to such purchases. He was very interested in incorporating Mr. Totten's analysis, if appropriate, into the formal system of the hospital. Unfortunately, he also had a very limited understanding of the techniques of financial analysis. Everyone other than Mr. Totten has become accustomed to the use of budget constraints and subjective evaluation as the only limitations or criteria in making such program and project decisions. Thus, Mr. Totten's educational as well as analytic jobs were cut out for him as he prepared for the board meeting the following week.

NOTE

1. Title XX is a Medicaid-related funding program of the federal government designed to pay for social services rendered to indigent patients or those who are disabled. Like most other federal reimbursement programs, it is cost-based but with no guarantee that payment might not be restricted to less-than-full cost due to legal constraints on taxation or legislative funding decisions.

17

Bay Health Plan

Stephen S. Hyde

Lunch was over, and Ray Stewart was relieved to have finally a full afternoon before him without scheduled meetings or the possibility of interrupting telephone calls. He turned his attention to preparing a financial plan for his new health maintenance organization (HMO), the Bay Health Plan (BHP). He reflected on the events that had led to his appointment as President and Chief Executive Officer only three months earlier, and all that had occurred since.

Ray had been the chief financial officer of a very successful HMO in the Rocky Mountain West and, after four years, had decided it was time to advance his career by using his skills to develop a new HMO. Through contacts in the HMO industry, he had been introduced to the president of Coastline Medical Group in Bay City, Florida. The medical group had recently decided to sponsor the development of a captive HMO, and was looking for an experienced person to manage the development and operations of the new venture. After the usual rounds of interviews and salary and benefit negotiations, Ray had accepted Coastline's offer.

After moving to Bay City, Ray had initially immersed himself in 14-hour days of market surveys, benefit design, physician education, meetings with state and federal regulatory officials, preliminary hospital negotiations, and discussions with various consultants. After three months of this process, Ray felt he had gathered sufficient information to be able to prepare preliminary forecasts of income and cash flow. He wanted these so that he could begin to estimate how much capital he would need to develop and operate the HMO until it achieved financial self-sufficiency.

Today, Ray barricaded himself in his office and his files and his personal computer to take a first crack at estimating those capital needs. He knew that while these estimates would be subject to substantial refinement by his own chief financial officer (CFO) — once he had the means to hire one — the figures he developed on this hot, muggy Florida afternoon would provide the basis for his ensuing negotiations with the investors who would be providing the needed start-up capital. This capital would support the two major phases of beginning the

HMO: (1) developing the HMO over a six-month period (September 1982 through February 1983) to the point just prior to beginning actual enrollment, and (2) operating BHP prior to its gaining sufficient enrollment to achieve profitability. The Phase 1 development costs are provided in Table 17.1.

Table 17.1

BAY HEALTH PLAN DEVELOPMENT BUDGET
September 1982 — February 1983

Expense Category	Estimated Expense
Personnel	$104,700
Rent	11,000
Telephone	3,000
Advertising	8,000
Actuary	2,500
Legal	10,000
Printing	20,000
Equipment	25,000
Travel	13,000
Postage and supplies	6,000
HMO management consultants	50,000
Total expense	$253,200

Before proceeding with his financial projections, Ray reviewed the Summary Business Plan (Appendix 17.1), a document he had prepared for the medical group physicians who were to provide the capital for the HMO. He also reviewed the letter he had recently received from Arkady Darrell, his consulting actuary, in which Ms. Darrell provided preliminary assumptions regarding expected utilization rates and unit costs for the major categories of health care services (Appendix 17.2).

From his meetings with colleagues and his periodic review of the literature, Ray felt that the HMO industry tended to focus too much on health services utilization control as the primary determinant of an HMO's success or failure. While Ray agreed that utilization control was an essential element of HMO success, he felt that tight control of administrative expenses was an area frequently overlooked by HMO managers, and with equally frequent fatal results. Therefore, Ray had been particularly careful in developing his estimates of administrative costs for the development period and initial three years of operations. Ray estimated that once BHP was solidly in the black, he would be able to operate the administrative component for about 12.5 percent of revenue.

As a former finance director, Ray knew only too well that financial results based on accrual accounting techniques did not necessarily reflect the ability of an HMO (or any other organization) to pay its bills when due. He placed a high priority on using his vendors as sources of permanent financing while not allowing his customers to do the same thing. His unofficial motto had long been "minimize receivables, maximize payables." (His official motto was "never make a decision until you need to.")

In preliminary discussions with the medical group's administrator, Enzo Paganinni, Ray had discussed the possibility of delaying BHP's monthly capitation payment to the medical group by up to 90 days (i.e., delay to the first of the third month following the month of service) for the first three years of operations, before moving to payment at the end of the month of service on a permanent basis. Ray justified this to Enzo on the basis that the medical group's accounts receivable on its fee-for-service business normally ran about 90 days, and that similar treatment for BHP — at least initially — would help the HMO get on its feet that much faster. Without committing himself fully, Enzo agreed that such an arrangement could probably be worked out. Ray was obviously concerned about the effect of Enzo's final decision on BHP's financing needs.

Ray next turned his attention to hospital expenses and when he would have to pay them. He expected that, unless he was able to work out arrangements for faster payment in exchange for discounts or fixed per diem rates, most of the hospitals would bill BHP at the end of each month for services provided during that month. He would pay those bills 30 to 60 days later, depending upon each hospital's collection policy. On average, he expected to pay BHP's hospital expenses 45 days after the end of each month of service. Ray realized, however, that he might have to or want to make earlier payment, depending upon each hospital's willingness to accept BHP's creditworthiness and upon its possible desire to provide discounts for prompt payment.

Ray knew from experience that enforcement of a reasonably firm policy on accounts receivable would tend to assure collection of substantially all of BHP's premium income during the month due. Ray planned to invoice each enrolled employer group on the twentieth of each month, with the billed amount being due on the first of the following month — the month of service. Ray knew that while certain accounts, most notably the U.S. government, were chronically late payers, most would pay during the month due. Indeed, a significant portion tended to pay before the due date of the first of the month. Ray concluded that the net effect would be that BHP would collect pretty close to 100 percent of its premiums in the month due, although he admitted to himself that he might not be quite as conservative in this area as he usually tended to be.

Since the bulk of administrative expenses (i.e., salaries, rent, etc.) were not subject to payment after the month expensed, Ray assumed that all such items would be paid in the month incurred.

As Ray booted up the "electronic worksheet" software on his personal computer to begin his financial projections, he set as his goal the preliminary determination of BHP's capital financing needs to cover development and initial operations to the point where BHP would begin generating, rather than consuming, cash. He also wanted to identify additional analytical and operational issues to be further refined by himself and his as-yet nonexistent executive staff (i.e., directors of marketing, finance, and medical care delivery) during actual development of the HMO. Ray hoped that, with the help of his microcomputer, he would be home by 5:30. He wasn't.

Appendix 17.1

SUMMARY BUSINESS PLAN

INTRODUCTION

Bay Health Plan (BHP) is to be a new health maintenance organization (HMO) sponsored by the Coastline Medical Group (CMG) and its member physicians, and developed by professional management staff employed by BHP.

BHP is to begin operations in March 1983 after a six-month development period. It will provide a wide range of health care services on a prepaid basis to members who voluntarily join the plan through employer groups. The business will be regulated as an HMO by agencies of the state of Florida and the federal government. It will be organized as a partnership to optimize tax advantages.

Prepaid health plans, or HMOs, have operated in the United States for over 50 years. There are now approximately 260 plans providing services for over 10 million members nationwide. The industry has grown rapidly during the past 10 years as the federal government, insurers, and employers have encouraged their development.

In Bay City there is currently only one HMO, CompreNet. BHP will market its services to employees in Bay City in direct competition with CompreNet. Competition will be based on medical delivery systems, locations, price, and benefits.

Marketing projections for the end of each of the first three calendar years of operations are:

Year	Members
1983	4,800
1984	10,450
1985	15,925

These projections are based on enrollment of groups of employees only. However, recent changes in the Medicare law may provide substantial financial incentives for HMOs to enroll Medicare individuals, and Bay City is ideal for rapid growth of prepaid Medicare services under these new rules.

BACKGROUND

Since the mid-1960s, the cost of health care has consistently risen faster than the consumer price index. The nation's total expenditure for health care is now in excess of 10 percent of the gross national product and is a major cost element of employee fringe benefits, thereby adding to the cost of all goods and services produced.

Both government and employers have been increasing their efforts to discover ways to control these ever-increasing costs. In 1969, a study was conducted comparing the experience of the Kaiser-Permanente Health Plan, a California-based HMO, and Blue Cross. Results of the study indicated that those enrolled in the Kaiser Plan were hospitalized half as much as those in Blue Cross, and that the total cost of services was lower. Since that time, other studies of prepaid plans have consistently shown that health care costs can be reduced in a prepaid health plan without sacrificing quality of care. Hospital services are reduced by use of outpatient surgery and testing, and by avoiding unnecessary services whenever possible.

The federal government began promoting the development of HMOs in 1973 as a way to slow the rate of increase in health care costs. As employers and insurers gained experience with the new concept, many began encouraging it themselves. During the past decade, growth of this industry has been significant. In 1970, there were only 30 plans with 2 million members. By the end of 1981 there were 260 plans with over 10 million members. Beginning on the West Coast and in the Northeast, the concept has now spread throughout the country. Eight plans now operate in the state of Florida.

Prepaid health plans differ significantly from traditional health insurance in how services are paid for and how services are received. First, most HMOs offer their comprehensive services for a fixed monthly fee. This means that services are paid for in advance. In comparison, insurance reimburses covered expenses after they have been incurred. Second, the delivery of health care services is never the responsibility of an insurance plan. It is up to the individual to find physicians and other providers as they are needed. HMO members receive care from physicians who are under contract with the HMO. In this way, all care is coordinated through the HMO. Preventive services, such as immunizations, are covered, as are hospital services and specialty care such as surgery, obstetrics, and gynecology. Because HMOs are able to reduce out-of-pocket expenses, their members can receive a wider range of benefits for less total cost per year than from an insurance plan.

DESCRIPTION OF SERVICES

An HMO provides the services of physicians, hospitals, and other providers to its members on a prepaid basis. Members are required to use only the providers affiliated with the HMO, except in cases of emergency. For an HMO to be attractive to prospective members, it must offer (1) perceived economic advantage, (2) perceived high-quality service, and (3) perceived convenience. BHP will be able to meet these needs for most working people in Bay City. Benefit plans are designed to have an economic value for the average person. Significant premium differentials with competing insurers will be avoided to reduce the chance of adverse selection of a high proportion of sick members. Total costs (i.e., premiums plus out-of-pocket costs for noncovered items, deductibles, and coinsurance) will be higher for insurance plans in most cases.

Of course, the main factor inhibiting HMO enrollment is the need to change doctors, to use only those affiliated with the plan. This is why perception (and, of course, the reality) of high-quality service is so important. If someone is willing to change doctors for economic reasons, he/she must be confident that the quality of service will be at least as good. Physician services are the strongest sales advantage of BHP because Coastline Medical Group will provide those services.

The CMG is a well-established, multispecialty group with a total of 35 physicians. It has attractive, well-equipped medical facilities, and can offer a wide range of services under one roof. Since its founding in 1967, CMG has provided the community with a wide range of high-quality services. Specialties include internal medicine, cardiology, endocrinology, pediatrics, orthopedics, obstetrics-gynecology, urology, general surgery, gastroenterology, nephrology, oncology, neurology, and pulmonary diseases. CompreNet, on the other hand, currently provides only primary care in its two facilities and has limited in-house capabilities. CMG's present 44,000-square foot facility opened in 1970. The group also has a branch office in the Southgate Mall shopping center.

CMG's interest in developing Bay Health Plan is to bring new patients to the group. This will allow CMG to utilize its facilities better and to grow in a planned and careful way. It will also diversify the group's patient base and reduce future dependence on Medicare, a dominant factor in Bay City.

In addition to physician services, high-quality hospital services are essential to an HMO's benefit package. BHP intends to contract with Bay City General Hospital, Children's Medical Center, and Three Palms Hospital. These are among the largest and best-known hospitals in the city.

Convenience is another important part of the plan's services. Each of the two CMG clinics is conveniently located. Approximately 191,000 people under age 65 live within three miles, and 401,000 within five miles, of the service locations currently available. This means that over three-quarters of Bay City residents below the age of 65 live within five miles, and no one lives beyond 30 minutes' travel time. Travel distance and time are considered to be important convenience factors.

The convenience of seeing a doctor without a long wait is important as well. Because CMG has in place well-developed systems responsive to its fee-for-service patients, members of BHP will be able to see a doctor just as readily as fee-for-service patients. There is also a choice of doctors in most specialties. A final element of convenience is reduction of paperwork. Members of BHP will not routinely have claim forms to file. Since services are provided directly by the plan, no claim forms are required. The only exception is for emergency services received outside of Bay City.

Marketing Strategy

BHP will initially provide services to residents of Bay City, Florida. Bay City is attractive for HMO development for several reasons: (1) population continues to increase; (2) the city is part of a larger SMSA which can allow future expansion; (3) there is a base of approximately 2,800 employers with 11 or more employees, and a total of 195,000 employees; (4) benefit levels and premiums are sufficient for an HMO to be competitive; and (5) major employers already offer CompreNet and will offer BHP to satisfy federal requirements. To become profitable, BHP must attain market penetration of less than 3 percent.

As of the 1980 census, there were 728,000 residents, 526,000 under 65. The city's population grew by 39.5 percent from 1970 to 1980 and current projections indicate continued growth, with a population base of 776,000 to 846,000 by 1985. In addition, most of the present growth is in younger age groups. Median age has dropped by two years over the last decade.

There are currently approximately 250,000 persons employed by 16,000 employers in Bay City. The distributions by industry type and firm size are shown in Table 17.2.

The actual market for BHP, as we define it, is limited to employers with 11 or more employees. There are approximately 2,800 employers with 195,000 employees in this category.

Table 17.2

DISTRIBUTION OF BAY CITY EMPLOYEES BY INDUSTRY TYPE AND FIRM SIZE

Industry Type	Percent of Employees
Service	27.0
Trade	26.3
Manufacturing	14.7
Government	12.7
Construction	7.9
Financial, insurance, real estate	7.6
Commercial utilities	3.8

Firm Size	Number of Firms	Percent of Employees
1-10	13,250	22
11-25	1,590	13
26-50	610	11
51-100	345	12
101-250	160	12
251-500	51	10
500+	29	20

Because the risk of adverse selection and the marketing costs are high for firms with fewer than 11 employees, these employers are not considered attractive. Medicare eligibles are also excluded from the initial marketing strategy, although recent changes in legislation promise substantial improvements in reimbursement for Medicare eligibles who belong to HMOs.

Other groups excluded from the market definition are hospital employees (14,000), who are traditionally high utilizers of health care services, and federal employees (7,000). Federal rules require that retired federal workers be enrolled at the same premium rate as nonretired workers. In Bay City, there are more than twice as many retired federal workers as active workers, so the risk in this group is unacceptable.

A current survey of over 250 Bay City employers representing approximately 60,000 employees (38 percent of the total) indicates that 63 percent of employees are covered by plans with premiums within $12 per month of our preliminary estimate of BHP's family premium rate. An additional 10 percent are between $12 and $18, and could receive a "low option" BHP benefit package. The conclusions of these findings are that approximately 75 percent of the employees are covered by plans with rates acceptable to BHP, and that the plan can be successfully marketed on a price-competitive basis in Bay City. BHP should become more competitive as rates for alternative plans increase at a faster rate over time. For BHP to be successful in the long run, it must reduce use of hospital services. Part of the savings can be used to reduce premiums, thereby making the plan more competitive.

Federal rules will be a significant advantage in dealing with major employers. Section 1310 of the federal HMO Act requires employers, under specific conditions, to offer the HMO option to their employees. Further, two types of HMOs are defined in the act and at least one of each type must be offered, if available. Most major employers have developed policies requiring compliance with these rules before they will offer the HMO option. For this reason, it is important for BHP to become qualified under the federal rules as a group-practice model. Since CompreNet is qualified as an IPA (Independent Practice Association) model HMO, both types will be represented in the city, and major employers currently offering CompreNet will also be required to offer BHP. This represents a substantial marketing advantage, and BHP's strategy is to make optimum use of it.

The strategy to be used to achieve marketing objectives is multifaceted. Within the first two years, approximately two-thirds of the large employee groups (i.e., 250 or more employees) are expected to enroll. Multiple benefit plans will be available to optimize enrollment in each group to reduce the risk of negative selection. Marketing to medium (100–250) and small (10–100) groups will begin in the first year and accelerate in years 2 and 3. During the first two years of operation, 20 large employer groups with over 34,000 employees are expected to enroll. CompreNet has enrolled 10 to 50 percent of the employees in these groups and BHP projects an average of 7.4 percent.

The marketing expense involved in acquiring new members in large groups should be relatively low because of the large number of potential members per group. However, penetration rates are generally higher in smaller groups because direct access to employees is more frequently available.

Part of the strategy includes enrolling smaller groups, which diversify the membership base. BHP will be sold to these smaller groups by a staff of sales and service personnel. They will be supported by a community awareness advertising program. This is an important element of the marketing strategy because the buying decision is often made by an employee's spouse who seldom hears the sales presentation directly. This is where the credibility of the long-established medical group is invaluable.

Groups will be enrolled only when they meet multiple selection criteria. Premium rates of current health insurance must be within competitive limits for the group to be acceptable from a risk perspective. Other criteria include group size, financial stability, management receptivity, equal premium contribution by the employer, and acceptable rating structure (e.g., not based on age categories). Each criterion is designed to assure that an enrolled group will contribute to BHP's profitability.

The plan will enroll employees and their families. This means that, on average, 2.3 members are expected to be enrolled for each contract (i.e., each employee). Approximately 30 percent of the plan's members will be children under the age of 20.

The standard approach in the HMO industry is to enroll members under contracts for one year. Once each year, employees are given the opportunity to change from one plan to the other without evidence of insurability. Experience in the industry indicates that HMO membership tends to grow each year as the HMO becomes better understood among employees. BHP expects to increase membership each year by 10 percent of the prior year's enrollment.

New members will also come from new employees hired by enrolled groups. However, an element of conservatism is reflected in the fact that no recognition has been given to this factor in the marketing plan.

Long-term growth may require expansion into new markets. Geographic expansion into contiguous counties is a logical step which will be continually evaluated. It is also important to grow in an orderly and planned way. Since member satisfaction and ability to control costs are so important, too rapid expansion could be detrimental to the plan's long-term profitability.

With the population growth potential of the SMSA, it is possible that BHP could serve a membership of 100,000 within ten years. This would represent less than 5 percent penetration of the SMSA's population by that time.

Appendix 17.2

CONSULTING ACTUARY'S ASSUMPTIONS ABOUT UTILIZATION RATES AND UNIT COSTS

Arkady Darrell, F.S.A.
Actuarial Consultant

August 8, 1982

Mr. Raymond Stewart, CEO
Bay Health Plan
83 Coast Highway
Bay City, Florida

Dear Ray:

You have asked me for preliminary health service utilization assumptions in support of initial financial projections to determine capital financing needs for Bay Health Plan (BHP). Using information provided by you and other sources, I have derived assumptions that I feel to be reasonable as a starting point in establishing financial projections. These assumptions are included in this letter. I must emphasize, however, that these are preliminary assumptions of a rather gross nature, and do not include the sort of detailed utilization and unit cost assumptions by type of service which will be necessary for BHP's rate filings with the Florida Insurance Commissioner. I look forward to working with you in the near future to develop these detailed assumptions.

REVENUE

It is my understanding that BHP will begin providing health care services to its members in March 1983. The plan will be marketed to employee groups in Bay City. On the basis of preliminary analysis, I would suggest initial monthly premiums which will yield revenues of $51.66 per member per month. This should result in rates which are within $12 and $33 of the single and family rates charged to most major groups in Bay City by their indemnity insurance carriers. CompreNet's rates are currently at approximately the same levels.

I would recommend that BHP plan to increase its premium rates each quarter for groups enrolling for the first time, and for those reenrolling after each full year of enrollment. Rates in each group, once established, would then be effective for one year. To be on the conservative side, I would recommend an assumed premium inflation rate of 12 percent per year over the next three years.

As you know, a basic unit of calculation for HMOs is the "member-month." A person who is a member for one year represents twelve member-months. Most revenue and cost items are projected on this basis. Using your enrollment projections for the first three years, I have calculated the following average revenue per member per month (pmpm) for those years:

Year	Member-Months	Average Revenue pmpm
1983	23,200	$52.56
1984	94,300	57.03
1985	161,400	64.23

The attachment to this letter provides a detailed breakout of these figures by month for each of the three years.

MEDICAL GROUP CAPITATION EXPENSE

Except for administrative expenses, the major cost items anticipated for BHP will vary directly with the level of membership. Compensation to the Coastline Medical Group (CMG) will be based on the number of members enrolled in BHP, and will be paid in the form of a monthly "capitation" payment. This "capitation" rate will be effective on a calendar-year basis, and will be included as part of the contract between BHP and CMG.

Services to be covered by this capitation rate will include all physician and professional services, laboratory, x-ray, and other diagnostic procedures, emergency room, and home health services. The initial capitation is projected at $21 pmpm. This is based on the utilization rates experienced by other HMOs in my data and adjusted for the age and sex characteristics of Bay City.

Service	Visits/Member/Year
Outpatient Visits	3.14
Lab	2.52
X-ray	0.67

I have estimated each year's capitation rate to CMG to be as follows:

Year	Capitation
1981	$21.00
1982	23.52
1983	26.34

HOSPITAL EXPENSE

The largest single expense item is hospitalization. This expense must be controlled for BHP to be successful. The unit of measure used among HMOs is days of hospitalization per 1,000 members per year. The national average for Blue Cross plans is approximately 750 days per 1,000 members per year. For HMOs, the national average is 425, with well-run, group-practice model HMOs operating consistently below 400 days/1,000 members/year. These reductions are possible because of the commitment of physicians to seek the most cost-effective approach to solving a patient's problem. Outpatient testing and outpatient surgery are used whenever possible. Avoiding unnecessary surgery and non-medically-necessary extra days before and after surgery also contributes to savings. It will be the job of the medical director, of course, to assure that such alternatives are taken by the physicians.

I recommend that your financial projections conservatively anticipate an ultimate utilization rate of 420 days/1,000 members/year, which should be achieved in 1985. Higher rates of 460 days and 435 days should be used for the years 1983 and 1984, respectively. Efficiency should increase with experience and as the number of patients gets larger. Many HMOs actually start out with very low hospital utilization rates, but with small membership the rate can be quite volatile. Therefore, I feel my recommended utilization rate assumptions build an element of conservatism into the financial plan.

I have assumed that the cost per day of hospital service will be $560 in 1983. Inflation will add 12 percent per year.

Year	Utilization Rate (days/1000)	Cost/Day	Cost pmpm
1983	460	$560	$21.47
1984	435	627	22.73
1985	420	702	24.57

PHARMACY EXPENSE

A pharmacy benefit will be separately capitated to a local pharmacy. The cost of drugs is expected to be offset by a $3 copayment per prescription, which will be collected from each member by the pharmacy. The initial net cost of providing the benefit is expected to be $2.05 pmpm, or four scripts per member per year, at a net (i.e., after copayment) cost of $6.15 each.

Year	Cost pmpm
1983	$2.05
1984	2.30
1985	2.57

ADMINISTRATIVE EXPENSE

Based on schedules of administrative cost provided by you, I have calculated the following summary administrative cost figures:

Year	Total Administrative Cost	Cost pmpm	Percent of Revenues
1983	$540,000	$23.28	44.3
1984	845,000	8.96	15.7
1985	1,296,000	8.03	12.5

We have not discussed cash-flow considerations regarding receivable and payable timing. You should be the best judge in that area, however. Also, while the above represent what I believe to be conservative assumptions, you may wish to build in a separate contingency reserve for Murphy's Law in your capital financing plans.

Ray, I hope this information is sufficient for your preliminary financial projection needs. I look forward to working with you to refine these estimates as your progress warrants.

My bill for services provided to date will be sent separately.

Sincerely,

Arkady Darrell, F.S.A.

Attachment

BHP MEMBERSHIP AND REVENUE PROJECTIONS

Month	Members	Average Revenue/Member	Total Revenue
Jan. '83	0	$0.00	$0
Feb.	0	0.00	0
Mar.	500	51.66	25,830
Apr.	700	51.66	36,162
May	900	51.66	46,494
Jun.	1,100	51.66	56,826
Jul.	1,300	51.90	67,468
Aug.	2,100	52.40	110,036
Sep.	3,150	52.67	165,906
Oct.	4,150	52.80	219,116
Nov.	4,500	52.83	237,739
Dec.	4,800	52.85	253,702
Total		$52.56	$1,219,279
Jan. '84	5,600	$53.57	$299,967
Feb.	5,900	53.78	317,325
Mar.	6,300	54.53	343,568
Apr.	6,700	55.03	368,709
May	7,100	55.47	393,850
Jun.	7,500	55.87	418,990
Jul.	7,900	56.31	444,872
Aug.	8,425	57.27	482,468
Sep.	8,950	58.30	521,750
Oct.	9,475	59.29	561,753
Nov.	10,000	59.73	597,275
Dec.	10,450	60.07	627,723
Total		$57.03	$5,378,251
Jan. '85	10,975	$60.80	$667,308
Feb.	11,425	61.32	700,635
Mar.	11,875	61.81	733,962
Apr.	12,325	62.34	768,376
May	12,775	62.84	802,789
Jun.	13,225	63.30	837,202
Jul.	13,675	64.10	876,614
Aug.	14,125	64.85	916,026
Sep.	14,575	65.55	955,438
Oct.	15,025	66.28	995,909
Nov.	15,475	66.97	1,036,379
Dec.	15,925	67.62	1,076,850
Total		$64.23	$10,367,487

18

Brant Clinic, A, B, and C

J. B. Silvers

BRANT CLINIC (A)

For some time now, Dr. Atwood (Woody) Brant, chairman of the Brant Clinic, and his administrator, Allen Grush, had discussed the idea of adding a satellite family practice clinic in Sandusky, Ohio. Twenty years ago, they had established their now-thriving, multispecialty group practice in Toledo, Ohio, and they now hoped to create a network of medical services in the northwest Ohio area. Currently, the Toledo setting consisted of several clinic buildings and a small hospital for a group practice of 40 physicians. The current financial statement is shown in Table 18.1.

Referral Patterns

The ever-increasing patient referrals that had sustained the clinic's growth seemed to have been dropping off in recent years. This worried Dr. Brant and the entire staff. For the first time they began to consider the source of their referrals and to analyze carefully their patient load. Out of this analysis, they concluded that the clinic was more vulnerable to the establishment of other practices in neighboring communities than they had ever realized. In fact, as new primary-care and specialty physicians moved into surrounding communities, clinic volume appeared to be dropping significantly. While overall population growth had sustained them, this new mix of physician-practice patterns was unfavorable. It seemed like an excellent idea to establish a more captive referral network for the clinic.

The specific proposal was to establish a small, two-person practice in Sandusky (several miles from Toledo) to capture a portion of that community's referrals. Mr. Grush also noted that the clinic had received a fair number of basic-care patients from this area in the past who presumably could be better served by a satellite family practice unit. Without the satellite, he considered it unlikely that the primary-care practice that the clinic had received would continue, given the increased number of new physicians moving into this area.

Table 18.1

BRANT CLINIC (A)

INCOME STATEMENT FOR YEAR ENDING DECEMBER 31, 1979

Revenue
Gross patient revenue	$18,997,000
Other revenue (contributions, securities, etc.)	1,348,000
Total revenue	20,345,000
Less: Contractual allowances	985,000
Uncollectible accounts	1,012,000
Net revenue	18,348,000

Expenses
Total salaries and wages	9,266,000
Pensions benefits and payroll taxes	1,311,000
Supplies	2,413,000
Depreciation	534,000
Rental and maintenance	376,000
Contributions and fellowships	922,000
Other expenses	3,784,000
Total expenses	18,606,000
Net income (deficit)	(258,000)

BALANCE SHEET AS OF DECEMBER 31, 1979

Assets
Cash and liquid assets		2,545,000
Accounts receivable	5,734,000	
Less: Allowance for doubtful account	(670,000)	5,064,000
Inventories		179,000
Investments in securities		1,304,000
Plant and equipment original cost	13,959,000	
Less: Accumulated depreciation	(4,582,000)	9,577,000
Land at cost		1,349,000
Other assets		262,000
Total assets		20,080,000

Liabilities and capital
Accounts payable		1,427,000
Notes payable		2,235,000
Accrued expenses		1,651,000
Total liabilities		5,313,000
Funds balance — Unrestricted	12,674,000	
Restricted	1,371,000	
Endowment	722,000	
Total funds balances		14,767,000
Total liabilities and capital		20,080,000

Volume/Cost Estimates

One major problem was making some estimate as to the potential volume of patients. Likewise, estimating costs appeared to be a challenge. Since this was a significantly different practice than what was now the pattern at the large Brant Clinic, there was considerable uncertainty. However, for lack of better data, Mr. Grush chose the figures represented in Table 18.2.

For the first year, he thought that 10,000 patient visits would be possible for the two-man practice. In the second year 20,000 seemed reasonable, and in the third year 30,000

Table 18.2

BRANT CLINIC (A):
Satellite Family Practice Clinic Forecast

Revenues and Expenses	Year 1	Year 2	Year 3
Operating revenues			
Number of patient visits/year	10,000	20,000	30,000
Average charge per visit	x$22.50	x$22.50	x$22.50
Gross revenue	225,000	450,000	675,000
Less: Bad debts	(22,500)	(45,000)	(67,500)
Net revenue	$202,500	$405,000	$607,500
Operating expenses			
Salaries and benefits			
Physicians and dentists	$200,000	$200,000	$200,000
Doctors' benefits	25,000	25,000	25,000
*Administrative	20,000	40,000	60,000
*Paramedical	10,000	20,000	30,000
*Technician	8,000	16,000	24,000
*Employees' benefits	9,000	16,000	23,000
*Laboratory and x-ray fees	1,500	3,000	5,000
*Medical and surgical supplies	8,000	16,000	24,000
Building and occupancy	35,000	35,000	35,000
Furniture and equipment	4,500	4,500	4,500
*Office supplies and services	4,000	8,000	12,000
*Legal and accounting	2,000	3,000	4,000
*Telephone	2,000	4,000	6,000
Insurance	5,000	5,000	5,000
Other	8,000	8,000	8,000
Total expenses	$342,000	$403,500	$465,500
Net income (loss)	(139,500)	1,500	132,000
Expense Analysis			
Expenses variable with volume (*)	$ 65,250	$126,000	$188,000
(as percentage of operating revenues)	(29%)	(28%)	(28%)
Expenses fixed with volume	277,500	277,500	277,500
(as percentage of operating revenues)	(123%)	(62%)	(41%)
Revenue Analysis			
Blue Shield volume (50%)	$112,500	$225,000	$337,500
Private insurance, self pay, and others	112,500	225,000	337,500
Less: Bad debts estimated (20%)	(22,500)	(45,000)	(67,000)
Net revenue	$202,500	$405,000	$607,500

*Expenses variable with volume.

should be attainable. To make the cost analysis simple, he decided to do it all in "constant dollars," which would eliminate the impact of inflation on the numbers. This way, he could make a pure analysis without being biased by specific inflation estimates. The $200,000 flat doctors' salary schedule would probably be reasonable for the first three years, since he felt this practice could be sustained in the near term by just the two resident physicians plus some rotation from the main clinic. He was not at all sure, however, what the variation should be in other personnel on the basis of this volume.

Fees and Payments

Preliminary fees were also a subject of great internal debate. Other physicians on the executive committee argued strongly that the $22.50 figure used by Mr. Grush was entirely out of line. A much higher fee would be feasible and imperative for such a project, they thought. Mr. Grush countered that the Sandusky-Huron area had a great number of retirees and working-class people. Income levels simply were not very high and the larger fees that were feasible in Toledo would not be possible at the new site. Mr. Grush estimated that with high fees, volume would be considerably lower than what was necessary. Also, because of the large number of small businesses in the area, insurance coverage was not as good as it might be. It was Mr. Grush's guess that about 50 percent of the volume would come from self-pay patients and private insurance companies, while the remaining 50 percent would come from more comprehensive Blue Shield plans. While Blue Shield usually paid the full amount of the bill, it often took more than 90 days on average to collect. On the other hand, private-pay patients (both self-pay and commercial insurance) had a bad debt rate of up to 20 percent as well as taking 90 days or more to pay. This meant that the calculated gross income would not be realized either imemediately or in its entirety by the clinic. Mr. Grush appreciated the additional cash financing need this placed on the satellite project.

In terms of payments, Mr. Grush knew physicians were paid monthly for the previous month's work while other employees were paid weekly. Supplies and other expenses would usually allow about a month's delay in payment. Since the clinic planned initially to lease all the needed equipment, only a small cash outlay would be needed for this purpose. In addition, office space would be rented until the operation had proven itself to be profitable.

Other Opportunities

In the economic environment of the 1980s, the clinic had many alternative investments to building a satellite — some of which offered a very profitable return. Mr. Grush estimated that 15 percent was a minimum return on investment but that 20 percent might be a more reasonable guideline for a new venture such as this. He also knew that the tax law that was likely to pass might make it worthwhile for the clinic to own its facility and equipment, to better utilize the depreciation tax shields that were available.

Financing could be a problem. By choice, the Brant Clinic was not currently using debt under a loan agreement that allowed them to borrow at 2 percent over the prime lending rate (now close to 20 percent), and therefore it did not seem proper to think about debt financing for the satellite. In any case, Mr. Grush was not certain that the bank would make a loan on the basis of just this one satellite unless all the other assets of the clinic were also pledged and available. He concluded that if the new satellite was to be, it would have to be financed independently by the clinic as long as sufficient funds were available.

The Decision

Woody Brant and Mr. Grush met to review the situation before the next day's executive committee meeting at which a final decision would be made. They were not certain about several points. First, it was not clear whether this proposed use of the clinic's money was superior to leaving it in the alternative investments now available. Profitability for the new venture simply was not clear. Likewise, the risk that they might encounter in the additional cash investment which was required bothered both of them. They were also concerned about how much money would actually be needed to finance the start-up and growth of this satellite. Without sound answers to these concerns, Dr. Brant was very skeptical as to whether the clinic's executive committee would vote for it. While he felt he could probably force it through if need be, he was not sure that this was even the proper strategic direction for the clinic at this point in time. With these items in mind, the two men planned to get together again in late afternoon to go over a final outline for the executive committee meeting.

BRANT CLINIC (B)

In addition to the planned expansion satellite clinic discussed in Brant Clinic (A), Dr. Atwood Brant and Mr. Grush frequently faced questions involving the use of new technologies at the clinic. Of all the capital requests generated by the management and physicians of the clinic, this area presented a particular challenge. At this point in time, they were faced with a choice regarding three pieces of equipment: the replacement of an existing computerized tomography (CT) scanner with a newer model, the renovation of their cardiac catheterization lab, and the purchase of a brand new piece of technology called digital subtraction angiography (DSA). Together the costs of these three items could total between $1.5 and $2 million. Thus, there was some concern about which, if any, would be the most appropriate purchase(s) for the clinic.

CT Scanner Replacement

The computerized tomography proposal was fairly straightforward. Brant Clinic had been one of the earliest to obtain CT technology when it first became available. It had proven to be a very profitable investment from both a medical and a financial point of view. Furthermore, clinic physicians now considered it to be an essential tool. The cost for almost any scanner was high — in the neighborhood of $500,000. At the volume of related service currently experienced by the clinic, there would be little difficulty in recovering operating costs plus a reasonable markup on CT procedures on a new machine. Perhaps more important, the physicians involved felt a new machine was essential to stay at the cutting edge of this technology. This raised an interesting question, however. Since such great improvements had been made in scanners in recent years, Dr. Brant wondered if it might not make more sense to wait until the next generation of machines came on the market before purchasing a new one.

Cardiac Catheterization Laboratory

The second major proposal cost was of the same order of magnitude as the scanner project. Expansion of existing facilities in the main building with the addition of a $600,000 catheterization lab in an adjacent outpatient building had been proposed by Dr. Clifton Jones, a leading cardiologist on the staff. Although cardiology was experiencing some growth and the existing cardiac catheterization lab was approaching capacity, Dr. Brant still had questions about the timing of this investment. Existing facilities would suffice for at least three or four more years at current rates of growth. However, Dr. Jones was very insistent. He was sure that he could produce three catheterizations per day (although Mr. Grush's market analysis indicated one per day would be more feasible). The numbers revealed that at current charges, three per day would produce a reasonable return on the investment, while one per day would fall somewhat short.

Another point to be considered was that Dr. Jones was one of the most revenue-producing cardiologists on the staff. His work generated almost $500,000 for the clinic each year. On the other hand, Dr. Jones had been something of a rebel on the medical staff and had caused some serious disruptions in the management process. Few would regret his leaving the clinic if that were a result of a negative decision with respect to the lab project. However, given his importance both medically and financially, Dr. Brant realized this was not a decision that could be taken lightly.

Digital Subtraction Angiography

The third proposal had to do with the new imaging technique of digital subtraction angiography (DSA). The new DSA machine would also cost around $500,000, although because of its newness, the amount of volume that could be assured was much less certain. The head of radiology felt that ten images per day could be achieved almost immediately. Within a short time, he felt that 20 patients per day would be feasible. To produce this volume, the accountants had estimated a total salary and wage cost of $96,000. Supplies at the 20-patients-per-day volume would run around $130,000 per year. In addition, indirect costs associated with radiology were calculated at 70 percent of direct cost. (This was based on the Medicare cost allocation.) Over a five-year depreciation life, the cost would be substantial. Dr. Anker, the chief of radiology, estimated the procedure should be done for about $200, including the professional component. This would be a substantial drop from the current charge for conventional angiography of $650.

Dr. Anker also noted that of existing cerebral arteriograms for two vessels, 126 should be replaceable each year with the quality levels of DSA. This was important since DSA involved only a general contrast medium and did not require invasion of the carotid artery with local contrast material. The difference in time and pain for the patient was substantial. Typically, this meant that a day of hospitalization could be avoided as well. Furthermore, in renal arteriography, he estimated that over 1,100 conventional angiograms could be replaced with DSA. The two added up to substantial savings for the patient.

Dr. Brant's main concern revolved around usages that did not currently exist. Studies had shown that the CT scanners had induced treatment to a very large extent. Although this may have been perfectly appropriate, it did result in a very large volume of scans that had not been predicted. He suspected that this might also be the case with DSA. From a financial point of view this would be favorable, but in terms of obtaining Health Systems Agency approval for the capital expenditure, it might be an important negative.

As with the CT proposal, Dr. Brant also wondered about waiting for future generations of DSAs. On the other hand, since this was the first generation, it might pay just to be the first one in the city with this new technique.

The Decision

In order to obtain some perspective on these three proposals that were roughly alike in terms of the capital involved, Dr. Brant asked his executive committee of physicians and administrators to rank the three proposals and provide some rationale for their rankings. He thought this would provide a good starting point for a discussion and analysis of the objectives implicit in such major capital investment decisions.

BRANT CLINIC (C)

Shortly after the satellite family practice opened in Sandusky, Ohio, the Brant Clinic was approached by a representative of the General Control Corporation, a manufacturing firm in the area with over 10,000 employees. It was by far the largest employer in the area. Its employees and dependents made up a very large proportion of the total potential patient population in the area. In fact, the plant had recently expanded to almost twice its original size. Its internal health care system for in-plant accidents and illness had not kept pace with this expansion. Thus, the representative of General Controls wanted to explore possible connections and an arrangement between the Brant Clinic and the newly expanded plant.

General Controls' representative first proposed that the Brant Clinic set up a special new branch on the plant grounds to provide occupational and emergency medical care to employees. Dependents would also be allowed to come to the site and get medical care. With a work force of 10,000 plus dependents as a captive population, Dr. Brant thought that it would be an interesting possibility to start up a clinic immediately.

As he and Mr. Grush thought about the matter more carefully, however, it occurred to them that a good portion of the patients they would see at the plant would be ones they were already taking care of at their own satellite facility. In fact, looking through the records, they concluded that perhaps 50 percent of the volume would come from dependents and others currently using Brant Clinic services. Thus, if 20,000 patient visits were generated by this group (roughly one visit per employee and dependent each year), only 10,000 of them would represent new patients. Obviously, if a plant site were opened, it might subtract up to 10,000 patients from the practice, which had so far been following the scheduled outline in the Brant Clinic (A) case fairly well. This "cannibalization" could be very serious and could certainly throw a curve into their financial calculations.

As an alternative, Dr. Brant thought that it might be wise for them to counterpropose that the existing satellite might simply be expanded to a capacity sufficient to take care of this additional load. Physicians could then visit on the plant site (which was about one-quarter of a mile away) to take care of the on-site difficulties. This arrangement would have the financial advantage of not necessitating duplication of the fixed cost of the satellite in another location. Presumably, only the variable cost of care would be added to pick up the additional patients.

About this time, the representative of General Controls suggested that in either case, since the company would be essentially guaranteeing a certain fixed volume, they should be granted a 20 percent discount from normal charges. While the Brant Clinic had never granted such a discount, it seemed to Mr. Grush that this might be feasible if the only additional costs were the variable costs of providing that extra service. However, the broader ramifications scared Dr. Brant and he was fairly negative on the idea. At this point the meeting broke up with the agreement that it would resume within a day or two. The General Controls executive further indicated that he had had preliminary discussions with other physician groups and wanted to come to some sort of conclusion within two weeks. Thus, the Brant Clinic was under pressure to come to a decision.

19

Manchester Community Hospital

L. William Katz

YOUR HOSPITAL

You have just been employed as Executive Director of the Manchester Community Hospital. When announcing your appointment, the Chairman of the Board stated that you were employed to reverse the financial situation of the hospital. For the last fiscal year, the hospital's financial statements showed an operating loss of $975,157. Of this amount, $204,103 was incurred during October 1982, the last month of the hospital's fiscal year. During previous years, the hospital reported an average monthly net income ranging between $40,000 and $65,000 and an annual net income of more than $650,000.

Manchester Community Hospital was chartered as a not-for-profit corporation in 1961 and, after successfully obtaining $4 million in grants, loans, and donations, opened with 110 beds in November 1967. The hospital completed a second building program in 1974 with a $10-million addition and remodeling, bringing the bed complement to 233. The hospital expects to complete its third building program in January 1983, two months from now. This program will bring the total number of beds to 405. (See Tables 19.1 through 19.3 for detailed summaries of the financing of the building programs, the hospital's debt service, and the number of beds available by year.)

The hospital facilities are located on a 30-acre site in a residential neighborhood at the outskirts of Manchester. The existing 363-bed hospital is composed of three major structures. The original 110-bed hospital consisted of a four-story patient wing and a one-story ancillary services building, which now houses surgery, radiology, laboratory, emergency room, central services, medical records, and pharmacy. In 1972, a 14-bed intensive-care unit was added to the one-story building, and in 1974, a four-story nursing wing was constructed, which pro-

The development of the original case study was supported by a grant from the W. W. Kellogg Foundation to the Hospital Research and Educational Trust. Copyright 1977 by the Hospital Research and Educational Trust. Revised and reprinted 1981, 1982, and 1983 with permission from the Hospital Research and Educational Trust, 840 North Lake Shore Drive, Chicago, Illinois 60611.

vided 109 additional beds and expanded service areas, including administrative offices, kitchen, business office, physical therapy, and storage areas. The present construction program began in 1980 and includes:

— A new five-story patient wing with space for four additional patient floors. (When all floors are completed, the hospital will have 600 inpatient beds.)

— A completely new surgical suite sufficient to support the hospital's projected surgical volume, based on its 600-bed capacity.

— A mental health unit providing 41 inpatient beds and service for outpatients.

— A new 11-story elevator tower providing two elevators and shafts for another two to be added later.

— Modernization of the ancillary services building and of the administrative offices.

— Expanded parking.

The hospital is currently negotiating the sale or lease of five acres of its site to a church-affiliated, nonprofit group for the construction of a 140-bed, skilled-nursing-care facility. It is expected that the project will be financed through the sale of tax-exempt revenue bonds secured by the revenue of the nursing home.

The hospital's building programs have been financed largely through intermediate- and long-term borrowing. The hospital borrowed $4 million in 1967, $9 million in 1974, and $15 million in 1980. Bonds and notes now mature each year through 1995, as shown in Tables 19.2. Bonds mature four times per year. Maturities in 1983 include $435,000 in March and April and $445,000 in September and October. Debt service in 1983 is approximately $3,120,000. According to the hospital Board's Chairman, "The Board is concerned that the hospital will be unable to meet debt service payments when they are due if the hospital's financial situation is not soon reversed."

THE COMMUNITY

Manchester Community Hospital is located in Manchester, a rapidly growing suburban community that is approximately 30 miles from the business center of Excelsior City. Interstate Highway 95 passes within two miles of the hospital; the Excelsior Airport is eight miles north of the hospital. The hospital serves Manchester, adjoining communities to the north and northwest, and portions of adjoining towns to the east and south. This hospital service area spans some 300 square miles.

Manchester and adjoining communities are experiencing some typical suburban growth patterns. Land development is occurring at a fast pace, and industrial sites in the nearby towns of Waverly and Chestertown are filling rapidly, which appears to ensure the continued growth of the area.

From 1970 to 1980, Manchester's population more than doubled, and the population of the hospital service area grew by 136 percent, from 128,829 to 304,218. The State Department of Human Resources forecasts continued growth through 1990 for both Manchester (160,000) and the hospital service area (546,000). Population figures are shown in Table 19.4. Generally, the population is young, middle-class, and very mobile. As such, many persons do not have a regular family doctor and seek a physician only when services are required. Average yearly visits to the hospital's emergency room have risen from 28,000 in 1975 to more than 40,000 in fiscal year 1982.

Manchester Community Hospital shares its service area with three church-affiliated, short-term general hospitals and a proprietary psychiatric hospital. St. Joseph's Hospital and Broadmoor Hospital, the psychiatric hospital, are in Raven Rock, six miles east of Manchester; Deaconess Hospital is in Hazelgreen, ten miles southeast of Manchester; and Holy Name Hospital is in Crab Orchard, five miles south of Manchester (see Figure 19.1). Statistics on the number of beds and on utilization for each of the five hospitals are given in Table 19.5. Approvals, facilities, and services of the four general hospitals are shown in Table 19.6, and patient origin data for Manchester Community Hospital are given in Table 19.7.

Figure 19.1

LOCATION OF AREA HOSPITALS, 1982

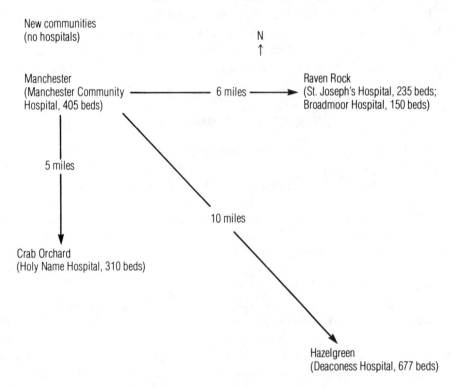

THE BOARD OF TRUSTEES

Composition of the Board

Manchester Community Hospital is governed by a 30-member Board of Trustees that represents a cross-section of professional and business leaders in the hospital's service area. There are no physicians on the Board, although the president of the medical staff attends board meetings ex officio. (The medical staff has requested at least ten board seats for its membership.) The president of the women's auxiliary also attends ex officio.

One-third of the Board is elected annually. Nominees are selected not only on the basis of their interest in the hospital but also on the basis of their place of residence and their religious affiliation, in order to maintain a geographic and religious balance in the composition of the Board. The original hospital Board was composed of community leaders who contributed much time and money to obtain a hospital for the community. Six members of the present Board were founding board members, and another ten have served for ten or more years.

One of the original members, I. Tate Charge, became board Chairman last year. Mr. Charge is also Chairman of the Board of the Whitnor Corporation, a large manufacturing concern headquartered in Excelsior City, but he has all but retired from this business. He has begun to assume a more active role in the affairs of the hospital than did past chairmen. He can be found frequently in the hospital board's office, located in the administrative suite, or in the medical staff lounge. Mr. Charge recently commented, "Lately, meetings of the Board and of the Executive Committee—the 17 of us on this Committee really do much of the Board's work—seem less well attended than I remember them to have been in the past."

The Board operates with five standing committees: executive, finance, financial development, building and grounds, and nominating. Five special committees also meet: pension and personnel, which are subcommittees of the Finance Committee; special gifts, a subcommittee of the Financial Development Committee; public relations; and house and property.

FINANCIAL COMMITTEES

The Financial Development Committee is charged with long-term capital funds acquisition; the Finance Committee is concerned with current operations. The personnel subcommittee of the Finance Committee reviews the personnel programs and the wage, salary, and employment practices of the hospital. The ten-member Finance Committee is chaired by A. L. Audit, a senior partner in a large national accounting firm. The committee's responsibilities as outlined in the hospital's bylaws are shown in Appendix 19.1. In addition to the functions outlined in the bylaws, the Finance Committee is responsible for reviewing the performance of the hospital controller and for fixing his compensation and benefits. Interhospital comparisons of charges and wages are shown in Tables 19.8 and 19.9.

In practice, many finance committee activities have been delegated to the Controller and the Executive Director. The Controller, Herman Marken, prepares a financial statement and a hospital statistical report each month for submission to the Finance Committee. Although the contents of the financial statement have been revised periodically to reflect requests of committee members, the statement has remained basically the same since Mr. Marken joined the hospital in 1976. A current statistical report, a comparative statement of revenue and expenses, a comparative balance sheet, and a statement of changes in financial position are presented in Tables 19.10 through 19.13, respectively.

The Finance Committee is responsible for preparing and submitting an annual budget to the Board. In consultation with the Executive Director, Mr. Marken drafts a budget that reflects his forecast of hospital utilization for the coming year and gives his estimate of revenue and expenses. Occupancy is estimated for each month, and revenue and expenses are budgeted on the basis of these estimated figures. Recommendations for revising charges and for adding new services are also submitted with the budget. The Finance Committee reviews the draft and at the same time considers the urgent needs expressed by department heads, medical staff members, the president of the women's auxiliary, and the Executive Director. The committee then sends a recommended budget to the Board of Trustees for approval.

At its monthly meetings, the Finance Committee reviews the hospital's financial and statistical reports and requests that the Executive Director and the Controller explain material variations from the budget. The Controller prepares a written summary of financial highlights, which normally covers most inquiries (see Tables 19.11 through 19.13). Since July, when the financial reports began showing an operating deficit, the board meetings have increased in length as members questioned the Executive Director and as he defended his adherence to the approved budget.

Interview with Board Chairman

Last week, just prior to your assuming the position of Executive Director, Mr. Charge discussed the Board's concern with the current state of hospital affairs. He stated:

> Many current members of the Board have been active members for over 10 years. The Executive Director had been here for nearly 14 years and was our personal choice to lead the organization. We were fond of him and respected his capabilities. However, this past year, we began to question his business acumen and to suspect that he was incapable of adjusting to meet his expanding responsibilities. Nevertheless, we were reluctant to interfere with his conduct of the hospital's daily affairs for fear of offending him. I felt that the hospital's financial situation was deteriorating rapidly and that drastic remedial actions were needed. Therefore, I had copies of the current hospital financial reports sent directly to my office for analysis by my accountant. I also felt obliged to take a more active role in operations and to spend more time at the hospital. I found that the medical staff and the heads of service departments had many complaints about how the hospital was being run.

First the Assistant Director, then the Director of Nursing and her assistant, and finally, in late August, the Executive Director left the hospital. A Director of Nursing Services was hired by me last month, but the three other positions are still vacant. Mr. Marken has been serving as acting administrator, but he is scheduled to return to his controller's position as soon as a new Executive Officer is on board.

THE MEDICAL STAFF

The hospital's medical staff consists of 200 physicians, 102 of whom are on the active staff. Of the active staff physicians, 43 each admit over 100 patients per year. Of the active staff members, 45 percent are under 50 years of age, and only 18 percent are over 60 years. The medical specialties are widely represented among the staff, and the hospital is confident that staff membership will increase approximately 10 percent annually over the next decade.

Half of the active staff members have been with the hospital for over ten years. Many of the physicians are young, recently board-certified specialists who are aggressive in their demands upon the hospital. They feel that the physicians should be responsible for determining what services are provided for their patients. The elected president of the medical staff explained the staff's position: "Let hospital administration take care of the nonmedical areas and leave the practice of medicine where it belongs—in the hands of the physicians."

So that you might quickly become more familiar with medical organization and procedures, Miss Bales, the medical staff secretary and a member of your office staff, assembled some summary information, shown in Appendixes 19.2 and 19.3. Two physicians also expressed their views to you.

Dr. Barnum, president of the medical staff, stated:

> Most active members have been on this staff for more than ten years. We consider Manchester to be *our* hospital, and so we are vitally interested in its operation. We have had increasing difficulty in communicating our concerns to the administration. I am the only medical representative on the board and find it difficult, as an internist, to communicate effectively the needs and priorities of my many colleagues. It is for this reason that we want ten seats on the board reserved for physicians elected by the staff.

Dr. Carpenter, chairman of the department of surgery, said, "You may have heard from the staff members that our department is a 'closed shop.' This is far from the truth. Our department has accepted new members and will continue to do so."

Miss Bales informed you that Dr. Carpenter technically is correct. Three surgeons have been added to the staff since 1980.

HOSPITAL DEPARTMENTS

The annual budget figures (Table 19.11) and the hospital's staffing figures (Table 19.14), which cover all departments, are available for your review. In addition, you have talked with several department heads, whose remarks follow.

The Controller

Mr. Marken said:

> As I stated in the October 1982 Financial Highlights, "the October deficit resulted from funding our pension plan contribution and from recording depreciation on the newly opened facilities. These expenses were recorded at a convenient time — the end of the fiscal year — and do not adversely affect the cash accounts. Therefore, the hospital does not have a serious financial problem, and our figures will be reversed as the new facilities are occupied."
>
> To cover our monthly cash fluctuations, we have a $500,000 line of credit at First National Bank. Our rate is prime plus 2 percent and we maintain a compensating balance of 15 percent of the outstanding loan. Today we are paying 20 percent because prime is at 18. We pay down as much as we can at the end of each month depending on cash flow. The bank expects us to clear the loan for at least 30 days a year, which we have always done.
>
> With interest rates the way they are, one of my first priorities is to bring our borrowing down as soon as the new building is occupied. Therefore, we are planning to hold the contractor's 10 percent retainage through April so we can pay the bank.

Mr. Marken also explained that Blue Cross patients represented 14 percent of patient days and approximately 13 percent of revenue. Medicare patients were responsible for 32 percent of patient days and 28 percent of revenues and Medicaid patients for 3 percent of patient days and 2 percent of revenues. Blue Cross pays the hospital for inpatient services at the lesser of charges or 105 percent of routine and ancillary service costs plus depreciation and capital projects' interest at cost.

Mr. Marken stated:

With the passage of the Tax Equity and Fiscal Responsibility Act (TEFRA), our reimbursement picture has changed considerably. In the past, we were not concerned with the limitations. However, this year's cost report will be subject to the routine cost limitation because of the costs we incurred in acquiring staff and supplies for the new building. Our routine cost limit for this cost report is $155.39. I have anticipated this problem by reserving over $700,000 for Medicare and Medicaid.

Next year we face additional limitations. Limitations are on cost per case and our case-mix index is unfavorable because it was computed on data collected before we were equipped to handle the complicated cases for which our new building is designed. We will need to reassess our budget once we have a handle on our target rate and our per case cost limits.

Also, United Airlines, a major employer in these parts, has approached us and Deaconess Hospital to develop a preferred provider agreement. They indicated they would guarantee payment for 14,600 patient days of care, provided we gave them a discount of 10 percent off our posted charges. Their employees were responsible for 8,020 days of care here last year and twice that amount elsewhere in the area. I am sure Deaconess is negotiating, so we need to prepare to answer United soon.

The Director of Nursing

The new Director of Nursing stated:

I have been here only one month and therefore have made very few changes. However, some of the head nurses have explained that we usually have difficulty in finding and keeping floor nurses because so many have family responsibilities. As a result, we regularly schedule many nurses on a part-time basis, and we are looking for more full-time and part-time staff to cover the new floors. I feel we should increase our recruitment efforts *now* so that we have time to train new nurses and nursing aides before all of the new beds are opened.

The Purchasing Agent

The purchasing agent stated that purchasing is done centrally except for the dietary department. He further stated that policy dictates that any purchase over $2,000 must have administrative approval. The purchasing agent is assisted by two secretaries. Storage facilities are in several locations throughout the hospital.

The Dietician

The dietician stated that she is proud of her operation. She explained: "I feel that I save the hospital a great deal of money in the area of purchasing supplies. This is evidenced by the periodic rebate checks that the hospital receives from my main suppliers. Usually, an administrator will be more inclined to cooperate fully with a department head when he knows that the department head is concerned with economy."

PROBLEMS AND ISSUES

As the new Executive Director, you are confronted with these conditions. You now must analyze the conversations that you have had and the information that you have collected to determine how you want to proceed.

At your last position, you put together a list of financial and productivity ratios which were helpful in reviewing the hospital's performance. These are provided in Table 19.15.

Appendix 19.1

RESPONSIBILITIES OF THE MANCHESTER COMMUNITY HOSPITAL FINANCE COMMITTEE

The Finance Committee shall be responsible for the management of all funds of the hospital. The committee shall be responsible for the following:

1. Ensuring that all endowment and trust funds are deposited with a responsible trust company or comparable agency for investment; securing prompt reports of such investments; seeing that income, after deduction of legitimate expenses, is paid into the proper fund of the hospital and that both principal and income are used in accordance with the terms of the trust.

2. Examining the monthly financial reports and requiring an explanation from the Executive Director for any material variations from the budget.

3. Arranging for adequate insurance coverage, such as fire, physical plant, Workmen's Compensation, comprehensive, public and professional liability insurance, and so forth.

4. Making recommendations to the Board of Trustees regarding policies and salaries of all employed staff members of the hospital.

5. Preparing and submitting to the Board of Trustees at its last meeting before the end of the fiscal year a budget showing the expected receipts and expenditures for the ensuing year.

6. Appointing an auditor, subject to the approval of the Board of Trustees.

Source: Manchester Community Hospital Bylaws.

Appendix 19.2

MANCHESTER COMMUNITY HOSPITAL
MEDICAL STAFF COMMITTEES

Clinical and Departmental Committees

1. General practice
2. Internal medicine
3. Obstetrics-gynecology
4. Pediatrics
5. Surgery
6. Dentistry
7. Diagnostic and therapeutic service

Standing Committees

1. Joint conference
2. Executive
3. Credentials
4. Constitution
5. Medical records
6. Tissue and audit
7. Professional standards*
8. Education
9. Nominating
10. Patient care
11. Emergency, trauma, and disaster
12. President's advisory
13. Infection control
14. Utilization

Special Committees

1. Financial audit
2. Library
3. Therapeutics
4. Dietary
5. Research and experimentation
6. Planning
7. Entertainment
8. Memorial
9. Radioisotope
10. Publications
11. Sterilization and therapeutic abortion
12. Intensive care
13. Tumor
14. Foreign education and aid

---

*The professional standards committee is the executive committee and the credentials committee in joint session.

Appendix 19.3

MANCHESTER COMMUNITY HOSPITAL MEDICAL STAFF ORGANIZATION: SUMMARY OF CERTAIN BYLAW PROVISIONS REGARDING MEDICAL STAFF

1. Medical staff officers are elected annually.

2. Each department elects its own chairman.

3. The president of the medical staff, following election, appoints all standing committees except the executive committee, the credentials committee, the joint conference committee, the tissue and audit committee, the departmental committees, and the nominating committee and selects the balance of the committee chairmen. Membership of the specified committees is set by the bylaws.

4. The president also appoints all special committees and designates the chairmen of such committees. He reports to the staff on the meetings of these committees.

5. All committees are required by the bylaws to meet at least monthly. However, the joint conference, research, radioisotope, planning, professional standards, and dentistry committees have been meeting quarterly.

6. Each medical department has a chairman, a vice chairman, and a secretary. Each clinical department has a departmental committee composed of attending members of the medical staff. Each department may have one or more sections with officers.

7. All decisions made by medical staff committees are reviewed by the executive committee.

Table 19.1

SOURCES OF CAPITAL FUNDS

Phase I, 1967	
Hill-Burton grant	$ 600,000
1967 Series A bonds	4,000,000
Bank loans, notes to suppliers[1]	345,000
Donations, memorials	905,000
Total	$ 5,850,000
Phase II, 1974	
Hill-Burton grant	$ 900,000
From operations	690,000
Donations	410,00
1974 Series A bonds[2]	9,000,000
Total	$11,000,000
Phase III, 1980	
Hospital equity funds	$ 5,136,000
Bonds and notes	
1980 Direct obligation notes[3]	15,000,000
Total	$20,136,000

[1]Repaid from operations

[2]Serial bonds sold at par. Interest rates: early maturities — 9 percent; late maturities — 10 percent; net interest cost — 9.8 percent. Bonds mature serially each year to October 1, 1990, in amounts ranging from $70,000 to $110,000. A final balloon maturity of $6,704,000 occurs in October 1990.

[3]Serial notes sold at par, maturing serially each year from 1983 to 1996 in amounts ranging from $280,000 in 1983 to $425,000 in 1993 and $7,275,000 in 1996. Interest rates range from 8.5 percent on early maturities to 9.5 percent on late maturities.

Table 19.2

SCHEDULE OF SERIAL MATURITIES AND INTEREST RATES:
1967, 1974, and 1980 Serial Bonds and Notes
($ in thousands)

Date	1967 BONDS Amount	Coupon	1974 BONDS Amount	Coupon	1980 NOTES Amount	Coupon
March, April 1983	$ 85	5.35	$ 70	9.0	$ 280	8.5
Sept., Oct. 1983	85	5.35	70	9.0	290	8.5
March, April 1984	85	5.35	75	9.0	290	8.5
Sept., Oct. 1984	85	5.35	75	9.0	300	8.5
March, April 1985	95	5.35	75	9.0	310	9.0
Sept., Oct. 1985	95	5.50	78	9.5	320	9.0
March, April 1986	95	5.50	80	9.5	320	9.0
Sept., Oct. 1986	95	5.50	85	9.5	330	9.0
March, April 1987	95	5.50	85	9.5	330	9.0
Sept., Oct. 1987	95	5.50	90	9.5	340	9.0
March, April 1988	145	6.00	95	9.5	350	9.0
Sept. Oct. 1988	145	6.00	100	9.5	350	9.0
March, April 1989			103	10.0	360	9.0
Sept., Oct. 1989			105	10.0	370	9.0
March, April 1990			110	10.0	370	9.5
Sept., Oct. 1990			6,704	10.0	380	9.5
March 1991					390	9.5
Sept. 1991					390	9.5
March 1992					400	9.5
Sept. 1992					410	9.5
March 1993					420	9.5
Sept. 1993					425	9.5
Sept. 1995					7,275	9.5
Total	$1,200		$8,000		$15,000	

Notes:
1967 Bonds: interest payable and maturities in March and September.
1974 Bonds: interest payable and maturities in April and October.
1980 Bonds: interest payable and maturities in March and September.

Table 19.3

BEDS AVAILABLE, 1967–1983

Date	Beds
1967	110
1974	233
1980	261
1982	
April	285
May	321
June	335
October	351
November	363
December	363
1983	
January	405

Table 19.4

SERVICE AREA POPULATION

Township	1970	1980	1985	1990
Manchester	58,910	119,218	139,000	160,000
Raven Rock	31,456	54,817	108,000	133,000
Crab Orchard	27,876	79,642	87,000	125,000
Hazelgreen	10,587	50,541	60,000	128,000
Total service area	128,829	304,218	394,000	546,000

Sources: U.S. Census for 1970 and 1980. Projections for 1985 and 1990 made by the State Department of Human Resources based on the U.S. Department of Commerce formula.

Table 19.5

BEDS AND UTILIZATION IN MANCHESTER SERVICE AREA

Hospital	YEAR ENDING SEPTEMBER 30		
	1979	1980	1981
Manchester Community Hospital:			
Beds	261	261	261
Admissions	13,100	13,991	14,546
Average census	216	230	254
Occupancy (percent)	95.2	88.1	97.3
St. Joseph's Hospital, Raven Rock:			
Beds	236	236	235
Admissions	8,648	8,544	7,830
Average census	194	188	172
Occupancy (percent)	82.2	79.7	73.1
Holy Name Hospital, Crab Orchard:			
Beds		(Opened in 1981)	310
Admissions			5,934
Average census			178
Occupancy (percent)			57.5
Deaconess Hospital, Hazelgreen:			
Beds	660	675	677
Admissions	20,385	21,458	21,751
Average census	579	583	579
Occupancy (percent)	87.3	86.2	85.7
Broadmoor Hospital, Raven Rock:			
Beds	135	144	150
Admissions	1,074	1,084	1,220
Average census	128	122	133
Occupancy (percent)	94.8	84.7	88.7

Source: *Hospitals, J.A.H.A.*, Guide Issue, August 1, 1980, 1981, 1982.

Table 19.6

APPROVALS, FACILITIES, AND SERVICES
for Year Ending September 30, 1981

Approvals	Manchester	St. Joseph's	Holy Name	Deaconess
JCAH accreditation	X	X	X	X
Cancer program	X	—	—	X
Residency	—	—	—	X
Internship	—	—	—	X
Professional nursing school	—	—	—	X
Blue Cross participation	X	X	X	X
Medicare certification	X	X	X	X
Facilities (Selected)				
Clinical laboratory	X	X	X	X
Postoperative recovery room	X	X	X	X
Cardiac care unit	X	—	X	X
Intensive care unit	X	X	X	X
Open-heart surgery facilities	—	—	—	X
X-ray therapy	—	X	—	X
Cobalt therapy	X	—	—	X
Organ bank	—	—	—	—
Blood bank	X	X	—	X
Inhalation therapy	X	X	X	X
Renal dialysis	—	—	—	—
Pharmacy (with registered pharmacist)	X	X	X	X
Physical therapy unit	X	X	X	X
Psychiatric inpatient unit	X	—	X	X
Psychiatric outpatient unit	—	—	—	—
Organized outpatient department	—	—	—	X
Emergency department	X	X	X	X
Home care department	X	—	—	X
Hospital auxiliary	X	—	X	X

Source: *Hospitals, J.A.H.A.*, Guide Issue, 1982.

Table 19.7

PATIENT ORIGINS

Town of Origin*	Percent of Discharges
Manchester	30
Waverly	20
Chestertown	12
Midland	10
Brunswick	8
Crab Orchard	5
Raven Rock	4
Hazelgreen	2
Other state residents	8
Out-of-state patients	1

Source: Manchester Community Hospital discharge records, FY 1982.

*Waverly, Chestertown, Midland, and Brunswick are located north and northwest of Manchester.

Table 19.8

REPRESENTATIVE HOSPITAL CHARGES
October 1, 1982

	Manchester	St. Joseph's	Holy Name	Deaconess
BEDS	351	235	310	677
ROUTINE SERVICES:				
Private room	196	178	186	190
Semiprivate room	170	165	165	178
Cardiac intensive care	310	325	325	325
Intensive care	310	325	360	375
Mental health	211		230	262
NURSERY:				
Mother in hospital	95	93	122	114
Mother out of hospital	170	137	—	114
PEDIATRICS:	170	170	224	202
OPERATING ROOM:				
Minimum charge				
First half hour				
Minor surgery	116	106	190	176
Major surgery	167	146	226	229
RECOVERY ROOM:				
Minimum charge				
First half hour	55	88	100	46
EMERGENCY ROOM:				
Base fee	12	30	40	26

Table 19.9

SALARY SURVEY OF AREA HOSPITALS:
Hourly Wage Rates, July 1982

Position	Manchester	HOSPITAL				Average of 72 Area Hospitals	Manchester Projected 12/1/82*
		Excelsior City	St. Joseph's	Holy Name	Deaconess		
Head Nurse, R.N.	$9.53	$10.69	$10.12	$9.02	$10.23	$9.63	$10.96
Staff R.N.	8.38	8.98	9.01	8.04	8.98	7.78	9.47
LPN II	6.50	5.32	6.93	5.96	7.10	5.93	7.21
Surgical Technician	6.17	6.09	7.24	6.11	6.09	5.86	7.15
Nursing Assistant	5.18	4.60	5.46	5.46	4.96	4.83	5.70
Food Service Supervisor	5.55	6.73	6.96	5.82	6.22	6.47	6.41
Food Service Worker I	4.64	4.36	4.79	4.10	4.19	4.23	4.96
Housekeeping Supervisor	7.24	5.96	7.19	7.11	5.63	5.81	7.96
Housekeeper I	4.74	4.21	4.83	4.68	4.45	4.67	5.00
Accountant (Staff)	7.52	10.85	7.08	7.08	7.03	7.73	8.12
Accounting Clerk I	5.52	4.88	6.62	6.17	6.40	5.56	6.07
Admitting Clerk	5.83	4.83	5.52	5.22	5.58	5.22	6.40
Cashier	5.61	4.96	5.97	4.81	4.76	4.88	5.94

Source: State Hospital Association Survey, July 1982.

*These increases are representative of the increases proposed for all nonsalary staff.

Table 19.10

MANCHESTER COMMUNITY HOSPITAL STATISTICS
October 1982 and 12 Months Ended October 31, 1982

	Beds	%	October 31, 1982 Actual	October 31, 1982 Budget	12 MONTHS ENDED October 31, 1982 Actual	12 MONTHS ENDED Budget	October 31, 1981 Actual
Admissions:							
Short stay			41		435		422
Intensive care and cardiac care					688		636
Medical-surgical			651		8,151		8,920
Mental health			31		540		403
Obstetrics			145		2,439		3,894
Pediatrics			200		3,187		3,319
Total			1,068		15,440		17,594
Infants-newborn			139		1,515		1,675
Patient Days:							
Short stay			240	130	1,131	1,275	1,268
Intensive care and cardiac care				349	3,794	4,106	3,630
Medical-surgical			4,820	6,346	53,392	59,325	50,845
Mental health			488	668	7,749	7,388	7,387
Obstetrics			544	822	7,806	10,313	11,293
Pediatrics			680	739	10,519	10,535	11,965
Total			6,772	9,054	84,391	92,942	86,388
Infants-newborn			670	610	7,305	7,612	7,683
Occupancy:							
Short stay	6	2	51.6%	69.9%	62.1%	70.0%	57.9%
Intensive care and cardiac care	15	4		75.0	69.3	75.0	66.3
Medical-surgical	230	66	67.6	89.0	95.4	87.9	99.5
Mental health	22	6	71.6	98.0	96.5	92.0	92.0
Obstetrics	34	10	51.6	78.0	62.9	83.1	91.0
Pediatrics	44	12	51.0	54.2	65.9	65.6	74.5
Total	351	100	62.2%	83.2%	78.9%	85.2%	90.7%
Infants-newborn	24	100	90.1%	82.0%	83.4%	86.9%	87.7%
Average Census:							
Adult			218.0	292	231	255	237
Infant-newborn			22.0	20	20	21	21
Average days stay—adult			7.1	—	6.5	—	5.7
Per diem inpatient income:							
room, board, and nursing care			$196.92	$149.77	$184.43	$166.55	$175.32
Ancillary services income			139.14	104.93	151.14	138.32	130.22
Total per diem income			$336.06	$254.70	$335.57	$304.87	$305.54

Table 19.11

COMPARATIVE STATEMENT OF REVENUE AND EXPENSES
October 1982 and 12 Months Ended October 31, 1982

	October 1982		12 MONTHS ENDED October 31, 1982	
	Actual	Budget	Actual	Budget
Revenue				
Patient Services:				
Room, board, and nursery care	$1,333,524	$1,356,000	$15,564,195	$15,479,419
Ancillary Services:				
Inpatient	942,267	950,000	12,755,011	12,856,000
Outpatient	273,686	275,000	3,294,224	3,465,000
Total billing to patient	2,549,477	2,581,000	31,613,430	31,800,419
Deductions From Revenue:				
Contractual adjustments	101,810	110,952	773,751	881,237
Bad debt allowance	52,264	53,000	648,075	678,523
Bad debt recovery (credit)	(18,250)	(17,500)	(226,308)	(326,500)
Total deductions from revenue	135,824	146,452	1,195,518	1,233,260
Net Revenue From Patients	2,413,653	2,434,548	30,417,912	30,567,159
Other Revenue	16,667	18,000	200,000	335,000
Total Revenue	2,430,320	2,452,548	30,617,912	30,902,159
Expenses				
Salaries and benefits	1,580,614	1,315,369	18,967,368	17,809,811
Fees and commissions	167,617	150,500	2,011,404	1,995,836
Drugs	82,631	80,631	991,568	952,372
Medical and other supplies	151,017	145,955	1,812,200	1,807,821
Food	65,791	60,900	789,492	785,000
Purchased services	54,397	51,000	652,764	648,789
Repairs and maintenance	68,048	63,050	816,576	803,500
Utilities	82,474	75,681	969,684	952,871
Interest and amortization of debt expense	187,431	185,900	2,249,172	2,159,000
Depreciation	110,309	109,500	1,323,715	1,325,000
Other	84,094	75,000	1,009,126	989,576
Total Expense	2,634,423	2,313,486	31,593,069	30,229,576
Excess of Revenues Over Expense (Deficiency)	$ (204,103)	$ 139,062	$ (975,157)	$ 672,583

Table 19.12

COMPARATIVE BALANCE SHEET:
October 31, 1982, and October 31, 1981

ASSETS	1982	1981
Current Assets:		
Cash	$ 21,733	$ 180,421
Short term investments	500,632	50,954
Accounts receivable, less allowance for uncollectible accounts of $421,767 and $397,524 in 1982 and 1981, respectively	7,159,941	6,292,477
Inventories, at cost	368,108	374,802
Current funds restricted for debt service	92,729	7,000
Prepaid expense	143,187	160,286
Total current assets	8,286,393	7,065,940
Funded Depreciation and Restricted Funds For Capital Improvements	809,315	526,241
Property, Plant, and Equipment, at Cost:		
Land and improvements	3,250,000	1,350,000
Buildings	8,309,040	6,804,040
Fixed equipment	7,973,200	6,496,800
Moveable equipment	3,466,960	2,871,960
Construction in progress	5,000,000	1,067,650
Total	27,999,200	18,590,450
Less: accumulated depreciation	8,155,557	6,831,842
Total property, plant, and equipment	19,843,643	11,758,608
Unamortized Financing Costs	549,065	1,376,500
Future Third-Party Reimbursement	455,700	1,125,700
Debt Service Reserve	1,002,779	12,516,365
TOTAL ASSETS	$30,946,895	$34,369,354

LIABILITIES	1982	1981
Current Liabilities:		
Current maturities of long-term obligations	$ 880,000	$ 310,000
Notes payable (short-term)	550,000	500,000
Accounts payable	1,194,721	2,049,514
Accrued expenses	1,926,611	1,266,016
Estimated amounts due to third-party payers	710,708	1,510,000
Construction contracts payable	1,522,165	2,725,977
Unexpended restricted contributions	18,740	24,982
Total current liabilities	6,802,945	8,386,489
Long-Term Obligations:		
Serial bonds issued in 1967, due in March and September to 1988, 5.35% to 6.0%	1,200,000	1,380,000
Serial bonds issued in 1974, due April and October to 1990, 9.0% to 10.0%	8,000,000	8,120,000
Serial notes issued in 1980, due in March and September to 1995, 8.5% to 9.5%	15,000,000	15,000,000
	24,200,000	24,500,000
Less: current maturities	880,000	310,000
Long-term debt	23,320,000	24,190,000
Fund Balance:		
Balance, beginning of year	1,792,865	1,622,294
Restricted contributions	6,242	19,900
Net income	(975,157)	150,671
FUND BALANCE	823,950	1,792,865
TOTAL LIABILITIES AND FUND BALANCE	$30,946,895	$34,369,354

Table 19.13

STATEMENT OF CHANGES IN FINANCIAL POSITION
for the Year Ending October 31, 1982

Funds Provided by:
Operations:

Net income	$ (975,157)
Items not requiring working capital	
Depreciation	1,323,715
Funds provided by operations	348,558
Restricted contributions	6,242
Unamortized financing costs	827,435
Future third-party reimbursement	670,000
Funds restricted for debt service	11,513,586
Nonoperating funds provided	13,017,263
Total funds provided	13,365,821

Funds Used for:

Funded depreciation and restricted funds for capital improvements	283,074
Additions to property, plant, and equipment	9,408,750
Current maturities of long-term debt	870,000
Total funds used	10,561,824
Increase in working capital	$2,803,997

Increase (decrease) in components of working capital:

Cash	$ (158,688)
Short-term investments	449,678
Accounts receivable	867,464
Inventories	(6,694)
Current funds restricted for debt service	85,792
Prepaid expenses	(17,099)
Current maturities of long-term debt	(570,000)
Notes payable	(50,000)
Accounts payable	854,793
Accrued expenses	(660,595)
Amounts due to third parties	799,292
Contracts payable	1,203,812
Unexpected restricted contributions	6,242
Increase in working capital	$2,803,997

Table 19.14

MANCHESTER COMMUNITY HOSPITAL STAFFING
October 1982

Department	Full-time Equivalent (FTE) Employees
Administration	91.5
Medical records	16.0
Dietary	66.8
Housekeeping	42.8
Linen[1]	3.6
Physical plant	17.6
Nursing service[2]	452.2
Laboratory	31.0
Radiology	17.6
Physical therapy	3.4
Pharmacy	4.7
Emergency department physicians[3]	8.7
Electroencephalography and cast room	3.3
Total FTE personnel[4]	759.2

BREAKDOWN OF ADMINISTRATIVE STAFFING

Department	FTE Employees	Personnel Included
General administration	13.4	Executive director and assistant directors, controller, medical staff secretary, patient representative, secretaries, and clerks
Admitting	11.5	Supervisors and clerks
Information office	1.6	
Business office	33.0	Supervisors and clerks
Financial development office	2.2	Financial development officer and secretary
Personnel	6.5	
Purchasing and stores	9.1	
Print shop	1.5	
Switchboard	8.3	
Volunteer office	0.9	Volunteer coordinator
Security guard	3.5	
Total FTE administrative personnel	91.5	

1. Laundry service is provided by an outside contractor.
2. Personnel mix: 55 percent licensed practical nurses, nursing aides, and orderlies; 45 percent registered nurses.
3. Coverage provided by salaried physicians.
4. Total number of employees: 554 full-time; 535 part-time.

Table 19.15

SELECTED INDUSTRY FINANCIAL AND PRODUCTIVITY RATIOS
For Hospitals of 200-399 Beds in the Region

FINANCIAL RATIOS (1)	Area Median	U.S. Median
Deductible ratio	.112	.135
Operating margin	.026	.023
Nonoperating revenue as percentage of		
net income	.329	.334
Current ratio	1.872	1.897
Quick ratio	1.553	1.567
Days in patient accounts receivable	54.016	59.361
Average payment period	47.488	47.748
Days cash on hand	14.061	12.499
Equity to total assets	.533	.538
Long-term debt to equity	.611	.574
Long-term debt to net fixed assets	.478	.485
Times interest earned	3.449	3.292
Debt service coverage	2.733	2.914
Total asset turnover	.990	.991
Current asset turnover	4.366	4.193

FINANCIAL RATIOS (2)	High	Median	Low
Solvency			
Current ratio	2.8	2.0	1.5
Current liabilities to net worth	14.7%	22.5%	36.5%
Fixed assets to net worth	80.9%	112.7%	169.9%
Efficiency			
Collection period (days)	47.8	57.3	67.5
Assets to sales	83.9	105.2	137.4
Sales to net working capital (times)	12.9	8.2	5.4
Profitability			
Return on sales	6.6%	4.0%	1.9%
Return on assets	5.8	3.7	1.5
Return on net worth	12.5	7.7	3.4

PRODUCTIVITY RATIOS (3)	Area Median
Cost per patient day	$208.51
Nursing service	
Nursing MH per patient day	6.25
Percent RN	32.20
Percent LPN	21.70
Salary expense per patient day	$ 39.12
Support Services	
Administrative and fiscal direct cost per patient day	25.85
Administrative MH per bed	14.04
Housekeeping and laundry direct cost per patient day	21.65
Full-time equivalent employees	
Per occupied bed	3.02
Per bed	2.49
Total MH per patient day	15.88
Salaries as a percentage of total expenses	50.76

1. HFMA Financial Analysis Service, 1982.

2. Dun & Bradstreet, Hospitals with total costs over $10 million, 1982.

3. MONITREND, American Hospital Association, area medians for the six months ended June 30, 1981.

20

The CCD Cost-Sharing Case

Jay Wolfson

INTRODUCTION

This case provides insight into some of the financial management problems faced by public-sector health service programs. It focuses on the institution of a cost-sharing policy in response to financial shortfalls. The case provides a basis for discussing the impact of new fiscal policies on service users and on programs, and serves as an opportunity to explore the topics of billing, accounting, and collection systems.

THE PROGRAM

The Crippled Children's Division (CCD) is part of the state Department of Health and is one of the oldest components of the public health service delivery system in a southeastern state. It has been funded through a combination of federal dollars and state-appropriated, categorical funds. As in other states, the CCD evolved from a limited set of services for crippled children to a wide spectrum of programs and services for more than 11,000 children annually. These children come from all socioeconomic levels, with handicapping disorders including clubfeet, cleft lips, sickle cell, burns, faulty hearts, and developmental disabilities. The range of diagnoses treated by the CCD is shown in Appendix 20.1.

Persons having or suspected of having handicapping conditions which may fall under the scope of the program's services are eligible under federal regulations to receive a diagnostic evaluation without charge, regardless of their income. If, however, the family has some form of third-party insurance, that insurance may be billed for these services. Persons receiving services through the CCD are the responsibility of their local county health departments, which maintain and route financial and clinical information for general case management.

The CCD operates several of its own clinics throughout the state but it contracts for many specific services with local physicians and institutional providers. Where contracting occurs, the state pays prenegotiated fees directly to providers and, where applicable, the CCD is supposed to bill third-party payers.

THE FINANCIAL PROBLEM

In mid-1979, the Department of Health expressed concern over the CCD's ability to accurately project utilization, costs, and expected revenues from program operations. Financial management problems had plagued the program for many years. In the past, the program had faced numerous financial shortfalls well before the conclusion of the fiscal year, but had been successful in securing additional, mid-year monies from the state legislature and the federal program.

In November 1977, during a serious mid-year funds shortage, the CCD found that state funding sources refused to yield to requests for additional, mid-cycle dollars. By January 1978, only six months into the fiscal year, 85 percent of the program's operating funds would be gone. The state, itself feeling the pinch of economic conditions, was neither prepared nor willing to continue the tradition of simply bailing out programs in financial distress. The CCD was instructed by the state to demonstrate that it was taking steps to achieve a greater degree of financial and operational self-sufficiency before additional funds would be provided.

CCD'S RESPONSE

Initial Response: Service Cuts

CCD responded to the state's demands in a dramatic, though rather typical, fashion. The administrators determined that service cutbacks would be the quickest way to reduce costs (see Appendix 20.2). Elective surgical procedures and occupational therapy, services thought to be "less necessary" or more "discretionary," were temporarily discontinued and general dental care was temporarily restricted. No plans were made at that time to examine the CCD's third-party receivables as a sleeper cash-flow source. Internal resource management practices were not discussed, nor was attention directed to the budget and budgeting process.

Cost Sharing

In late 1977, an additional step was taken to improve the program's financial status. A cost-sharing requirement to be put in place in February 1978 was announced. For years, CCD consumers had received care without having to incur any out-of-pocket expense. The new cost share would require direct financial participation from all service users for the first time. By this time, the state had responded to CCD's financial crisis, and some additional funds were appropriated. All services were reinstated, but cost sharing remained a permanent fixture.

The new cost-sharing provision included two sets of fees that were scheduled by family size and median monthly family income (see Tables 20.1 and 20.2). The clinic fee was a per-visit fee based on family size and income and ranging from $10 to the total clinic charge. This fee could be collected from service users no more than once a month and by no more than one clinic. An additional fee was charged to three family-size/income category groups of non-Medicaid eligible consumers. It ranged from $35 to the full cost of laboratory services, appliances, x-rays, surgery, and other items.

THE COST-SHARING ISSUE

There has been considerable debate over the effects of cost sharing on both service users and programs.[1] Cost sharing is designed to accomplish several goals. First, it operationalizes the insurance concept of shared risk and liability. Health insurance creates risk pools which are meant to reduce personal liability should illness occur. Through deductibles and copayments, the insurance pool does not assume all costs. Cost sharing permits relatively low premiums accompanied by a wide range of benefits.

But in the wake of Medicare and Medicaid, cost sharing emerged as a potential deterrent to the use of unnecessary services. As access to and demand for services increased among the new class of Medicare and Medicaid recipients, it was viewed as a way to reduce the use of "unnecessary" services. Medicare's cost sharing takes the form of an annual deductible for both Part A and Part B and copayments for all services received beyond the payment of the deductible in Part B. Most private insurance policies also contain some form of cost sharing. The Medicaid program, designed to provide health care for the medically indigent, and many categorical programs such as crippled children's programs, have not generally included cost sharing.

Cost sharing has also been heralded as a potential boon to cash flow. It is argued that if consumers pay the program something at or near the time services are received, providers can gain rapid access to a portion of their revenues in cash, and can collect the remaining portion from third-party payers.

CONSULTANT'S OBSERVATIONS

In mid-1979, CCD contracted for management consulting services to help remedy its chronic financial problems. In addition, the administrators were concerned about the effects of the new cost-sharing policy on service users. They feared that people in financial need might be discouraged from using medically needed services by the cost-share requirement. For the most part, these administrators were clinical social workers and social service staff who had been elevated to positions of management responsibility.

During the consultant's initial contact with program staff, there was no reference to receivables, collections policies and practices, or budgeting practices. Extended, structured staff interviews and reviews of extant service and billing records revealed a number of problems related to the management of CCD's finances:

1. Inaccurate information was kept about the methods, sources, and occurrences of payment for services. This included the lack of:
   —updated, readily available information on the financial status of service users (e.g., monthly incomes, sources of income)
   —reliable follow-up reports on referrals and payments to medical consultants
   —updated summaries on how much the program had spent within service categories
   —ability to project program expenditures, other than fixed salary costs

2. Insufficient information was maintained about the characteristics of service users. This included the inability to:
   —report, on a timely basis, the type of diagnoses, treatments, and financial-status categories of service users
   —generate profiles of individual cases without having to review pages of hard copy files
   —cost-out treatment and diagnosis categories serviced by the program

Accessible information about service users and utilization was very limited. Data which were stored on the program's computerized current index file of active cases could not be merged with data on expenditures or revenues.

Records indicated that the program was authorizing payments for services which were not reimbursable under its guidelines. The authorization process for payment to service providers, especially those on contract, was poorly controlled, and program staff were frequently unsure about the specific services covered by the program.

Among the most revealing findings were the facts that CCD did not always bill third-party payers when appropriate and that determinations of eligibility for Medicaid and other assistance programs were not always made. As a consequence, large but undeterminable amounts of program dollars, rather than third-party dollars, were used to pay for care.

Effects of the Cost-Sharing Policy

In mid-1980, a retrospective analysis of available CCD financial and medical data was initiated. The study focused on the effects of the new cost-sharing policy on the program and its service consumers. Time-series analytical techniques were used to produce trend data. Pre-post analytic techniques were also employed to examine changes in the mix of services offered by the program and changes in the characteristics of service users following the new policy.

Some of the initial questions which were asked about the cost share included: Was the program doing anything different under the cost share to conserve additional resources? Were service consumers affected in any detrimental fashion?

Table 20.3 shows the number of encounters analyzed within each of the seven collapsed diagnostic categories used in the study for fiscal years 1977 to 1979. Family income was specified as the variable which best reflected changes in use patterns of program participants. Were the mean family income to increase following the cost-sharing policy, it might suggest that lower-income consumers were deterred from service use. In order to explore the impact of the cost share on consumers, the mean monthly income of those using program services was analyzed across and within major service categories.

Figure 20.1 is a time-series analysis graph that was constructed to reflect the income of service users for the entire 30-month study period. Figure 20.2 is the autocorrelation function of this time-series plot, which displays the range of lagged correlation coefficients for each observation.[2] Figure 20.3 is an example of the time-series graphs that were constructed for income within each major diagnosis category. It reflects changes in income of service users within the diagnosis category of "orthopedic" (representing the largest single diagnosis category). Figure 20.4 is the corresponding autocorrelation function analysis. Figure 20.5 proved to be an insightful time-series chart showing the proportion of examinations performed to all services performed for the study period. The peaks at 12 and 24 months were traced back to a policy of dumping funds available at the end of the fiscal year into service provision. This pattern held for each type of service category, and reflects in part a management-by-crisis practice of the program. Figure 20.6 is the corresponding autocorrelation function. The pattern on the time-series chart is reflected in the decay in the lagged correlation coefficients. Since available data on program costs, types of services, consumer characteristics, and details about the agency's budget were not available, it was not possible to conduct meaningful analyses on costs per unit of service.

Table 20.4 displays the mean monthly family income for CCD cases in the sample for the pre- and postpolicy periods. The figures presented represent income adjusted and nonadjusted for both inflation and earnings increases for the period and for the geographic region within which the CCD operated.

In order to gain insight into things which the program itself might have been doing differently as a response to financial problems, the percentage of each service to all services provided was analyzed, as shown in Table 20.5. To contain costs, programs may exercise administrative discretion in a number of different ways. Administrative discretion represents efforts by staff to tighten up on eligibility or entitlement requirements or to discourage use of "less necessary" services among consumers. Previous studies of large-scale fiscal policy changes have revealed that administrative discretion in the form of more diligent gatekeeping can be pervasive within programs attempting to contain costs.[3]

In order to examine certain aspects of administrative discretion within CCD, closed cases were analyzed. Table 20.6 shows the percentage change in the rates of closed CCD cases by major reason for closure between the pre- and postpolicy periods.

Following the analysis of changes in services provided and in the mix of service consumers, a management question concerning effects of the cost-sharing policy on the program itself surfaced. The program was not billing private insurance companies and Medicaid where appropriate. Furthermore, the program lacked the capability to monitor, bill, and account for cost-share receivables. Medical and billing records indicated sporadic instances where cost-share amounts had been collected. However, there was no place on billing forms, medical records, or within CCD's limited financial accounting system to reflect cost-share receivables or actual collections. In addition, there was no system in place to bill service consumers for the cost-shared dollars which they owed. But preliminary findings from a 1983 study of cost sharing reveal important differences in rates of collection across major payer sources.[4] Table 20.7 is an hypothetical example of the total dollar receivables (billed) versus collected amounts by major payer sources.

While CCD program management agreed that third-party reimbursement should be more aggressively pursued, they were hesitant about actively collecting cost-share dollars from service consumers. Program managers and staff felt that aggressive follow-up on cost share could deter users from seeking care. Financial support staff in the program were more concerned about the mechanics of cost-share monitoring, accounting, and collections. Many of these financial staff members felt that the limited cost-share dollars involved would not justify a more sophisticated financial accounting system to deal with these receivables.

NOTES

1. The following articles discuss various effects of cost sharing: J. Wolfson, A. Kapadia, M. Decker, et al., "Effects of Cost-Sharing on Users of a State's Health Service Program," *Medical Care* 20 (1982): 12, 1178–1187, 1166–1167; E. Peel and J. Scharff, "Impact of Cost-Sharing on Use of Ambulatory Services under Medicaid, 1969," *Social Security Bulletin* 10 (1973): 3; A. Scitovsky and N. Snyder, "Effect of Coinsurance on Use of Physician Services," *Social Security Bulletin* 6 (1972): 3; A. Scitovsky and N. McCall, "Coinsurance and the Demand for Physician Services: Four Years Later," *Social Security Bulletin* 5 (1977): 19; E. Brian and S. Gibbens, "California's Medical Copayment Experiment," *Medical Care* (1974 supp.): 12; S. Jonas, "National Health

Insurance," in *Health Care Delivery in the United States,* ed. S. Jonas (New York: Springer, 1977); S. R. Garfield, "Prevention of Dissipation of Health Services Resources," *American Journal of Public Health* 61 (1971): 1499; J. P. Newhouse and C. E. Phelps, "New Estimates of Price and Income Elasticities of Medical Care Services," in *The Role of Health Insurance in the Health Services Sector,* ed. R. N. Rossett (New York: National Bureau of Economic Research, 1961): 261; J. P. Newhouse, C. E. Phelps, and W. Schwartz, "Policy Options and the Impact of National Health Insurance," *New England Journal of Medicine* 290 (1974): 1345; J. P. Newhouse, W. Manning, L. Orr, et al., "Some Interim Results from a Controlled Trial of Cost-Sharing in Health Insurance," *New England Journal of Medicine* 305 (1981): 1501.
2. For a detailed discussion of time-series analysis, see G. E. P. Box and G. M. Jenkins, *Time-Series Analysis, Forecasting and Control* (San Francisco: Holden-Day, 1970); T. D. Cook and D. T. Campbell, *Quasi-Experimentation: Design and Analysis Issues for Field Settings* (Chicago: Rand-McNally, 1979).
3. C. E. Hopkins, F. Proctor, F. Gartside, et al., "Cost-Sharing and Prior Authorization Effects on Medicaid Services in California": Part I, "The Beneficiaries' Reaction," *Medical Care* 12 (1975): 583; Part II, "The Provider's Reaction," *Medical Care* 13 (1975): 613.
4. J. Wolfson, "Cost-Sharing Effects on Providers," *Hospitals,* February 16, 1982, p. 46.

Appendix 20.1

DIAGNOSTIC CATEGORIES FOR WHICH CCD PROVIDES DIAGNOSTIC AND EVALUATION SERVICES

ORTHOPEDIC
Tuberculosis of bones and joints
Acute poliomyelitis including late effects
Malignant neoplasms of bone
Cerebral palsy
Rheumatoid arthritis and allied conditions
Osteomyelitis and periostitis
Legg-Perthes disease
Slipped femoral epiphysis, nontraumatic
All other osteochondrosis
Craniostenosis
Certain other diseases of bones and organs of movement
All other diseases of the bones and joints
Progressive muscular dystrophy
Curvature of the spine
Flatfoot
Hallux valgus and varus
Metatarsus varus

Clubfoot
Tibial torsion
Genu valgum and genu varum
All other diseases of musculoskeletal system
Congenital dislocation of hip
Chondrodystrophy
Osteogenesis imperfecta
Congenital limb deficiencies
All other congenital malformations of bones and joints
Webbed fingers and/or toes
All other congenital orthopedic malformations
Fracture of bone due to birth injury
Congenital torticollis

RHEUMATIC FEVER
Rheumatic fever

Rheumatic fever (latent, under
  prophylactic care)
Chronic rheumatic heart disease

EPILEPSY
Epilepsy

CLEFT LIP AND CLEFT PALATE
Cleft palate
Cleft lip
Cleft lip and palate

SICKLE CELL
Sickle cell

HEMOPHILIA
Hemophilia

METABOLIC DISORDERS
Diabetes mellitus
Rickets, active and late
PKU
Galactosemia
All other endocrine system diseases
All other metabolic and nutritional
  diseases

CYSTIC FIBROSIS
Cystic fibrosis
All other diseases of respiratory system

HEARING IMPAIRMENT
Otitis media (with or without mention of
  mastoiditis)
Mastoiditis (with or without mention of
  otitis media)
Conductive hearing loss
Sensory-neural hearing impairment
All other hearing impairments
All other diseases of the ear and mastoid
  process
Organic speech disorders

*NEUROSURGICAL AND
NEUROLOGICAL*
Late effects of acute infectious
  encephalitis
Malignant neoplasms, CNS
Nonorganic speech disorders
Vascular lesions affecting CNS
Late effects of intracranial abscess or
  pyogenic infections
Multiple sclerosis
All other diseases of nervous system
Spina bifida and meningocele
Congenital hydrocephalus
Intracranial and spinal injury at birth

UROLOGICAL
Malignant neoplasms, urinary organs
Nephrosis
Nephritis
All other diseases of genitourinary system
Undescended testicle
Epispadias and hypospadias
All other congenital malformations,
  genitourinary system

CONGENITAL ANOMALIES
Congenital hypertrophic pyloric stenosis
Imperforate anus
Congenital deformity of intestine
Congenital absence or atresia of bile duct
Tracheo-esophageal fistula
All other congenital malformations,
  digestive system
Congenital cataract
Congenital ptosis of eyelid
Congenital malformation of ear

PLASTIC SURGERY
Burns
Poisoning by corrosive aromatics, acids,
  and caustic alkalis

HEART
Acute and subacute endocarditis
All other diseases of circulatory system
Congenital malformation of heart
Congenital malformation of great vessels
All other congenital malformations,
    circulatory system

OTHER OR UNSPECIFIED
All other tuberculosis
All other infective and parasitic diseases
Leukemia and aleukemia
All other malignant neoplasms
Hemangioma and lymphangioma
All other neoplasms
Asthma
All other allergic disorders
All other diseases of blood and blood-
    forming organs
Mongolism
All other mental deficiency
All other mental, psychoneurotic, and
    personality disorders
Refractive errors
Strabismus

Blindness
All other diseases of sense organs
Hypertrophy of tonsils and adenoids
Dental caries
Disorders of eruption, occlusion, tooth
    development
Hernia of abdominal cavity
Intestinal obstruction (without mention of
    hernia)
All other diseases of digestive system
Deliveries, complications of pregnancy,
    childbirth, puerperium
Diseases of the skin and cellular tissue
All other birth injuries
Neonatal disorders
Hemolytic disease of newborn
All other of certain diseases of early
    infancy
All other codes in symptoms, senility and
    ill-defined conditions
All other poisoning
All other conditions due to accidents and
    violence
Provisional or deferred diagnosis
Examination made, no abnormality
    reported

Appendix 20.2

CCD'S INITIAL RESPONSE TO FUNDS SHORTAGE

MEMORANDUM   20 December 1977

TO: All CCD clinics and providers
FROM: Director, CCD program
SUBJECT: Service Provision during Budget Problems

Effective immediately, and until further notice, the following CCD services will be discontinued: dental services, outpatient diagnostic services, inpatient admitting and related services (without formal approval from this office), and prosthetic appliance maintenance. We can no longer guarantee reimbursement for any of these services.

MEMORANDUM   12 January 1978

TO: All CCD clinics and providers
FROM: Director, CCD program
SUBJECT: Institution of a Fee Schedule for CCD Services

Effective 13 February 1978, a fee schedule for CCD services will be put into effect. Each clinic will be responsible for conducting financial screens on all CCD patients according to guidelines that will be sent under separate cover. In order to ensure the financial viability of the program, we will have to start collecting a small fee from all users.

MEMORANDUM   18 January 1978

TO: All CCD clinics and providers
FROM: Director, CCD program
SUBJECT: Resumption of Certain Services

As of this date, inpatient admissions of CCD patients for preauthorized procedures are to be resumed. Outpatient diagnostic testing will require approval from district offices of the Health Department. At this time, only emergency authorized dental services will be provided. All prosthetic maintenance will resume as before.

Table 20.1

FEE SCHEDULE FOR CRIPPLED CHILDREN'S CARE
February 1978 – April 1979

Family Size	A Monthly Income	B Monthly Income	C Monthly Income	D Monthly Income	E Monthly Income	F Monthly Income
1	$ 241 - 360	$ 361 - 420	$ 421 - 481	$ 482 - 691	$ 692 - 902	$ 903 or more
2	393 - 471	472 - 549	550 - 629	630 - 904	905 - 1179	1180 or more
3	476 - 582	583 - 679	680 - 777	778 - 1117	1118 - 1457	1458 or more
4	578 - 693	694 - 808	809 - 925	926 - 1329	1330 - 1734	1735 or more
5	671 - 804	805 - 938	939 - 1073	1074 - 1542	1543 - 2012	2013 or more
6	763 - 915	916 - 1067	1068 - 1221	1222 - 1755	1756 - 2289	2290 or more
7	781 - 936	937 - 1092	1093 - 1249	1250 - 1795	1796 - 2342	2343 or more
8	798 - 957	958 - 1116	1117 - 1277	1278 - 1835	1836 - 2394	2395 or more
9	816 - 978	979 - 1141	1142 - 1305	1306 - 1876	1877 - 2447	2448 or more
10	833 - 998	999 - 1165	1166 - 1332	1333 - 1915	1916 - 2498	2499 or more
11	850 - 1019	1020 - 1189	1190 - 1360	1361 - 1955	1956 - 2550	2551 or more
12	868 - 1040	1041 - 1214	1215 - 1388	1389 - 1995	1996 - 2603	2604 or more
13	885 - 1061	1062 - 1238	1239 - 1416	1417 - 2036	2037 - 2655	2656 or more
14	902 - 1081	1082 - 1262	1263 - 1443	1444 - 2075	2076 - 2706	2707 or more
15	920 - 1102	1103 - 1286	1287 - 1471	1472 - 2115	2116 - 2759	2760 or more
Clinic Fee	0	0	0	1/3	2/3	Full
Other	$10.00	$15.00	$20.00	$35.00	$50.00	Full

Table 20.2

FEE SCHEDULE FOR CRIPPLED CHILDREN'S CARE
April – December 1979

Family Size	A Monthly Income	B Monthly Income	C Monthly Income	D Monthly Income	E Monthly Income	F Monthly Income
1	$ 334 - 401	$ 402 - 468	$ 469 - 534	$ 535 - 768	$ 769 - 1002	$1003 or more
2	437 - 524	525 - 612	613 - 699	700 - 1005	1006 - 1311	1312 or more
3	540 - 647	648 - 755	756 - 863	864 - 1241	1242 - 1619	1620 or more
4	643 - 771	772 - 900	901 - 1028	1029 - 1478	1479 - 1928	1929 or more
5	745 - 894	895 - 1043	1044 - 1192	1193 - 1714	1715 - 2235	2236 or more
6	848 - 1018	1019 - 1187	1188 - 1357	1358 - 1950	1951 - 2544	2545 or more
7	868 - 1041	1042 - 1215	1216 - 1388	1389 - 1995	1996 - 2603	2604 or more
8	887 - 1064	1065 - 1241	1242 - 1418	1419 - 2039	2040 - 2660	2661 or more
9	906 - 1087	1088 - 1268	1269 - 1449	1450 - 2083	2084 - 2717	2718 or more
10	925 - 1110	1111 - 1295	1296 - 1480	1481 - 2128	2129 - 2775	2776 or more
11	945 - 1133	1134 - 1322	1323 - 1511	1512 - 2172	2173 - 2834	2835 or more
12	964 - 1157	1158 - 1350	1351 - 1542	1543 - 2217	2218 - 2892	2893 or more
13	983 - 1179	1180 - 1376	1377 - 1572	1573 - 2260	2261 - 2948	2949 or more
14	1002 - 1202	1203 - 1403	1404 - 1603	1604 - 2305	2306 - 3006	3007 or more
15	1022 - 1226	1227 - 1430	1431 - 1634	1635 - 2349	2350 - 3065	3066 or more
Clinic Fee	0	0	0	⅓	⅔	Full
Other	$10.00	$15.00	$20.00	$35.00	$50.00	Full

Table 20.3

CALCULATED SAMPLE SIZE
for Fiscal Years 1977 – 1979 by Diagnostic Strata*

Diagnostic Category	July 1977– June 1978 (Number)	July 1978– June 1979 (Number)	July 1979– December 1979 (Number)
Orthopedic	334	331	369
Heart	173	164	192
Neurologic	108	106	123
Hearing	99	108	126
Congenital	58	58	69
Metabolic	30	35	45
Other	176	176	203
Total for Fiscal Year	978	978	1127

*Total number calculated for sample = 3,083.

Table 20.4

COMPARISON OF MEAN MONTHLY FAMILY INCOME FOR CCD FAMILIES SELECTED IN THE SAMPLE FOR PRE- AND POSTPOLICY PERIODS WITH ADJUSTMENT FOR EARNINGS INCREASES* AND INFLATION**

Mean Monthly Family Income	Prepolicy Period July 77–January 78	Postpolicy Period March 78–December 79
Earnings Increases and Inflation Adjusted†	$537.61	$507.16

*The earning increase rate for the postpolicy period was 0.17 (U.S. Department of Labor, Personal Correspondence, 1981.)

**The inflation rate for the postpolicy period was 0.19 (U.S. Department of Labor, Personal Correspondence, 1980.)

†Earnings increased/inflation adjusted mean monthly family income, $t = 3.60$ $1\,d.f.$, $0.20 > p > 0.10$.

Table 20.5

COMPARISON OF PERCENTAGE OF EACH SERVICE TO ALL SERVICES PROVIDED TO CCD SERVICE USERS IN PRE- AND POSTPOLICY PERIODS.

Service Category*	PREPOLICY PERIOD JULY 77–JANUARY 78 (Percent)	POSTPOLICY PERIOD MARCH 78–DECEMBER 79 (Percent)
Exam	40.6	40.5
Tests	11.3	11.0
Followup	9.4	9.2
Appliances	5.1	5.8
Social work	3.1	4.1
Evaluations	6.4	6.6
Closure	18.3	15.4
Surgery	4.0	3.3
Prescriptions	3.1	4.1
	$n = 379$ 100.0	$n = 2612$ 100.0

*Change in the percentage of each service to all services provided, $\chi^2 = 2.37$.
8 $d.f.$, $0.97 > p > 0.95$.

Table 20.6

PERCENTAGE CHANGE IN THE RATES OF CLOSED CCD CASES BY REASON FOR CLOSURE FOR PRE- AND POSTPOLICY PERIODS.

Reason for Closure*	CASE CLOSURE RATE/100 Prepolicy Period July 77–January 78	Postpolicy Period March 78–December 79	Percentage Change
Medically ineligible	5.3	2.4	−54.7
Financially ineligible	0.8	0.4	−50.0
No further CCD care necessary	1.6	0.9	−43.8
Condition corrected	3.2	3.0	−6.3
Under care of another agency	0.3	1.3	+433.3
Under private care	0.6	1.3	+216.7
Moved out of state	2.1	1.2	−42.9
Dead	3.2	0.6	−81.3
Parent's request	1.6	1.2	−25.0
Cannot locate	0.6	0.5	−16.7
Over age	1.6	1.3	−18.8
Other	0.6	1.5	+250.0
	$n = 379$	$n = 2612$	

*Change in the distribution of reasons for case closure, $\chi^2 = 0.31$.
11 $d.f.$, $p > 0.50$.

Table 20.7

HYPOTHETICAL COST-SHARE COLLECTIONS BILLED
VS. COLLECTED AMOUNTS
by Payer Source for 1981

| | PAYER SOURCE | | | | |
	Blue Cross	Private Insurance	Medicare	Medicaid	Private Pay
Billed amount	$5,950,200	$7,321,000	$3,226,300	$18,950,700	$1,223,000
Patient cost share	$1,785,060	$2,342,720	$1,129,205	$1,895,070	$1,223,000
Cost share collected (6 months)	$1,517,301	$1,944,457	$903,364	$966,495	$1,002,860
Percentage of billed amount actually collected	85%	83%	80%	51%	82%

Figure 20.1

TIME-SERIES PLOT OF MEAN INCOME OF CCD SERVICE USERS
Over Thirty-Month Study Period

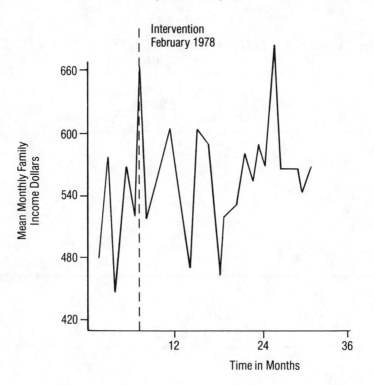

Figure 20.2

AUTOCORRELATION FUNCTION OF MEAN INCOME OF CCD SERVICE USERS
Over Thirty-Month Study Period

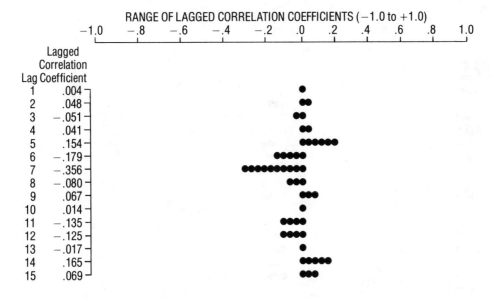

Figure 20.3

TIME-SERIES PLOT OF MEAN INCOME BY DIAGNOSIS
Orthopedic

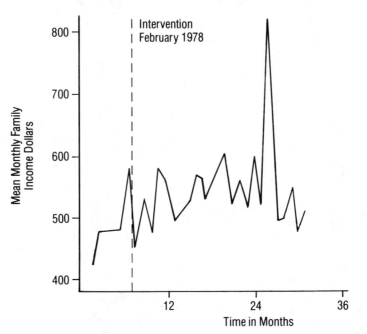

Figure 20.4

AUTOCORRELATION FUNCTION OF MEAN INCOME BY DIAGNOSIS
Orthopedic

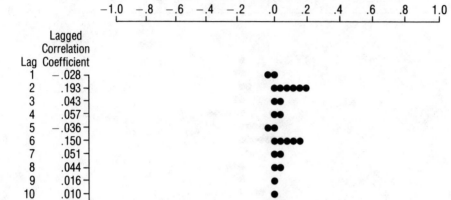

Figure 20.5

TIME-SERIES PLOT OF PROPORTION OF EXAMS
TO ALL SERVICES PROVIDED EACH MONTH

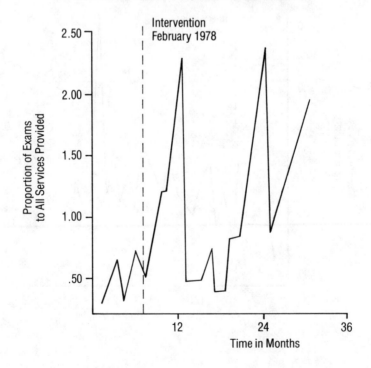

Figure 20.6

AUTOCORRELATION FUNCTION OF PROPORTION OF EXAMS
TO ALL SERVICES PROVIDED EACH MONTH

Range of Lagged Correlation Coefficients (−1.0 to +1.0)

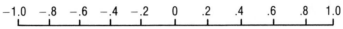

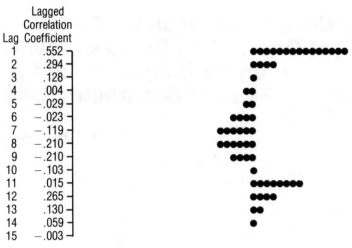

Lag	Lagged Correlation Coefficient
1	.552
2	.294
3	.128
4	.004
5	−.029
6	−.023
7	−.119
8	−.210
9	−.210
10	−.103
11	.015
12	.265
13	.130
14	.059
15	−.003

21

Failure to Orchestrate An HMO: The Case of One HMO's Reorganization under Chapter 11 of the Federal Bankruptcy Law

A. Kay Keiser

INTRODUCTION

In early December 1979, two representatives from the federal government's Office of Health Maintenance Organizations (OHMO) reported to the Board of Directors of the Nevada Health Plan:

> We can only reiterate to you, as Board members, what has been outlined in the letter of noncompliance sent to you by our (OHMO) office on November 30, 1979. The Nevada Health Plan (NHP) has failed to establish effective procedures to monitor utilization and cost controls. . . . Management must exercise control over the costs of hospitalization and referrals to specialist consultants. . . . Administrative costs are too high. . . . Disenrollment of members exceeds that of similar HMOs. . . . The plan has incurred operating deficits averaging $71,000 per month; therefore, it must concurrently raise revenue and lower costs. . . . There is no evidence to support either the assumptions or projections about when this plan will reach break-even. . . .
>
> Quite frankly, our major concern is whether NHP has adequate time to reverse its losses. In our experience, the process of "turning around" a plan as deeply in debt as NHP takes about six months and your federal funding, at present levels, will last only four months. . . . NHP must, therefore, submit a corrective action plan to our office which sets forth the methods by which you propose to achieve compliance. . . . If you do not submit the plan within 30 days, or if it is not satisfactory to us, the director of OHMO is empowered under federal legislation to take further action.

BACKGROUND

The Nevada Health Plan (NHP) is a community-sponsored, federally-qualified, staff model health maintenance organization (HMO). In December 1979, it was providing a full range of health care services, including ambulatory and hospital care, to about 8,200 members from the Greater West Nevada Metropolitan Area, an SMSA of about 300,000 residents. Its services are provided by a salaried staff of physicians and other coprofessionals in a 15,000-square-foot health center, a renovated facility which contains doctors' offices, x-ray and laboratory services, a pharmacy, and administrative offices. It can accommodate 15,000 members in its present space.

Other specialty care is provided by community-based consulting physicians upon referral by NHP's core of basic specialists (internal medicine, pediatrics, and obstetrics-gynecology). All hospital care is provided by both the HMO and consulting physicians to HMO members at one of three local community hospitals. NHP also has contractual agreements for care of its members with skilled nursing homes, a rehabilitation center, and several home health care agencies.

NHP is one of the country's 225 prepaid medical practice plans referred to as HMOs, many of which were funded by the federal government under the HMO Act of 1973 (P.L. 93-222). Under this legislation, the HMO ensures a full range of health services to a voluntarily enrolled population in a defined geographic area. These enrolled members pay a fixed monthly premium (or have it paid on their behalf by their employers) regardless of the numbers or kinds of services they use.

Among other requirements, NHP must assure that its services are of high quality and that they are being provided in a fiscally responsible way in order to be in compliance with the HMO Act and to be designated as a "federally qualified" HMO. NHP became operational on March 1, 1977, and was federally qualified only 15 days later. Thus, when it received its notice of noncompliance in early December 1979, NHP was less than three years old and facing loss of its federal qualification.

DOCUMENTING THE FACTS

The Call for a Management Staff Meeting

Of all of the Board members, the Vice Chairman and unpaid Acting Executive Director, Professor Bill Wilson, found the OHMO noncompliance news most difficult to accept. Immediately after the meeting between the OHMO representatives and the NHP Board, Bill called NHP's three senior management staff members together. They included Scott Stratton, the Director of Finance; Mark Long, M.D., Medical Director; and Catherine Jackson, the Director of Marketing. Bill advised them that the purpose of the meeting was to get their ideas about what had contributed to NHP's present status and to prepare a strategy for developing a corrective action plan. He urged them to bring along any documentation they had about their respective departments. Bill Wilson was determined to get to the bottom of this situation by getting "facts," especially about NHP's continued shortfall in revenue due to persistently low enrollment of members.

Bill Wilson and His Staff Meet

Bill Wilson opened the meeting with the following comment:

> I have concluded that launching an HMO is one of the most complex and formidable tasks in which I have ever participated. I have thought a great deal about the many national and local

events that have influenced NHP's organizational life. I would therefore like to review with you some of my perspectives and then ask that you share your views with me. Perhaps in this way we can develop a list of our major problems, their causes, and their potential solutions. The latter will be incorporated into the corrective action plan we must submit to OHMO.

I suggest that to keep the discussion orderly, we might use the three phases of NHP's development as the basis for examining our present financial status, which to me appears to be due to our having fewer members enrolled than projected. "Feasibility," "planning-development," and "initial operations" may be arbitrary designations of our organizational phases, but at least for me, they will help to put the issues in perspective. Since none of you were with NHP during its feasibility phase, let me begin the discussion.

Phase I: Feasibility (1971–1972)

Bill Wilson explained:

Yesterday's meeting with OHMO certainly makes me wonder whether the local and national environments before and just after passage of the HMO legislation in 1973 were really conducive to establishing an HMO. Locally, the 1971 feasibility study was undertaken by the administration and medical staff of Barnes Hospital, only to result in a vote by the medical staff at the end of the one-year study that a "hospital-sponsored HMO was not feasible for the area." At the time, the community Board I called together learned that Barnes Hospital's medical staff and the local medical community generally were opposed to any HMO, regardless of the sponsor. The vote taken by the Barnes Hospital staff was a concession made out of fear of the community's possible reaction to physician opposition to an HMO as an alternative delivery system committed to reducing health care costs. As I look back I wonder whether we won a battle but lost the war. We had to go outside the area to recruit a medical staff for NHP and the local physicians have since sponsored a competing Individual Physician Association (IPA) HMO to serve the same area as NHP.

And nationally, the original HMO legislation in 1973 mandated a very comprehensive range of benefits which certainly made it difficult for early HMOs to be price-competitive in the marketplace with Blue Cross-Blue Shield and commercial health insurance carriers. It took two sets of amendments to the original HMO law, first in 1976 and then in 1978, before HMOs really began to grow. Maybe we simply entered the HMO field too early; we needed changes in the benefit package, community rating, and open enrollment provisions of the 1973 act, as well as the HMO management training programs and increased funding which the amendments also made possible.

Phase II: Planning and Initial Development (1972–1976)

Bill Wilson then recalled for the management staff that when the present community Board of Directors was formed to take over NHP's sponsorship from Barnes Hospital (one of the three local community hospitals), he became Chairman of the Board. During that time, NHP submitted its first five-year financial plan as required by OHMO. Not only was that plan rejected, but in June 1975, the OHMO staff called a special meeting with NHP's Board of Directors and made any future financial support contingent upon NHP's recruiting a new President-Chief Executive Officer (CEO).

It took the Board's search committee six months to recruit Martin Carpenter, who joined the plan in December 1975. Martin Carpenter's name was one of six acceptable candidates for the position provided by OHMO to NHP's search committee. Martin had very impressive academic credentials and work experience in health care, but no actual experience in HMOs. The HMO industry at the time was sufficiently small and relatively new so that seasoned CEOs simply were not available; many HMO executives were recruited from business.

Bill Wilson addressed his next question to Scott Stratton. "Scott, wasn't it soon after Martin became President-CEO that you joined NHP? Perhaps you can fill in some of the details here, with as much documentation as you have. But remember, my background is in philosophy and not finance, so I ask that you keep things as simple as possible. I don't have the other members of the Board who are bankers and C.P.A.s here to help me translate the financial statements as they usually do."

Scott Stratton, NHP's Director of Finance, explained that he had joined NHP in April 1976, about four months after Martin Carpenter was appointed President-CEO. He also confirmed that one of his first tasks was to develop a revised five-year financial plan.

By way of explanation, Scott began:

Like any other business, an HMO's financial plan consists of ongoing revenue and expense items which are related to the cost of, and payment for, the range of benefits the HMO offers. Stated simply, the *cost* of providing all services offered by the HMO is related to enrolled members. It is referred to as a "capitation" and is usually expressed on a "per-member-per-month" basis to reflect a period of time. On the *revenue* side, premiums represent the major source of an HMO's income. Thus, the level at which NHP's total revenue and total costs are equal represents the HMO's "break-even" membership.

The concept of break-even membership can be seen from the graph I just gave you (see Figure 21.1). The fixed costs, represented by the horizontal broken line, exist regardless of how many members we enroll. But total cost is the sum of both fixed and variable costs. So it is represented on the graph by a slanted line because, by definition, variable costs increase as new members are enrolled. And finally, revenue that is derived primarily from members' premiums is also shown as a slanted line. Thus, the break-even point is where the revenue and total cost lines cross. In other words, operating revenue is equal to operating costs.

However, it is important to understand that although break-even is a function of fixed and variable costs, deciding on a break-even membership level is not as easy as it sounds. Since our capitated cost of providing services determines what our premiums will be, we must be sure that the premium is competitive in the market; we must also minimize fluctuations in the capitation so that premiums will be relatively stable over the first few years. This is done by setting the break-even enrollment goal in advance, which can be done somewhat arbitrarily. . . . The next two tables (Tables 21.1 and 21.2), identify the differences between the first two five-year financial projections and highlight some of the consequences.

If you look at the "membership" and "expense" portions of the first table (21.1), you'll see that my predecessor, Carl Slatter, shows NHP's break-even membership at 24,000 members in year 4, with total expenses of $7,849,966 resulting in a capitation of $27.26 per member per month pm/pm. That capitation would certainly have been very competitive in the marketplace.

The problem is that Carl placed his membership level too high in order to derive a low capitation. He assumed a beginning enrollment of 1,000 members in year 1. Given the many employer groups in NHP's large service area, that is a conservative estimate. But from there on he went wild. For example, his projection of 1,000 members in year 1 to 7,000 members in year 2 represents an annual increase of 600 percent.

From year 2 at 7,000 members to year 3 at 16,000 members is almost another 130 percent increase. I don't care how many employer groups there are out there in the service area as our

Figure 21.1

THE BREAK-EVEN MEMBERSHIP CONCEPT

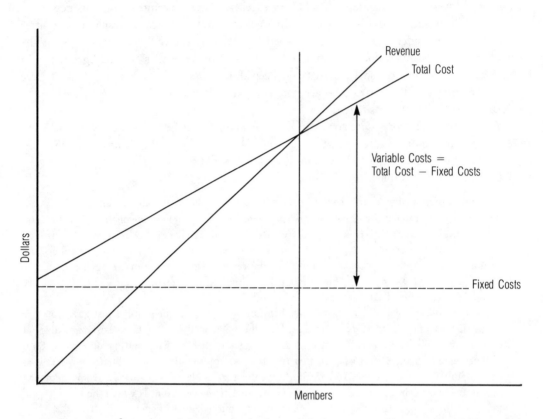

major source of members, it is just completely unrealistic to expect *any* marketing staff to bring in so many members in such a short time. But Carl shows income of $7,893,345 in year 4 offsetting the $7,849,966 costs, for a surplus of 15 cents per member per month. Now, let's compare that with my projections.

According to the table before you (Table 21.2), when I revised the projections, I showed that NHP needed only 15,000 members in year 4 as a break-even membership, with a capitation of $35.30. I figured 15,000 members as a more realistic break-even level, based on the HMO industry's rule of thumb which sets break-even enrollment at the health center's membership capacity. I figured our health center of 15,000 square feet could accommodate 15,000 members. You'll notice that I offset total costs by projecting increased income over the five years from two sources in addition to premiums: fee-for-service and pharmacy.

Martin assured me that he would recruit some local community physicians who would bring some of their private patients into NHP until they could enroll as members through their places of employment. I also estimated higher income from pharmacy than Carl did because although some members don't have the prepaid prescription benefit, they can purchase their medications at the health center's pharmacy. Of course there are some disadvantages in setting break-even membership too low. But after all, the final decision about break-even is a policy decision, not a technical one. I only participated in it in working with Martin Carpenter as the president-CEO.

Table 21.1

FIRST FIVE-YEAR PROJECTIONS OF INCOME AND EXPENSE
February 1976 – February 1980

	Year 1 (1976)	Year 2 (1977)	Year 3 (1978)	Year 4 (1979)	Year 5 (1980)
Membership					
Members	1,000	7,000	16,000	24,000	30,000
Expense					
Medical	$ 891,938	$1,355,477	$2,080,113	$2,705,382	$ 3,464,063
Hospital	327,205	1,373,623	2,589,000	3,763,000	5,082,000
Administrative	809,221	899,596	1,210,838	1,381,584	1,465,916
Total	$2,028,364	$3,628,696	$5,879,951	$7,849,966	$10,011,979
Capitation					
Per member per month	$169.03	$43.20	$30.62	$27.26	$27.81
Income					
Premiums	$ 675,456	$2,718,676	$5,200,050	$7,718,345	$10,532,933
Fee-for-service	175,000	175,000	175,000	175,000	175,000
Total	$ 850,456	$2,893,676	$5,375,050	$7,893,345	$10,707,933
Surplus (Deficit)					
Total	($1,177,908)	($ 735,020)	($ 504,901)	$ 43,379	$ 695,954
Cumulative	($1,777,908)	($1,912,928)	($2,417,829)	($2,374,450)	($1,678,496)
Per member per month	($98.16)	($8.75)	($2.63)	$0.15	$1.93

Table 21.2

SECOND FIVE-YEAR PROJECTIONS OF INCOME AND EXPENSE
July 1976 – July 1981

	Year 1 (1976)	Year 2 (1977)	Year 3 (1978)	Year 4 (1979)	Year 5 (1980)
Membership					
Members	1,000	5,000	10,000	15,000	21,000
Expense					
Medical	$ 580,356	$ 796,639	$1,203,438	$1,692,620	$2,174,016
Hospital	409,328	1,111,545	2,028,208	3,194,982	4,500,067
Administrative	612,944	794,884	1,150,435	1,466,045	1,828,318
Total	$1,602,616	$2,703,068	$4,382,079	$6,353,649	$8,502,401
Capitation					
Per member per month	$133.55	$45.05	$36.52	$35.30	$33.74
Income					
Premiums	$ 772,532	$2,027,524	$3,784,568	$5,999,280	$8,428,054
Fee-for-service	189,000	252,000	362,000	635,000	732,000
Pharmacy	7,000	7,000	7,000	7,000	7,000
Total	$ 968,532	$2,286,524	$4,153,568	$6,641,280	$9,167,054
Surplus (Deficit)					
Total	($ 634,084)	($ 416,544)	($ 228,511)	$ 287,633	$ 664,653
Cumulative	($ 634,084)	($1,050,628)	($1,279,139)	($ 991,506)	($ 326,853)
Per member per month	($52.84)	($6.94)	($1.91)	$1.60	$2.64

Bill Wilson didn't respond to Scott's comments, but he made a note to pursue the matter of fee-for-service income because, despite continued opposition to NHP by the local medical community, NHP had been successful in recruiting Barnes Hospital's former Director of the Department of Medicine. Dr. David Aaron, a board-certified specialist in internal medicine, had closed his very prestigious and active practice in the community and agreed to join NHP as its Medical Director. But neither he nor his two colleague internists had ever joined NHP's medical staff. Only six months after Martin Carpenter arrived, he and Dr. Aaron reported that they simply could not work together, and the Board decided it had no alternative but to accept Dr. Aaron's resignation, before NHP had even become operational.

Phase III: Early Operations (1977 to Reorganization in 1980)

Bill Wilson also recalled the near euphoria among the Board and staff when NHP finally opened its doors to its first members on March 1, 1977.

OHMO was very supportive at that time. In quick succession it awarded a $2.5-million loan (February 1977) to cover operating deficits for NHP's first three years and also designated NHP as a "federally qualified" HMO (March 15, 1977).

In looking back on 1977 and 1978, Bill Wilson was convinced that if only NHP had met its projected membership, many of its early problems would have been solved. "Sure, there were other problems," he told himself, "but every new business faces problems during its first three to five years." He asked Catherine Jackson, Director of Marketing, to review with the group some background information. Catherine began:

> I took over as Director of Marketing during 1978. One of the first things I did was review NHP's marketing and enrollment experience. I found that on day 1 of NHP's operations (March 1977), it actually had 265 members against a projection of 1,000 members. And, for the first year, *actual* monthly membership averaged 329 members against *projections* of 333. So the negative variance between actual and projected members for the first year was insignificant. But there were no clear marketing objectives or strategy for enrolling members. I had to devote most of my time to marketing tasks that should have been done during the planning and development phase.
>
> For example, in year 2 (March 1978) my predecessor projected an increase from the 333 members to 416 members per month. And at the same time Scott and Martin decided on an 11-percent premium increase beginning with year 2. The consequence of these decisions can be seen in the exhibit before you (Table 21.3). It compares NHP with two other local staff model HMOs and shows terminations as a percentage of net enrollment. You can see how our terminations shot up in the second quarter of 1979 just after the 11-percent premium increase took effect in March. That higher premium and the increase in projected enrollment from 333 to 416 members per month continue to plague us, but my marketing staff is doing the best it can. They are bringing in close to the *gross* projected membership of 416 members; but because disenrollment is so high, the actual *net* enrollment falls short of its target. As a result, when NHP entered its third operational year in March 1979, actual enrollment was at 7,000 members rather than the 10,000 members Scott had projected in his revised five-year plan.
>
> My marketing staff is working as hard as it can. As best as I can determine, members are disenrolling because they find the premiums too high, thanks to Scott's high capitation. Quite frankly, it's very discouraging to have been told repeatedly that NHP could not afford to undertake a survey to document why members are disenrolling, to expand the marketing staff so they would have time to go back and service those employer groups from which they enrolled members, and to pay an incentive bonus to the marketing staff. But Martin always refused such requests. So, since marketing can't control disenrollment, NHP needs to look at the other side of the coin — its costs.

Bill Wilson was inexperienced about marketing and enrollment and didn't quite know

Table 21.3

TERMINATIONS AS A PERCENTAGE OF NET ENROLLMENT BY QUARTERS FOR NHP AND TWO LOCAL STAFF MODEL HMOs, 1979

		STAFF MODELS	
1979 Quarters	NHP	HMO #1	HMO #2
January – March	9.6%	5.0%	6.3%
April – June	25.1	3.4	5.5
July – September	11.9	7.3	6.1
September – December	8.0	5.5	6.7
Total	13.5	5.4	6.2

*Includes only the first two weeks of December 1979.

how to respond to Catherine's comments. But since OHMO had also said that NHP's expenses had to be reduced, Bill asked Scott if he would address this issue.

Scott explained:

Based on OHMO's notice of noncompliance, I have broken out selected expenses on a per-capita basis and compared them with the staff model HMO nearby. According to the exhibit before you (Table 21.4), which takes our experience up to September 30, 1979, we don't compare very favorably. NHP's total costs at $37.51 are about $2 more than those of the other HMOs at $35.14. But the cost items contributing to total expenses are quite different. Our administrative costs are higher because of the unfavorable rent we had to agree upon at the last minute when we couldn't find another facility to lease.

And in terms of health delivery, both our referrals to specialists and inpatient hospital care are much higher. The reasons are easy to explain. We don't have accurate records on referrals. And inpatient care, one of the most expensive health care costs, is just too high because Mark Long, as Medical Director, doesn't control it. There is no reason to believe that our members are any sicker than those who join the other HMO, and yet our hospital experience between 1978 and 1979 went up from 397 days to 505 days per 1,000 members. The latter figure compares with 320 days for the other HMO and when I talked to them, they thought their utilization was high!

Table 21.4

COMPARATIVE EXPENSE ITEMS PER MEMBER PER MONTH FOR NHP AND A LOCAL STAFF MODEL HMO
Fiscal Year Ending September 1979

	PER MEMBER PER MONTH			
	NHP		Staff Model HMO	
Expense	*(Dollars)*	*(Percent)*	*(Dollars)*	*(Percent)*
Specialist referrals	$ 3.41	9.1%	$ 1.79	5.1%
Hospitalization	11.33	30.2	8.50	24.2
Administration	8.40	22.4	5.48	15.6
All others	14.37	38.3	19.37	55.1
	$37.51	100.0%	$35.14	100.0%

Dr. Mark Long, the Medical Director, was a young pediatrician without any training or experience in medical management. He interrupted at this point, "Scott, I'm trying to monitor current hospitalization as best I can. But then I discovered that when Blue Cross pays our members' bills directly to the hospitals on our behalf, it takes two months for them to notify us what expenses we have incurred. In other words, when you give me a copy of the Blue Cross report you get, it shows NHP members for whom Blue Cross paid hospital claims, but their figure is based on hospitalizations that happened two months earlier. So, if NHP's hospitalization costs increase, I don't know it until two months later."

Scott tried to be patient with Dr. Long, saying Mark obviously didn't know the difference among prospective, concurrent, and retrospective utilization review. Scott said, "What you need, Mark, is to review your medical staff hospitalization requests *before* the patient is admitted. Then, after admission, keep a daily record of what NHP patients are at what hospitals, for what reasons, and for how long. A nurse discharge coordinator might help."

Scott then added:

No wonder Blue Cross informed us that because NHP's hospital utilization was higher than projected, they had to pass on a 30-percent increase in the monthly hospital payment we had been making to them for inpatient care. The increase became effective with our third operational year (March 1979). I remember we discussed this in the senior management staff meeting. But Martin Carpenter reminded us about the disenrollment we had in March 1978 with our first premium increase of 11 percent, and he didn't want to implement another one.

Catherine also insisted that with another rate increase in 1979, she would be placed at an even greater competitive disadvantage in the marketplace against Blue Cross and commercial health insurance carriers. Both sell their health insurance policies with less comprehensive benefits; they also can sell at a lower price by using copayments and deductibles, even though that means subscribers pay more out of pocket as their share of total costs.

I have the minutes of that staff meeting here which show that we decided to use the OHMO loan available for underwriting our deficit, instead of passing on the increased hospital costs to our members. That's why by August of this year (1979), I had to report to the Board that NHP's deficit of about $60,000 per month remained constant. Then, the two-month lag in Blue Cross reporting caught up with us. And quite frankly, I was embarrassed to have to go back to the Board and report that at the same time revenues were down, referrals to specialists and hospitalizations had increased, so that in fact my earlier deficit figure was wrong; it was really $90,000 a month, not $60,000. The rest is history. OHMO made a site visit and told Martin that unless he got better control, they would put us in noncompliance. Bill, that's when you took over for Martin.

Indeed, Bill Wilson and the Board had been stunned when, soon after the OHMO site visit in late October 1979, Martin Carpenter had resigned abruptly. Although Bill had stepped down from Chairman to Vice-Chairman of the Board for health reasons, he agreed reluctantly to serve as the unpaid Acting Executive Director until the Board's search committee could find a new President-CEO.

At this point Bill Wilson decided he had better close the staff meeting. He certainly had more "facts" than had ever been given to him or the Board previously. But many of them simply did not make sense to him. He decided to call NHP's auditor, Tom Smith.

In response to Bill's inquiry, Tom explained that his firm had just closed NHP's books for the fiscal year ending September 1979. With some concentrated effort, his firm would need about two weeks to do a quarterly audit which would extend their report to the end of December 1979. After briefing Bill, the auditors agreed to meet with NHP's executive committee which was called into special session. Bill also suggested that NHP's attorney join them.

The auditors reported that, in fact, NHP's monthly deficit was neither $71,000 as reported by OHMO nor $90,000 as reported by Scott Stratton. Rather, they placed it at $100,000 per month, with some reservation that it might be even higher because of incurred but undocumented expenses. Their spot check of medical records and accounts payable revealed major discrepancies, especially with several hospitalizations for which there were no financial records of incurred expenses.

NHP's management practices and information system were grossly inadequate. For example, on the expense side, the Medical Director did not adequately monitor referrals to specialists. No limitation was placed on a specialist's services, so he/she often saw a patient several times, and performed expensive diagnostic studies as part of a patient's visits, without notifying the Medical Director. At times a consultant also hospitalized a patient, but NHP did not know about it until either the patient returned to the health center for follow-up care or the business office received a bill from the consultant and the hospital.

Scott Stratton, as Director of Finance, was essentially running a cash operation. No provisions were made to identify incurred but unbilled expenses for either specialists' referrals or hospitalizations. There was indeed a two-month lag time in identifying hospital inpatient costs. And when Scott was interviewed by the audit team, he reported proudly that NHP had had a good reputation for keeping current with its accounts payable to specialists and other vendors such as pharmaceutical supply houses until recently, when cash flow had become a problem. However, many vendors' bills had not been entered in accounts payable.

Finally, Tom Smith reported that NHP's *total* income was grossly inadequate for several reasons. First, members' premiums as the major source of income were much less than projected because of the negative variance between actual and projected members. Second, premium increases were either inadequate when implemented, or deferred despite escalating costs. Third, other sources of income, especially fees for physicians' services, were never achieved; NHP had apparently never overcome the local medical community's opposition. Instead of recruiting physicians from community-based practices, NHP hired salaried physicians from outside the area. And although NHP was entitled to recover income from such sources as workmen's compensation and automobile accidents, there were no provisions for such coordination of benefits.

Tom Smith noted that his firm also audited the books of the other staff model HMO in the area. Although its financial data for the quarter ending December 1979 were provisional, he thought they would be helpful when compared with NHP. He revised the September 1979 information previously reported by Scott Stratton and updated it to the end of the year. The results are displayed in Table 21.5.

Tom Smith finally concluded, "As best as we can determine from an audit which is still preliminary, NHP owes a total of $3.2 million to 150 creditors. Jointly or individually, these creditors can file a claim and/or an injunction against NHP which essentially would force it to close its doors. Except for the federal government, Blue Cross, which has been paying NHP's hospital claims, is the largest debtor with an estimated indebtedness of $350,000."

Bill Wilson and the executive committee were incredulous, but with this documentation

Table 21.5

COMPARATIVE ANALYSIS OF INCOME, EXPENSE, AND DEFICIT FOR NHP AND A LOCAL STAFF MODEL HMO
Last Two Quarters of 1979

| | PER MEMBER PER MONTH | |
Quarter Ending September 30, 1979	NHP	Staff Model HMO
Income	$27.97	$36.70
Expense	39.66	35.14
Deficit	($11.69)	$ 1.56
December 30, 1979		
Income	$26.39	$38.20
Expense	38.36	38.43
Deficit	($11.97)	($ 0.23)
Quarter Ending September 30, 1979		
Sources of income		
As a percentage of total:		
Premiums	97.0%	91.3%
Fee-for-service	1.6	2.3
All other	1.4	6.4[1]
Total	100.0%	100.0%

1. Includes income from such sources as pharmacy and office visit copayments, coordination of benefits, and interest earned.

in hand, the Board chairman called a special meeting of the full Board. NHP's attorney also attended the meeting, held in early January 1980.

On recommendation of the attorney, the Board authorized NHP's officers to meet with Blue Cross. They explained that if the Board were to declare bankruptcy with dissolution, Blue Cross and other creditors would be paid 16 cents for every dollar due them. As an alternative, NHP proposed to Blue Cross, as its largest creditor, that the plan be placed in receivership with the objective of reorganization rather than dissolution.

Further, since the state's courts had a history of demanding immediate liquidation of financially distressed for-profit firms, NHP's attorney recommended that the plan, as a non-profit agency, submit a petition for reorganization rather than dissolution under Chapter 11 of the Federal Bankruptcy Code, which had been revised only recently. Thus NHP gained the questionable distinction of becoming the first qualified HMO to be reorganized under federal legislation.

The decision to file for reorganization required approval of Blue Cross and NHP's other major creditors. A series of negotiations ensued among NHP, Blue Cross, and OHMO, which culminated in a Blue Cross takeover of NHP. The major provisions of the Blue Cross-OHMO agreement included the following:

1. Blue Cross would provide NHP with a $1 million line of credit to be used to offset further deficits until break-even occurred.

2. Blue Cross would provide the necessary working capital to pay all creditors of record

in full (except the federal government and Blue Cross) since it assumed that NHP was unable to do so.

3. Blue Cross would waive collection of its $350,000 outstanding debt and the interest on that debt until it could be repaid out of NHP's earned surplus.

4. NHP would have to seek and obtain approval for a 26-percent premium increase from the state Commissioner of Insurance.

5. As part of its reorganization, NHP would be required to give Blue Cross a "significant" but not a "majority" representation on the NHP Board.

6. NHP would be required to enter into a formal management contract with Blue Cross under which Blue Cross would recruit and appoint an Executive Director for NHP.

7. OHMO would have to agree to a three-year deferral of payment on the principal of its $2.5-million federal loan, as well as agree to waive the accrual of interest during the three-year period.

8. OHMO would also have to agree to continuation of NHP's federal qualification status.

NHP and Blue Cross signed their agreement on February 29, 1980, the last day of the month in a leap year.

ISSUES AND PROBLEMS

1. Identify the evidence presented in the case which substantiates the deficiencies cited by OHMO as reasons for NHP's noncompliance.

2. Of the several reasons for NHP's noncompliance, which would you identify as contributing most to NHP's need to reorganize under Chapter 11 of the federal bankruptcy law?

3. NHP's Director of Finance, Scott Stratton, claimed that although there is an HMO-industry rule of thumb to follow in setting break-even membership levels, the ultimate decision is a "policy" matter rather than a "technical" one.

    A. Why would break-even levels vary among HMOs?

    B. As a board member, what issues would you consider in establishing a policy about break-even membership level for your HMO?

    C. What individual staff members would you hold accountable for implementing your policy?

4. As a board member, what action would you take concerning Catherine Jackson's claims that the persistent differences between projected and actual membership:

    A. were due primarily to disenrollment over which her marketing staff has no control?

    B. would be ameliorated by her suggestion of a bonus incentive plan for her marketing representatives?

    C. were due in part to the fact that she did not have sufficient marketing staff to expect them to make follow-up calls on those employer groups from which they initially enrolled members?

5. What policies and procedures would you recommend to Scott Stratton, the Director of Finance, and Mark Long, the Medical Director, to control inpatient hospital utilization and costs?

6. For the fiscal years (ending September 30) 1980 and 1981, the Nevada Health Plan reported the following information to the state Commissioner of Insurance:

	1980	1981
Average members per year	8,635	8,316
Member months	103,620	99,792
Income		
Premiums	$3,094,087	$3,397,711
Fee-for-service	172,267	217,427
All other[1]	35,236	159,205
Total income	$3,301,590	$3,774,343
Expenses		
Medical[2]	$2,095,922	$2,297,938
Hospital	1,166,138	1,021,361
Administration/marketing	795,905	893,232
Total expenses	$4,057,965	$4,212,531

1. Includes about $129,000 interest earned by NHP on a loan from Blue Cross.
2. Includes both NHP provider salaries and all referrals.

Calculate NHP's surplus (deficit) for 1980 and 1981 by:

A. total, year-end

B. per-member-per-month, year-end

7. Assess the progress made by NHP between 1980 and 1981 in its several areas of noncompliance by recasting the above data on a per-member-per-month basis using the following format:

**Per-Member-Per-Month Income and Expenses,
by Components, and Percentage Change, between
1980 and 1981**

	1980	1981	Percent Change (1980– 1981)
Average members	8,635	8,316	
Member months	103,620	99,792	

	Per Member Per Month		Percent Change (1980– 1981)
	1980	1981	
Income			
Premiums			
Fee-for-service			
All other income			
Total income			
Expenses			
Medical			
Hospital			
Administration/ marketing			
Total expenses			

IV

Investment Decisions

Overview

Investment decisions typically involve the commitment of large sums over long periods of time. As a result, capital investments can have a major impact on the health care organization's ability to meet its financial goals. Appropriate evaluation and ranking of competing projects require application of time value of money concepts, an estimate of the cost of capital, and financial projection techniques. The cases in this section focus on several types of capital investment projects in varying health care organizations.

The first case, "Dr. Baggins and the Cardiac Cath Lab," highlights a potential investment in expensive equipment which may help to counter some competition. The role of the physician and the relationship of services in health care organizations are crucial aspects of the decision to be made. Also present are political and social factors.

The managers of the "Denver Visiting Nurse Association" face a common problem in health care delivery — how to assist clients unable to pay for needed durable medical equipment. At the same time, the agency is interested in acquiring additional revenues. Several alternatives must be evaluated in light of complex Medicare regulations.

A large teaching hospital, "Upton University Hospital," provides the political setting for analysis of facility expansion plans. Medical needs and whether a hospital master plan can be implemented in the foreseeable future are interpreted differently by the key actors in the case. Substantial quantitative analysis can be performed for each alternative investment presented.

"Inspiration Medical Center and National Hospital Corporation," the fifth case, takes a detailed, rigorous look at financial analysis techniques for evaluating competing expansion proposals. The case allows evaluation from both institutional and societal perspectives. It also involves consideration of the political ramifications surrounding consolidation of a city-owned hospital with another hospital.

Potential responses to a survival threat are the subject of the final case, "Implementing Hospital Acquisition and Diversification Strategies." Managers must decide among hospital acquisition and diversification alternatives — often-cited "cures" for financial woes. Complicating matters is the interaction between financial analysis and political and behavioral factors.

22

Dr. Baggins and the Cardiac Cath Lab

J. B. Silvers

"Dr. Baggins is at it again, and now the tab will run over half-a-million dollars," exclaimed Mr. Sam Gangee as he returned to his office from the capital equipment planning meeting of St. Ambrose Hospital. As Administrator of the 455-bed, suburban, church-owned, not-for-profit hospital (see Table 22.1 for 1976 summary statistics), Mr. Gangee had played an important role three years previously in recruiting Dr. Baggins, a 35-year-old board-certified cardiologist, after he had finished his residency at a nearby hospital.

But the price had been high. Already St. Ambrose had equipped a new cardiac care unit and facilities for ECG, treadmill testing, and echocardiogram interpretation at a considerable expense for the sole use of Dr. Baggins—the only cardiologist on the staff. However, the inconvenience of doing his cardiac catheterization tests at a better-equipped hospital four miles away had prompted Baggins to request the purchase of a full cardiac cath lab.

ANOTHER MAJOR INVESTMENT

Complying with Dr. Baggins's request would require an additional equipment investment of $475,000 plus $85,000 for renovation. The out-of-pocket costs per procedure were estimated to be $42. In addition, other direct operating costs of $46,000 per year for two technicians and a specially trained nurse and depreciation of $80,000 per year over the seven-year expected lifetime would inflate costs by at least $126,000 annually. Indirect overhead costs allocated to the project would add another 35 percent to this yearly amount. The Director of Finance thus hoped that hospital charges could be set at a level sufficient to produce revenue equal to the total per-year cost (direct plus allocated) of $170,000.

Of course, pricing would depend upon the volume and on prices at other hospitals currently accepted by Blue Cross for full payment. The volume could eventually rise to three procedures per day (260 per work year), according to Dr. Baggins. However, Mr. Gangee thought that one per day was a more realistic initial level and, depending on the response of other hospitals, might be all that could ever be achieved.

Table 22.1

1976 STATISTICS FOR ST. AMBROSE HOSPITAL

Patient Volume

Inpatient admissions	18,000
Outpatient visits	30,000
Emergency room visits	35,000
Patient days of service	143,000
Occupancy rate	86%

Ancillary and Surgical Volume

Surgical cases	12,000
Diagnostic radiology	80,000
Laboratory tests	650,000
Pharmacy orders filled	480,000
EKG exams	18,000
[1]Treadmill exams	1,100
[1]Echocardiograms	1,100
[2]Holter monitoring (24 hr. EKG)	400

1. The patient charge for each treadmill and each echocardiogram (usually conducted together) was $30, $15 of which went to the cardiologist as the professional component.
2. The portable 24-hour EKG holter monitoring equipment had recently been purchased by the hospital for $30,000. It required a technician's partial attention (following special training) and a specially equipped room. Patient charges for this were $125 each, with $50 going to the physician.

At the break-even level where cost equaled revenue, the payment from all reimbursement sources would be the same on a per-test basis. In a more normal situation, 33 percent of typical patient volume (covered by Medicare and Medicaid) was reimbursed on the basis of the lower of allowable costs or charges. Other patient services in this state (under Blue Cross and other third-party sources) were paid on the basis of charges. Charges could be revised at a negotiated rate equal to full cost plus a small additional margin. Other third-party sources were also charged the Blue Cross rate. The current average hospital charge in the area for a right or left catheterization was $330 (range $250 to $360) or for both together, $350 (range $260 to $390). New rates were less constrained by the voluntary rate review system. However, Mr. Gangee knew that, despite break-even considerations, the state rate review authorities would expect a rate near the mean of about $340. This charge would not include the physician's professional fee.

THE MEDICAL SIDE

Dr. Baggins described cardiac catheterization as a proven procedure for examining in detail many components of the circulatory system. It involved inserting a small flexible tube or catheter into a vein or artery, and observing, through fluoroscopic and radiographic imaging, various structures of the blood vessels and heart as the catheter was guided through the body. The major advantage of this over other current cardiac procedures, such as an electrocardiogram or echocardiogram, was its ability to visualize defects and to pinpoint and more accurately diagnose cardiac problems. As an added advantage, it provided measures of cardiac output and internal blood pressures. Unfortunately, it was an invasive procedure and thus carried with it some degree of risk and pain for the patient.

The current private office cardiac rehabilitation facilities maintained by Dr. Baggins took up one-half of one floor of a new five-story doctors' office building. The three-floor physicians' building plus a six-floor parking garage had been constructed three years previously for $3 million and a $1.5-million addition of two more floors was now underway. The tax-exempt subsidiary of St. Ambrose that owned this structure set rents just to break even.

Of the current 30 physicians with offices there, an overwhelming majority were new specialists like Baggins, recently attracted to St. Ambrose by the efforts of Mr. Gangee, the aggressive administrator who had come to the staff from the Stanford University Medical Center where he had been an associate administrator. He was proud of the fact that most of the attending staff physicians now called St. Ambrose their home base rather than regarding it as a secondary institution for admission of local neighborhood cases only.

Of course Dr. Baggins was not the only cardiologist in the area. However, of the 25 practicing in the general area, only 12 were board-certified. Dr. Baggins was planning to establish a cardiology group practice, starting with one associate the following year and adding another the next year. The hope was to attract these board-certified specialists directly from their residencies. St. Ambrose had its only residency program in family practice.

THE COMPETITIVE ENVIRONMENT

As the administrator of one of the seven major hospitals (including a major university medical center) in a metropolitan area with a population of approximately 1 million, Mr. Gangee was not at all sure he could justify establishing a sixth cardiac catheterization service. He also knew that, of the five other hospitals with this capability, all were equipped for open-heart surgery, although only four maintained active programs. This was important since the proposed test often led to such surgery. At the present time, cardiac patients were transferred to another hospital for testing and surgery or further treatment. With the lab, patients would be transferred only for surgery. However, Mr. Gangee knew, as these matters went, that pressure would mount for St. Ambrose to expand eventually into open-heart surgery if this first step were taken.

He also knew that while the local Health Systems Agency had turned down very few projects in its brief existence, it might reject this proposal as an unnecessary duplication. The pressure was growing for planners and regulators to hold the line, especially on "status symbol" technology. Nevertheless, on the basis of the record to date, Mr. Gangee thought that with concerted effort he could force through an approval. In fact, the hospital nearest to St. Ambrose had just received planning approval for a $300,000 modernization of its eight-year-old cath lab.

On the other hand, fiscal reality might dictate that this outlay would preclude another competing project — the most visible of which was a CAT scanner desired by the hospital's radiological and medical staff. Computerized Axial Tomography (CAT) procedures represented

Table 22.2

BALANCE SHEET FOR ST. AMBROSE HOSPITAL,
December 31, 1976
(Thousands of Dollars)

ASSETS			LIABILITIES AND FUND BALANCES		
Cash	40		Accounts payable	1,430	
Securities	120		Lease contracts payable	200	
Accounts receivable	4,100		Accrued payroll	850	
Inventory	700		Advances from		
Prepaid expenses	480		third parties	930	
Total current assets		5,440	Long-term debt due		
			within year	770	
Endowment investments		1,100	Total current liabilities		4,180
Land	900		Long-term debt		4,950
Buildings	9,500				
Equipment	14,200		General fund balances		13,610
Total (at original cost)	24,600				
Less: accumulated					
depreciation	(8,400)				
Total net fixed assets		16,200	Total liabilities and		
Total assets		22,740	fund balances		22,740

Table 22.3

INCOME STATEMENT FOR 12 MONTHS
Ending December 31, 1976
(Thousands of Dollars)

Income		
Inpatient services		
Room and board	12,097	
Other services	11,433	
		23,530
Outpatient services	4,197	
Less charity	(1,816)	
Other income	1,806	
	4,187	
Total revenue		27,717
Expenses		
Salaries	12,829	
Physicians' fees	2,192	
Drugs	538	
Food	964	
Supplies and services	6,895	
Utilities	728	
Building improvements	1,466	
Depreciation of buildings and equipment	1,134	
Interest	539	
Total expenses		27,285
Net income		432

a dramatic, but unproven, breakthrough in x-ray technology and, more importantly, would require about the same amount of dollar investment. Of course, if the need for both projects and/or other capital investments were strong enough, additional debt beyond the approximately $5 million currently outstanding (Table 22.2) could perhaps be obtained at the 8 percent interest rate paid on existing debt. However, since 40 percent of total assets were currently financed by liabilities of one sort or another, the conservative hospital board might be reluctant to make such a move.

Some evidence on the strength of feeling regarding the internal and external competitive pressures came out during the fall fund drive in September 1977. The auxiliary chose the expansion of the St. Ambrose "heart program" as the theme of its campaign and mentioned a cardiac cath lab as a basic component. The surgeons and radiologists quickly questioned this priority and other hospitals, as well as the local Health Systems Agency, inquired about this yet unannounced and unapproved program.

THE COMPETITIVE RISK

Finally, Mr. Gangee was concerned about the possibility that another hospital, most likely the already fully equipped hospital where Dr. Baggins currently did his cardiac catheterizations, might woo away St. Ambrose's only cardiologist. This would mean a loss of his 222 direct admissions and the 2,200 procedures he conducted on a consulting basis for other medical staff in a typical year. At an average revenue of $1,865 per admission for the hospital, his admissions produced $414,000 of revenue while other consulting procedures brought the total revenue for St. Ambrose to about $550,000. The only supporting staff *directly* tied to Dr. Baggins were technicians who were each paid about $10,000 per year. Table 22.3 presents St. Ambrose's income statement for 1976.

THE DECISION

With the assurance of a break-even operation, Mr. Gangee felt that the board would support the proposed cardiac cath lab. They might even go further into debt to support it if they understood the importance of Dr. Baggins's patient volume for the hospital. On the other hand, although other medical staff members supported this project in addition to other capital investments proposed, he doubted whether the project was really needed or was even financially justified. Opposing it, however, would be politically difficult.

With this in mind, he started to work on an analysis and report for the planning committee which was to reconvene in two weeks at Dr. Baggins's insistence.

23

Denver Visiting Nurse Association

Bettina D. Kurowski
Bruce R. Neumann

INTRODUCTION

Ginny Tulga is Director of the Denver Visiting Nurse Association (VNA), a private, nonprofit (government-affiliated), Medicare-certified home health care agency with a staff of more than 100 health care professionals. (In 1981 the agency provided 130,000 multidisciplinary home health care visits including general nursing, speech therapy, occupational therapy, physical therapy, social work, and home health aide services.) Ginny recently received a call from Tica Bowman, the nursing supervisor of one of the several VNA branch offices situated in the four-county Denver metropolitan area which the VNA serves. Tica was concerned with the growing problem for Medicare patients in obtaining necessary medical equipment, such as walkers or wheelchairs, because of worsening general economic conditions.

In discussing the problems of the elderly with her staff, Tica had found that Medicare patients were often unable to pay the out-of-pocket expenses associated with needed durable medical equipment (DME) purchased or rental through an outside agency. She wondered whether anything could be done to help the patients more easily obtain needed DME, while at the same time supporting the agency's financial objective of establishing new and reliable revenue sources.

Tica had checked into a few of the relevant issues with some of her contacts at other agencies that had DME programs of their own. She suggested that the VNA could choose to offer DME to its patients as a direct supplier (maintaining its own inventory) or as an intermediary (contracting with suppliers in the area). Such arrangements would qualify DME as a home health benefit under Medicare, offering significant financial advantages to VNA Medicare patients.

The authors would like to acknowledge the assistance and advice of the following former students who helped in collecting data and in preparing and reviewing preliminary drafts of the case: Robert Asinof, Betsy Graef, and Michael Hoffman.

Tica explained that primary among these advantages is reimbursement for home health services, since DME received under the auspices of a home health agency is paid for under Medicare Part A. Since Part A pays 100 percent of reasonable charges for home health benefits, the patient incurs no out-of-pocket expenses. In contrast, DME received directly from a supplier is paid for under Medicare Part B. Part B pays only 80 percent of reasonable charges less any unmet deductible. (In not receiving DME as a Part A benefit, the patient is responsible for 20 percent of the charges under the coinsurance provisions of the policy and for any portion of the annual deductible ($75) which has not yet been applied to his medical expenses.) Tica stressed that the copayment obligations under Part B impose financial hardships on many of the VNA's Medicare patients who require DME.

Tica also argued that Part A coverage of DME as a home health benefit could prevent inappropriate equipment rental. While the beneficiary may choose to purchase or rent, existing payment plans may discourage his selection of the most advantageous option. Suppliers rarely offer lease-purchase arrangements; thus, if the patient's share of the total expense is high under his Part B policy, he may choose to rent when purchase would otherwise have been less costly. In renting, patients would also lose Medicare coverage for separately itemized repairs and replacement as well as for certain essential accessories, since this coverage applies only to purchased equipment.

She went on to say that patients requiring DME also benefit from the more flexible definition of equipment which is under the aegis of a home health agency. DME is generally defined as equipment which is "primarily and customarily used to serve a medical purpose . . . and which generally is not useful to a person in the absence of illness or injury." However, the inclusion of medical appliances as covered items under home health benefits may meet additional equipment needs of patients. Medical appliances are items that customarily serve a medical purpose, but they may also include items which, although customarily serving a nonmedical purpose, may serve a medical purpose in a specific case. These types of equipment may be covered under home health benefits if they are noted specifically in a physician's care plan.

Tica added that issues of quality and convenience were factors to consider in judging the merits of VNA participation in the provision of DME. For example, the active involvement of the VNA in the provision of durable medical equipment would give the agency a role in informing its patients of the options available to them in arranging for DME. As a concerned supplier or intermediary to suppliers, the VNA could ensure that its patients were aware of their options and the advantages of each. The VNA would also provide its patients with a personal and immediate avenue for redress should problems with their equipment arise. (Such problems often stem from the client's receipt of equipment that, for some reason, does not meet the client's medical needs.)

Finally, Tica suggested that should the VNA decide to establish contracts with suppliers, patients would benefit by being served by suppliers who are guaranteed payment. Such contracts could better ensure supplier reliability. Contract provisions for delivery guarantees and for equipment repair might also improve the quality and convenience of supplier service to VNA patients.

VNA'S DURABLE MEDICAL EQUIPMENT OPTIONS

Ginny thanked Tica for her concern and for taking the time to investigate the issues. She assured her that she would give serious consideration to the options. When she hung up the telephone, she knew that Tica had raised a potentially advantageous patient care option. However, she wasn't entirely convinced of the financial soundness of the ideas from the agency's perspective, although she did reflect that the added DME services would provide an opportunity to improve the visibility of the agency among potential clients for whom competitors were bidding.

Ginny then called her Chief Financial Officer, Dick Anderton, to ask him to follow up on the ideas and report back to her within the next three months. Dick turned the project over to one of his new staff assistants, Betsy Graef, a recent graduate of the University of Colorado Graduate Program in Health Administration. Dick asked Betsy to prepare an analysis of each of the following options with a recommendation for a VNA decision on the matter.

1. Continue the status quo, with all VNA patients obtaining needed DME from commercial vendors.

2. The VNA would purchase sufficient DME for use by its patients.

3. The VNA would subcontract with selected commercial vendors to serve as an intermediate source of DME for its patients. For example, the VNA could purchase its annual DME requirements and dropship them to commercial vendors who would repair, deliver, and bill (collect) the equipment to patients for 25 percent of the monthly rental fee. In this case, the DME costs would be reimbursed under Medicare Part A.

When Dick gave Betsy the assignment, he reminded her of the financial and utilization data that was already available, encouraging her not "to reinvent the wheel."

FINANCIAL OFFICER'S REPORT

Synopsis of Medicare Regulations Covering DME

The Health Care Financing Administration (HCFA) of the Department of Health and Human Services reimburses the purchase or rental of durable medical equipment (DME) under both Medicare Part A and Part B. Acquisition of DME directly from a supplier is reimbursed through the patient's Part B coverage. It is therefore subject to the standard $75 annual deductible, less any portion of the deductible which has already been paid, and the 20 percent coinsurance provision of the Part B policy. Medicare pays for 80 percent of the supplier's reasonable charges. The coinsurance provision is waived with respect to the purchase of used equipment whenever the purchase price is at least 25 percent less than the reasonable charge for comparable new equipment. Acquisition of DME through a home health agency is paid under the patient's Part A coverage. Part A pays 100 percent of reasonable charges for home health benefits, and therefore the patient incurs no out-of-pocket expenses.

Reimbursement is allowed only if the following three requirements are met:

1. The equipment meets the definition of durable medical equipment. For purposes of Medicare coverage, durable medical equipment is equipment which (a) can withstand repeated use, (b) is primarily and customarily used to serve a medical purpose, (c) is generally not useful to a person in the absence of illness or injury, and (d) is appropriate for use in the home.

    Equipment which primarily and customarily serves a medical purpose: Items such as hospital beds, wheelchairs, hemodialysis equipment, iron lungs, respirators, intermittent positive-pressure breathing machines, medical regulators, oxygen tents, crutches, canes, trapeze bars, walkers, inhalators, nebulizers, commodes, suction machines, and traction equipment primarily constitute medical equipment. (Although hemodialysis equipment is a prosthetic device, it also meets the definition of durable medical equipment, and reimbursement for the rental or purchase of such equipment for use in the beneficiary's home will be made only under the provisions for payment applicable to durable medical equipment.)

Equipment which primarily and customarily serves a nonmedical purpose: Equipment which is primarily and customarily used for a nonmedical purpose is not considered "medical" equipment for which payment can be made under the Medicare program. This is true even though the item may be medically useful. For example, in the case of a cardiac patient, an air conditioner might possibly be used to lower room temperature to reduce fluid loss in the patient and to create an environment conducive to maintenance of proper fluid balance. Nevertheless, because the primary and customary purpose of an air conditioner is a nonmedical one, the air conditioner cannot be classified as medical equipment reimbursable under Medicare.

Other devices and equipment used for environmental control or to enhance the environmental setting in which the beneficiary resides are not considered durable medical equipment. These include such items as room heaters, humidifiers, dehumidifiers, and electric air cleaners. Equipment which basically serves comfort or convenience functions or is primarily for the convenience of a person caring for the patient, such as elevators, stairway elevators, posture chairs, and cushion lift chairs, do not constitute medical equipment. Similarly, physical fitness equipment (e.g., an exercycle), first-aid or precautionary-type equipment (e.g., portable oxygen units), self-help devices (e.g., safety grab bars), and training equipment (e.g., speech teaching machines and braille training texts) are considered nonmedical in nature.

2. The equipment is necessary and reasonable for the treatment of the patient's illness or injury or to improve the functioning of a malformed body member. These requirements will bar payment for equipment which cannot reasonably be expected to perform a therapeutic function and will permit only partial payment when the type of equipment substantially exceeds that required for the treatment of the illness or injury involved. In most cases, the physician's prescription for the equipment is sufficient to establish its medical necessity.

   In determining the reasonableness of the equipment in question, the intermediary considers whether (a) the expense of the item is disproportionate to the therapeutic benefits to be derived, (b) the item is substantially more costly than a medically appropriate and feasible alternative method of care, and (c) the item serves essentially the same purpose as equipment already available to the beneficiary. If these conditions exist, Medicare will reimburse an amount based on the reasonable costs for the equipment or alternative treatment which meets the patient's medical needs.

3. The equipment is used in the patient's home. For purposes of rental or purchase of DME, a beneficiary's home may be his own residence, an apartment, a relative's home, a home for the aged, or some other similar type of institution. However, an institution is not considered a beneficiary's home if it is either a hospital or a skilled nursing facility.

Repairs, Maintenance, Replacement, and Delivery

Repairs to equipment purchased by the beneficiary are covered when necessary to make the equipment serviceable and when the repair expense does not exceed the estimated expense of purchasing or renting another item of equipment for the remaining period of medical need. Routine maintenance is not covered; however, extensive maintenance based on manufacturers' recommendations and requiring authorized technicians is covered.

Replacement of equipment purchased by the beneficiary is covered in cases of loss or irreparable damage or wear and when required because of a change in the patient's condition. Reasonable delivery costs are covered if the supplier customarily makes separate charges for delivery and this is a common practice among other local suppliers.

Suppliers and Accessories

Reimbursement may be made for supplies only when they are essential to the effective use of DME. Essential accessories are reimbursed only if the beneficiary purchased the equipment.

Payment for Durable Medical Equipment

The intermediary decides whether an item of equipment will be rented or purchased on the basis of medical necessity forms prepared by the beneficiary's physician. Items with a purchase allowance of $120 or less are always purchased. For items costing more than $120, HCFA determines on the basis of medical information whether the expected duration of need warrants a presumption that purchase would be less costly and more practical than rental and, if so, reimburses on the basis of a lump-sum or lease-purchase arrangement. Nevertheless, rental of the equipment may be authorized if the required purchase would impose an undue financial hardship on the beneficiary. A lease-purchase arrangement is applicable to high-cost items where the risk to the Medicare program of outright purchase is not justified but rental of the equipment may possibly extend for a long period of time. The intermediary cannot require lease-purchase arrangements but is directed to process claims involving lease-purchase arrangements offered by suppliers that are equitable and meet the above conditions.

Expenses for DME are incurred as of the date of delivery with expenses for subsequent months incurred as of the same day of the month as the date of delivery. In determining whether an item is covered, the entire expense of the item is considered to have been incurred on the date of delivery.

When the beneficiary is at home part of a month and is in an institution for part of the same month, payment will be made for the entire month. Where a supplier charges for only part of a month in such a case, payment will be made on a prorated basis. No payment will be made for any month in which a patient with purchased equipment is in an institution. Upon return to the home, payments resume without loss of monthly installments because of the institutionalization.

Demand Estimates for DME at Denver VNA

The DME expected to be required by VNA patients during a one-year period was developed by assigning probable equipment needs to the primary diagnostic categories of a sample of VNA patients discharged between July 1, 1981, and June 30, 1982. The DME requirements for a one-year period were extrapolated from the number of patients within each of these diagnostic categories and were based on the average length of stay experienced within each of these diagnostic categories.

There were approximately 11,445 cases discharged by the VNA during this time period. Of these cases, 1,426 (12 percent) were not assigned to a diagnostic category and could not be used to establish expected equipment needs. They were eliminated from the sample. Twenty-five percent of the remaining cases were reviewed.

A number of diagnostic categories in which DME might be expected to be found were not included in the base for the equipment extrapolation. These included certain diagnostic categories in which the likelihood of DME need is difficult to establish because of the probable variation in case intensity associated with such categories. Those diagnostic categories for which DME need was not routinely expected were also excluded from the sample. In addition, the analysis of DME options was limited to VNA patients insured by Medicare, which represented 48.9 percent of VNA patients for the year. The final sample consisted of 932 cases.

Establishing an average length of stay within the selected diagnostic categories posed a difficulty because of the substantial variation in length of stay among patients within certain diagnostic categories. In addition, some categories featured only one case during the year, making the reliability of the length of stay associated with each category suspect. Therefore, the merit of the extrapolations which were derived from the average length of stay must be viewed with caution. However, two procedures were used to modify these potential problems:

1. In those categories which could be grouped together on the basis of having the same DME requirements, average length of stay was computed on the basis of diagnostic clusters.

2. In the remaining categories which exhibited high variation in average length of stay, professional clinical judgment was used to determine the most likely average length of stay.

The patient discharge sample resulted in detailed monthly worksheets which were aggregated as shown in Table 23.1. These worksheet summaries were prepared for ambulatory equipment (chairs, walkers, canes, and crutches) and for nonambulatory equipment (beds and lifts). The total demand, extrapolated for all DME needs for a one-year time period, is summarized in Table 23.2.

Rental and purchase prices for six types of DME were obtained from three Denver-area commercial vendors. The averages of these prices are shown in Table 23.3. The cost to the agency for purchasing this equipment, including delivery, was also obtained, in the event that the Denver VNA should decide to purchase these items in quantities of ten or more. Selected data for determining the VNA's potential DME cost follows:

1. Assume a useful economic life and reimbursement life for all DME of three years.

2. The Denver VNA's current cost of capital is 12 percent and it is expected to increase to 14 to 15 percent in the next several years.

3. The Denver VNA has storage space in the basement of its main building and in two clinics which cannot be used for patient care or offices. This space is currently unoccupied, has no commercial value, and is not included in the Medicare cost allocation statistics. Similar commercial warehouse space would rent for $4 a square

foot per month. About 10,000 square feet would be required for the storage and rental of sufficient DME to satisfy the agency's annual needs.

4. The U.S. General Accounting Office has estimated that DME acquisition decisions are made primarily by the following parties:

Patient	25%
Family and others	15%
Physician	32%
Hospital	18%
Supplier	10%
	100%

5. A summary of Part B DME utilization by all Medicare intermediaries is shown in Table 23.4. This data illustrates the duration of DME rental periods for all Medicare beneficiaries in the 1976 fiscal year.

6. Estimates of why patients do not obtain "prescribed" DME are as follows:

Too costly	35%
No access to supplier	30%
Unfamiliar reimbursement rules	25%
Other	10%
	100%

These estimates are based on an estimated 20 to 25 percent of all patients who fail to obtain recommended DME, of the six types discussed above, and who just "make do" without the specialized equipment.

7. Delivery charges from commercial vendors vary from 0 to $10 per item. Delivery charges are usually built into the rates for any items whose rental fee exceeds $20.00 per month. Flat rates are usually charged for delivery on all other items. No fees are charged for pickups at the end of the rental period.

8. Maintenance and repairs would cost the agency approximately $40,000 per year ($20,000 staff, $20,000 parts and equipment).

9. Billing and collection activities are expected to cost $10 per episode.

VNA's Financial Statements

The financial statements of the Denver VNA are summarized in Tables 23.5 through 23.11. Table 23.5 is the audit report of the combined statement of revenues and expenses for 1981 with summary comparisons to 1980. Table 23.6 is a supplementary schedule showing details of the operating fund. Table 23.7 indicates the annual functional expenses for 1980 and 1981. Table 23.8 contains comparative balance sheets. A summary of functional expenses, classified by HCFA cost categories (Worksheet B), from the 1981 Medicare Cost Report is shown in Table 23.9. Table 23.10 is a reproduction of Worksheet C from the 1981 Medicare Cost Report. Table 23.11 is from the agency's monthly and year-to-date financial statement for December 1981. This statement indicates the full scope of line-item data available to agency managers.

Table 23.1

SUMMARY OF VNA MEDICARE PATIENT CATEGORIES BY DIAGNOSIS
1981–1982 Discharge Survey

Discharge Diagnosis	# Thirty-Day FTE Patients*	Approximate Length of Stay (Days)	AMBULATORY DME EQUIPMENT Wheelchair Estimate* %	#	Walker Estimate* %	#	Cane Estimate* %	#	Crutch Estimate* %	#
Multiple sclerosis	40	50	15	6						
CVA	196	52	70	137			55	108		
Osteoarthrosis	8	27					10	1		
All femur reductions	248	77			60	149	40	99		
All tibia reductions	247	59			85	210				
All ankle/foot diagnoses	28	46			25	7			30	8
Patellectomy, knee replacements	45	58			58	26	42	19		
Hip repair/replacements	85	47			40	34				
Amputations, lower limb	35	44							25	9
Total	932			143		426		227		17

*Calculated on the basis of 30-day full-time-equivalent (FTE) patient encounters.

Table 23.2

ESTIMATE OF DME NEEDS FOR DENVER VNA

	DME 25% Sample Estimates	Projected Needs	10% Safety Stock	Total Annual DME Needs
Chairs	143	572	56	628
Walkers	426	1,704	171	1,875
Canes	227	908	91	999
Crutches	17	68	7	75
Beds	103	412	42	454
Lifts	33	132	14	146
				4,177

Table 23.3

SUMMARY OF 1982 DME PRICES
(Average of 3 Commercial Vendors in Denver)

Equipment Type	Client Rental Per Month	Client Purchase Price	Home Health Agency Purchase Price
Canes, J type, rubber tip	N.A.	$ 7.00	$ 5.00
Crutches, aluminum, adjustable	$ 10.00	32.00	22.40
Walkers, non-folding	15.00	53.00	38.20
folding	16.00	62.00	42.00
Wheelchair, fixed arms, detachable footrest	30.00	400.00	276.00
Beds, standard, full, electric	105.00	1,250.00 plus freight	875.00
Lifts	50.00	800.00	600.00

Table 23.4

RENTAL DURATION OF PART B DME EPISODES FOR U.S.
(Fiscal 1976)

Length of Episode (Months)	Number of Episodes	Percent	Number of Cumulative Percent	Number of Rental Months
1	75,086	43.37	43.37	75,086
2	26,520	15.31	58.68	53,020
3	15,506	8.96	67.64	46,518
4	10,538	6.06	73.73	42,152
5	7,885	4.55	78.28	39,425
6	6,393	3.69	81.97	38,358
7	4,817	2.78	84.75	33,719
8	3,995	2.28	87.03	31,640
9	3,279	1.89	88.92	29,511
10	2,993	1.73	90.65	29,930
11	2,375	1.37	92.02	26,125
12	2,557	1.48	93.50	30,684
13	1,573	.91	94.41	20,449
14	1,328	.77	95.18	18,592
15	1,344	.78	95.96	20,160
16	1,161	.67	96.63	18,576
17	890	.51	97.14	15,130
18	881	.51	97.65	15,858
19	757	.44	98.09	14,383
20	765	.44	98.53	15,300
21	784	.45	98.98	16,464
22	561	.32	99.30	12,342
23	566	.33	99.63	13,018
24	624	.36	99.99	14,976
	173,178			671,416

Table 23.5

COMBINED SUPPORT AND REVISED EXPENSES FOR OPERATING FUND
FOR THE YEAR ENDED DECEMBER 31, 1981
(WITH COMBINED 1980 TOTALS FOR COMPARISON)
AND BUDGET FOR THE YEAR ENDED DECEMBER 31, 1981

	Budget 1981	Visiting Nurse Association General Operating Fund	CITY AND COUNTY OF DENVER Public Health Nursing Fund	Other Allocated Costs[1]	Elimi-nations	Combined 1981	Combined 1980
Public Support and Revenue:							
Patient service revenue— net	$4,076,928	$4,026,650				$4,026,650	$2,099,934
Visiting Nurse Association— contractual commitment			$4,002,409		$(4,002,409)		
City and County of Denver	1,626,504	1,042,755	1,626,500	$773,739	(1,042,755)	2,400,239	2,314,878
Mile High United Way	135,816	122,024				122,024	95,075
Special grants, agency reimbursements, and other	57,060	77,519				77,519	62,398
Total	5,893,308	5,268,948	5,628,909	773,739	(5,045,164)	6,626,432	4,572,285
Expenses:							
Salaries	3,943,907		3,610,045			3,610,045	2,996,720
Payroll taxes and employee benefits	897,025		800,645			800,645	631,175
City and County of Denver Public Health Nursing Fund— contractual commitment		4,002,409			(4,002,409)		
Administrative, general, and other	1,545,180	593,469	738,187	773,739	(543,549)	1,561,846	1,323,049
Total	6,386,112	4,595,878	5,148,877	773,739	(4,545,958)	5,972,536	4,950,944
Public Support and Revenue over (under) Expenses	$ (492,804)	$ 673,070	$ 480,032	$ -0-	$ (499,207)	$ 653,896	$ (378,659)

1. Allocated costs are estimated by the Visiting Nurse Association.
   Final 1981 allocated costs will not be determined by the City and County of Denver until approximately September 1982.

Table 23.6

STATEMENT OF INCOME AND EXPENSES AND CHANGES
IN OPERATING FUND BALANCES

For Years Ended December 31, 1981 and 1980

	General Operating Fund 1981	General Operating Fund 1980
Public Support and Revenue:		
Contributions	$ 22,470	$ 13,952
Grant — Mile High United Way	122,024	95,075
Special grants and agency reimbursements	23,020	33,130
Contractual reimbursement from City and County of Denver Public Health Nursing Fund	1,042,755	260,825
Total public support	1,210,269	402,982
Patient service revenue	4,599,267	3,088,603
Less: Unreimbursed services	(471,657)	(509,985)
Contractual adjustments	(21,929)	(314,671)
Bad debts	(79,031)	(53,013)
Net patient service revenue	4,026,650	2,099,934
Investment income	22,551	13,085
Miscellaneous	9,478	2,231
Total revenue	4,058,679	2,115,250
Total public support and revenue	5,268,948	2,518,232
Expenses:		
Program expenses — contractual commitment to City and County of Denver Public Health Nursing Fund	4,002,409	2,639,611
Supporting services — administrative, general, and other	593,469	260,825
Total	4,595,878	2,900,436
Public Support and Revenue over (under) Expenses	673,070	(382,204)
Fund Balances, Beginning of Year	654,841	1,037,045
Fund Balances, End of Year	$1,327,911	$ 654,841

Table 23.7

STATEMENT OF FUNCTIONAL EXPENSES FOR OPERATING FUND
for the Years Ended December 31, 1981 and 1980

	1981 General Operating Fund	1980 General Operating Fund
Program Expenses—		
Contractual commitment to City and County of Denver Public Health Nursing Fund	$4,002,409	$2,639,611
Supporting Services—		
Salaries and benefits	96,972	39,272
Payroll taxes	7,761	2,569
Total	104,733	41,841
Contractual services:		
Temporary help	86,604	64,335
Security escort	41,975	25,065
Medical personnel	56,755	
Printing and stationery	56,323	19,608
Depreciation	49,920	
Professional services	44,570	15,750
Medical supplies	34,929	15,761
Rental of equipment	27,894	4,627
Committee expense		
Meetings and travel	17,141	15,018
Telephone and utilities	11,976	6,520
Building maintenance	11,685	8,955
Publications and education	11,182	10,562
Postage	9,350	6,427
Advertising	9,079	16,852
Equipment repair and maintenance	8,171	3,486
Office supplies	5,529	1,106
Insurance	4,148	4,912
Miscellaneous	1,505	
Total supporting services	593,469	260,825
Total Expenses	$4,595,878	$2,900,436

Table 23.8

THE DENVER VISITING NURSE ASSOCIATION BALANCE SHEETS
December 31, 1981 and 1980

ASSETS	1981	1980
General Operating Fund:		
Cash	$ 1,415	$ 92,296
Commercial paper	49,000	60,000
Patient receivables (less allowance for uncollectible accounts: 1981, $123,927; 1980, $59,132; less allowance for contractual adjustments: 1981, $25,929; 1980, $50,969)	1,758,386	867,394
Property and equipment (net of accumulated depreciation of $49,920)	449,286	
Other assets	14,791	10,760
Total General Operating Fund	$2,272,878	$1,030,450
Investment Fund:		
Cash	$ 9,695	$ 3,321
Investments	486,152	460,980
Miscellaneous receivables	1,030	5,983
Total Investment Fund	$ 496,877	$ 470,284

LIABILITIES AND FUND BALANCES	1981	1980
General Operating Fund:		
Accounts payable and accrued liabilities	$ 46,123	$ 34,118
Contractual commitment to City and County of Denver Public Health Nursing Fund	713,890	288,510
Estimated payable — contractual agency	184,954	52,981
Total liabilities	944,967	375,609
Fund balance	1,327,911	654,841
Total General Operating Fund	$2,272,878	$1,030,450
Investment Fund:		
Fund balance	$ 496,877	$ 470,284
Total Investment Fund	$ 496,877	$ 470,284

Table 23.9

GENERAL SERVICE COSTS, WORKSHEET B
1981 Medicare Cost Report

1.	General service cost centers	
2.	Depreciation — building and equipment	$ 66,000
3.	Depreciation — movable equipment	109,000
4.	Plant operation and maintenance	343,000
5.	Transportation	-0-
6.	Administrative — general	1,133,700
		$1,651,700
7.	Reimbursable services	
8.	Skilled nursing care	$2,763,000
9.	Physical therapy	554,700
10.	Speech pathology	48,000
11.	Occupational therapy	160,600
12.	Medical social services	19,000
13.	Home health aide	624,100
14.	Medical appliances	-0-
15.	Durable medical equipment	-0-
16.	Supplies	-0-
		$4,169,400
17-25.	Title XVIII nonreimbursable services	-0-
26.	Other nonreimbursable costs	
	Public health	484,600
	Nonvisit	439,100
	Seniors program	121,000
	Subtotal	$1,044,700
	Total	$6,865,800

Table 23.10

APPORTIONMENT OF PATIENT SERVICE COSTS, TITLE XVIII ONLY
January 1– December 31, 1981

Patient Service	Total Visits	Average Cost Per Visit	MEDICARE VISITS		COST OF SERVICES		
			Post Hosp. Plan-Part A	Medical Plan-Part B	Post Hosp. Plan-Part A	Medical Plan-Part B	Total Medicare Cost
1. Skilled nursing	81,680	45.18	43,276	6,418	$1,955,210	$289,965	$2,245,175
2. Physical therapy	17,572	41.13	11,644	1,935	478,918	79,587	558,505
3. Speech pathology	1,169	53.67	705	113	37,837	6,065	43,902
4. Occupational therapy	4,074	51.61	2,654	328	136,973	16,928	153,901
5. Medical social services	227	109.48	226	37	24,742	4,051	28,793
6. Home health aide services	27,501	28.81	19,753	2,874	569,084	82,800	651,884
7. Total (lines 1-6)	132,223		78,258	11,705	$3,202,764	$479,396	$3,682,160

Table 23.11

GENERAL OPERATING FUND—STATEMENT OF NET REVENUE (LOSS)
December 1981

Expenses	CURRENT MONTH Actual	Budget	Variance	1981 YEAR-TO-DATE Actual	Budget	Variance	1980 YEAR-TO-DATE Actual	Budget	Variance
Salaries:									
Director and Adm. Assts.	$ 13,491			$ 193,188			$ 212,162		
Clinical Specialists	4,634			87,773			125,141		
Supervisors	16,463			254,497			269,949		
Prof. Services	198,001			2,249,893			2,146,044		
PT, OT, ST	48,355			506,788			107,887		
LPNs	11,567			138,496			129,614		
Clerical Staff	72,841			872,434			841,430		
Serving Seniors	7,653			107,621			102,479		
Total Salaries	$373,005	$403,411	$ (30,406)	$4,410,690	$4,840,932	$(430,242)	$3,934,706	$4,145,916	$(211,210)
Other Expenses									
Audit, Legal, and Mgmt. Fees	17,225	41,291	(24,066)	430,655	495,492	(64,837)	116,286	25,716	90,570
Data Processing	1,476	458	1,018	5,591	5,496	95	8,001	36,612	(28,611)
Postage and Mailing	723	980	(257)	9,130	11,760	(2,630)	7,039	7,656	(617)
Auto Mileage	10,794	20,092	(9,298)	132,225	241,104	(108,879)	98,457	103,200	(4,743)
Travel		823	(823)	8,171	9,876	(1,705)	11,742	6,456	5,286
Conferences and Meetings	380	786	(406)	5,595	9,432	(3,837)	6,119	4,596	1,523
Printing and Duplication	277	968	(691)	7,522	11,616	(4,094)	5,879	8,700	(2,821)
Microfilm	157	667	(510)	4,071	8,004	(3,933)	51	9,996	(9,945)
Insurance		882	(882)	5,597	10,584	(4,987)	3,901	10,584	(6,683)
Repair and Maintenance	1,960	75	1,885	8,827	900	7,927	3,031	996	2,035
Stationery Supplies	6,714	9,466	(2,752)	77,807	113,592	(35,785)	28,740	11,184	17,556
Inservice and Workshops	1,332	158	1,174	1,062	1,896	(834)	1,987	2,100	(113)
Advertising	351	250	101	10,015	3,000	7,015	10,917	9,900	1,017
Dues and Subscriptions	350	457	(107)	10,113	5,484	4,629	5,893	1,452	4,441
Janitorial Services	1,055	833	222	12,002	9,996	2,006	10,188		10,188
Publications	1,111	600	511	208	7,200	(6,992)	1,543	5,796	(4,253)
Surgical & Clinical Supp.	2,361	8,858	(6,497)	90,669	106,296	(15,627)	42,861	12,636	30,225
Off-Street Parking	469	292	177	3,897	3,504	393			
Temp. Office Personnel	4,815	9,750	(4,935)	86,680	117,000	(30,320)	71,341		71,341
Guard and Courier	6,933	3,454	3,479	38,995	41,448	(2,453)	22,518	24,996	(2,478)
Office Furniture and Equip.	373	4,017	(3,644)	28,896	48,204	(19,308)	53,641	32,904	20,737
Telephone	1,561	939	622	12,136	11,268	868	6,991	3,612	3,379
Rental — Lease Land and Bldg.	3,494	3,750	(256)	31,491	45,000	(13,509)	20,409	54,996	(34,587)
Rental Equipment	5,318	3,542	1,776	33,237	42,504	(9,267)	25,158	24,996	162
Equipment Charges/Services	705	5,137	(4,432)	2,790	61,644	(58,854)	7,897	17,004	(9,107)
Other Interfund Transfers	35	500	(465)	2,221	6,000	(3,779)	31,540	29,496	2,044
Program Operation Svs.	28,091	9,740	18,351	168,805	116,880	51,925	42,176	14,004	28,172
Total Other Expenses	98,060	128,765	(30,705)	1,228,408	1,545,180	(316,772)	644,306	459,588	184,718
Total Expense	471,065	532,176	(61,111)	5,639,098	6,386,112	(747,014)	4,579,012	4,605,504	(26,492)
Net Revenue (Loss)	$129,357	$(41,067)	$170,424	$ 216,084	$ (492,804)	$ 708,888	$ (513,338)	$ (916,440)	$ 403,102

24

Upton University Hospital

Hugh W. Long

INTRODUCTION

The telephone was ringing as Joseph L. Kent, M.D., Director of the Upton University Hospital, came into his office. He answered it and heard a familiar voice.

"Good morning, Joe. This is Courtney. I just got the proposal your staff worked up for a freestanding clinical lab. It seems a bit premature to me."

"Courtney" was R. Courtney Hill, M.D., the Dean of the College of Medicine at Upton University. He was widely respected for his many accomplishments during the 20 years he had been dean.

Joe Kent realized the importance of the dean's support if the proposal for the new laboratory (Appendix 24.1) was to be accepted. He weighed his response carefully.

"Yes, Courtney, I've been wanting to sit down with you and talk about the lab proposal. I think my people have done a pretty good job of putting it together. And I'm not quite sure I understand what you mean when you say it's 'premature.' "

"Well, you know, Joe, we've really put in a lot of effort on Roy Webb's master plan, and I think he is a damned fine architect," the dean began. "Webb has guaranteed that we can phase the master plan, so that we can begin by producing a permanent lab facility right next to the present hospital building, and have it on line by mid-1985."

"Courtney, I appreciate your confidence in Webb, and you know I want to see this hospital right at the forefront of medical care. We can do that with the proper design for the new building; but I still believe that the way to plan a hospital is from the top down," the hospital director said.

This case was originally commissioned by the Hospital Administrative Services Program of the American Hospital Association supported by a grant from the W. K. Kellogg Foundation through the Hospital Research and Educational Trust, which published the case in 1973. The current 1983 version was supported in part by the W. K. Kellogg Foundation and the Association of University Programs in Health Administration. The case is intended for classroom use only, and is not intended to illustrate either effective or ineffective handling of a management situation. Copyright 1983. All rights reserved.

"That's a nice theory, Joe, but Webb assures me that starting the lab right away won't affect any other aspects of the plan. He also tells me that we could have the new ICU facility by early 1986, as a trailer to the first phase of the plan."

"But, Courtney, that's all at least three years away, even if we broke ground for the first phase tomorrow," Joe Kent replied. "We can have a freestanding lab operational by the end of this year. This could free up the ICU space right away, and could generate some really good cash flow. Then, when the permanent facility is ready, we could move into it and lease out the freestanding building, which we probably would own free and clear by then. Besides, Courtney, to be quite frank, I think you and Webb are overly optimistic about getting the master plan off the ground so soon. The fellow who analyzes our property projects, Henry Groton, thinks there will be some serious difficulties in getting Webb's preliminary drawings into compliance with the codes."

"Look, Joe, those aren't serious problems," the dean answered. "Webb can work them out in no time at all. You can rest assured that the master plan is on the way. By the time you arrange for the necessary financing, it will all be ready to go."

"Well, Courtney, let's look at the financing aspect, too. Money's awfully tight right now. We can swing the freestanding lab, and we even have a reasonable prospect in the offing for an interest-free loan. But the master plan is going to call for a lot more money; it's hard to tell just how much, with construction costs escalating 10 to 15 percent every year. We can have the freestanding lab in gear in two weeks, but it seems to me that it's going to be hard to have the master plan ready for the final financial planning within even six months."

"But, Joe, that's really why your proposal seems out of place. Don't you see that the freestanding lab is going to hurt the chances of the master plan all the way down the line? It's not only going to absorb loans and donations that would otherwise go into permanent facilities, but it's a release valve as well. When you take off some of the pressure for new facilities with a stopgap like this, you automatically prejudice an early starting date for the master plan. Besides, many of the faculty members have very strong feelings about this separation of the lab from the mainstream. They think this would make it much more difficult to attract the best people to come here for research, and I tend to agree. I've sent you a memo from Dr. Shattuck [Appendix 24.2] that spells out the faculty position pretty well. Remember, it's their laboratory, after all."

"I'm glad you're sending me a copy of that memo, Courtney. I need to know how the faculty is thinking. Look, why don't we get the key people together—you get Webb, Shattuck from the labs, and Dr. Loomis from pathology, and I'll bring along Groton, Buckley, and Cranbrook. Let's meet in the board room—say, tomorrow afternoon—and let's have a go at this whole thing."

"Joe, I really don't know what we can accomplish. I myself certainly want the first priority, in planning and finances, to go to the master plan; and the faculty really doesn't want the lab moved until it's moved to the new permanent building. But perhaps Webb can convince you that he can do what he says, so let's get together."

"Thanks, Courtney. I'll have my secretary work with your secretary to set it up."

Joe Kent hung up the telephone, leaned back, and gazed at the calendar on his desk. "January 20, 1983," he said to himself. "We've been talking about the master plan for four years now, and we're still at least a year away from turning the first shovelful of dirt."

BACKGROUND

Upton University Hospital had been constructed only a little over a decade before. At that time it had been the very latest word in medical care. The teaching hospital now operated 600 beds, serving a metropolitan commercial and manufacturing area with a population of just under a million people.

The hospital's financial statements (as subsequently audited) for 1981 and 1982 are shown in Appendix 24.3. For the year ended December 31, 1982, occupancy for all beds had averaged 88 percent. For 1983, average occupancy for medical-surgical beds was projected to be approximately 95 percent.

Ancillary Service Revenues

As is the case in most hospitals, the cash flow and income from ancillary services at Upton were its financial lifeblood, which ensured the institution's at least breaking even on patient care. This was true even though Medicare and other governmental plans paid substantially less than posted charges, indeed in most instances less than costs.

Historically, the hospital had not accounted for ancillary revenue by payment or diagnostic type of patient, or by type of bed, but it had become clear that this information would be of value. Consequently, Gene Buckley, an associate director of the hospital, had requested an estimate of ancillary revenues attributable to the existing intensive-care unit (ICU) activity. The response from Barry Choate, C.P.A., the hospital's financial analyst, is shown in Appendix 24.4. On the basis of this information, Buckley had prepared the projected 1983 ancillary service budget for the 18 existing ICU beds (Table 24.1), along with the daily service budget for those beds.

Origin of Freestanding Laboratory Proposal

Gene Buckley and Henry Groton had been primarily responsible for the preparation of the formal proposal document (Appendix 24.1) to which Courtney Hill had referred in his telephone conversation with Joe Kent. Most of the backup information attached to the proposal had been developed by Henry Groton with support from Barry Choate. Copies of the proposal had been provided to Director Kent, to Dean Hill, and to the Alumni Information Office of the College of Medicine.

PERSONAL COMMENTS

Henry Groton—Hospital Planner and Developer of the Proposal

Henry Groton elaborated on several points of the proposal. "There's no doubt that I can demonstrate the need for this package. For example, a reasonable standard for a laboratory is 30 square feet of lab space for each hospital bed. This means that we should have 18,000 square feet of lab, rather than our present 8,000. And an appropriate standard for ICU coverage is 8 percent of the total beds. For us that would be 48 beds—we have 18. Furthermore, the new ICU would be strategically located right across the hall from the operating rooms instead of down at the end of the building. Across from surgery, we would have sufficient space to go into some new concepts of intensive care.

"You see, our present ICU was not built for this purpose originally, but was converted from regular medical-surgical beds. This, incidentally, is why there is essentially zero cost associated with converting them back to regular beds.

"The idea for the freestanding lab goes back to 1979, when we began looking for beds. We wanted to find out how we could get additional beds in this building without major new construction. My staff and I took all of the floor plans and tried to figure out how many beds we could get out of the system — out of the existing facility. We came up with a program whereby we *could* get beds — easy beds and difficult beds. One of the ideas that I had was to convert the lab to beds — namely ICU beds — because the criteria for ICU beds are different from those for regular beds. You see, under the state law requirements, patient rooms must have an outside exposure with the windows equal to 15 percent of the floor area; but the law allows you to have ICU beds without windows (and I know of two hospitals that have windowless ICUs), provided that there is an awareness of outside light and of the time of day. So the lab seemed logical to me in that it has only two windows; from that point of view, it is a natural ICU location. As we've indicated in the proposal, we would use 7,000 of the 8,000 square feet for the ICU, and leave the remaining space for a small surgical-pathology lab.

"It is also necessary to understand that the proposed freestanding-lab building is to be designed under the team concept, from the ground up, by bringing together our technical staff with a building designer and a contractor. Then we'll 'fast-track' the construction; that is, we will begin building the shell before the inside design is completed. This is what we did for the business office building we mentioned in the proposal. That building cost us $750,000 under the team concept and with 'fast-tracking,' which was $200,000 under the lowest outside bidder.

"Finally, I think that we can't overestimate the potential value of financing a portion of the project with an interest-free loan, particularly in these times of tight money. Of course, we don't have anything in writing yet, but it is my understanding that the pledge of a $2.5 million loan without interest, from a friend of the school, is essentially assured."

Gene Buckley—Associate Director and Developer of the Proposal

Gene Buckley emphasized certain facets of the proposal that he hoped would help the faculty to understand it. "An important point is that all of this is going to add very little to overhead and administration; even the new lab building won't require any additional employees, except for some housekeeping personnel. Of course, we'll need a few more R.N.'s, nursing aides, and orderlies, but that's just a standard direct cost associated with any bed increase of whatever kind. And I think we'll need at most three additional office personnel to handle the administration of the expanded lab and the 28 additional beds. But even the utilities, housekeeping, insurance, and such on the new lab should only be around $100,000 a year.

"We didn't include the specifics of the effect of this proposal on the income or cash flow of the hospital — the proposal seems to me to be rather long as it is — but I understand that the figures Barry Choate worked up show that the income of the hospital will go up by about $200,000 a year, which is good news since we slipped a bit in that respect last year. I do have his sheet on indirect expenses [Table 24.2]; the incremental excess of revenues over direct costs should be a direct projection of the current figures for daily and ancillary services for both ICU and regular beds, since, fortunately, private insurers pay charges and the 'Blues' reimburse us on a prospective charge basis rather than on costs."

Barry Choate—Hospital Financial Analyst

Barry Choate, a C.P.A., had recently moved from an office in the main hospital, adjacent to the emergency room ramp, to the new "fast-tracked" business office building. He observed that the new building was nice enough, but that he missed hearing and seeing the ambulances come and go. "It's as if I really weren't working for a hospital anymore," he said. "I'd think that the lab technicians might feel that way, too, if they were moved to another building."

Excerpts from Barry Choate's worksheets for indirect expenses and excess of revenues over direct costs are shown in Table 24.3. Because the financial analyst had not been told of the possibility of an interest-free loan, he had assumed that all funds for construction would be borrowed. Information on cost estimates of the new facilities given to Choate by the housekeeping department is shown in Table 24.4.

John Cranbrook—Associate Director
for Patient Care Services

John Cranbrook had administrative responsibility for such activities as the blood bank, radiology, emergency services, operating room, pharmacy, and the clinical laboratories. "My responsibility as I see it," he said, "is to keep the labs within reasonable financial boundaries in terms of the net surplus or deficit they are supposed to create, and to see to it that the services being provided are satisfactory, by whatever indicators I, as a nonphysician, can use. However, the medical qualities of the lab are judged by the physician-users and by the lab director, and the administrative characteristics of the lab are the responsibility of the lab manager and me. I don't have the power to hire or fire—that belongs to the faculty director of the labs, Dr. Shattuck—but, of course, I can recommend.

"I've talked to several of the lab people personally—mostly supervisory personnel; I think they like the idea of a better physical facility. But the remoteness will bother many of them simply because they might be a little more isolated. There will be fewer people walking through the lab—and that includes everybody from a messenger to a surgeon. From the standpoint of productivity, I consider it an advantage that there wouldn't be so many people trafficking through the labs; and it might even result in an advantage of greater job satisfaction. But for most of the lab employees, the immediate reaction to a separate facility is: 'Gee, we're going to be way out there. I won't get to see people and I won't be quite in the center of things the way I am now. And I won't have the feeling of being necessary that comes when someone leans over my shoulder and asks what the result is. So the job will be a much less personal experience than it is now.'

"I feel strongly, though," Cranbrook continued, "that there can be job satisfaction in this kind of arrangement. It would be different, there's no question about that; but, you know, we're not trying to perpetuate all the old patterns — a lot of the time, we'd like the doctors to stay out of the labs because they *are* disruptive.

"Now, as to the proposal, what we're talking about as far as the economies you would gain by making this a freestanding building is not related to the fact that it's a laboratory building. If you move a laboratory, people think that just because you moved it, it's going to make more or less money. That's not the case at all. The economies that are to be achieved, the savings, the cash flow from this decision will come from having the space that the clinical laboratories now occupy freed up for beds. The beds themselves don't generate a great deal of money, but the volume of ancillary services that will be ordered for the patients occupying those beds, particularly the ICU beds, is enormous. These services, like it or not, are priced in such a way that they generate a surplus — simply from the historical pricing formulas that were established when hospitals really didn't understand their costs, and nobody else did either.

"We are pretty sure we can keep 28 ICU beds full. As it is now, cardiac surgery alone is allocated 14 of the 18 available beds. Physicians in other specialties who might like to do surgery that would require postoperative care in the ICU have to either postpone surgery or send their patients elsewhere."

Mark Loomis—Chairman
Department of Pathology
Upton University College of Medicine

Mark Loomis, M.D., found himself largely supporting the academic viewpoint, although he clearly appreciated Joe Kent's perspective, and even talked of taking a sabbatical leave in the near future to attend a graduate school of business. "There's no question that a hospital must look at a lab in terms of dollars under the existing structure of charges. I personally believe that those charge structures are overdue for revision to put them more in line with costs; but if that happens, the hospitals are in real trouble. The pathologists get about 25 percent of the net, while the hospital gets the other 75 percent. The faculty, of course, see the lab as a teaching resource. And, frankly, I don't know how you evaluate a proposal that might be viewed as the best financially and the worst academically.

"It is clear to me that it would be very difficult to attract academically qualified people to run an operation that was housed off in a separate area from the main hospital. It would relegate the supervisory personnel to a kind of out-of-house operation — like a laundry that could be set up in the next town, for example, and just deliver sheets and linens. This would really downgrade the academic qualities of the laboratory.

"And we must recognize that the people involved in the laboratory have a real concern with the patient care aspects — the logistics of physically getting the specimens and of providing the feedback data efficiently — if the lab is removed from a location fairly close to the emergency room, the intensive care unit, and so forth. To us, it would be more nearly ideal to have the lab physically close to the place where the specimens are being collected, particularly in a hospital like this where so much of our work is *Stat.* — that is, it can't be nicely scheduled, but rather it's emergency things that get requested at all hours of the day and night because of some critical situation involving patients. This kind of thing is different from just having routine laboratory work done as part of an annual physical exam, where you just collect specimens and it doesn't really matter whether you get the results next week or three weeks later."

Meanwhile, in the director's office . . . When Joe Kent's secretary brought him the morning's interoffice mail, she told him that the meeting with Dean Hill was confirmed for the following afternoon, but that Drs. Shattuck and Loomis would be unable to attend because they were both leaving in the morning to deliver papers at a professional meeting in Miami. In the mail was the promised copy of the memo from Dr. Shattuck to the dean (Appendix 24.2), together with a copy of a letter from Dr. Loomis to the dean (Appendix 24.5).

Joe Kent wondered how he might best counter Dean Hill's opposition to the freestanding building the next afternoon. He also wondered if the proposal was as sound on a dollar basis as his staff had assured him. He had noted the recent introduction of legislation to set rates prospectively for Medicare on the basis of diagnoses. Although the media gave the bill little chance for passage, he was concerned about its implications for capital expenditures at such time as it might become law. He was also uncertain as to the real effects of the Tax Equity and Fiscal Responsibility Act (TEFRA) on Upton's Medicare payments. The hospital was now three weeks into its first TEFRA year and he really didn't know how that might affect the proposal. He decided it was time to put sharp pencil to paper.

Appendix 24.1

A PROPOSAL FOR A NEW CLINICAL LABORATORY AND ADDITIONAL INTENSIVE-CARE BEDS

Two fundamental problems face the Upton University Hospital and reduce its ability to serve the needs of the College of Medicine: a shortage of beds and a lack of space in support facilities. The purpose of this presentation is to ask for your support of a program to move the clinical laboratory into a new building and to remodel the vacated area into an intensive-care unit that would accommodate approximately 28 beds.

The total facilities for inpatient teaching are inadequate, although many patients of physicians in the community are observed for educational purposes. In addition to the 200 faculty members with patient contact, there are over 250 interns, residents, and clinical fellows, plus 300 medical students. Lack of beds forces many cancellations of scheduled patient admissions, particularly in the department of surgery. Consequences could be the drying up of referral sources and the loss of an adequate inflow of teaching material.

The demand for nonbed services that support inpatients has increased substantially since the hospital opened in June 1973. Among the services that have expanded greatly as a result is the clinical laboratory.

The main clinical laboratory for the hospital is an overcrowded facility with a rapidly expanding output. It is occupying approximately 7,900 gross square feet of space (5,800 usable) directly across from the operating rooms. During a typical day, approximately 90 full-time personnel occupy the space. Plumbing, ventilation, and emergency power are inadequate. All bench space is used, and there is no space for development of new procedures. There is little space for storage of supplies, dishwashing, and clerical support. Major equipment additions have been made to increase output, but they have reduced usable space still further.

It is remarkable that the quality of output and the morale of the employees are both at high levels. Morale is partly a result of the belief that the situation is so bad that something must be and will be done. Also, we have attempted to involve key laboratory personnel in our planning and analysis.

The laboratory has not always been so crowded. Five years ago there were 42 technicians; now there are more than twice that many. Five years ago 456,000 determinations were performed; in the coming year 1.4 million will be done. (Part of the increase is due to additional automated techniques introduced in 1980, and even if 1981 is used as a base year, there was a 22 percent increase in 1982 and another 23 percent increase is expected next year.)

The laboratory clearly needs more space. There is no way to expand sufficiently in its present location. If it can be relocated, intensive-care beds can be installed with excellent proximity to the operating rooms, and the laboratory would benefit as follows:

1. Space would be available for:
    a. *Stat.* procedures — no designated space available now
    b. Bone marrow studies — no designated space available now
    c. Conference room, library, and lecture room — none now, despite the fact that 10 medical technology students are trained each year
    d. Immunology — now done in College of Medicine research space
    e. Bacteriology and serology — now done in College of Medicine research space
    f. Special hematology and coagulation laboratory — now done in College of Medicine research space
    g. Locker and lounge facilities — no lounge now and lockers are on the main corridor through the lab
    h. Expanded blood bank and donor facilities
    i. Thyroid testing
    j. Central receiving and storage — deliveries now clog work areas
    k. Reagent preparation room
    l. Office space for chief technologists and supervisors — only one chief technologist has office space now
    m. Office and laboratory space for needed M.D. staff — no space now

2. Bench space to accommodate more medical technology students would be available.

3. The facility could be designed to provide for computerization and rapid communication of library information. Recent applications at other medical centers have demonstrated considerable success in this area. The hospital is presently installing advanced computer equipment for general hospital use, and the laboratories could utilize this resource with properly designed facilities.

We have attempted to deal with the problems of beds and support space as quickly and economically as possible. To date we have relied on internally generated cash to meet our requirements and have borrowed at the floating rate of one-half of one percentage point over the prime rate. We have attempted to remove services not directly related to patient care from high-cost space usable for beds. For example, the laundry, previously done at the hospital, has been centralized with six other hospitals, and the former laundry space will be converted into a 20-bed psychiatric unit. Similarly, all business office functions for the hospital and outpatient clinics are being centralized in a new 15,200-square-foot building just north of the hospital. The cost of these projects ($1,400,000) has been financed by seven-year bank loans to be paid from the hospital cash flow.

The ability of the hospital to finance future projects depends either on gift funds (there is no fund-raising program in operation for the hospital at the present time, and the hospital has no endowment) or on identifying projects in which capital investments will generate savings sufficient to amortize necessary debt financing. This proposal is of the latter type, but the current shortage of loan money and high interest costs make a large loan difficult to obtain and service. However, if no-interest (or low-interest) funds could be obtained to the extent of 75 to 80 percent of project costs, it would be feasible to repay such a loan over a 15-year period from the incremental cash flow of the project.

Specifically, our proposal is as follows:

It is recommended that a 20,000-square-foot freestanding laboratory be constructed, connected to the hospital by pneumatic tubes, television, data printout, computer cable, and other communication and information devices and systems. Further, it is recommended that this construction be followed by the construction of an intensive-care facility and a small surgical-pathology laboratory within the existing laboratory area. All of this could be accomplished within 18 months at a cost of approximately $3,132,000. Alternatively, a two-story office/laboratory building could be constructed in which the first floor could be leased at $12 per square foot per year, with a possible four-year payoff for the leased 20,000 square feet. This would assist in providing a "self-paying" facility (program) and could be used when required for laboratory expansion to 40,000 square feet.

There are at present a sufficient number of renters within the university family who are currently leasing facilities within one-half mile of the proposed building site (one block from the present hospital) who might be interested in leasing space from the hospital. The hospital would have to protect its nonprofit status; however, this could be arranged.

To proceed with the master plan would demand a commitment of funds amounting to $4,978,000, and intensive-care beds would not be available for at least 39 months. A review of the summary analysis (cost/time comparisons) and back-up data attached to this proposal will illustrate this point more clearly.

As mentioned above, the proposal includes the conversion of the area currently occupied by the laboratories to a 28-bed intensive-care unit. Intensive-care patients generate ancillary revenue at a substantially higher rate per day than other patients. At the present time, there are 18 intensive-care beds with an average occupancy of over 90 percent, with frequent overflow of these patients into other beds. It is our opinion that an occupancy rate of 85 percent could be maintained in an intensive-care unit of 28 beds.

The existing 18 ICU beds would be returned to their original function, that of medical-surgical beds. As such, they would come on line against a projected occupancy rate of 95 percent for all medical-surgical beds, and they would also provide a cushion for the flow-through of patients from the expanded ICU, who occupy such beds when they no longer require intensive care.

In addition, the freestanding building program will provide the time needed to push the relocation of purchasing; to assist in the solution of space needs of other departments such as radiology, nuclear medicine, pharmacy, etc.; and to allow the detailed planning of the master plan to proceed in a more orderly fashion.

At such time as the master plan is completed, and it is possible to move the laboratory to the space provided in the plan, the freed space in the freestanding building might be available for lease arrangements or for one or more of the following:

Purchasing
Community blood reserve
Social services
Print shop
Student bookstore
Personnel department
Psychiatry outpatient clinic
Medical record storage

It is proposed that this project in the one-story form be financed as follows:

Cash from the hospital	$ 92,000
Bank loan — 9-year term at 12-percent interest	540,000
No-interest-bearing loan — 15-year term	2,500,000
Total project cost	$3,132,000

Debt service, including interest, under this arrangement would range from $291,467 in the initial year to $233,867 in the ninth year, at which time the bank loan would be liquidated. For the remaining term of the no-interest-bearing loan (six years) the annual debt service would be $166,667 per year. As an alternative to this arrangement, the annual debt service could be evened out to $224,267 per year over the entire 15 years, by reducing the payments on the no-interest-bearing loan during the first nine years and increasing them in the remaining six years from the $166,667 proposed above to $224,267. It is estimated that the incremental annual cash flow from the project will be sufficient to fund the required debt service.

January 15, 1983

SUMMARY ANALYSIS
FREESTANDING LAB/28 ICU BEDS versus MASTER PLAN
COMPARISON OF COST AND TIMING

FUNCTION	Size (Sq. Ft.)	$/Sq. Ft.	Total $	Months to Complete*
Freestanding lab/ICU:				
Lab (incl. parking)	20,000	104.30	2,086,000†	10†
ICU (incl. surgical-pathology lab)‡	8,000	130.76	1,046,000	18
Total program	28,000		3,132,000**	18**
Master plan††:				
Lab	20,000	140.00	2,800,000	30
Equipment and lab furniture			320,000	
Footings for future construction	24 ea. @ 7,000		168,000	30
Temporary site conditioning			100,000	
Landscape			100,000	30
Fees and overhead (12 percent)‡‡			392,000	
ICU (incl. surgical-pathology lab)‡	8,000	130.76	1,046,000	38
Parking			52,000	7
Total program	28,000		$4,978,000	38

*Engineering estimate.

†"Fast-tracking" construction.

‡Placed in space currently occupied by laboratory.

**For 40,000-square-foot lab/office building, add $990,000 and two months.

††First phase representing 10 to 15 percent of the total master plan.

‡‡Architect—8 percent; university overhead—4 percent.

FREESTANDING LABORATORY BUILDING

A. Laboratory building
Budget cost for 20,000 sq. ft. (single-story), "fast-tracked"

Item		Total
Basic building (incl. air conditioning) @ $44/sq. ft.		$ 880,000
Mechanical @ $20/sq. ft.		400,000
Electrical @ $5/sq. ft.		100,000
Services: Electric	$16,000	
Water	2,000	
Gas	2,000	
Sewer	2,000	
Air compressor	4,000	
Vacuum pump	4,000	
Telephone	6,000	
Communication	26,000	
Pneumatic tube	30,000	92,000
Total construction costs		1,472,000
Construction cost per sq. ft.	$73.60	

Continued

Driveway and parking (140 stalls)	90,000
Landscaping	40,000
Planning and engineering	140,000
Fees, permits, bonds, etc.	24,000
Equipment	180,000
Furniture	140,000

Total cost for project		$2,086,000
Total cost per sq. ft.	$104.30	

Allow four months for planning and six months for construction from time of concept approval.

Depreciation

Building, etc., @ 3 percent of	$1,766,000	=	$52,980	
Equipment and furniture @ 15 percent of	320,000	=	48,000	
Total	$2,086,000		$100,980	

B. Laboratory/leased office space (optional addition to A.), "fast-tracked"

Construct a two-story building with 20,000 square feet of office space and 20,000 square feet of laboratory space:

Item	Total
Basic building @ $44/sq. ft.	$ 880,000
Stairs	10,000
Landscaping	12,000
Parking (100 stalls)	40,000
Planning and engineering (4 percent)	40,000
Fees, permits, bonds, etc.	8,000

Total construction costs		990,000
Total cost per sq. ft.	$49.50	
Total cost for project A		$2,086,000

Allow four months for planning and eight months for construction of laboratory/office building for a total cost of: $3,076,000

Income from rental space may be estimated at $1 per square foot per month ($12 per square foot per year). This space may allow for future uninterrupted expansion of laboratory space.

Annual rental = $240,000

Payback period, excluding financing and operating costs:

Leased space: $\dfrac{\$990,000}{\$240,000} = 4.125$ years

Entire building: $\dfrac{\$3,076,000}{\$\ 240,000} = 12.8$ years

December 17, 1982

PROPOSAL FOR INTENSIVE CARE UNIT

Budget Cost

Construct a 28-bed unit in present clinical laboratory space and relocate surgical-pathology lab:

Item		Total
Architect's estimate 6/15/80 @ $72.70/sq. ft.		$ 509,000
Escalation (30 percent) 1980 – 1983 @ $21.80/sq. ft.		152,600
Fees (13 percent) @ $12.30/sq. ft.		86,400
Monitor equipment		162,000
Beds		48,000
Total construction costs		$ 958,000
Total cost per sq. ft.	$136.80	
Relocation of surgical-pathology lab* @ $88/sq. ft.		88,000
Total cost for project		$1,046,000

Depreciation:

Building conversion (25-year life)	4 percent of	$836,000 =	$33,440
Monitor equipment (5-year life)	20 percent of	$162,000 =	32,400
Beds (10-year life)	10 percent of	$ 48,000 =	4,800
		$1,046,000	$70,640

*Would be part of the cost for conversion — must be relocated to the south end of the new ICU unit.

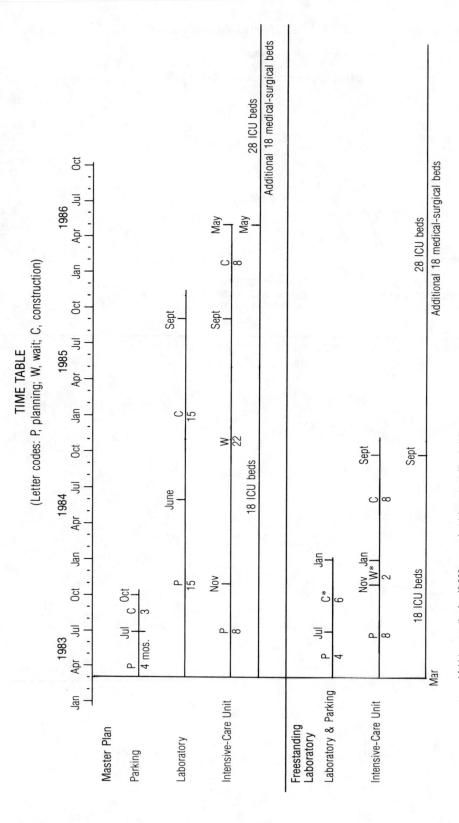

TIME TABLE

(Letter codes: P, planning; W, wait; C, construction)

*Add two months for 40,000 square feet laboratory/office building.

Appendix 24.2

MEMO FROM DR. SHATTUCK TO DR. HILL

DATE: December 20, 1982

TO: R. Courtney Hill, M.D.

FROM: Stephen Shattuck, M.D.

SUBJECT: Problems that may be encountered by placing the clinical laboratories in their own building

If the clinical laboratories are removed from their present sites and are reestablished in their own building, space problems of several operations in the hospital may be aided, but a number of difficulties may be compounded for the clinical laboratories. What follows is a provisional attempt on my part to describe some of these difficulties.

1. It must be remembered that approximately two-thirds of the total hours during the year in which the laboratory is functioning are at night, on weekends, and on holidays. During these times, we have a partial staff to draw the blood and do the hematology, chemistry, and blood banking. It is essential at these times that the laboratory personnel be centralized in their activities, and very close to those who make requests upon them and to whom they must return data. This is especially true during an emergency situation, and nowhere is this more true than in blood banking. I have a horrible vision of a nighttime technician doing a chemical procedure, typing blood, trying to get specimens, and trying to get information or bottles of blood back to a doctor or a nurse from a block away.

2. Although laboratory requests and reports could probably be handled satisfactorily from a distance, I think that even at times when the lab is fully staffed it would be very hard to collect blood, transport urine, and perform certain other operations from the distance of the proposed site. Also, it should be noted that certain outpatient clinics, principally hematology and oncology, which depend on very rapid blood counts on patients in order that therapeutic decisions may be made at once, would find it very difficult to operate at such a distance from the lab.

3. Of very major concern to us is a probable drop in the educational function of the laboratory if we were to be moved to a separate building. It is hard to estimate the number of medical students, community practitioners, house staff, and faculty who drop into the laboratory; nevertheless, I think it would be hard to overestimate the educational importance of these contacts. I know how often I meet a resident in the hall, and we fall to discussing a particular patient's problem, and then we take a couple of minutes to run upstairs to look at a particular smear or biopsy in order to make a major decision on a case. I very much fear that if the laboratory were at a distance, this kind of contact would seriously diminish.

These are just a few of the difficulties I see with the removal of the clinical laboratories to their own building, and perhaps other people will bring up other problems. I certainly cannot say that these problems could not be overcome, even in the case of a distant laboratory, but they seem to me to represent serious problems that must be considered before we make a major decision of this kind.

Appendix 24.3

AUDITED FINANCIAL STATEMENTS

BROOK, IDELWILD, RAINIER AND COMPANY

One Brook Square
Upton, Centralstate

The Board of Directors
Upton University Hospital

We have examined the accompanying balance sheet of Upton University Hospital at December 31, 1982, and the related statements of revenues and expenses and fund balances for the year then ended. Our examination was made in accordance with generally accepted auditing standards, and accordingly included such tests of the accounting records and such other auditing procedures as we considered necessary in the circumstances. It was not practicable to confirm accounts receivable for patients undergoing hospital treatment or to confirm outstanding claims for services provided to patients covered by federal and state health insurance programs, as to which we satisfied ourselves by means of other auditing procedures. We have made a similar examination of the financial statements for the prior year.

In our opinion, the statements mentioned above present fairly the financial position of Upton University Hospital at December 31, 1982, and December 31, 1981, and the results of its operations for the years then ended, in conformity with generally accepted accounting principles applied on a consistent basis during the two-year period.

March 18, 1983

BALANCE SHEET
Fiscal Years Ending December 31, 1982 and 1981

ASSETS	1982	1981
General Fund		
Cash	$ 220,146	$ 454,628
Patient accounts receivable, less Medicare current financing ($1,122,000 in 1982 and $1,270,000 in 1981) and allowance for doubtful accounts ($955,278 in 1982 and $701,442 in 1981)	9,967,018	7,112,378
Other accounts receivable	150,012	210,546
Pharmacy inventory, at cost	346,374	305,508
Minor equipment and operating supplies	740,604	735,180
Prepaid expenses and deposits	41,958	144,790
	$11,466,112	$ 8,963,030
Plant fund (Note 1)*		
Time deposits and short-term investments, at cost	$ 3,400,000	$ 2,993,260
Due from general fund	3,056,610	2,668,092
Hospital plant and equipment, less accumulated depreciation	22,265,998	20,935,116
Investment in and advances to central laundry, at cost (Note 3)*	425,000	—
	$29,147,608	$26,596,468
Special funds		
Trust funds cash	$ 178,574	$ 164,798
	$40,792,294	$35,724,296

LIABILITIES AND FUND BALANCES	1982	1981
General Fund		
Accounts payable and accrued liabilities:		
Vendors	$ 1,753,330	$ 1,210,708
Professional fees	309,768	291,492
Accrued payroll	423,810	595,142
Payroll and sales taxes payable	39,704	28,114
Allowance for adjustments to costs under government health insurance plans (Note 2)*	2,352,948	864,000
Other accrued expenses	352,010	245,264
Payable to Upton University for services and advances, net	527,400	709,686
Due to plant fund	3,056,610	2,668,092
Fund balance (working capital equity)	2,350,532	2,350,532
	$11,466,112	$ 8,963,030
Plant Fund (Note 1)*		
Bank loan, payable in monthly installments of $9,902 to March 1, 1986, including interest at .5% above prime rate		
Bank loans, payable in monthly installments of $16,072 to March 1, 1989, thereafter in monthly installments of $7,117 to May 1, 1989, plus interest at .5% above prime rate	295,846	378,064
Fund balance (owner's equity)	1,219,634	380,000
	27,632,128	25,838,404
	$29,147,608	$26,596,468
Special Funds		
Trust funds balance	178,564	164,798
	$40,792,294	$35,724,296

*See accompanying notes.

STATEMENT OF REVENUES AND EXPENSES
Fiscal Years Ended December 31, 1982 and 1981

	1982	1981
Operations:		
Revenues (Note 2)*:		
Hospital daily service	$27,665,054	$24,198,348
Hospital ancillary and other services:		
Inpatient	20,296,302	18,528,098
Outpatient	3,014,766	1,850,016
Emergency	863,574	722,160
Cafeteria	837,290	902,464
	$52,676,986	$46,201,086
Less:		
Allowances, charities, and provision for collection losses	1,575,738	942,510
Provision for Medicare and state programs (Note 2)*	1,705,162	1,523,168
	3,280,900	2,465,678
	$49,396,086	$43,735,408
Expenses:		
Hospital daily service	26,773,766	23,985,730
Hospital ancillary and other services:		
Inpatient	17,197,010	14,792,212
Outpatient	2,603,588	1,734,134
Emergency	1,078,414	839,222
	$47,652,778	$41,351,298
Excess of operating revenues over operating expenses	1,743,308	2,384,110
Other income:		
Interest — net	125,636	59,606
Other — net	193,038	46,748
Excess of revenues over expenses — designated for plant fund (Note 1)*	$ 2,061,982	$ 2,490,464

Depreciation deducted in the above statement: $1,564,848 in 1982 and $1,452,298 in 1981

*See accompanying notes.

STATEMENT OF FUND BALANCES
Fiscal Years Ended December 31, 1982 and 1981

	1982			1981		
	General Fund	Plant Fund	Special Fund	General Fund	Plant Fund	Special Fund
Fund balances, beginning of year	$2,350,532	$25,838,404	$164,798	$2,350,532	$23,331,388	$211,678
Additions:						
Excess of revenues over expenses		2,061,982			2,490,464	
Donated equipment		190,212			129,344	
Contributions and trust income			302,960			173,304
Total available	$2,350,532	$28,090,598	$467,758	$2,350,532	$25,951,196	$384,982
Reductions:						
Fund balance applied to payment of accounts receivable from Upton University		$29,320			$36,164	
Payment to Upton University for bond retirements and interest related to its ownership of hospital facilities (Note 1)*		429,150			76,628	
Expenditures for patient charges			42,124			30,934
Other expenditures			247,060			189,250
	—	$ 458,470	$289,184	—	$ 112,792	$220,184
Fund balances, end of year	$2,350,532	$27,632,128	$178,574	$2,350,532	$25,838,404	$164,798

*See accompanying notes.

NOTES TO FINANCIAL STATEMENTS
December 31, 1982

1. Ownership and basis of presentation

Upton University Hospital is a nonprofit corporation that operates facilities owned by Upton University. The hospital facilities, accumulated depreciation, and the university's related equity therein are included under the plant fund, based upon original costs. Obligations of the university that are related to its ownership of the properties, which are not obligations of the hospital, are not included in the financial statements. Plant and equipment in the accompanying balance sheet are comprised as follows:

	1982	1981
Buildings	$13,054,950	$11,356,332
Fixed equipment	11,816,856	11,637,354
Land improvements	1,320,282	1,222,808
Equipment	9,001,646	7,953,314
Construction in process	343,132	419,712
	$35,536,866	$32,589,520
Less accumulated depreciation	13,270,868	11,654,404
	$22,265,998	$20,935,116

In accordance with a policy adopted in 1978, the net balance of revenues over expenses has been transferred to the plant fund.

Certain balances from December 31, 1981, have been restated to conform to classifications used for December 31, 1982.

2. **Reimbursements under federal and state programs**

A substantial portion of hospital services is provided to patients covered by Medicare and other government programs under which the hospital is reimbursed on the basis of its costs. These costs are subject to examination by the interested government agencies, and the management of the hospital believes that adequate provision has been made for possible adjustments resulting from such examinations.

During the year ended December 31, 1982, an examination of costs covered by Medicare and other government programs from inception to December 31, 1979, was completed. Although the settlement of this examination has not been finalized, the proposed adjustments have been adequately covered by the hospital's allowance for such adjustments. Examinations of the hospital's reimbursement computations for Medicare and other programs since December 31, 1979, have not been completed.

3. **Contingencies and commitments**

Upton University Hospital and certain other hospitals are members of a corporation, which provides central laundry services. The laundry's facilities are financed by a long-term loan, secured by substantially all the laundry's assets, under which the hospital is contingently liable as guarantor for approximately $1,440,000.

As of December 31, 1982, the hospital was contingently liable for approximately $280,000 as guarantor of bank loans made to certain individuals for the payment of their hospital charges.

Appendix 24.4

ANCILLARY REVENUE GENERATED BY ICU PATIENTS

January 9, 1983

TO: Joseph L. Kent, M.D., Director
        Eugene Buckley, Associate Director

FROM: Barry Choate, Financial Analyst

For the purpose of determining the amount of ancillary revenue generated by our intensive-care patients, a special study of these patients was undertaken, which covered approximately 6 percent of total annual patient days in the intensive-care unit. The sample was a random selection and was considered statistically adequate to be representative of the whole.

This study indicated that ancillary revenue is generated by ICU patients at a rate of about

4.6 times that for all patients. If the ancillary operations were added to the daily service for the six months ended December 31, 1982, the combined results would be as follows:

	Daily Service	Ancillary Service	Total
Revenue	$ 940,000	$1,488,000	$2,428,000
Expenses	1,096,000	1,326,000	2,422,000
Net income (loss)	$ (156,000)	$ 162,000	$ 6,000
Percentage of revenue	−17%	11%	

On this basis, the present ICU is about a break-even operation — not satisfactory, but not as bad as it might first appear. This has been the extent of our investigation to date. Routine reporting does not provide such data, and considerable time is involved in getting it. Other units may show a similar pattern. For example, the coronary-care unit shows expenses about equal to revenue for daily care. However, it could be that above-average ancillary revenue is produced, and net income on a combined basis is a quite different result.

BC:was

Appendix 24.5

MEMO FROM DR. LOOMIS TO DR. HILL

January 19, 1983

TO: Dr. R. Courtney Hill, Dean

FROM: Dr. Mark Loomis, Pathology

SUBJECT: Clinical Laboratory Space

Following several discussions that we had last fall concerning the present difficulties with the clinical laboratories and the urgent need to develop plans for new laboratory facilities, I called a meeting of those individuals whom I thought were directly involved in laboratory activities to initiate planning discussions.

Twelve faculty members, plus myself, were in attendance. We presented some of the ideas that we were generating in the pathology department concerning appropriate development of certain laboratory functions that could be automated; we discussed the various new space proposals that were current; and I invited all of the major laboratory divisions to submit proposals to me outlining their optimal space requirements in a new building.

During the subsequent two months, a number of written responses were generated in which several of the divisions of the laboratory projected their needs as they foresaw them. On the evening of January 17, the second meeting of the group was called, at which time John

Cranbrook was also invited. I reviewed the proposals that had been submitted to me by the various division chiefs, and we also had a long discussion concerning the realistic probabilities relating to the development of the master plan as opposed to the more rapid construction of a freestanding building somewhere in close proximity to the present hospital building. A large portion of the discussion was concerned with which activities could reasonably be moved into a freestanding building and which could not be moved because of their relation to critical clinical care activity.

I should emphasize to you that all of us are in agreement that an ideal laboratory development plan would call for consolidation of all of the various laboratory units in a well-organized space that was close to areas of critical patient care (such as the operating room, the intensive care unit, etc.). On the other hand, we generally agreed that expansion of laboratory facilities was an urgent matter, and we are also aware of the desire of some of the clinical departments to use the present laboratory core space for the development of a better intensive-care facility. With these considerations in mind, we generally agreed that if a freestanding building could be adequately designed and rapidly constructed to provide badly needed space, certain laboratory functions could be housed in such a structure without detriment to clinical activities.

Those laboratory units which could be moved to a freestanding building are the following: chemistry, including urine and stool analyses; serology; the school of medical technology; a tissue bank, which could be a central resource for an expanded program in clinical genetics; and a number of facets of a large and expanded blood bank facility that would, at the minimum, serve the needs of this hospital and might even be designed as a central blood resource for an entire region. Such blood bank activities as the donor unit, facilities for the preparation of blood components, and adequate back-up storage could all be housed in a freestanding building.

Those laboratory functions which would have to remain in the present core space include a somewhat expanded surgical-pathology laboratory, morphologic-hematology laboratory, co-agulation laboratory, a small *Stat.* laboratory, and some aspects of blood bank activity, including typing, cross-matching, and short-term storage of blood materials needed for emergency situations. We estimate roughly that some 75 or 80 percent of the present core space would thus be freed up for future development, and even more than this would be possible, if, for example, there were plans to move the hospital administration offices to another site. It was also considered that a freestanding clinical laboratory could handle a good deal of the laboratory volume generated at the VA Hospital, contingent, of course, on the development of adequate specimen transportation mechanisms and data communication systems. However, clinical microbiology, a coagulation laboratory, and a *Stat.* facility would have to remain at the VA Hospital. This, of course, is consistent with ideas that I have discussed with you previously concerning the advisability of making full use of a heavily automated university laboratory facility, rather than duplicating expensive equipment and space development at the VA Hospital itself.

The group also agreed that it should be clearly recognized that other functions of the clinical laboratory that could not be moved to a freestanding building were nonetheless urgently in need of increased space and facilities. These include particularly microbiology, clinical immunology, and the major coagulation laboratories. Accordingly, we considered briefly the possibility that, if a freestanding building were feasible, it might be possible to plan a structure that could also house such activities as the purchasing department, the engineering and carpentry departments, etc. If this were possible, then part of the space vacated by these units could be allocated to housing some of these other laboratory units.

I think that one of the most urgent matters at this time concerns a realistic appraisal of the possibility of beginning to implement the master plan. If this really does not seem to be a near-term possibility, the group agrees that a prompt decision to go ahead with the planning of a freestanding building should be made at the earliest possible time.

I would be happy to discuss this report in more detail at your convenience. I am looking forward to your response.

ML:cm
cc: Dr. Joseph L. Kent

Table 24.1

1983 BUDGET FOR 18 ICU BEDS
($ in thousands)
(Dollar totals may not add due to rounding)

Daily Service			Ancillary Services		
Gross revenues[1,2]	$2,129	100.0%	Gross Revenues[5]	$3,075	100.0%
Bad debt allowance	53	2.5%	Bad debt allowance	77	2.5%
Net revenues	$2,075	97.5%	Net revenues	$2,998	97.5%
Direct expenses			Direct expenses	$2,112	68.7%
Salaries and staff benefits	$1,575	74.0%			
Materials and services[3]	192	9.0%			
Total direct expenses	$1,767	83.0%			
Excess of revenues over direct expenses	$309	14.5%	Excess of revenues over direct expenses	$886	28.8%
Indirect expenses allocated[4]	711	33.4%	Indirect expenses allocated	246	8.0%
Net income	$ (402)	(18.9%)	Gross income	$640	20.8%
			Less 35% not reimbursed by Medicare and other government programs[6]	224	7.3%
			Net income	$415	13.5%

1. 18 beds @ .90 occupancy x 365 days = 5,913 patient days
2. 5,913 x $360/day rate
3. Includes 10% inflation over 1982 experience
4. Includes $20,000 depreciation
5. 5,913 x average daily gross revenue of $520/ICU bed (1982 study showed about $450/bed)
6. Although all governmental reimbursement was cost-based, all other third-party contracts (including those with Blue Cross Plans) were either charge-based or prospective rates.

Table 24.2

FINANCIAL ANALYST'S ESTIMATE OF PROPOSAL'S
INCREMENTAL INDIRECT EXPENSES

($ in Thousands)

(Totals may not add due to rounding)

Item	10 ICU beds	18 medical-surgical beds	Freestanding building	Total
Utilities*	NC	NC	$ 30+	$ 30
Engineering and maintenance*	NC	NC	40	40
Dietary*	$ 43	$ 87	NA	131
Housekeeping*	10	19	20+	49
Laundry and linen*	15	28	NA	43
Insurance*	2‡	NC	3	5
Depreciation				
Building	33‡	NA	53	86
Equipment	37‡	NC	48**	85
Interest cost on construction loans*	63	NA	125	188
Administration and other				
allocated overhead††	30	60	60	150
TOTAL	$235	$194	$378	$807

*See accompanying back-up material (Tables 24.3 and 24.4).

+Expenses typically paid by a leasee.

‡Based on 28 new ICU beds.

**Laboratory-related equipment.

††Includes $30,000 for three additional clerks; remainder is reallocation of overheads.

NC — no change.

NA — not applicable.

Table 24.3

EXTRACTS FROM FINANCIAL ANALYST'S WORKSHEETS

			$(000)
Insurance			
1. Fire and natural disaster: $1,232/million face value			
Lab 2,086 ⎫ 3.132 million			3.9
ICU 1,046 ⎭			
2. Public liability and malpractice			
Rate is $38.02 per average daily occupancy for inpatients.			
28 new beds times .85 occupancy rate equals 22.8			
average daily occupancy.			0.9
Insurance coverage based on inpatient visits and the			
number of residents is insignificant.			

	$(000)
Utilities — based on 1982.	
Cost/sq. ft. for entire hospital/year = $1.46	30.0
Engineering and maintenance	
Estimated at $2/year/sq. ft. in new facility	40.0
Dietary $14/patient day (net of overhead)	

Interest on construction

Item	ICU	Labs
Cost of construction — amount of loan	1,046	2,086
Total interest @ 12% for 10 years	628	1,252
Interest per year	63	125

Excess of ancillary revenues over direct expenses per
medical-surgical bed per day occupied:

Item	Amount
Gross excess (1983)	$27.50
Average not reimbursed by Medicare and	
other third parties	6.00
Net excess	$21.50

Incremental Annual Effect of 18 Medical-Surgical Beds (Daily Service)

Item	$(000)	%
Gross daily revenue	840	100.0
Bad debt allowance	20	2.5
Net daily revenue	820	97.5
Direct expenses		
Salaries and staff benefits	368	43.8
Materials and services	84	10.0
Total direct expenses	452	53.8
Net excess of daily revenues over direct expenses	368	43.7
Indirect expenses allocated	536	63.8
Net income	(168)	(20.0)

Table 24.4

HOUSEKEEPING DEPARTMENT'S COST ESTIMATES

I. Laboratory Relocation—20,000 Sq. Ft.

Supplies			$ 7,310.54
Equipment			2,669.30
Payroll			12,450.00
Total annual cost			$22,429.84

Supplies (per year)			
Toilet tissue	35	cases	$ 385.00
Paper towels	145	cases	2,525.90
Bar soap	10	cases	415.00
Soap dishes	500	each	21.12
Liners, large	3,120	each	312.00
Liners, medium	26,000	each	1,040.00
Toilet seat covers	20	cases	627.20
Wet-mop heads	24	each	50.08
Wet-mop handles	6	each	25.56
Dry mops	104	each	33.28
Cleaner, toilet	26	each	41.60
Cleaner, floor	150	gals	600.00
Floor wax	60	gals	432.00
Cleanser, powdered	104	each	52.00
Miscellaneous items			749.80
Total			$ 7,310.54

Equipment			
2 trucks, refuse	@ $130.90		$ 261.80
2 mop units	@ 115.60		231.20
2 carts, maids	@ 219.80		439.60
1 machine, floor			810.60
1 vacuum, 5 gallons			743.40
1 truck, hand			182.70
Total			$ 2,669.30

Payroll—1.5 janitors	@ $8,300 per year		$12,450.00

II. 28-Bed ICU—7,000 Sq. Ft.

Supplies			$ 9,910.20
Equipment			2,887.40
Linen-laundry			43,221.36
Payroll			19,250.00
Total annual cost			$75,268.96

Supplies (per year)			
Toilet tissue	30	cases	$ 330.00
Paper towels	150	cases	2,325.00
Bar soap	4,500	each	315.00
Soap dishes	2,300	each	90.00
Liners, large	4,500	each	450.00
Liners, medium	22,500	each	900.00
Toilet seat covers	165	pkg	204.60
Wet mops	25	each	73.00
Dry mops	800	each	1,120.00
Cleaner, toilet	150	cans	495.00
Cleaner, floor	450	gals	1,800.00
Soap, disinfecting	78	boxes	561.60
Floor wax	55	gals	374.00
Cleanser, powdered	12	cases	288.00
Miscellaneous items			584.00
Total			$ 9,910.20

Continued

Table 24.4 Continued

Equipment		
Cart, housekeeping maid	3 each	$ 425.28
Floor machine	1 each	722.00
5 gallon microstatic vacuum	2 each	1,486.80
Mopping unit, janitor	1 each	121.40
Mopping unit, maid	2 each	100.00
Step ladder, 6 ft.	1 each	31.92
Total		$ 2,887.40
Linen-laundry (per year)		
Estimated linen usage		
28 beds @ 15 lbs. per bed	420 lbs. per day	
420 lbs. × 365 days	153,300 lbs. per year	
153,300 lbs. @ .17 laundry cost		$26,061.00
153,300 lbs. @ .10 linen service		15,330.00
		$41,391.00
Disposable laundry bags @ 25 lbs. per bag	6,132 bags per year	
6,132 disposable bags @ .19		$ 1,165.08
Disposable pillows (336) @ 1.98 per pillow		665.28
Total		$43,221.36
Payroll — 2.5 maids	@ $7,700 per year	$19,250.00

25

Inspiration Medical Center and National Hospital Corporation Case Study: Present Value of Cost Approaches to Competing Capital Projects

Thomas M. Tierney, Jr.
Douglas A. Conrad

PREFACE

Recent dramatic growth in the investor-owned sector of the American hospital industry provides difficult challenges for health planning. At a general level, health planners and policy-makers will soon need to make explicit judgments about the relative merit of continued acquisitions by investor-owned chains. Neither nationally nor at local levels have health planners faced up to the fact that the growth of those corporations will result in profound changes in the industry for which they are making their plans. More immediately, the boom in acquisitions requires improvement of planning techniques. Planners and capital investment regulators will see fewer simple one-hospital expansion projects, since an area's need for expanded hospital capacity is increasingly seen by the large hospital corporations as a chance for geographic diversification and horizontal expansion.

This case does not discuss the relative merits of investor-owned and nonprofit corporations; the corporate structure of the two facilities in the case is irrelevant. But the case is nonetheless germane to the general issues of acquisition and diversification, focusing as it does on the analytical methods planners and regulators must learn to employ as they encounter an increasing number of expansion proposals from competing applicants.

BACKGROUND HISTORY OF THE CASE

In 1980, Inspiration Medical Center (IMC) was a 230-bed, general acute-care hospital in Capital City. The hospital was moved to its present site of 40 acres on the northeast outskirts of town in 1972. Since then, the hospital has expanded five times in response to rapid population growth in the area. The only hospital in the county (population 120,000), IMC is part of a nonprofit multi-institutional system operated by a Catholic order.

Early in 1980, IMC unveiled its plan to undertake Phase VII of its capital expansion program, an expansion that was planned to meet the area's hospital needs throughout the decade of the 1980s. Initially speculating that Phase VII might cost as much as $50 million, the hospital created quite a stir in the community as it sought a certificate of need (CON) to spend approximately $500,000 on planning the project. Even the politically active local Health Systems Agency (HSA) agreed there was a need for more hospital beds in the area, but there was considerable disagreement over both the justification for planning a $50-million project and the continuation of Capital City as a "one-hospital town."

A small ad hoc committee of citizens therefore encouraged the National Hospital Corporation (NHC) to take a look at Capital City as a possible future market. NHC concluded that development of a second hospital on the west side of town would be an appropriate investment.

As IMC undertook the development of their architectural plans, NHC set about "selling" their concept to the community. They encountered resistance from the medical community, most of whom were located in a complex of medical offices surrounding IMC (and felt reluctant to move or to open second offices on the west side). A large regional HMO also had a clinic immediately adjacent to IMC. Nevertheless, the concept of a second hospital seemed appealing to a segment of the community; some wanted an alternative to a Catholic hospital, some wanted a facility on the west side of town (where there had been significant commercial development in recent years), and some felt the encouragement of competition was always beneficial.

In January 1981, IMC and NHC both submitted CON applications, to be reviewed concurrently as competing proposals. (Although nothing prohibited the approval of both proposals, both applications assumed only one would be approved.) So, the issue of this case is, which proposal should be approved? The *should* in this instance poses a problem of analytical approach; people look at the question in various ways and therefore come up with different judgments. The student is asked to adopt some principles of investment analysis to reach a decision in the case.

DESCRIPTIONS OF THE PROPOSED PROJECTS

Inspiration Medical Center

Table 25.1 describes the proposed increases in bed capacity by service for IMC. The IMC proposal also sought 11 surgical recovery beds, 2 obstetric recovery beds, and 28 nursery bassinets, all of which were nonlicensed bed increases.

IMC would acquire space for the additional beds by constructing an attached two-story nursing tower to house the expanded obstetric and surgery departments. The second floor of this addition would be shelled in for potential future expansion of 30 to 40 beds. Space for the remaining general medical-surgical beds would be gained via relocation and remodeling of existing space. The expanded psychiatric service would be relocated in a newly constructed one-story, freestanding unit.

The IMC project also sought to increase space and service capacity in several clinical and nonclinical support areas including, but not limited to, surgery, physical therapy, respiratory therapy, social services, dietary/cafeteria, admitting, energy management, and parking.

The total capital cost for the project, including construction and equipment, was estimated to be $34,349,000. Of that amount, IMC proposed a share of $8,572,000 (25 percent) to be financed through funds generated internally and $25,917,000 (75 percent) to be financed through a 20-year note at 11 percent interest.

National Hospital Corporation

The NHC sought a license for a general acute-care hospital. They proposed initial licensure of 142 beds, with 110 beds in operation when the hospital opened, and the remaining beds to be added in increments as the planning area occupancy rate increased. Table 25.2 describes NHC's proposed schedule.

NHC proposed adult medical and surgical services, including ten beds dedicated to intensive care and coronary care. A dedicated pediatric unit was not proposed; however, the applicant stated that "pediatric inpatient care will be available." Obstetric and psychiatric care were not proposed.

Proposed ancillary and clinical support services were surgery, radiology, laboratory, pharmacy, emergency, physical therapy, respiratory therapy, and social services. Nonclinical support included dietary and laundry services, the latter to be provided by an outside contractor.

The total capital cost of the NHC project, including construction and equipment, was estimated to be $20,632,854. In keeping with general corporate policy, 40 percent of the project would be equity-financed with cash from the parent company (secured from internally generated funds, commercial paper, and a credit line with commercial banks). The remaining 60 percent of capital costs ($12,379,712) would be financed through a 20-year loan at 14.5 percent interest. Note that neither applicant offered a persuasive argument about the difference in their forecasts of interest rates. NHC, with superior borrowing power due to their corporate affiliation and their conservative use of leverage, would normally be expected to pay lower debt costs. IMC was not proposing the issuance of tax-exempt bonds (which could lower their cost of borrowing). This issue, unresolved, is important to the analysis of the case.

Area "Bed Need"

Using the forecasting method prescribed in their own Health Systems Plan and in the state Health Plan, the HSA planning staff forecast total patient volumes in selected future years as follows:

	1983	1984	1985	1986	1987	1988
Areawide Patient Days (All Services)	77,661	79,758	81,911	84,123	86,394	88,727

In a refinement of those service volume forecasts, the HSA staff also projected the area's need for beds, classified according to service. Table 25.3 shows the bed-need forecasts of the HSA, the NHC, and IMC. The HSA forecasts differ slightly from those of IMC. The

NHC proposers predicted significantly greater service volumes in the area and, therefore, a larger need for bed capacity.

Essentially, the different forecasts result from different expectations about market shares. Over the past years, the HSA and IMC had seen facilities growing in rural neighboring counties to the point that they were attracting specialists and retaining patient loads in their own communities instead of seeing patients referred to Capital City. The market share controlled by IMC in outlying counties had dropped substantially between 1977 and 1980. The outlying hospitals, as well as both the HSA and IMC, considered the change in market shares desirable.

NHC argued to the contrary that the reason for IMC's loss of market share in outlying counties from 1977 to 1980 was the hospital's strained capacity. If there had been sufficient capacity in Capital City, NHC argued, patients would have continued to travel from less-populated counties, and Capital City residents would have been served at home instead of traveling to bigger cities to the north. Thus, NHC reasoned that with an easing of "suppressed demand" (by construction of a new facility on the west side), the market share of facilities in Capital City would grow again to their 1977 percentages.

> Problem: Evaluate NHC's inference that increased capacity in Capital City will result in increased market shares. Look at the issue from both institutional and regional perspectives.

PART 1: HSA's ANALYSIS OF THE PROBLEM

As can be seen in the previous project descriptions, the capital costs of the two proposals differed significantly. IMC proposed a capital expenditure of $34 million, approximately $340,000 per bed, while NHC would commit $20 million in capital, approximately $140,000 per bed. Recognizing that a judgment of costs would necessarily go beyond capital costs, but not knowing how to add capital and operating costs, the local HSA brought in a consulting analyst to look at the economic implications of the two projects. The analyst perceived the issue to be one of adding capital costs to the present value of future operating costs for each of the projects to determine which option represented the lesser commitment of total resources. That is, his primary objective was the minimization of total cost (although he also included a nonfinancial discussion of benefits in terms of the area's "needed" beds, reasoning that only "needed" beds produced benefit).

In looking at future costs of the projects, the analyst limited his observations to the years 1983 to 1988. The projects would not come "on line" until 1983. But hospital technology and the industry's structure under regulation were changing so rapidly that the HSA and its consultant agreed that to look beyond 1988 as a "planning horizon" would create a false impression that it was possible to judge what hospital needs and costs would be in later years.

In this section the student is asked to follow the general steps taken by HSA's consultant, questioning both the assumptions and mechanics of his method. He began with an analysis of the NHC proposal (rounding off to thousands of dollars).

National Hospital Corporation

Step A 1

The pro forma estimates of revenues and expenses in NHC's application (Table 25.4) were based on their own projections of volumes. As was seen in Table 25.3, the HSA disagreed with those projections, so an estimate was needed of NHC's future costs at lower volumes. The HSA staff argued that without a reason to expect a large market shift from IMC to NHC (after all, the town's physicians all practiced near the IMC complex), they would allocate to NHC only the days over and above IMC's capacity of 78.4 percent occupancy.

Using a fixed and variable cost ratio for each expense category, NHC planners provided revised expense estimates for lower service volumes, as shown in Table 25.5.

> Problem: The total costs do not change dramatically with a change in volume. What does that suggest to you about the ratio of fixed and variable costs? What does it suggest about the sensitivity of cost estimates to volume differences? Incidentally, no inflation is included for the cost estimates. Think about that; it will be an issue later.

Step A 2

Reasoning that he would add the project's total capital costs to the present value of future operating costs to estimate full project costs, the HSA analyst subtracted depreciation expenses from each yearly total in Table 25.5, lest the capital costs be counted twice. He also subtracted the annual tax estimates, because a tax represents a transfer from one group to another, not a true economic cost. He left the interest costs of the project in with the other expenses.

> Problem: Capital costs for construction and equipment are funded partly by debt, partly by equity. Interest costs are a repayment for a source of debt funds. Distinguishing between equity and project cash flows, and recognizing that you will compute the present value of future operating costs in order to account for the "time value" of money, decide for yourself whether to retain the interest costs in your calculation of future operating costs. Follow your own advice.

Step A 3

For the estimates of *real* (1983 dollar) noncapital operating expenses obtained in Step A 2, discount to 1983 present value, using a 10-percent discount rate. (Assign 1983 as year 0; then the formula for present value is to multiply the annual estimate by $[1/(1 + r)]^n$ where r is the real discount rate and n is the year for which the computation is made. Alternatively, consult a "Present Value Table" for the appropriate discount factor for each year.)

> Problem: Are you satisfied with the choice of a 10-percent discount rate (remembering that it is a *real* discount rate, i.e., future costs are calculated in real dollars)? Calculate the discount rate you believe appropriate in this case, and show your reasoning. Discount the operating expenses in Step A 2 to 1983 present value, using your chosen discount rate. Store that information for the time being.
>
> By convention many analysts perform the present value calculation with several alternative discount rates, reporting the outcomes from each of those calculations to show the outcome's *sensitivity* to the choice of discount rate, commonly called a sensitivity analysis. That may be adequate; however, we urge you to develop a supportable rationale for the use of one rate (using, perhaps, the capital asset pricing model or simply a reasoned argument of what should influence the real discount rate).

Step A 4

Calculate the sum of the stream of costs for NHC from 1983 through 1988. (The HSA analyst obtained a total of about $33.2 million; if you subtracted interest expenses in Step A 2, your total will be lower, of course.)

Continuing Costs at IMC, without Phase VII

The cost estimates for NHC represent roughly the incremental costs of running that facility in Capital City in addition to continuing services at IMC. The HSA analyst concluded that those incremental costs should be compared with the incremental costs of the IMC project. However, all of IMC's projections of future costs involved total operations, not just those resulting from the proposed project. The analyst considered it necessary, therefore, to establish a baseline for the costs of services at IMC, *without* Phase VII.

This treatment of incremental costs ignores some issues of shifting patient volumes from IMC to NHC, with ramifications for IMC's costs. To simplify the analysis, the consultant assumed that none of IMC's current market would shift to NHC (as noted in Step A 1, above). To estimate IMC's costs without Phase VII, the analyst took the following steps, making a series of assumptions.

Step B 1

Record the past experience of annual operating expenses in the years 1976– 80, from Table 25.6.

Step B 2

Deflate the estimates obtained in Step A 2 to constant (1976) dollars, using average Hospital Cost Index increases of 9 percent.

Step B 3

The real operating costs obtained in Step B 2 were associated with the following patient service volumes, measured in "adjusted patient days."

	1976	1977	1978	1979	1980
Adjusted Patient Days	65,110	69,422	70,560	77,229	78,390

Calculate the real expenses per adjusted patient day. Then calculate the average annual compound growth rate for those daily expenses from 1976 to 1980.

Problem: Remembering that you have adjusted for inflation and for volume increases, interpret the meaning of the growth rate just calculated.

Step B 4

Assume no growth in IMC service volumes after 1982 since they would be at capacity and NHC would be open to take up the slack. Assume, however, that costs continue to grow at the real, volume-adjusted growth rate calculated in Step B 3. Thus, 1983 expenses are assumed to equal 1982 expenses ($29,357,000 from Table 25.6) multiplied by $(1 + g)$, where g is the growth rate.

Estimate the yearly real costs of ongoing operations at IMC from 1984 through 1988, using the same assumptions as for 1983.

Step B 5

For the estimates obtained in Step B 4, discount to present value, using a 10-percent discount rate (or a rate you think more appropriate).

Step B 6

Sum the present value of real expenses for ongoing operations at IMC from 1983 through 1988. The HSA analyst obtained an estimate of about $163 million.

> Problem: Discuss the validity and reliability of the estimates obtained so far. At which points may there have been estimating error?

Costs at IMC, with Phase VII

Step C 1

From Table 25.7, estimate yearly operating expenses, treating interest and depreciation for Phase VII as you did for the NHC estimates. (Note that Phase VII costs are distinguished from other interest and depreciation.)

Step C 2

For the estimates obtained in Step C 1, deflate to constant 1983 dollars, assuming a 9-percent annual rate of inflation.

> Problem: Both the NHC and IMC operating expenses are calculated in constant dollars (that is, they are real costs). Why does this analysis ignore the "cost increases" that are the ravages of inflation? Explain for yourself very clearly the cost impact of inflation.

Step C 3

For the estimates of real, noncapital operating costs obtained in Step C 2, discount to present value using a 10-percent discount rate.

> Problem: Recall any misgivings you had about the choice of discount rates for the NHC proposal. Calculate the present value of IMC expenses using the alternative discount rate you calculated in Step A 3 for NHC. Again, store that information for later comparison of results.

Step C 4

For the estimates in Step C 3, calculate the sum of the present value of IMC costs from 1983 through 1988. The consulting analyst calculated a sum of approximately $181 million. Your answer may be lower, depending on your treatment of Phase VII interest costs. (The consultant retained those costs in annual cost estimates.)

Step C 5

From the sum obtained in Step C 4, subtract the baseline of costs of IMC's ongoing operations *without* Phase VII. The remainder is the *incremental cost* of Phase VII. The analyst obtained a figure of about $17.5 million for the present value (in 1983) of the real incremental noncapital costs of IMC's proposed project for the years 1983 through 1988. (Again, your estimate may differ from his depending on your treatment of interest costs.)

Comparison of the Projects

The steps taken above led to a cost comparison of the two projects that involved adding the capital costs of construction and equipment to the present value of future operating costs. The results are shown in Table 25.8.

In a report to the HSA board, the consulting analyst concluded that the cost comparisons show that "development of a new hospital in the area will involve higher costs, even though NHC could build a facility with considerably lower construction costs than IMC appears to believe are achievable." On the other hand, he reminded the board that "the difference in total costs between the two projects amounts to only about 4 percent of either project estimate. We know that no one's estimates of future costs will have less than a 4-percent margin of error." He continued, "We are comfortable enough in the accuracy of our projections, however, to dismiss the impression that the NHC project is intrinsically less costly because of its lower capital costs. Your decision in this case should, therefore, rest more on benefits obtainable from the two projects than on differences in costs."

ISSUES AND PROBLEMS (PART 1)

1. The analyst included capital and operating costs only for the years 1983 through 1988. What would you expect to be the result if a longer view were taken? Do you accept the validity of limiting an analysis in 1980 to a planning horizon of 1988?

2. Discuss the relationship of general price inflation and project resource costs. That is, why did the analyst not compute costs in nominal dollars?

3. The analyst discounted to present value using a (real) discount rate of 10 percent. How would the decision in the case be affected if your alternative discount rate were used? Justify your choice of rates in terms of finance theory.

PART 2: OTHER VIEWS OF THE PROBLEM

In June 1981 the HSA passed a recommendation to the state's Department of Social and Health Services (DSHS) that the IMC application be approved and the NHC proposal be denied. Sure that they would be sued regardless of their decision in the case, DSHS obtained permission from the interested parties in the case to extend the time period for review. DSHS staff then embarked on their own analysis of the case.

The focus of that analysis centered on patient volume projections. The staff concluded that service volumes would be higher than HSA's projections for the years 1983 through 1988. DSHS staff also used some assumptions different from those of HSA to divide projected areawide volumes between the two facilities (if NHC were approved).

Now to the point for this case study: DSHS forwarded those patient volume projections to the staff of the state rate review commission for an analysis of the costs and the allowable rates that would result from each of three options. The commission staff looked at approval of either project alone and approval of both, based on DSHS volume projections.

The commission staff's analysis of future operating costs varied from that of the HSA consultant in several ways. First, the commission adjusted to volume forecasts from DSHS (assuming that 30 percent of total costs varied with volume). Second, they subtracted professional fees from the hospital's cost projections, but included depreciation expenses. Third, they deflated to 1981 constant dollars (instead of 1983), applying different inflation rates to the various cost categories.

Subtracting depreciation expenses from the commission's estimates, the present value of real operating costs for the years 1983 through 1988 is $10.3 million less for the IMC project than at NHC, given the commission staff's assumptions. However, adding capital costs tips the balance slightly toward NHC, where *total* project costs would be about $3.5 million lower, according to this analysis. In other words, the volume revisions from DSHS and the changes in estimates by the commission made NHC appear slightly more favorable in terms of the objective of cost minimization. However, NHC's advantage in this analysis is smaller even than IMC's advantage in the HSA's analysis. In either one you may legitimately argue that there is no true difference in costs between the two projects.

The Commission's Rate Review

On the basis of their own forecasts of operating costs and on an allowance for the development of future equity capital, the commission staff estimated the rates that would be allowed in each of three approval scenarios. Table 25.9 presents annual total rate-setting revenues at NHC if that proposal were approved alone. To obtain the total rates community-wide for an NHC approval, the commission staff estimated baseline revenues for IMC and added the annual baseline estimates to NHC's. Table 25.10 presents the annual total rate-setting revenues at IMC if that project were approved alone. (The state rate review commission determined the allowable rates presented in Tables 25.9 and 25.10 by considering appropriate cost levels and adding a margin to provide equity capital for future expansion. The appropriateness of the costs is determined by comparison with similar, "peer group" hospitals. As a result, hospitals that offer similar services will be allowed to charge roughly similar rates.)

Focusing on the allowable revenues per adjusted patient day, the commission staff concluded that in 1984 the "IMC only" option would result in a community-wide average per adjusted patient day of $370.49, compared to $393.23 resulting from the "NHC only" option. However, for 1985 through 1988, the estimated average rate per adjusted patient day for the "NHC only" option is lower than that estimated for IMC. By 1988 it is estimated that the "NHC only" community rate would be $395.75, compared to an "IMC only" community rate of $417.37.

In the end, the commission voted to recommend approval to DSHS of both projects, concluding that either one or both would be financially feasible (although rates from any of the scenarios would be out of line compared with similar hospitals in similar communities).

In a final decision in the case, DSHS awarded approval to the IMC project alone, denying NHC its project on the grounds that both facilities were not needed and that the IMC service mix better fit the community's hospital needs. Two years later, as this case study is being written, the state's decision is still being appealed by NHC.

ISSUES AND PROBLEMS (PART 2)

1. In their presentations at public meetings, NHC representatives argued that *consumer* costs (i.e., allowable rates) are the important choice variable — not *operating* costs, which were the focus of the HSA's consulting analyst. Discuss the merits of those arguments in terms of finance theory.

2. Calculate the present value of allowable community-wide rates for the alternatives (1983 through 1988). How would you decide the case if your objective function is

to minimize rates (that is, the "costs" to consumers)? Does it matter whether you look at "total rate-setting revenues" or "revenues per adjusted patient day"?

3. Remembering that revenues achievable by a project in a free market should reflect consumers' evaluations of benefits, what would you conclude about the benefits of the proposed alternatives? What other measures of benefits would you propose?

Table 25.1

PROPOSED INCREASE IN BED CAPACITY BY SERVICE FOR IMC

Clinical Service	Existing Beds, 12/80	Proposed Beds, 1988	Additional Beds Proposed
Adult Medical/Surgical	191	246	55
Pediatric Medical/Surgical	13	20	7
Obstetrics	18	36	18
Psychiatry	8	26	18
Totals	230	328	98

Table 25.2

NHC'S PROPOSED SCHEDULE FOR DEVELOPMENT OF BED CAPACITY

Indicator	ESTIMATED YEAR OF OPERATION 1983	1986–87	1989–90
Facility — Opening Occupancy = 42.5%	110	—	—
Area Occupancy = 80%	—	+ 20	—
Occupancy Returns to 80%	—	—	+ 12
Totals	110	+ 20	+ 12

Table 25.3

FORECAST BED NEED FOR PLANNING AREA
(Residents and In-migrants)

FORECAST BED NEED[1]

	1985		1988			1990			1993	Current Planning Area Beds in Service[2]
	HSA	NHC	HSA	NHC	IMC	HSA	NHC	IMC	IMC	
Total needed:	71	105	92	127	94	106	142	109	131	230
Medical/surgical	39	—[3]	55	—	55	66	—	66	83	191
Pediatric	7	—	8	—	7	9	—	7	7	13
Obstetric	10	—	12	—	14	13	—	16	18	18
Psychiatric	15	—	17	—	18	18	—	20	23	8
Total bed need forecast in planning area (needed + 230)	301	335	322	357	324	336	372	339	361	

1. Occupancy rates: HSA = 75% all services; NHC = 80% all services; IMC = 82% all services

2. Planning Area has 239 beds licensed and 230 currently in service. Figures are based on the 230 beds in service.

3. NHC does not calculate beds separately for each service.

Table 25.4

PRO FORMA OPERATING STATEMENTS, NHC

	FY 1983	FY 1984	FY 1985
PATIENT DAYS	16,441	22,696	29,354
ADJUSTED PATIENT DAYS	18,907	26,100	33,757
ADMISSIONS	2,936	3,982	5,150
ADJUSTED ADMISSIONS	3,376	4,579	5,923
OCCUPANCY[1]	42.5%	58.7%	75.9%
REVENUES:			
Routine	$2,448,025	$ 4,380,532	$4,372,284
Ancillary	4,258,893	5,881,199	7,606,577
Total inpatient	$6,706,918	$ 9,261,731	$11,978,861
Outpatient	1,004,869	1,383,937	1,789,945
Total patient	$7,711,787	$10,645,668	$13,768,806
Other	77,897	107,532	139,078
Gross revenues	$7,789,684	$10,753,200	$13,970,884
REVENUE DEDUCTIONS:			
Contractual adjustments[2]	$ —	$ —	$ —
Charity, bad debts, etc.	171,373	236,570	305,973
Total deductions	$171,373	$ 236,570	$ 305,973
NET REVENUE	$7,618,311	$10,516,630	$13,601,911
OPERATING EXPENSES:			
Salaries and wages	$3,562,948	$ 4,193,408	$ 5,048,502
Benefits	552,238	691,912	833,002
Fees	238,723	329,546	426,220
Supplies	1,200,034	1,585,790	2,051,242
Utilities	163,094	221,286	276,515
Repairs, leases, rentals	59,844	78,856	93,895
Insurance	78,095	99,862	118,003
Nonincome taxes	150,000	160,000	175,000
Depreciation	861,393	871,740	892,454
Other	51,789	69,904	89,823
Total operating expenses	$6,918,168	$ 8,302,304	$10,004,656
NON-OPERATING INTERCOMPANY CHARGES:			
Management fees	$ 129,062	$ 178,164	$ 230,429
Interest	1,788,911	1,771,076	1,750,510
NET INCOME BEFORE TAXES	($1,217,830)	$ 265,086	$ 1,616,316
Provision for income taxes (or tax benefit)	(560,202)	121,940	743,505
Investment tax credit	(487,246)	—	—
NET INCOME AFTER TAXES	($ 170,302)	$ 143,146	$ 872,811

1. Based on 106 beds in service.
2. While cost-based patients are being served, the allowance for return on equity more than offsets the difference in revenues and expenses in 1984 and 1985. The carry-forward effect will diminish in 1986 and disappear in 1987.

Table 25.5

NHC'S EXPENSES, ASSUMING LOWER VALUES

	1983	1984	1985	1986	1987	1988
Salaries	$3,032,640	$3,032,640	$3,033,006	$3,034,977	$3,037,001	$3,050,764
Fringes	500,386	500,386	500,446	500,771	501,105	503,376
Fees	149,501	149,501	187,921	234,141	281,616	330,400
Supplies	770,199	905,271	1,043,927	1,186,391	1,332,607	1,482,855
Utilities	163,094	163,094	163,094	163,094	163,094	163,094
Repairs/rentals	55,000	55,000	55,000	55,000	55,000	55,000
Insurance	58,574	58,574	66,866	76,860	87,116	97,656
Taxes (nonincome)	150,000	150,000	150,000	150,000	150,000	150,000
Depreciation	861,393	861,393	861,393	861,393	861,393	861,393
Miscellaneous	33,576	41,174	48,973	56,987	65,211	73,663
Management fees	83,673	102,607	122,044	142,014	162,511	183,572
Interest	1,788,911	1,771,076	1,750,510	1,726,797	1,699,454	1,667,924
Total	$7,646,947	$7,790,716	$7,983,180	$8,188,425	$8,396,108	$8,619,697
Less interest	4,996,643	5,158,247	5,326,277	5,600,235	5,835,261	6,090,380

Table 25.6

SUMMARY OF FINANCIAL INFORMATION
1976– 1982, IMC
($ in Thousands)

	1976	1977	1978	1979	1980	1981	1982
Inpatient daily care revenues	$12,349	$14,487	$15,985	$19,208	$22,666	$26,856	$30,734
Outpatient daily care revenues	1,679	2,289	2,574	3,227	3,853	4,619	5,133
Total revenues	$14,028	$16,776	$18,559	$22,435	$26,519	$31,475	$35,867
Outpatient as % of inpatient	13.6%	15.8%	16.1%	16.8%	17.0%	17.2%	16.7%
Patient days	57,315	59,950	60,775	66,121	67,000	70,015	73,804
Adjusted patient days	65,110	69,422	70,560	77,229	78,390	82,058	86,129
Total revenues	$14,028	$16,776	$18,559	$22,435	$26,519	$31,475	$35,867
Less: Physician component	(399)	(470)	(516)	(658)	(699)	(807)	(935)
Rate-setting revenues	13,629	16,306	18,043	21,777	25,820	30,668	34,932
Operating expenses:							
Salaries and benefits	6,988	8,545	9,669	11,304	13,902	16,540	18,942
Supplies and other	3,914	4,880	5,678	6,925	7,859	8,816	10,067
Depreciation— Phase VII	—	—	—	—	—	—	—
Depreciation	564	652	842	1,144	1,426	1,581	1,631
Interest— Phase VII	—	—	—	—	—	—	42
Interest	474	527	453	673	797	831	223
Less: Physician component	(399)	(470)	(516)	(658)	(699)	(807)	(935)
Other operating revenues	(315)	(348)	(374)	(433)	(497)	(564)	(620)
	11,226	13,786	15,752	18,955	22,788	26,397	29,357
Deductions from revenue	1,602	1,644	1,369	1,611	2,081	2,773	3,328
Excess of op. rev. over exp.	$ 801	$ 876	$ 922	$ 1,211	$ 951	$ 1,498	$ 2,247
Per adjusted patient day:							
Salaries and benefits	$107.33	$123.09	$137.03	$146.37	$177.34	$201.57	$220.01
Supplies and other	60.11	70.29	80.47	89.67	100.26	107.44	116.88
Depreciation— Phase VII	—	—	—	—	—	—	—
Depreciation	8.66	9.39	11.93	14.81	18.19	19.27	18.94
Interest— Phase VII	—	—	—	—	—	—	.49
Interest	7.28	7.59	6.42	8.71	10.17	10.13	2.59
Less: Physician component	(6.13)	(6.77)	(7.31)	(8.53)	(8.92)	(9.84)	(10.86)
Other operating revenues	(4.84)	(5.01)	(5.30)	(5.61)	(6.34)	(6.87)	(7.20)
Expense per day	$172.41	$198.58	$223.25	$245.43	$290.70	$321.69	$340.85
Deductions from revenue	24.60	23.68	19.40	20.86	26.55	33.79	38.64
PCSC	12.30	12.62	13.07	15.68	12.13	18.26	26.09
Rate-setting revenues	$209.32	$234.88	$255.71	$281.97	$329.38	$373.73	$405.58
FTE's	625.0	718.8	749.0	802.0	879.2	915.9	953.4

Table 25.7

PRO FORMA OPERATING STATEMENTS
1983– 1988, IMC
($ in Thousands)

	1983	1984	1985	1986	1987	1988
Inpatient daily care revenues	$35,272	$39,843	$47,944	$53,744	$59,557	$66,203
Outpatient daily care revenues	5,820	6,455	7,479	8,492	9,470	10,593
Total revenues	$41,092	$46,298	$55,423	$62,236	$69,027	$76,796
Outpatient as % of inpatient	16.5%	16.2%	15.6%	15.8%	15.9%	16.0%
Patient days	77,592	83,260	88,379	90,708	93,173	96,535
Adjusted patient days	90,395	96,748	102,166	105,040	107,988	111,981
Total revenues	$41,092	$46,298	$55,423	$62,236	$69,027	$76,796
Less: Physician component	(1,076)	(1,233)	(1,405)	(1,593)	(1,798)	(2,020)
Rate-setting revenues	40,016	45,065	54,018	60,643	67,229	74,776
Operating expenses:						
Salaries and benefits	21,459	24,550	27,969	31,592	35,033	38,981
Supplies and other	11,433	13,055	14,649	16,700	18,656	20,869
Depreciation — Phase VII	253	1,041	1,791	1,791	1,791	1,791
Depreciation	1,737	1,847	1,966	2,095	2,235	2,385
Interest — Phase VII	293	1,345	3,064	3,019	2,858	2,802
Interest	211	516	679	523	573	541
Less: Physician component	(1,076)	(1,233)	(1,405)	(1,593)	(1,798)	(2,020)
Other operating revenues	(682)	(750)	(825)	(908)	(998)	(1,098)
	33,628	40,371	47,888	53,219	58,350	64,251
Deductions from revenue	3,848	3,278	4,111	4,893	5,704	6,723
Excess of op. rev. over exp.	$ 2,540	$ 1,416	$ 2,019	$ 2,531	$ 3,175	$ 3,802
Per adjusted patient day:						
Salaries and benefits	$237.39	$253.75	$273.76	$300.76	$324.42	$348.10
Supplies and other	126.48	134.94	143.38	158.99	172.76	186.36
Depreciation — Phase VII	2.80	10.76	17.53	17.05	16.59	15.99
Depreciation	19.22	19.09	19.24	19.94	20.70	21.30
Interest — Phase VII	3.24	13.90	29.99	28.74	26.47	25.02
Interest	2.33	5.33	6.65	4.98	5.31	4.83
Less: Physician component	(11.91)	(12.74)	(13.75)	(15.17)	(16.65)	(18.04)
Other operating revenues	(7.54)	(7.75)	(8.08)	(8.64)	(9.24)	(9.81)
Expense per day	$372.01	$417.28	$468.73	$506.65	$540.34	$573.77
Deductions from revenue	42.57	33.88	40.24	46.58	52.82	60.04
PCSC	28.10	14.64	19.76	24.10	29.40	33.95
Rate-setting revenues	$442.68	$465.80	$528.73	$577.33	$622.56	$667.76
FTE's	984.4	1,030.4	1,072.5	1,114.0	1,140.4	1,174.9

Table 25.8

COST COMPARISON OF THE TWO EXPANSION ALTERNATIVES

Alternative 1—Development of NHC	
Incremental construction and equipment costs	$ 20,633,000
Present (1983) value of incremental operating costs (including interest)	33,871,000
Incremental costs (1983–88) of Alternative 1	$ 54,504,000
Alternative 2—Expansion of IMC	
Incremental construction and equipment costs	$ 34,439,000
Present (1983) value of total operating costs	180,617,000
Less: baseline costs, without Phase VII	(163,031,000)
Incremental non-capital operating costs of Phase VII (including interest)	17,586,000
Incremental costs (1983–88) of Alternative 2	$ 52,025,000

Table 25.9

ALLOWABLE COMMUNITY-WIDE REVENUES AND AVERAGE RATES
1983–1988, GIVEN NHC APPROVAL

	1983	1984	1985	1986	1987	1988
NHC total rate-setting revenue (A-7, L4)	8,203,391	8,585,642	9,164,207	9,464,014	10,008,527	10,276,491
IMC total rate-setting revenue (A-8, L13)	29,318,678	29,221,923	30,125,824	31,777,632	33,046,736	34,396,294
Total rate-setting revenue, community (L1 + L2)	37,522,069	37,807,565	39,290,031	41,241,646	43,055,263	44,672,785
Total community adjusted patient days, DSHS (A-2, L9)	92,198	96,145	98,556	104,270	109,529	112,880
Average rate for community per adjusted patient day (L3/L4)	406.97	393.23	398.66	395.53	393.09	395.75

Table 25.10

ALLOWABLE REVENUES AND AVERAGE RATES
1982–1988, GIVEN IMC APPROVAL

	1982	1983	1984	1985	1986	1987	1988
Revised operating expense (A-2, L12)	26,726,817	28,272,166	31,199,551	34,406,383	35,599,537	36,422,256	37,484,062
Add planned capital and service component	2,247,000	2,540,000	1,416,000	2,019,000	2,531,000	3,175,000	3,802,000
Add deductions (charity and bad debts @ 1981 level)	3,328,000	3,736,000	3,005,000	3,656,000	4,297,000	4,967,000	5,827,000
Total estimated rate-setting revenue	32,301,817	34,548,166	35,620,551	40,081,383	42,427,537	44,564,256	47,113,062
Estimated average rate/adjusted patient days (L4/A-2, L9)	366.03	374.72	370.49	406.69	406.90	406.87	417.37

Implementing Hospital Acquisition and Diversification Strategies

Joseph S. Coyne

INTRODUCTION

Today, many nonprofit hospitals face a situation involving reduced inpatient census, tighter reimbursement regulations, need for capital renovation and replacement, and desire to consolidate and coordinate services. Many, such as HealthWest Foundation of Los Angeles, have pursued a strategy of acquisitions and diversification. In one community, River City, this strategy was pursued by Memorial Hospital, which is located across the street from River City Public Hospital. The management teams from the two hospitals have spent almost two decades attempting to alleviate some common financial problems through a merger. Because River City's economy has suffered severely as the result of a general decline in the city's largest industry, farm implement manufacturing, the managers of the two hospitals have realized that they must consolidate and create a financially sound medical center serving the Delta Valley region.

This case describes the steps involved in a comprehensive financial analysis of potential hospital acquisition and diversification alternatives. The midwestern community of River City depicts not only common hospital consolidation issues but also current economic conditions facing many medium-sized communities. The case focuses on these issues and identifies methods for analyzing mergers and acquisitions. Future trends in the hospital industry are discussed in terms of diversification alternatives and how these can be analyzed.

The River City Setting

River City is located in the heart of the Delta Valley region along the Delta River, close to major interstate thoroughfares. It is about a three-hour drive from the state capital and, in the other direction, from a major metropolitan area. The area consists of River City and Atwater on one side of the Delta River, and Bend and River View on the other side. The area's 1980 population was 375,000, which reflects an increase of more than 25 percent since 1970.

The River City and Atwater side of the river is rich in the culture and heritage of its earliest settlers, the American Indians, and also boasts large German and Swedish communities. The Bend and River View side of the river includes a large Irish-Catholic population with much interest in community growth and development.

Economy

The area is home to approximately 425 industrial firms, of which 35 percent are in the farm implement industry. The employment market encompasses a 30-mile radius, including more than 170,000 employable people.

Harsh economic conditions, brought about by the recession of the early 1980s, have caused a 13-percent unemployment rate. Major layoffs at all of the farm implement manufacturers and their suppliers have almost crippled the area. The once powerful and prosperous farm industry has been battered by these economic blows. The whole community, including hospitals, has felt the effects of the recession.

Size and Location of Hospitals

Seven hospitals operate in the area, four on one side of the river and three on the other side. The first four hospitals range in size from 150 to almost 400 beds, and are located within an eight-mile radius of each other. The other three hospitals range in size from 150 to almost 300 beds, and are located within a four-mile radius of each other.

The proportion of each hospital's patients that come from the hospital's local community varies significantly (Table 26.1). About 32 percent of the total patient census of Memorial and Public hospitals come from River City, while across the river 60 percent of the Bend hospitals' patients are from Bend. The likely reason for this variation is the availability of services; patients migrate outside their community when services are unavailable.

Hospital Ownership and Interests

The ownership and interests of the seven River City area hospitals differ markedly, as do the size and service ranges. On the River City side, the hospitals contrast sharply. Memorial Hospital is affiliated with a nationwide church and, as a church-sponsored body, its 15-member Board includes representatives from that church. The Memorial Hospital Board, under the direction of its chairman, Jack Fitzmorris, must seek approval from the church leadership for major capital expansion decisions. Conversely, River City Public Hospital is a city-owned hospital controlled by the city council. The Board traditionally has been small, about five members, and dominated by one prominent business executive, William Gable. The city has been proud of its hospital and is committed to maintaining it.

The management approach in the two hospitals is quite different. Memorial Hospital's Chief Executive Officer, Thomas Medley, is an affable and aggressive administrator who is interested in expanding and diversifying Memorial's service area, while River City Public's Chief Executive Officer, Michael Swenson, wants merely to maintain an adequate occupancy rate and protect the hospital's current market share.

The other hospitals on the River City side include the small, district-owned Sterling

Hospital and the large, nonprofit St. Francis Medical Center. The three hospitals on the other side of the river are also nonprofit, including two with religious affiliations (St. Mary's and Community) and one that is locally owned and operated (Doctors Hospital).

Financial and Utilization Characteristics

The local hospital inflation rates show some significant differences. Memorial Hospital has experienced increases in its inpatient revenue per day and expenses per adjusted day of 16 percent and 22 percent, respectively (Table 26.2). The area median has been 23 percent for inpatient revenue per day and 26 percent for expenses per adjusted day. All other hospitals have experienced higher inflation rates, with St. Mary's having realized the highest. The salary expenses per adjusted day and inpatient revenue per stay have displayed similar patterns across all area hospitals.

For Memorial Hospital and River City Public Hospital, patient admissions are roughly comparable, although Memorial has a higher number of patient days because of longer lengths of stay (Table 26.3). Memorial Hospital is shown to be larger in terms of revenue and expense statistics and balance sheet statistics (see financial statement for Memorial Hospital in Appendix 26.1 and for River City Public Hospital in Appendix 26.2). In addition, the occupancy rate is higher at Memorial because of a longer average length of stay, which in turn is due to a higher percentage of discharges over age 65. The personnel statistics help explain the differences in the financial statistics — Memorial has a lower staffing ratio to permit it to incur fewer expenses and to charge less per patient day (Table 26.4).

Based on the 1980 audited financial statements (Appendixes 26.1 and 26.2) from both River City hospitals, further differences are identified (see Table 26.5). Liquidity, activity, and composition are fairly comparable; however, capital structure and profitability are different. Memorial is significantly more leveraged, while River City Public is more profitable.

CHRONOLOGY OF EVENTS

The history of relations between Memorial and River City Public has been stormy. The two hospitals began discussing the possibility of merger or consolidation in 1966. Since then several major decisions have been made, but very little action has followed.

A 15-member Implementation Committee developed a ten-point policy statement in late 1970, which provided a plan for corporate membership, Board composition and terms, and subcommittee policies. The policy statement was helpful in bringing out the issues for discussion related to merger and acquisition between the two hospitals. However, it was not conducive to bringing about an actual merger or acquisition; Gable, chairman of Public Hospital, immediately presented a series of reservations that the Public Board had about the merging of the two hospitals. Ultimately, Memorial's Board voted for merger, while Public's Board voted three to two against merger.

From 1973 to 1974, there were many news releases that discussed the advantages and disadvantages of merger. In short, the community interest was increasing and merger and acquisition were viewed as a critical public issue.

After a lull in negotiations, discussion began again in 1978, when it was decided to build a bridge between Memorial and Public hospitals. In addition, it was decided that River City

Public would provide obstetric services for the two facilities, while Memorial would provide medical pediatric care. This trade agreement represented a big step toward consolidation.

In 1982, River City Public proposed a $15-million expansion, which was countered by an acquisition offer from Memorial Hospital to purchase River City Public. Following these proposals, a Hospital Services Coordinating Committee was formed by the River City council to examine the alternatives. This culminated in a decision to merge the facilities, but the specific steps toward merger were not agreed upon. At this point, because of the economic recession, the River City Public Hospital laid off 150 of its 800 employees. The chairman of Public's Board, Gable, indicated he was more willing than ever to discuss consolidation terms. Meanwhile, under the administrator, Medley, Memorial continued its efforts to diversify and expand.

THE KEY ISSUES

Several key issues pertain to the attempted merger/acquisition in River City. These issues identify the major areas of debate throughout the case. In considering these issues, a better understanding of the motives of the different parties can be achieved.

Issue 1: Duplication of Inpatient Services and Need for Consolidation of Inpatient Services

Both Memorial Hospital and River City Public Hospital have long recognized the need to consolidate services. The medical staffs, management, and trustees of both hospitals have all agreed (although not always at the same time) that a merger of the assets and revenues would be desirable. As with most mergers, the process is long and cyclical, with resolutions passed but later rejected.

A step was finally taken to reduce duplicate services: construction of a bridge linking the two neighboring hospitals and agreement on a service trade. Memorial Hospital closed its obstetric services and became the designated medical pediatric care facility, while River City Public Hospital closed its medical pediatric services and became the designated obstetric service center. In addition, Memorial is designated as the cancer therapy center, while River City Public Hospital is identified as the CAT-scanning facility. Although such service trades help, they are far from an adequate solution to the overall problem of duplicating services. Indeed, even with the bridge and service trades completed (as of early 1981), 66 percent of all services offered are still duplicated in the two facilities (see Table 26.6). An analysis of the potential savings from consolidating the nursing education program, surgery suites, and emergency services of the two hospitals showed an estimated annual savings of $1.1 to $1.6 million (see Table 26.7). The financial feasibility study, discussed later, expands on the importance of such savings.

Issue 2: Declining Inpatient Census and Need to Create New Corporate Structures

As with many community hospitals, the River City hospitals' inpatient census has experienced a significant decline since the mid-1970s. Patient days have declined from almost 77,000 in

1975 for both hospitals to 66,000 in 1981 for Memorial and 54,000 in 1981 for River City Public (see Table 26.8 and Figure 26.1). Faced with this gloomy information, the Board and management of Memorial Hospital formed a task force to examine alternative corporate structures that would permit isolation of nonreimbursable activities and movement into new businesses. A consultant who had guided several other nonprofit hospitals through the restructuring process was commissioned by Memorial.

Figure 26.1

PATIENT DAY TRENDS

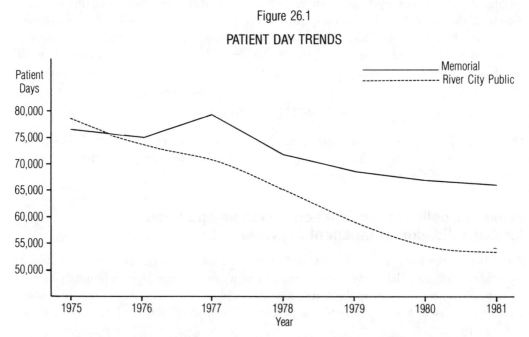

As a first step, the consultant worked with the task force to develop a strategic plan. A long-range goal and several operating objectives were adopted by the Board and management (Appendix 26.3). Comprehensive health care delivery was emphasized through development of a diverse health care network with other hospitals. Establishing a hospice program and creating a foundation for fund raising were also identified as initial steps.

Several alternative structures were considered (Table 26.9 and Figure 26.2). The first alternative, affiliation, was successfully pursued in 1980 and resulted in the services trade agreement between Memorial and Public. The second alternative, contracting, was considered less desirable since asset accumulation and financial security would not be realized. The third alternative, consolidation, was unsuccessfully pursued but still remains an alternative worthy of consideration. The fourth alternative was to create a parent corporation that would provide the organizational base for a highly diversified health care service network. A formal structure proposed by the consultant (Figure 26.3) allows for subsidiaries including the two hospitals, a medical office building, and a fund-raising foundation.

Issue 3: Assessing Potential Acquisitions

On the basis of the financial data discussed earlier, the consultant recommended the acquisition alternative in addition to continuing to pursue the third alternative, consolidation. After nu-

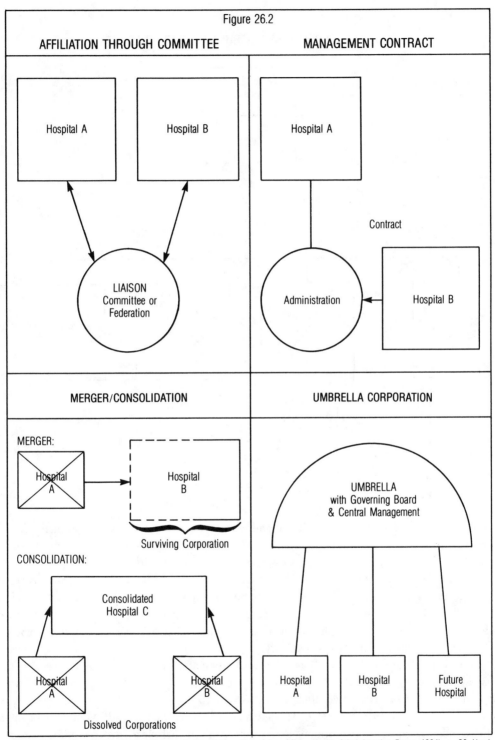

Figure 26.2

AFFILIATION THROUGH COMMITTEE

MANAGEMENT CONTRACT

Hospital A

Hospital B

LIAISON
Committee or
Federation

Hospital A

Contract

Administration

Hospital B

MERGER/CONSOLIDATION

UMBRELLA CORPORATION

MERGER:

Hospital
A

Hospital
B

Surviving Corporation

CONSOLIDATION:

Consolidated
Hospital C

Hospital
A

Hospital
B

Dissolved Corporations

UMBRELLA
with Governing Board
& Central Management

Hospital
A

Hospital
B

Future
Hospital

Source: Starkweather, David, *Hospital Mergers in the Making* (Ann Arbor, Mich.: Health Administration Press, 1981), p. 39. Used by permission; revised slightly for use in this Case.

Figure 26.3

A PROPOSED CORPORATE STRUCTURE FOR RIVER CITY

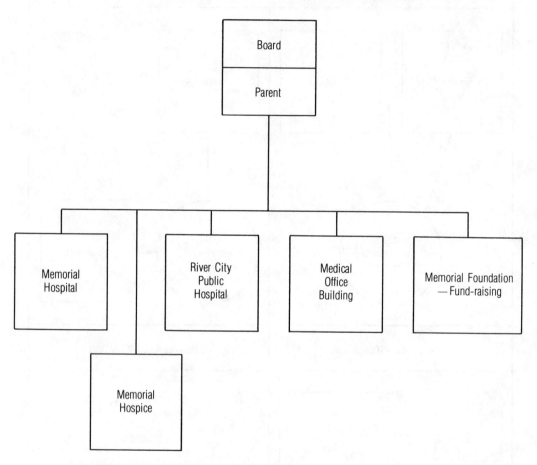

merous discussions with Memorial's Board and management, nearly a dozen reasons for Memorial to acquire River City Public were identified (Appendix 26.4).

The consultant then outlined the steps for assessing River City Public Hospital (Appendix 26.5), a necessary process before a firm purchase offer could be made. The purchase offer would be the end product of the assessment (Step II in the process outlined). The various phases of the assessment—including market, geography, operations, organization/structure, and architecture—lead toward the financial assessment. To determine the purchase price, a comprehensive financial analysis is necessary.

As a critical step in the overall assessment of a potential acquisition, a debt capacity study must be conducted. Appendix 26.6 identifies the assumptions used in the analysis, while Appendix 26.7 summarizes two alternatives used in the analysis. The financial results are shown in Appendixes 26.8 and 26.9. Appendix 26.10 shows the results if Memorial Hospital remains independent. The assumptions used in this analysis include a 12-percent, 30-year, tax-exempt bond issue to finance the acquisition. The rate increases are assumed to be 13 percent in the first year, with 68,500 patient days for Memorial and 115,000 for Memorial and River

City Public combined. Each of the alternatives includes a normal rate increase of about 13 percent and a special rate increase of about 14 percent. Hospital equity contribution equals $4 million, and all existing debt would be retired.

The first alternative provides an analysis when the anticipated borrowings are at either $16 million or $17 million (see Appendix 26.8). The two income statements show a net profit of about $1 million. The second alternative shows pro forma statements for anticipated borrowings of $20 million and $21 million (see Appendix 26.9). The income statements show a $700,000 net profit without a special price increase and a $1.4 million net profit with a special price increase.

AN UPDATE

At a city council meeting to discuss Memorial's proposal to purchase River City Public, Public also proposed to expand their obstetric services and emergency room. Through the long and powerful arm of Public's mentor, William Gable, the council voted against the acquisition while voting for Public's expansion. A Hospital Services Coordinating Committee was formed to explore all alternatives. The committee is made up of city government representatives, local business leaders, and hospital management. The major resolution is clear: consolidation of assets would be fine but not through an acquisition. The committee ultimately endorsed this option in its recommendation to the city council. The council, responding to the city's economic crisis, has now decided to rescind its earlier support for Public's expansion.

Interestingly, Gable has now suggested merger as a worthwile option just as Public was forced to layoff 150 of its 800 total employees because of low inpatient census resulting, in turn, from adverse economic conditions. Certainly, Public Hospital's problems have become apparent to everyone, and merger or consolidation appears desirable, even though still unattainable.

FINANCIAL ANALYSIS QUESTIONS

1. Analysis of Operating and Financial Data
   — What is the effect on recorded assets, liabilities, and income and expenses of differing accounting policies and practices?
   — What is the basis of recording operating statistical data at Memorial and River City Public hospitals? Are they consistent?
   — What levels of productivity are being achieved? Can these be improved?

2. Reimbursement
   — Is purchase price, fair market value, or some other basis to be used for depreciation?
   — What is the status of previously submitted reports for Medicare, Medicaid, and Blue Cross? Would any liability regarding acquisition be incurred?
   — Can any statistical bases be changed to maximize reimbursement for a combined institution?

3. Alternative Sources of Debt
   — What are the hospitals' alternative sources of debt financing?
   — What are the advantages and disadvantages of each source?
   — What are the implications of each of the debt source provisions on further debt financing?
   — Should nontraditional sources of financing be considered?

4. Acquisition Debt Capacity and Duration
   —How much can Memorial borrow and for how long?
   —What terms should be included in the debt instrument?
   —What is a fair interest rate?
   —Can Memorial's operations repay acquisition debt alone?
   —What contribution will each hospital have to make to debt retirement?
   —Should Memorial borrow more than acquisition debt to accomplish other objectives if capacity is available?
   —How should principal repayment be structured?
   —What terms should be included (i.e. working capital requirements, mortgages, additional borrowing provisions, prepayment penalties, etc.)?

5. Assessment of Future Capital Capacity
   —Given current operating characteristics and alternatives based upon economics, what is the maximum level of debt that:
     —Memorial could handle alone?
     —the combined institution could handle?
   —Using current lender ratios and requirements, as well as market conditions, how would maximum computed debt capacity be viewed by lenders?
   —Using estimates of current and projected construction costs for a 10-year period and the hospital's estimated debt capacity, what money would be available for capital replacement or addition to facilities?
   —What effect does the acquisition have on long-range borrowing capacity?

6. Capital Needs
   —Are there other capital requirements beyond the acquisition cost associated with this acquisition? What are the items and estimated amounts?
   —How can these additional capital requirements be financed? What are the alternatives? Pros and cons?
   —Does Memorial have the capital to finance these requirements internally?
   —Can any of these additional capital requirements be deferred? What is the impact?

Additional data that could be considered is shown in Alternative III (Appendix 27.10). This assumes that Memorial remains a freestanding facility. The assumptions for this alternative are the following:

1. Memorial's total patient days equal 68,500

2. Sources and uses under A
   a. Borrow $12.5 million
   b. Funds available = $5.8 million

3. Sources and uses under B
   a. Borrow $13.5 million
   b. Funds available = $6.6 million

In addition, data may be projected for several time periods, using a predetermined annual rate of increase in revenues and expenses. Also, only alternative I may be considered for analysis instead of both alternatives I and II.

GENERAL DISCUSSION QUESTIONS*

1. Implications of the acquisition on Memorial Hospital's existing mission, goals, and image
   — What are the hospital's objectives in the acquisition vis-à-vis its current mission and goals?
   — Will the resultant mission and goals conflict with the hospital/church role?
   — What are the community/political implications and considerations in the merger?

2. Review of areawide situation to assess implications of merger
   — What are the short- and long-range program/service implications — as separate institutions? as consolidated institutions?
   — What are the patient referral patterns of each institution and how will they be affected by the acquisition?
   — What facilities will be needed for consolidated operations?
     — Short-range — with two physical plants?
     — Long-range — with one physical plant?

3. Facilities planning considerations and evaluation of physical plant deficiencies on proposed operation
   — Are there outstanding deficiencies in physical plant and operations as determined by regulatory/accrediting agencies?
   — What is the functional capability of the two facilities to meet proposed operational objectives of the acquisition?
   — What are the health planning implications of the acquisition at the regional and state level?

4. Evaluation of major governance, managerial, and professional staff implications of the merger
   — What is the compatibility of the organizational structures/personnel with regard to roles, responsibilities, and reporting relationships?
   — Is the existing organizational structure appropriate for the resultant institutions?
   — What are other appropriate organizational alternatives for the resultant institution?

5. Legal implications/considerations of the acquisition
   — Bond covenants?
   — City ordinances?

6. Impact on medical staff organization and bylaws
   — What differences exist between the medical staff bylaws and policies of the hospitals? What are the legal considerations and implications of these?
     — Privileges?
     — Consultations?
     — Department specialties?
     — Organizational structure, committee, etc.?
   — Are there any problems regarding general practitioner versus specialist that will result from the consolidation of the medical staff?

---

*The author wishes to acknowledge the consulting firm of Ernst and Whinney for its contribution to these questions.

— Are there any differences in medical practice between the physicians primarily associated with either hospital which will present problems in the consolidation of the medical staff?
  — Utilization of diagnostic procedures?
  — Admission practices?
  — Professional referral patterns?

7. Evaluation of salary, benefits, and personnel policies
   — Is a salary and wage administration program in effect at both hospitals?
   — What would the financial impact be of adjusting all personnel to the highest wage of either hospital?
   — Are fringe benefits comparable?
   — What would it cost to have uniform fringe benefits?
   — What are the differences in personnel policies and what is needed to make them uniform? What is the financial impact?

8. Identification of staffing characteristics and potential problems/savings
   — What are the staffing patterns for each of the departments at each hospital?
   — How do the staffing patterns and ratios compare?
   — What are the functional relationships within and between operating departments at each hospital?
   — What functions and/or departments could be consolidated at one hospital? With what potential savings or improvements in service?

9. Identification of areas for potential improved economic benefit
   — Which departments and/or services should be physically combined or consolidated at either location? What are the expected economic benefits?
   — Are there any services or departments that should be discontinued? What are the potential savings?
   — Are there any contractual relationships that can be improved or discontinued? What are the potential savings?
   — Can prices be increased to make them uniform? Will this result in improved revenue flow?
   — Are billings and collections procedures and policies compatible? If not, what is the financial impact of uniformity?
   — Can insurance coverage premiums be affected favorably or unfavorably?

10. Contractual relationships
    — What are the contractual relationships that exist at the hospitals with hospital-based physicians?
    — How do the contractual relationships for hospital-based physicians differ between the two hospitals?
    — How will the differences be handled in an acquisition?
    — Are there other contractual relationships that exist for such services as:
      — Housekeeping?
      — Dietary?
      — Other ancillary or supportive services?
    — What leases exist?

Table 26.1

PATIENT ORIGIN DATA

Hospital	Community	Percentage
1. Memorial	River City	32.8
2. River City	River City	31.5
3. Sterling District	Sterling	14.2
4. St. Francis	Atwater	48.1
5. St. Mary's	Bend	62.5
6. Community	Bend	54.4
7. Doctors	Bend	59.1

Note: Availability of services offered is the primary reason for
patients migrating to hospitals outside their community.

Table 26.2

LOCAL HOSPITAL INFLATION RATES
1981 and 1982

Measures Used	Memorial Hospital	River City Public	St. Francis	Sterling District	St. Mary's	Doctors	Community	Area Median
Inpatient revenue per day	16%	26%	19%	NA	34%	NA	27%	23%
Expense per adjusted day	22%	26%	24%	NA	51%	NA	43%	26%
Salary expense per adjusted day	24%	30%	28%	NA	35%	NA	32%	31%
Inpatient revenue per stay	15%	18%	18%	NA	25%	NA	30%	22%

Source: "Three Month Data for Periods Ending January 1981 and January 1982", *Monitrend Reports* (Chicago: AHA).

Table 26.3

GENERAL COMPARISON OF MEMORIAL HOSPITAL
AND RIVER CITY PUBLIC HOSPITAL

Patient Statistics[1]	Memorial Hospital	River City Public
— Average number of beds in service	295	275
— Admissions	8,753	9,049
— Patient days	66,955	54,650
Revenue and Expense Statistics[2]		
— Total operating revenue	$18,383,587	$16,149,445
— Total operating expenses	$18,167,443	$15,486,725
— Net operating income	$ 216,144	$ 662,720
— Net income (excess of total revenue over total expenses)	$ 679,649	$ 608,213
Balance Sheet Statistics[2]		
— Current assets	$ 5,189,845	$ 4,256,137
— Net fixed assets	$15,057,253	$ 9,475,568
— Current liabilities	$ 2,255,924	$ 1,381,601
— Long-term debt	$11,463,603	$ 850,000
— Equity (fund balance)	$11,560,135	$11,373,256

1. Patient statistics are from the local Health Systems Agency, Aggregate Hospital Utilization Annual Report, 1980.

2. Financial statistics are from the 1980 audited financial reports from each hospital.

Table 26.4

COMPARATIVE STATISTICS
From Monitrend

STATISTIC	State[1] Norm	Memorial[2] Hospital (MH)	River City[2] Public (RCP)	Percent by Which MH Data Is Greater (+) or Less (−) Than RCP
Utilization				
— Occupancy percent	65.59	76.9	57.45	+34
— Average length of stay	7.21	7.35	5.74	+28
— Percentage of discharges over age 65	28.43	30.85	23.90	+29
— Discharges per bed per month	2.79	3.21	3.07	+5
— Emergency-room clinic visits/day	54.52	70.66	39.26	+80
Personnel				
— FTE/adjusted occupied bed	3.56	3.38	4.41	−23
— Paid medical-surgical nursing hours/ patient day	7.12	6.91	6.37	+11
— Overall average hourly salary	7.69	8.16	8.17	0
— Nursing units average hourly salary	7.78	8.27	9.36	−12
Financial				
— Revenue/patient day	378.73	312.20	393.17	−21
— Expense/adjusted patient day	309.83	305.74	379.83	−20
— Salary expense/adjusted patient day	155.62	155.62	203.35	−24
— Days net revenue in accounts receivable	51.01	63.22	56.94	+11

Source: *Monitrend Report* (Chicago: AHA, 1981).

1. The state norm is an average for all 200 to 299 bed hospitals for the three months ended December 31, 1981.

2. The MH and RCP statistics are an average for the three months ended December 31, 1981.

Table 26.5

SELECTED RATIO CALCULATIONS FOR MEMORIAL
AND RIVER CITY PUBLIC

RATIO	Median Value	Memorial	River City Public
Liquidity			
1. CA/CL	1.8	2.3	3.1
2. C + MS/CL	.2	.4	.4
3. CL/FB	.4	.2	.12
4. NAR × 365/NOR	60	69.7	73.8
Activity			
5. NOR/CA	3.6	3.5	3.8
6. NOR/I	52	39.4	44.5
7. NOR/NFA	1.3	1.2	1.7
8. NOR/TA	1	.8	1.2
Composition			
9. NFA/TA	.6	.7	.7
10. CA/TA	.2	.2	.3
Capital Structure			
11. TA/FB	1.9	1.9	1.2
12. LTD/FB	.53	.99	.07
13. LTD/NFA	.53	.8	.09
14. NI + DE/CL + LTD	.19	.12	.6
15. AD/FB	.6	.6	.6
Profitability			
16. NOI/TA	.03	.01	.05
17. NOI/FB	.06	.02	.06
18. NI/NOR	.03	.04	.04
19. NOI/NOR	.02	.01	.04

Source: Financial statements of two hospitals and median values from Financial Analysis Service,
Ohio State University, 1980.

Table 26.6

MEMORIAL AND RIVER CITY HOSPITAL SERVICES

Service	Memorial Hospital	River City Public	Duplication
1. Postoperative recovery room	X	X	X
2. Intensive-care unit (cardiac care only)		X	
3. Intensive-care unit (mixed or other)	X	X	X
4. Open-heart surgery facilities			
5. Pharmacy with FT-registered pharmacist	X	X	X
6. Pharmacy with PT-registered pharmacist			
7. X-ray radiation therapy	X		
8. Megavoltage radiation therapy	X		
9. Radioactive implants	X	X	X
10. Diagnostic radioisotope facility	X	X	X
11. Therapeutic radioisotope facility	X	X	X
12. Histopathology laboratory	X	X	X
13. Organ bank			
14. Blood bank			
15. Electroencephalography	X	X	X
16. Respiratory therapy services	X	X	X
17. Premature nursery		X	
18. Self-care unit			
19. Skilled nursing or other long-term-care unit			
20. Hemodialysis (inpatient)		X	
21. Hemodialysis (outpatient)			
22. Burn-care unit			
23. Physical therapy services	X	X	X
24. Occupational therapy services	X	X	X
25. Rehabilitation inpatient unit			
26. Rehabilitation outpatient services			
27. Psychiatric inpatient unit			
28. Psychiatric outpatient services			
29. Psychiatric partial hospitalization program			
30. Psychiatric emergency services			
31. Psychiatric foster and/or home care program			
32. Psychiatric consultation and education services			
33. Clinical psychology services			
34. Organized outpatient department		X	
35. Emergency department	X	X	X
36. Social work services	X	X	X
37. Family-planning service			
38. Genetic counseling service			
39. Abortion service (inpatient)			
40. Abortion service (outpatient)			
41. Home care program			
42. Dental services	X	X	X
43. Podiatric services			
44. Speech pathology services	X	X	X
45. Hospital auxiliary	X	X	X
46. Volunteer services department	X		
47. Patient representative services	X	X	X
48. Alcoholism/chemical dependency inpatient unit			
49. Alcoholism/chemical dependency outpatient services			
50. TB and other respiratory diseases unit	X		
51. Neonatal intensive-care unit			
52. Pediatric inpatient unit	X	X	X
53. CT scanner		X	

Source: *Guide to the Health Care Field* (Chicago: AHA, 1981).

Note: Of a total of 27 services offered, 18 (66%) are duplicated services.

Table 26.7

POTENTIAL ANNUAL SAVINGS* FROM CONSOLIDATING SERVICES

Consolidated Program	Annual Savings
—Nursing residence and education program: One nursing program in River City will sufficiently supply the need for registered nurses in the community, reducing from four to three the number of programs in the River City area.	$500,000— $700,000
—Surgery salary savings: Reduce one operating room suite at one of River City's hospitals to serve combined patient volume.	$400,000— $600,000
—Emergency room medical doctor salary savings: Contract for one less emergency room medical doctor.	$200,000— $300,000
Total savings	$1,100,000— $1,600,000

*Based on *Monitrend Cost Reports* and Memorial Hospital Financial Report.

Table 26.8

CENSUS DATA:
Patient Days

Year	Memorial Hospital	River City Public Hospital
1975	76,071	77,858
1976	74,675	73,595
1977	79,606	70,941
1978	71,202	58,869
1979	68,243	54,769
1980	66,955	54,650
1981	66,244	54,684

Source: Local HSA, *Aggregate Hospital Utilization Annual Reports*, 1975–1981.

Table 26.9

FOUR ALTERNATIVE METHODS OF JOINING THE TWO HOSPITALS

	Affiliations	Management Contracts	Merger/ Consolidation	Acquisition/Parent Corporation
Definition	Combinations among institutions designed for specific and limited undertaking, such as to share or trade-off services	Agreements wherein a management company is retained for several years to manage a facility in part or in total	Combination of previously separated entities in which at least one organization is dissolved and absorbed by another or by a new corporation	New corporation is formed that spans but does not replace the prior entities with full authority (parent-sub)
Example	Carolinas Hosp. and Health Services (Shared Services Organization)	Hyatt Medical contract to manage Cook County	Rush-Presbyterian St. Lukes	Lutheran General Hospital
Legal Bonds	Formal agreements with escape clauses	Contract typically for several years	Replacement agreements abolish prior entities	Assets are transferred with prior corporate entities intact
Geography	Dispersed or local	Same or separate communities	Often a common geographic location	Sometime serve same population and often regionally organized
Services Combined	Support, logistic	Administrative, broadly defined	Administrative, professional, direct patient care services	Administrative, professional
Benefits	Coordination of planning for and development of services in an area and sharing costs	Efficiency improvements in administration of hospitals involved	Duplication of services reduced or eliminated	Services developed at a medical center base for an entire region with ability to add facilities that retain identity
Costs	Time of administrative staffs consumed in planning and coordinating services	Management fees to the managed hospital and sometime difficult relations between parties	Lack of separate community identity and sacrifice of independence	Legal costs of corporation formulation and administrative staff time in creating new structure

Adapted from: Starkweather, D. "Health Facility Mergers: Some Conceptualizations," *Medical Care*, November-December 1971, p. 473.

Appendix 26.1

MEMORIAL HOSPITAL FINANCIAL STATEMENTS

BALANCE SHEETS
September 30, 1980 and 1979

ASSETS	1980	1979
Unrestricted Fund		
Current assets:		
Cash, including time deposits (1980, $145,838; 1979, $238,853)	$ 788,076	$ 243,246
Receivables:		
Patients, less allowance for doubtful accounts (1980, $470,000; 1979, $401,600)	3,508,506	4,201,822
Medicare and public aid	100,000	—
Other	54,036	68,048
Supplies and materials	466,557	405,583
Funds held by trustee and restricted by loan agreement, held for payment of current principal and interest	231,355	231,220
Other, primarily prepaid expenses	41,315	44,805
Total current assets	$ 5,189,845	$ 5,194,724
Board designated funds for improvements and replacements	$ 1,622,985	$ 1,048,168
Funds held by trustee and restricted by self-insurance agreement	$ 1,069,073	$ 730,324
Funds held by trustee and restricted by loan agreement	$ 2,110,195	$ 2,189,792
Property and equipment:		
Land and land improvements	$ 959,350	$ 928,436
Buildings	15,352,021	14,882,233
Furniture, fixtures, and equipment	5,792,284	5,666,314
Construction in progress	—	237,456
	$22,103,655	$21,714,439
Less accumulated depreciation	7,046,402	6,168,120
	$15,057,253	$15,546,319
Other assets:		
Bond issuance expenses	$ 424,111	$ 439,975
Contracts receivable	43,500	47,500
	$ 467,611	$ 487,475
	$25,516,962	$25,196,802

LIABILITIES AND FUND BALANCES	1980	1979
Unrestricted Fund		
Current liabilities:		
Current maturities of long-term debt	$ 196,165	$ 190,642
Accounts payable, trade	535,720	505,767
Medicare, Blue Cross, and public aid	135,000	420,000

Continued

BALANCE SHEETS Continued

Accrued salaries, wages, and payroll taxes	542,887	420,368
Accrued earned time	569,880	480,240
Accrued interest payable	185,472	186,940
Unearned tuition	90,800	97,897
Construction contracts payable	—	156,184
Total current liabilities	$ 2,255,924	$2,458,038
Long-term debt	$11,463,603	$11,660,778
Deferred third-party reimbursement, net	$ 237,300	$ 197,500
Fund balance	$11,560,135	$10,880,486
Commitments and Contingencies		
	$25,516,962	$25,196,802

STATEMENT OF REVENUE AND EXPENSES
UNRESTRICTED FUND
Years Ended September 30, 1980 and 1979

	1980	1979
Patient service revenue	$18,947,822	$17,168,147
Less discounts, allowances, and contractual adjustments	1,199,115	1,633,766
Net revenue from services to patients	$17,748,707	$15,534,381
Other operating revenue	634,880	753,518
	$18,383,587	$16,287,899
Operating expenses:		
Salaries and wages	$ 8,698,884	$7,642,177
Supplies and other expenses	7,762,370	6,709,928
Depreciation	944,311	901,754
Interest	761,878	769,350
	$18,167,443	$16,023,209
Operating income	$ 216,144	$ 264,690
Nonoperating income:		
Investment income, dividends, and interest	$ 437,061	$ 396,324
Unrestricted contributions	26,444	62,156
	$ 463,505	$ 458,480
Revenue over expenses	$ 679,649	$ 723,170

Appendix 26.2

RIVER CITY PUBLIC HOSPITAL FINANCIAL STATEMENTS

BALANCE SHEETS
March 31, 1980 and 1979

UNRESTRICTED FUNDS

ASSETS	1980	1979
Current:		
Cash	$ 96,256	$ 272,306
Investments, at cost (market $456,583)	468,070	—
Receivables, less estimated uncollectibles and allowances of $502,431 and $541,688	3,262,844	2,906,792
Inventories	362,879	392,861
Prepaid expenses	66,088	88,734
Total Current Assets	4,256,137	3,660,693
Property, plant, and equipment	16,801,940	16,325,909
Less accumulated depreciation	7,326,372	6,600,658
Net property, plant, and equipment	9,475,568	9,725,251
	$13,731,705	$13,385,944

LIABILITIES AND FUND BALANCES	1980	1979
Current:		
Current installments of long-term debt	$ 275,000	$ 275,000
Accounts payable	334,398	294,429
Accrued expenses	522,986	439,311
Contracts payable	197,994	409,361
Deposits	6,965	6,331
Due to restricted funds:	45,268	74,966
Total current liabilities	1,381,601	1,499,398
Deferred revenue — third party reimbursement	126,848	235,493
Long-term debt — revenue bonds	850,000	1,125,600
Fund balance	11,373,256	10,525,453
	$13,731,705	$13,385,944

STATEMENT OF REVENUE AND EXPENSES
Years Ended March 31, 1980 and 1979

	1980	1979
Patient service revenue	$16,515,506	$14,756,134
Allowances and uncollectible accounts: net of retroactive adjustments of $108,504 and $389,593	838,459	110,191
Net patient service revenue	15,677,047	14,645,943
Other operating revenue (including $58,479 and $3,619 from restricted funds)	472,398	409,601
Total operating revenue	16,149,445	15,055,544
Operating expenses:		
Nursing services	5,389,329	5,144,812
School of nursing	415,922	369,293
Ancillary services	3,458,313	3,260,021
Medical records and library	232,251	264,721
Dietary	1,151,888	1,151,106
Maintenance	933,311	840,400
Housekeeping and linen	483,104	436,953
Laundry	190,169	196,521
Administration	3,232,438	3,039,056
Total operating expenses	15,486,725	14,702,883
Income from operations	662,720	352,661
Nonoperating expense (income)		
Interest expense	72,577	87,818
Interest income	(18,070)	—
Total nonoperating expense	54,507	87,818
Excess of revenue over expenses	$ 608,213	$ 264,843

STATEMENT OF CHANGES IN FUND BALANCE
Years Ended March 31, 1980 and 1979

	1980	1979
Unrestricted Funds		
Balance at beginning of year	$10,525,953	$10,356,969
Excess of revenue over expenses	608,213	264,843
Prior periods capitalized interest written off to comply with Medicare guidelines	—	(149,322)
Transferred from restricted gifts, bequests, and grant funds	239,090	53,463
Balance at end of year	$11,373,256	$10,525,953

Appendix 26.3

SUMMARY OF MEMORIAL HOSPITAL BOARD OF DIRECTORS AND ADMINISTRATION POSITION STATEMENT

The Board and management of Memorial Hospital have adopted the following long-range goal:

> To develop a comprehensive health care delivery system for the River City area and Delta Valley region through patient services in acute, ambulatory, and long-term care.

In pursuing this long-range goal, the Board and management will seek to achieve the following operation objectives:

— To create a comprehensive network with other healthcare facilities in the Delta Valley region that permits patient referrals and new physician relationships

— To develop a diverse healthcare system throughout the region providing outpatient services in the smaller communities of the area

— To enhance basic acute-care services, such as pediatrics and intensive care, through the use of new medical technology

— To increase medical staff recruitment and enhance these staff relations through improving medical staff facilities

— To establish a hospice program as well as other forms of intermediate and sub-acute care

— To create a foundation for fund-raising and development purposes to minimize reimbursement problems

Appendix 26.4

REASONS WHY MEMORIAL HOSPITAL SHOULD PURCHASE RIVER CITY PUBLIC

From an Operational Perspective

1. Memorial Hospital has maintained a greater and more stable service delivery volume over the past six years as measured by patient census trends, occupancy percents.

2. Memorial Hospital has maintained a greater asset and revenue base and therefore greater financial strength.

3. Memorial Hospital has charged patients 21 percent less per patient day.

4. Memorial Hospital incurred 20 percent lower overall costs per adjusted patient day, and incurred 24 percent lower salary expenses per adjusted patient day.

5. Memorial Hospital has utilized 23 percent less staff to service patients.

From a Capital Perspective

6. Memorial Hospital has successfully managed two major capital expansion projects in the past decade, and therefore is well experienced at this process.

7. Memorial Hospital has obtained its own credit rating from a public rating agency and is neither dependent on city government for its creditworthiness nor dependent on a potential tax liability upon the community.

8. Memorial Hospital has achieved higher than necessary levels of coverage for its principal and interest payments during the past decade.

9. Memorial Hospital is a not-for-profit community hospital that is free from the long-range difficulties of operating as a city-owned or public hospital.

From the Reverse Perspective

10. If River City were to purchase Memorial Hospital, River City's funds would have to be divested out of city activities and into the church.

11. If River City were to purchase Memorial Hospital, Memorial Hospital's 1977, 6 percent bonds would have to be retired and reissued at almost double the interest rates.

Appendix 26.5

STUDY PLAN OF MEMORIAL HOSPITAL FOR ASSESSING RIVER CITY PUBLIC

May 13, 1982

I. DEVELOP FORMAL PLAN FOR ASSESSING RIVER CITY PUBLIC

    A. Identify specific products and time table

    B. Identify roles and responsibilities of all participants

    C. Identify and request specific documents and information needed from River City Public

    D. Establish cost estimate of study

    E. Establish benchmarks or criteria to be used in making decisions or determining purchase price

II. CONDUCT ASSESSMENT

A. Market and geographical
  1. Identify the future demographic characteristics
  2. Project volume levels for specific service areas
  3. Project future economic conditions for the River City area and their impact on hospital operations
  4. Collect patient destination and patient origin information, using the local Hospital Council study data when possible
  5. Identify new services to develop based on patient population data

B. Operational
  1. Identify departments for consolidation
  2. Identify functional implications of departmental consolidations
  3. Identify departments for elimination
  4. Identify departments for renovation or modernization
  5. Assess the cost savings from consolidation and elimination
  6. Identify salary/benefit structure
  7. Determine cost of establishing uniform salary/benefit structure

C. Organizational/Structural
  1. Identify reporting lines and structural hierarchy
  2. Identify board-administration relations
  3. Specify implications of consolidating operations on current structures: medical, staff, board, and management
  4. Develop legal and governance structures
  5. Develop interim organization and operating plans

D. Architectural
  1. Assess the design and layout of the physical plant
  2. Estimate cost of making necessary improvements to plant
  3. Identify the potential areas for conversion to alternate use
  4. Estimate cost of these potential conversions
  5. Identify areas for elimination after acquisition
  6. Summarize costs and savings of making architectural improvements and conversions
  7. Conduct legal due diligence activities to verify the assets

E. Financial
  1. Conduct financial analysis of all audited statements for past 5 years and project for next 5 years
  2. Analyze accounts receivable aging schedule and identify significant problems (potential or actual) or unique aspects of accounting techniques used
  3. Assess all contractual obligations and existing debt and determine how the acquisition would affect them

4. Assess the general condition of major fixed assets in terms of their:
   —Age
   —Expected life
   —Replacement cost
   —Possible elimination after acquisition
   —Projected volumes of service from continued operation
5. Identify necessary changes in financial operations to remedy problems and assess related costs of making changes
6. Make necessary adjustments to actual and projected financial statements
7. Establish a preliminary estimate of net worth less the necessary costs derived from the above analysis in financial and architectural analysis

III. ANALYZE AND REPORT ON ASSESSMENT
   A. Prepare formal report for presentation to City Council
   B. Provide further analysis as requested
   C. Prepare formal report to others as needed

Appendix 26.6

ASSUMPTIONS USED IN DEBT CAPACITY ANALYSIS

Related to Financing:
- Tax-exempt bond issue
- Hospital equity contribution of $4 million
- Underwriter's discount of 3 percent and additional issue espenses of $250,000
- Coupon rate on bonds of 12 percent
- Existing debt would be retired
- Issue life of 30 years
- Assets acquired to be depreciated over average life of 25 years

Related to Inflation:
- Rate increases of approximately 13 percent in 1981-82
- Inflation of approximately 12 percent in 1981-82

Related to Utilization:
- Patient days of 68,500 in 1982 for Memorial and 115,000 for Memorial and River City Public combined
- Outpatient visits of 28,000 in 1982 for Memorial and 29,000 for Memorial and River City Public combined

Appendix 26.7

TWO ALTERNATIVES USED IN THE ANALYSIS

I. BOTH FACILITIES COMBINED: *(115,000 patient days)*

    A. Sources and uses under A
        1. Borrow $16 million
        2. Funds available equal $10 million

    B. Sources and uses under B
        1. Borrow $17 million
        2. Funds available equal $9 million

    C. Special rate increase of 13 percent

II. BOTH FACILITIES COMBINED: *(115,000 patient days)*

    A. Sources and uses under A
        1. Borrow $20 million
        2. Funds available equal $13 million

    B. Sources and uses under B
        1. Borrow $21 million
        2. Funds available equal $13 million

    C. Rate increase of 16 percent

Appendix 26.8

ALTERNATIVE I

ANALYSIS OF ESTIMATED FINANCIAL AND OPERATIONAL CRITERIA
River City and Memorial Hospitals

	A	B
Utilization data:		
Patient days	115,000	115,000
Outpatient visits	29,000	29,000
Average daily census	315.07	315.07
Average number of beds in service	539.00	539.00
Occupancy	58.45%	58.45%
Cost-based expense (%)	50.00%	50.00%
Cost-based revenue (%)	50.00%	50.00%
Revenue requirements:		
Gross revenue per patient day	$344.49	$347.78
Percentage price increases:		
Normal annual	13.00%	13.00%
"Special" annual	(.41)%	.55%
Debt service percentage of gross revenue	5.06%	5.32%
Debt service coverage	2.00X	2.00X
Operating expense analyses:		
Operating expenses		
Per patient day	$294.49	$294.49
Employee benefits as a percentage of salaries	16.50%	16.50%
Capital cost analyses:		
Annual debt service	$2,003,903	$2,129,147
Debt service per patient day		
— Current	$.00	$.00
— Additional	$17.43	$18.51
— Total	$17.43	$18.51
Depreciation, interest, and		
amortization per patient day:		
— Current	$9.13	$9.13
— Additional	$19.96	$21.30
— Total	$29.09	$30.43

ESTIMATED SOURCES AND USES OF FUNDS
River City and Memorial Hospitals

	A	B
Sources of Funds:		
Anticipated borrowings	$16,000,000	$17,000,000
Funds to be provided at closing	4,000,000	4,000,000
Funds to be provided from operations	0	0
Interest to be earned on trustee-held funds	0	0
	$20,000,000	$21,000,000
Uses of Funds:		
Funds available for construction and related expenditures	$ 8,766,096	$ 9,610,848
Bond discount	480,000	510,000
Funds deposited in:		
Interest fund	0	0
Debt service reserve fund	2,003,903	2,129,147
Bond financing expenses	250,000	250,000
Debt retirement	8,500,000	8,500,000
	$19,999,999	$20,999,995

STATEMENT OF ESTIMATED REVENUES AND EXPENSES WITH SPECIAL PRICE CHANGE
River City and Memorial Hospitals

	A	B
Revenue from Services to Patients:		
Routine services	$19,212,864	$19,396,608
Ancillary services	17,504,480	17,671,934
Outpatient services	2,898,832	2,926,555
Gross patient service revenues	39,616,176	39,995,097
Deductions from Revenues:		
Contractual allowances	1,873,712	1,992,656
Uncollectible accounts and free service	990,405	999,877
Net patient service revenues	36,752,059	37,002,564
Other operating revenues	1,121,998	1,121,998
Total operating revenues	37,874,057	38,124,562
Operating Expenses:		
Salaries and wages	18,733,952	18,733,952
Employee benefits	3,091,100	3,091,100
Supplies and other expenses	11,201,221	11,201,221
Professional fees	840,000	840,000
	33,866,273	33,866,273
Net income available for debt service	4,007,784	4,258,289
Provisions for Depreciation:		
Existing	1,050,000	1,050,000
Additional	350,644	384,434
Interest Expenses:		
Existing	0	0
Additional	1,919,999	2,039,999
Amortization of Bond Issue Expense:		
Existing	0	0
Additional	24,333	25,333
	3,344,976	3,499,766
Income from operations	662,808	758,523
Nonoperating Revenue:		
Contributions	50,000	50,000
Interest earned on trustee-held funds	220,429	234,206
Other	0	0
Net income	$ 933,237	$ 1,042,729

STATEMENT OF ESTIMATED REVENUES AND EXPENSES WITHOUT SPECIAL PRICE INCREASE
River City and Memorial Hospitals

	A	B
Revenue from Services to Patients:		
Routine services	$19,291,056	$19,291,056
Ancillary services	17,575,712	17,575,712
Outpatient services	2,910,628	2,910,628
Gross patient service revenues	39,777,396	39,777,396
Deductions from Revenues:		
Contractual allowance	1,954,320	1,883,808
Uncollectible accounts and free service	994,435	994,435
Net patient service revenues	36,828,641	36,899,153
Other operating revenues	1,121,998	1,121,998
Total operating revenues	37,950,639	38,021,151
Operating Expenses:		
Salaries and wages	18,733,952	18,733,952
Employee benefits	3,091,100	3,091,100
Supplies and other expenses	11,201,221	11,201,221
Professional fees	840,000	840,000
	33,866,273	33,866,273
Net income available for debt service	4,084,366	4,154,878
Provisions for Depreciation:		
Existing	1,050,000	1,050,000
Additional	350,644	384,434
Interest Expenses:		
Existing	0	0
Additional	1,919,999	2,039,999
Amortization of Bond Issue Expense:		
Existing	0	0
Additional	24,333	25,333
	3,344,976	3,499,766
Income from operations	739,390	655,112
Nonoperating Revenue:		
Contributions	50,000	50,000
Interest earned on trustee-held funds	220,429	234,206
Other	0	0
Net income	$ 1,009,819	$ 939,318

Appendix 26.9

ALTERNATIVE II

ANALYSIS OF ESTIMATED FINANCIAL AND OPERATIONAL CRITERIA
River City and Memorial Hospitals

	A	B
Utilization Data:		
Patient days	115,000	115,000
Outpatient visits	29,000	29,000
Average daily census	315.07	315.07
Average number of beds in service	539.00	539.00
Occupancy	58.45%	58.45%
Cost-based expense (%)	50.00%	50.00%
Cost-based revenue (%)	50.00%	50.00%
Revenue Requirements:		
Gross revenue per patient day	$357.67	$360.96
Percentage price increases:		
Normal annual	13.00%	13.00%
"Special" annual	3.40%	4.36%
Debt service percentage of gross revenue	6.09%	6.34%
Debt service coverage	2.00X	2.00X
Operating Expense Analyses:		
Operating expenses		
Per patient day	$294.49	$294.49
Employee benefits as a percentage of salaries	16.50%	16.50%
Capital Cost Analyses:		
Annual debt service	$2,504,879	$2,630,123
Debt service per patient day		
— Current	$.00	$.00
— Additional	$21.78	$22.87
— Total	$21.78	$22.87
Depreciation, Interest, and Amortization per Patient Day:		
— Current	$9.13	$9.13
— Additional	$25.34	$26.69
— Total	$34.47	$35.82

ESTIMATED SOURCES AND USES OF FUNDS
River City and Memorial Hospitals

	A	B
Sources of Funds:		
Anticipated borrowings	$20,000,000	$21,000,000
Funds to be provided at closing	4,000,000	4,000,000
Funds to be provided from operations	0	0
Interest to be earned on trustee-held funds	0	0
	$24,000,000	$25,000,000
Uses of Funds:		
Funds available for construction and related		
expenditures	$12,145,120	$12,989,872
Bond discount	600,000	630,000
Funds deposited in:		
Interest fund	0	0
Debt service reserve fund	2,504,879	2,630,123
Bond financing expenses	250,000	250,000
Debt retirement	8,500,000	8,500,000
	$23,999,999	$24,999,995

STATEMENT OF ESTIMATED REVENUES AND EXPENSES WITH SPECIAL PRICE INCREASE
River City and Memorial Hospitals

	A	B
Revenue from Services to Patients:		
Routine services	$19,947,888	$20,131,680
Ancillary services	18,174,144	18,341,584
Outpatient services	3,009,732	3,037,462
Gross patient service revenues	41,131,764	41,510,726
Deductions from Revenues:		
Contractual allowances	2,349,488	2,468,464
Uncollectible accounts and free service	1,028,295	1,037,769
Net patient service revenues	37,753,981	38,004,493
Other operating revenues	1,121,998	1,121,998
Total operating revenues	38,875,979	39,126,491
Operating Expenses:		
Salaries and wages	18,733,952	18,733,952
Employee benefits	3,091,100	3,091,100
Supplies and other expenses	11,201,221	11,201,221
Professional fees	840,000	840,000
	33,866,273	33,866,273
Net income available for debt service	5,009,706	5,260,218
Provisions for Depreciation:		
Existing	1,050,000	1,050,000
Additional	485,805	519,595
Interest Expenses:		
Existing	0	0
Additional	2,399,998	2,519,998
Amortization of Bond Issue Expense:		
Existing	0	0
Additional	28,333	29,333
	3,964,136	4,118,926
Income from operations	1,045,570	1,141,292
Nonoperating Revenue:		
Contributions	50,000	50,000
Interest earned on trustee-held funds	275,537	289,313
Other	0	0
Net income	$ 1,371,107	$ 1,480,605

STATEMENT OF ESTIMATED REVENUES AND EXPENSES WITHOUT SPECIAL PRICE INCREASE
River City and Memorial Hospitals

	A	B
Revenue from Services to Patients:		
Routine services	$19,291,056	$19,291,056
Ancillary services	17,575,712	17,575,712
Outpatient services	2,910,628	2,910,628
Gross patient service revenues	39,777,396	39,777,396
Deductions from Revenues:		
Contractual allowance	1,672,288	1,601,792
Uncollectible accounts and free service	994,435	994,435
Net patient service revenues	37,110,672	37,181,169
Other operating revenues	1,121,998	1,121,998
Total operating revenues	38,232,670	38,303,167
Operating Expenses:		
Salaries and wages	18,733,952	18,733,952
Employee benefits	3,091,100	3,091,100
Supplies and other expenses	11,201,221	11,201,221
Professional fees	840,000	840,000
	33,866,273	33,866,273
Net income available for debt service	4,366,397	4,436,894
Provisions for Depreciation:		
Existing	1,050,000	1,050,000
Additional	485,805	519,595
Interest Expenses:		
Existing	0	0
Additional	2,399,998	2,519,998
Amortization of Bond Issue Expense:		
Existing	0	0
Additional	28,333	29,333
	3,964,136	4,118,926
Income from operations	402,261	317,968
Nonoperating Revenue:		
Contributions	50,000	50,000
Interest earned on trustee-held funds	275,537	289,313
Other	0	0
Net income	$727,798	$657,281

Appendix 26.10

ALTERNATIVE III

ANALYSIS OF ESTIMATED FINANCIAL AND OPERATIONAL CRITERIA
Memorial Hospital

	A	B
Utilization Data:		
Patient days	68,500	68,500
Outpatient visits	28,000	28,000
Average daily census	187.67	187.67
Average number of beds in service	290.00	290.00
Occupancy	64.71%	64.71%
Cost-based expense (%)	55.00%	55.00%
Cost-based revenue (%)	55.00%	55.00%
Revenue Requirements:		
Gross revenue per patient day	$358.42	$364.33
Percentage price increases:		
Normal annual	13.00%	13.00%
"Special" annual	(.88)%	.75%
Debt service percentage of gross revenue	6.38%	6.77%
Debt service coverage	2.00X	2.00X
Operating Expense Analyses:		
Operating expenses		
Per patient day	$296.23	$296.23
Employee benefits as a percentage of salaries	16.50%	16.50%
Capital Cost Analyses:		
Annual debt service	$ 1,565,549	$ 1,690,793
Debt service per patient day		
— Current	$.00	$.00
— Additional	$22.85	$24.68
— Total	$22.85	$24.68
Depreciation, Interest, and Amortization		
Per Patient Day:		
— Current	$15.33	$15.33
— Additional	$25.59	$27.85
— Total	$40.92	$43.18

ESTIMATED SOURCES AND USES OF FUNDS
Memorial Hospital

	A	B
Sources of Funds:		
Anticipated borrowings	$12,500,000	$13,500,000
Funds to be provided at closing	4,000,000	4,000,000
Funds to be provided from operations	0	0
Interest to be earned on trustee-held funds	0	0
	$16,500,000	$17,500,000
Uses of Funds:		
Funds available for construction and related		
expenditures	$ 5,809,451	$ 6,654,207
Bond discount	375,000	405,000
Funds deposited in:		
Interest fund	0	0
Debt service reserve fund	1,565,549	1,690,793
Bond financing expenses	250,000	250,000
Debt retirement	8,500,000	8,500,000
	$16,500,000	$17,500,000

STATEMENT OF ESTIMATED REVENUES AND EXPENSES WITH SPECIAL PRICE CHANGE
Memorial Hospital

	A	B
Revenue from Services to Patients:		
Routine services	$11,389,602	$11,577,476
Ancillary services	10,376,851	10,548,019
Outpatient services	2,785,520	2,831,468
Gross patient service revenues	24,551,973	24,956,963
Deductions from Revenues:		
Contractual allowances	1,301,459	1,446,640
Uncollectible accounts and free service	564,695	574,010
Net patient service revenues	22,685,819	22,936,313
Other operating revenues	736,999	736,999
Total operating revenues	23,422,818	23,673,312
Operating Expenses:		
Salaries and wages	11,158,921	11,158,921
Employee benefits	1,841,220	1,841,220
Supplies and other expenses	6,687,918	6,687,918
Professional fees	603,680	603,680
	20,291,739	20,291,739
Net income available for debt service	3,131,079	3,381,573
Provisions for Depreciation:		
Existing	1,050,000	1,050,000
Additional	232,378	266,168
Interest Expenses:		
Existing	0	0
Additional	1,499,999	1,619,999
Amortization of Bond Issue Expense:		
Existing	0	0
Additional	20,833	21,833
	2,803,210	2,958,000
Income from operations	327,869	423,573
Nonoperating Revenue:		
Contributions	50,000	50,000
Interest earned on trustee-held funds	172,210	185,987
Other	0	0
Net income	550,079	659,560

STATEMENT OF ESTIMATED REVENUES AND EXPENSES WITHOUT SPECIAL PRICE CHANGE
Memorial Hospital

	A	B
Revenue from Services to Patients:		
Routine services	$11,490,762	$11,490,762
Ancillary services	10,469,016	10,469,016
Outpatient services	2,810,261	2,810,261
Gross patient service revenues	24,770,039	24,770,039
Deductions from Revenues:		
Contractual allowance	1,421,394	1,343,830
Uncollectible accounts and free service	569,711	569,711
Net patient service revenues	22,778,934	22,856,498
Other operating revenues	736,999	736,999
Total operating revenues	23,515,933	23,593,497
Operating Expenses:		
Salaries and wages	11,158,921	11,158,921
Employee benefits	1,841,220	1,841,220
Supplies and other expenses	6,687,918	6,687,918
Professional fees	603,680	603,680
	20,291,739	20,291,739
Net income available for debt service	3,224,194	3,301,758
Provisions for Depreciation:		
Existing	1,050,000	1,050,000
Additional	232,378	266,168
Interest Expenses:		
Existing	0	0
Additional	1,499,999	1,619,999
Amortization of Bond Issue Expense:		
Existing	0	0
Additional	20,833	21,833
	2,803,210	2,958,000
Income from operations	420,984	343,758
Nonoperating Revenue:		
Contributions	50,000	50,000
Interest earned on trustee-held funds	172,210	185,987
Other	0	0
Net income	$ 643,194	$ 579,745

About the Editors

JAMES D. SUVER is professor of accounting and health administration at the University of Colorado—Denver School of Business. Previously he was professor and director of the master's degree program at the Department of Health Policy and Administration, University of North Carolina—Chapel Hill. A certified management accountant, Dr. Suver speaks, consults, and publishes extensively on the financial management of health care organizations. Among his publications are two textbooks. Dr. Suver holds an M.B.A. and a D.B.A. from Harvard Business School.

CHARLES N. KAHN III is legislative assistant to Senator Dan Quayle. Mr. Kahn previously served as director of the Offices of Curriculum Development and Financial Management Education of the Association of University Programs in Health Administration (AUPHA). Before joining AUPHA, he served as an administrative resident with the Association of American Medical Colleges and as an aide to the mayor of New Orleans. In addition to his health and policy experience, Mr. Kahn has managed two congressional campaigns and consulted on a number of others. He earned an M.P.H. in health systems management from Tulane University.

JAN P. CLEMENT is a doctoral candidate specializing in finance in the Department of Health Policy and Administration at the University of North Carolina—Chapel Hill. Previously, Ms. Clement was on the faculty of the University of Texas—Austin. She has also held positions in state government, hospital management, and community health organizations. Her M.S.P.H. was awarded by the University of Missouri—Columbia.